RHETORIC READINGS FOR ADVANCED WRITERS

COLORADO STATE UNIVERSITY | FORT COLLINS

COMPOSITION PROGRAM

FOUNTAINHEAD
PRESS

Our green initiatives include:

Electronic Products
We deliver products in non-paper form whenever possible. This includes pdf down-loadables, flash drives, & CDs.

Electronic Samples
We use Xample, a new electronic sampling system. Instructor samples are sent via a personalized web page that links to pdf downloads.

FSC Certified Printers
All of our printers are certified by the Forest Service Council which promotes environmentally and socially responsible management of the world's forests. This program allows consumer groups, individual consumers, and businesses to work together hand-in-hand to promote responsible use of the world's forests as a re-newable and sustainable resource.

Recycled Paper
Most of our products are printed on a minimum of 30% post-consumer waste recycled paper.

Support of Green Causes
When we do print, we donate a portion of our revenue to green causes. Listed below are a few of the organizations that have received donations from Fountain-head Press. We welcome your feedback and suggestions for contributions, as we are always searching for worthy initiatives.
Rainforest 2 Reef
Environmental Working Group

Cover Artwork by Courtney Putnam
See her work at:
http://thehealingnest.blogspot.com/
http://oriart.blogspot.com
http://www.cafepress.com/quietgirl

Cover Design by Doris Bruey
Design by Susan Moore

Books may be purchased for educational purposes.

For information, please call or write:

1-800-586-0330
Fountainhead Press
Southlake, TX 76092
Web Site: www.fountainheadpress.com
E-mail: customerservice@fountainheadpress.com

2011 Edition
ISBN: 978-1-59871-479-1
Printed in the United States of America

ACKNOWLEDGEMENTS

It is a commonplace that writing can be exceptionally hard work, and writing *Rhetorical Readings for Advanced Writers* (*RRAW*) proves the axiom. Putting together this book has been an enterprise that relied on the good will, intelligence, and creativity of a number of people. Special instructors in upper-division composition Christina Sutton and Debra Walker took the lead on this project, while Beth Lechleitner and Ed Lessor wrote the introductions to these articles. Special instructor Brad Benz assisted with the preliminary selection of articles in 2010. They and Bev McQuinn have been invaluable in making our advanced composition program the success that it is. Former English department chair, Bruce Ronda, has encouraged us throughout the project, and faculty members in the Composition Program—Sue Doe, Tobi Jacobi, Kate Kiefer, Carrie Lamanna, Lisa Langstraat, Steve Reid, and Sarah Sloane—have helped to select the contents of this book. Moreover, Sarah Sloane graciously agreed to shepherd this book through production and publication, and Lisa Langstraat helped develop the introductory materials for *RRAW*.

We are pleased to be working with Fountainhead Press on this project. Tim French and Susan Moore have been especially helpful, working out the logistics of producing this book from the initial concept through the final printing of this reader. With the press's Green Initiative program and their goal of being an eco-friendly publisher, Fountainhead's sustainable values are a perfect fit with Colorado State University's designation as "a green university." Not only is this book you are reading printed on recycled paper, Fountainhead Press gives money to environmental groups all over the country, including the Colorado State University Environmental Learning Center.

We do not offer thanks frequently enough to the instructors who are the primary teachers of CO300. They are the ones who inspire students, enliven a love of writing, and perform the hard, daily work of making better writers. They deserve all our thanks for making the CO300 classes and upper-division composition program the success that it is.

The copyright of this reader is not granted to any individual faculty member but is instead held by the Composition Program as a whole. Any funds earned through the sales of this book are returned to undergraduate and graduate students at Colorado State University through essay writing contests, professional development funds, GTA awards, student travel funds, CO300 faculty workshops, and many other initiatives that directly benefit CSU students.

Finally, these readings are offered as selections varied in rhetorical contexts, strategies, stakeholders addressed, and purpose and genre. They are included here to show the range of rhetoric available to all writers, and not to promote any one point-of-view.

C RHETORICA XXIII 73

Plate from Die Tarocchi. Zwei italienische Kupferstichfolgen aus dem XV. Jahrhundert (Cassirer, 1910: Berlin). Ascribed to the artist Andrea Mantegna.

INTRODUCTION

Consider the image of Rhetorica on the preceding page. In Mantegna's (ca. 1495) allegorical painting, Rhetorica looks like a warrior; she is armored and carries a sword to represent the power of words to command authority and action. She gazes directly at her viewer, her composed, open look fortified by her sword; the sword signifies the potential of discourse to cut to the heart of an issue and to influence grave decisions of state. Rhetorica here is certainly no pawn to language: her helmet and breastplate are jeweled, and she is someone who commands words and worlds. She is royalty, and she appears to be quite beloved royalty, at that. Note the cherubs who sound their trumpets to honor her arrival; they dance at her feet in veneration and respect. And note, too, that Rhetorica is poised for action; she gathers the hem of her skirt to suggest movement, progress. She is going to make things happen.

Whatever happened to Rhetorica? When we refer to "rhetoric" today, rarely do we have in mind a figure of such royal power, a beloved figure who effects change, who makes things happen. As the cartoon gallery on the next several pages suggests, today "rhetoric" is usually derided as empty, manipulative language. And, while we might certainly question the martial symbolism of Mantegna's vision of Rhetorica, we might also wonder why rhetoric and rhetorical studies have generally fallen into such low esteem.

Rhetorical Readings for Advanced Writers(RRAW) contains essays that ask us to reconsider and revalue rhetoric as an art of discourse that makes things happen. This advanced writing course gives you the opportunity to learn more about rhetorical theory as you gain vital practice in the art of writing arguments. Writing an effective argument is a complex and demanding act. It requires that we understand the rhetorical context in which we write. It requires that we understand our audiences' needs, values, and beliefs. It requires that we consider the purpose of our argument, and understand how to construct ethical, emotional, and logical appeals. Writing arguments requires an intellectual curiosity about how we'll engage various genres and modes to best convey our message and reach our audience. Critically reading these essays on rhetoric can be challenging for even the advanced student in an upper-division writing course. Rhetorica will most likely challenge you in many ways. However, whether you are writing proposals, technical reports, pamphlets, editorials, essays, or any other document, a genuine understanding of rhetorical theory will help you understand how to compose arguments with power.

RRAW is organized into three chapters. Essays in the first section, "Rhetorical Contexts," provide foundational information about the rhetorical situation, the cultural influences that shape common features of rhetoric, and the nature of public discourse. "Features of Argument" includes texts that provide insight into the central characteristics of argumentative writing, such as ethos, pathos, logos, evidence, and style. The third section in *RRAW* focuses on new media. "Multimodal Composing" recognizes that many of the arguments we encounter today are not written in traditional essay form but instead include visual, aural, and multimodal rhetorics that demand our special attention. Each chapter of *RRAW* includes multiple essays written for multiple audiences; these essays challenge us to read closely, to think critically, and to become more open to and aware of the ways rhetoric influences our daily lives. They ask us to consider what lessons Rhetorica might teach us today.

An image of "Rhetorica" From Margarita Philosophia, 1508. Note the way this emblem acknowledges the interconnectedness of various sources of ideas and information.

"Do you prefer rosy rhetoric or the plain truth that I'm firing you?"

"And now, for a rebuttal."

"Don't worry too much about math,
science, or history — just make
sure you get good marks in *rhetoric.*"

"I didn't feel answers were necessary.
All the questions seemed rhetorical."

TABLE OF CONTENTS

How Do We Know?: Students Examine Issues of Credibility With a Complicated Multimodal Web-Based Text

Mark Baildon and James S. Damico

CONSIDER AS YOU ARE READING:

One way writers establish credibility (and thereby appeal to ethos in their arguments) is to use credible source material. Determining the quality of a source is challenging even when the material is in a purely alphabetic mode (printed words on a page). But what happens when other modes—still or moving images, for instance—come into the mix? Do the skills we have developed, and continue to hone, apply to other modes or to discourse using multiple modes? Baildon and Damico suggest that this question is particularly germane today because the internet makes the integration of text, image, and now sound, more common and more accessible to all researchers, especially student writers. Rather than rushing into a treatise about how students should assess multimodal rhetoric, Baildon and Damico set out to understand how students determine credibility now. Their article is important, therefore, because it helps us read a wider range of texts more critically and compose more effectively across multiple modes. A broader understanding of how to assess the credibility of sources, and to establish your own credibility in our increasingly multimodal world, will help you develop as a writer.

1. *What do Baildon and Damico conclude are the three biggest challenges students faced when trying to judge the quality of the assigned multimodal argument (Loose Change)?*

2. *Think of the last time you encountered a multimodal text that was not credible. What could the author have done to make it more credible?*

3. *The authors note that the students in the study found images,
    especially eyewitness testimony, more credible than other
    information. Why might that be? Do you tend to trust a picture
    more than what someone says? Why or why not?*

CREDIBILITY IN AN AGE OF MULTIMEDIA AND MULTIMODALITY

Discerning the credibility of sources of information has become increasingly challenging because of the accelerated growth of networked information and communication technologies (ICT), especially the Internet with its varied text structures and formats, including nonlinear hypertext, multimedia texts, and interactive texts (Coiro, 2003). Identifying and evaluating claims and assessing the credibility of Web sources of information requires having enough background information to contextualize information and authorship, being able to read intertextually across assorted texts and modalities to consider the "vast network of relations of credibility" (Burbules & Callister, 2000) and corroborate claims and evidence, and developing the critical capacity to make judgments about claims and the qualifications of the author(s) or creator(s) of a source. Several sets of criteria have been offered to help teachers and students do this challenging work (Damico, Baildon, & Campano, 2005). However, people rarely use these criteria for assessing credibility and instead seemingly rely on seemingly more superficial qualities, such as visual cues, information design and structure, and information focus or use (Warnick, 2003).

Based on the argument that criteria typically used to evaluate credibility may no longer suffice with newly emergent texts, genres, and digital tools and formats found on the Web, Burbules (2001) notes, with the growth of the Internet and its decentered nature, the referencing and organizational systems that are available, for example, in libraries, do not exist here. The markers of institutional credibility and authority, the lines of tradition, that allow viewers to judge media sources, or publishers, for example, have not been settled yet; there is an even greater capacity to locate information that will tend to confirm one's existing views and prejudices, rather than challenge them. In all this, the scope of the network, and its deregulated content, overwhelm the ordinary idea that we can comparatively judge different sources, or that we can trust popular processes of selection to weed out the less credible, and give status to the survivors. (p. 443)

According to Burbules (2001), Internet users are more interested in getting the information they are looking for than assessing credibility. As a result, "judgments rely on attributions of trust— trust in individuals, trust in communities and collective (and largely invisible) processes of vetting information" (p. 451).

Furthermore, the Web is "a self-sustaining reference system" in which we must rely on other information gleaned within the network to determine credibility (Burbules, 2001). Not only must we be able to assess the claims and evidence in the source we are reading or viewing, we must also be able to assess the associations they make, such as external references and links and semiotic or textual references (images, sounds, symbols, metaphors, etc.) found within the text itself. In other words, there are issues of internal and external credibility that must be considered in determining credibility. The validity of claims based on supporting evidence within the text along with their internal logical consistency must be determined and issues of authorship and claims should be corroborated intertextually with other sources.

Multimodal texts, in particular, are challenging because they often mix images, music, graphic arts, video, and print to make claims or to provide supporting evidence. Different modes, defined here as representational and meaning making resources used to communicate meaning (Kress, 2003), are "braided" together to "create a different system of signification, one that transcends the collective contribution of its constituent parts" (Hull & Nelson, 2005, p. 225). Claims are often supported through multimodal arrangements that shift the nature of authorship, claims and evidence, and the logical structure of texts. The screen is now the dominant site of texts, as we move toward a "logic of the image," governed by a more spatial form of logic rather than the temporal or linear logic of written language (Kress, 2003). Each of the types of texts or modes used in the construction of a multimodal text may connect to students' prior knowledge and experiences in different ways, reference other texts, and require students to draw on a range of symbolic resources and strategies. The multiple texts used may need to be analyzed individually as well as considered together to determine their effects and issues of credibility. Given these "new mediascapes" (Appadurai, 1996; Dimitriadis & McCarthy, 2001), new ways of thinking about credibility and new practices for determining credibility are needed.

These new ways of thinking must also attend to epistemological issues related to the challenges of assessing credibility because "the very *status* of knowledge, learning, teaching and researching are currently in a state of profound upheaval under the double impact of rapid and far-reaching technological change and the massive assault on longstanding narratives of foundation and legitimation" (Lankshear, Peters, & Knobel, 2000, pp. 17–18; italics original). The digital age, the superabundance of information, the "legitimation crisis," and new information technologies have necessitated a shift in thinking about knowledge and knowing, especially in terms of literacy practices. A focus on epistemology means that the criteria, practices, and tools for determining credibility need to be made explicit and considered carefully.

Equipped with these understandings, we designed and enacted a study to examine empirically how a group of young adults in a ninth-grade Humanities classroom in an international school in East Asia would evaluate the credibility of a complicated Web-based video text, *Loose Change* (http://www.loosechange911.com/).

THEORETICAL FRAMEWORK

In contemporary contexts, new media and multimodal texts are altering conceptions of texts and textuality, thus providing new dynamics and challenges for readers (Nixon, 2003). Students have a range of experiences with digital technologies and multimedia texts (film, music, video games, Internet, television) in media culture and draw on a number of technologies, symbolic resources, and prior knowledge and experiences in their literacy practices to make meaning and determine credibility in increasingly multimodal and digital "mediascapes" (Dimitriadis & McCarthy, 2001). Guiding our attempts to better understand this meaning-making are three sets of perspectives: multimodality, intertextuality, and disciplined inquiry in social studies.

The logic of images is a logic of space and simultaneity and because visual images and the medium of the screen (e.g., television, computer, film) have become increasingly dominant in media culture, this requires a shift from linguistic theory to semiotics, a theoretical orientation that can better account for multiple modes and how meanings are produced and understood in multimodal and multimedia environments (Sonesson, 2002). Kress (2003) describes how multimodal texts combine a number of modes, such as print, visual images, music, sound effects, and spoken word. Because "modes are associated with particular media" (Fairclough, 1995, p. 77)—for example, the mode of writing is conveyed by the media of books and newspapers; the modes of gesture and music are often combined in the media of dance or music videos—each mode comes with different constraints and affordances and makes different epistemological demands in communicative interactions. In making "modality judgments" (Hodge & Kress, 1988), people draw on their knowledge of contexts, uses of media, textual representations, and modes of communication to evaluate the plausibility of claims made in a specific text.

To frame what types of reading multimodal texts promote, we turned to intertextuality, a theoretical perspective that posits the meaning of any text is shaped by other texts. Put another way, "meaning is not transferred directly from writer to reader, but instead is mediated through, or filtered by, 'codes' imparted to the writer and reader by other texts" (Kristeva, 1980, p. 66). Kristeva, drawing on Bakhtin (1973), also uses the term "ambivalence" (Kristeva, 1980, p. 68) to describe how two paths merge within texts: intertextual relationships within and outside of texts. For example, images create syntagmatic relationships or sequences within a multimodal text to create meaning, and images are related to other images and signifiers that exist outside of the text. Moreover, because of the "arbitrariness of the sign" (Derrida, 1974, p. 45), the signifier remains free-floating and unspecified, and always shaped by the given context and readers' knowledge and understanding of the signs that make up the text (Barthes, 1977). This helps us understand texts as "meaning-making events whose functions are defined by their use in particular social contexts" (Baldry & Thibault, 2006, p. 4). Reading multimodal texts, then, requires an understanding that signs and texts exist in relationship to other texts and contexts and that multiple, shifting, and competing readings are possible.

Similarly, there is a synergistic relationship between different modal elements in a text. Sipe (1998) argues that readers/viewers oscillate between sign systems in an ongoing process of transmediation in which content in each sign system is translated into the other sign systems. Drawing on the theory of transmediation, then, we, as readers/viewers, go back and forth in "a potentially endless process [in which] reviewing and rereading will produce ever-new insights as we construct new connections and make modifications of our previous interpretations" (Sipe, 1998, p. 106). Intentionally and systematically moving back and forth between modes or sign systems may provide new readings and allow for more critical understandings of multimodal texts and how they are constructed and received.

A third set of ideas that frames our work is disciplined inquiry in social studies, defined by Levstik and Barton (2001) as the purposeful act of seeking information or knowledge, activating prior knowledge, investigating significant questions, and constructing knowledge "within a community that establishes the goals, standards, and procedures of study" (p. 13). A core practice within the social studies classrooms in which we work, as well as broader communities of social scientists, is the careful evaluation of claims and evidence within and across sources of information. Historians or social scientists regularly have to evaluate, analyze, and interpret a range of texts, such as political cartoons, oral accounts, interviews, diaries/journals, images, sound recordings, and film. Also, utilizing multiple sources in historical inquiry requires levels of intertextuality "where readers absorb, transpose, and build a mosaic of intersecting texts" (Hartman, 1995, p. 521). The idea of intertextuality in disciplined inquiry points to how readers construct meaning from fragments, such as evidence found in primary sources, to build their own understanding of subject matter. An underlying assumption of our work is that a primary goal of history and social studies education is for students to become careful, critical readers of all texts, from textbooks, trade books, magazines, and newspapers to maps, videos, and architecture (Segall, 1999; Werner, 2002).

Carmen Luke (2003) unites and extends these theoretical perspectives as she makes a case for interpretive work with multiple modalities as "thinking across associations, accessing and integrating knowledge laterally" (p. 401) across modes. She argues multimodal texts require "a cognitive orientation akin to what is often termed *lateral thinking* . . . creative, critical, and aesthetic practices . . . [that] demand horizontal or lateral cognitive mobility across disciplines, genres, modalities and, indeed, cultural zones" (p. 401; italics original). In our study, we consider to what extent we see this in students' responses to the complex multimodal text, *Loose Change*.

CONTEXTS OF PRODUCTION AND RECEPTION OF *LOOSE CHANGE*

Fairclough (1989) argues that texts, social practices, and contexts are bound up in ideology, or the "'common sense' assumptions which are implicit in the conventions according to which people interact linguistically, and of which people are generally not consciously aware" (p. 2). Thus, to investigate the ways readers make meaning of the multimodal text *Loose Change*, it is important to understand the multidimensional nature of the video, the social practices that both constituted its production as well as the social practices used to make meaning of it as a text, and some of the social, historical, and political contexts and discourses that shaped both its production and reception.

LOOSE CHANGE, A COMPLEX MULTIMODAL TEXT

As the Web site http://www.loosechange911.com/, notes… [this] independent documentary has grown from a cult following to a grassroots organism that can no longer be contained. The central premise of Loose Change is that the United States Government was, at the very least, criminally negligent in allowing the attacks of September 11th, 2001 to occur. However, when one looks deeper into the evidence, one might come to the startling conclusion that our own government might have been directly responsible for the attacks themselves. Loose Change merely scratches the surface of information that points to a massive government cover-up regarding 9/11. We highly encourage you to take it upon yourself to research the events of 9/11 for yourself and come to your own conclusions. Loose Change is currently in two editions, with a third being developed for American theaters, intended to be released in 2007.

The video, first posted on the Web in April 2005, is 1 hour and 22 minutes long, written, directed, and narrated by Dylan Avery, produced by Korey Rowe, and based on research by Jason Bermas. All three are from Oneonta, New York, in their early 20s, and produced the video for $6,000 using a laptop computer (Sales, 2006). The movie consists of Avery narrating over still photographs, news footage, computer-generated simulations, diagrams, models, and other sources relating to 9/11, with an underscore of hip-hop and urban-style audio tracks. The film includes considerable video content from CNN, NBC, and FOX News as well as a number of interviews with eyewitnesses and "experts."

Effectively combining multiple modalities, the creators string together a range of claims and evidence to present a compelling narrative as well as invite viewers to engage in further inquiry. The video challenges viewers to question what they know about 9/11, specifically government and media accounts of 9/11. As Avery noted in a *Vanity Fair* interview, "You have to be a skeptic... You can't believe anything someone tells you just because they told you to. Especially your government, and especially your media—the two institutions that are put there to control you. And you're going to tell me you're going to take their word for everything? I don't think so" (Sales, 2006).

A range of historical, scientific, mathematical, and documentary evidence is marshaled to support the main claims of the film, which basically consist of the following assertions: (1) individuals within the U.S. government or with strong links to government officials (i.e., neo-cons, members of The Project for the New American Century) knew of the impending attacks and did nothing to stop them because they would serve as a catalyst for military buildup and imperial expansion; (2) the collapse of the World Trade Center buildings was not because of the airplane crashes, but was the result of explosives planted in the building; (3) a commercial airliner did not crash into the Pentagon; (4) the public has been misled about what really happened to the plane that crashed in rural Pennsylvania; and (5) the U.S. government has misled, misinformed, and kept information from the American public about 9/11.

THE 9/11 TRUTH MOVEMENT AND *LOOSE CHANGE* AS A CONSPIRACY THEORY TEXT

Loose Change is now an integral part of the 9/11 Truth Movement, which consists of a number of Web sites (e.g., www.911truth. org; www.911truthmovement.org), books (e.g., *The New Pearl Harbor; 9/11 The Big Lie*), and films (e.g., *9/11: Press for Truth*) that challenge mainstream accounts of the attacks. It has generated a great deal of response in the alternative press (e.g., www. alternet.org), spawned a group of people calling themselves Scholars for 9/11 Truth, and led to the online peer reviewed *Journal of 9/11 Studies* (www.journalof911studies.com). Various people in the movement usually point to evidence that neoconservatives since Reagan have had grand imperial designs, have willfully misled, misinformed, and lied to the American public by skillfully using the media and effective public relations tactics, and point to the body of evidence that should have warned the intelligence community and the Bush administration of the attacks. As the 911Truth.Org site notes, the mission of the movement is "to expose the official lies and cover-up surrounding the events of September 11th, 2001 in a way that inspires the people to overcome denial and understand the truth; namely, that elements within the US government and covert policy apparatus must have orchestrated or participated in the execution of the attacks for these to have happened in the way that they did" (www.911truth.org).

Because *Loose Change*, along with other texts of the 9/11 Truth Movement, aims to illuminate the ways the U.S. government "conspired" against the American people, it can be viewed as a conspiracy theory text, defined by Allen (2006) as "hypotheses [that] often consist of a vast pile of circumstantial evidence shaped into a seemingly coherent whole with the strong glue of faith." Because conspiracy theories produce "heroic strivings for evidence to prove that the unbelievable is the only thing that can be believed" (Hofstadter, 1964), even if a reader is able to "debunk one or even many allegations . . . the pile still stands, impressive in its bulk and ideological coherence." So, why do people gravitate to conspiracy theories? According to Allen (2006),

> There is something comforting about a world where someone is in charge—either for good (think gods) or evil (think Bush insiders plotting 9/11). Many people prefer to believe a Procrustean conspiracy rather than accept the alternative: Life can be random, viciously unjust, and meaningless; tragedy and joy alike flow from complex combinations of good and bad intentions, careful plotting, random happenstance and bumbling incompetence.

Hofstadter (1964) also contends that Americans seem particularly invested in conspiracy theories, pointing out a long American tradition of expressing popular discontent as sinister conspiracies where a main condition for these paranoid tendencies "is a confrontation of opposed interests which are (or are felt to be) totally irreconcilable, and thus by nature not susceptible to the normal political processes of bargain and compromise."

Regarding the events of 9/11, over 40% of Americans now think there was a government cover-up (Zogby News, www.zogby.com/search/ReadNews.dbm?ID=855) and the public's willingness to believe in 9/11 conspiracies has even been spoofed in a *South Park* episode (Stone & Parker, 2006) in which Kyle proves that the 9/11 conspiracy theories are actually the result of a government conspiracy to create a conspiracy because they want people to think the government is in control of everything. A whole industry around 9/11 conspiracy theories seems to have developed since 9/11, leading President George Bush to note in a speech to the General Assembly of the United Nations, "Let us never tolerate outrageous conspiracy theories concerning the attacks of September 11" (Sales, 2006). It has also generated efforts to identify erroneous evidence and faulty claims and generally debunk 9/11 conspiracy theories (e.g., the book, *Debunking 9/11 Myths*). Specific sites to debunk *Loose Change*

provide point-by-point critiques (e.g., www.911research.wtc7.
net; http://screwloosechange.blogspot.com/).

Our attention to conspiracy theory here aligns with Nixon's
(2003) argument that we need to investigate the cultural
mediation of information, especially new media accounts. We
must consider the contexts of texts and intertextual referents,
and how certain discourses and technologies contribute to
achieving and sustaining the dominance of particular strategies
and practices. This includes identifying certain social forces
and systems of ideas that shape dominant narratives and ways
of making meaning that have currency in the larger society.
Because conspiracy theory can be understood as a particular
genre, discourse, or style evident in *Loose Change*, it is important
to consider these discursive styles and broader contexts to
understand the ways students read this complex multimodal
text.

METHODS

Our study is situated in an international school in East Asia with
a predominately Asian-American student population of 2,200
K–12 students. All students must possess a foreign passport
and admittance priority is given to U.S. passport holders. There
is a strong college preparatory focus at the school with the
expectation that students will do well on Advanced Placement
(AP), International Baccalaureate (IB), and SAT tests and gain
admittance to top universities in the United States and other
places around the world.

The 32 students participating in the study were members of two
ninth grade Humanities (combined social studies and language
arts) classes. The Asian Studies curriculum that makes up the
ninth-grade Humanities program is an integrated curriculum
comprised of five units of study: Geography and Identity;
Beliefs and Values; Conflict and Change; Contemporary Asian
Challenges; and an experiential learning unit based on trips
to nearby Asian countries. Each unit is designed using the
Understanding by Design framework (Wiggins & McTighe,
1998) and throughout the curriculum there is an emphasis on
students identifying and evaluating claims and evidence in a
range of texts (e.g., Web sites, primary sources, literature, visual

texts, etc.) as well as having students make their own claims (in writing and other textual formats) supported with evidence, sound reasoning, and elaboration.

The ninth-grade students in this study viewed *Loose Change* on the last regularly scheduled class of the 2005–2006 school year. Five students had seen the video before their viewing in class. Mark Baildon was the teacher in this interdisciplinary Asian Studies course. At this point in the school year, the students had recently completed research papers on Contemporary Asian Challenges and a primary focus during their research was identifying and evaluating claims and evidence and determining the credibility of the Web sources of information they located in their research (Damico & Baildon, 2007).

Mark first found out about *Loose Change* from his 15-year-old son (who was also a student in the study). Mark was initially reluctant to watch the video; he was aware of some of the conspiracy theories circulating about 9/11 and usually quickly dismissed them. It wasn't until Mark received the following e-mail from one of his students that he finally decided to watch the video: "hey doctor b. look what I found on Google video! http://video. google.com/videoplay?docid=-8260059923762628848. I think it's pretty convincing!" Because the video did seem to make convincing claims and raised issues of credibility in the age of video, photo, and information doctoring, manipulation, and spin, conspiracy plots, fear and distrust, information and data overload, skepticism toward truth claims, and the willingness of people to believe almost anything, Mark decided to share the video with his students to see how they made sense of it and, specifically, how they determined whether it was credible.

Using the Understanding by Design framework (Wiggins & McTighe, 1998), Mark identified two "desired results" or "enduring understandings" that guided his pedagogical approach with the video: (1) Evaluating claims (and evidence) and credibility with multimodal texts, such as *Loose Change*, requires careful and critical analysis of specific components of the video as well as how these component parts are combined to create meaning; and (2) This careful and critical analysis is best done in a community of inquiry where different perspectives and meanings can be shared and developed.

These desired results led to the development of four "essential questions" to guide classroom activity with the video:

- What is believable about this text?

- What isn't?

- How do you know?

- What might make the text more or less believable?

Evidence collected for assessment purposes as well as for our study included three primary data sources: (1) Mark's field notes, a "running record" of what transpired during the class discussion as well as his reflections during and after the class; (2) an audio and video tape of the class discussion with parts transcribed; and (3) students' written responses to the four questions noted above, which were posed at the end of the full-group discussion of the video.

Based on these pedagogical moves, we developed our primary research question: How do students think about and evaluate credibility in this multimodal text (*Loose Change*)? We used an exploratory case study research design (Stake, 1994) to document and explain the complexities of student thinking about credibility. Using a constant comparative method of analysis (Strauss & Corbin, 1990), data sources were coded to discern initial patterns and themes which were refined and modified during the analysis to generate "both descriptive and explanatory categories" (Lincoln & Guba, 1985, p. 341). For example, Mark's notes were an attempt to record students' comments and ideas during the discussion, as well as his own insights and reflections written during his planning period immediately following the class. During this planning period, Mark noted items that he found puzzling and started to develop what he thought were themes and issues that emerged during the lesson. These were later refined and developed as we looked across all of the data.

Situating the *Loose Change* video in broader social, historical, and ideological contexts (as described in the previous section) also led to categories that frame our findings as key challenges that students struggled with during the class discussion and in their written responses to the four questions. These challenges speak directly to concerns about evaluating credibility with a complicated multimodal Web-based conspiracy theory text. This analytical approach also helped us understand students' responses to the video and make connections between students' responses and these broader discursive contexts, because meaning is a part of society and not external to it (Fairclough, 1989).

STUDENTS DETERMINE CREDIBILITY IN *LOOSE CHANGE*

Our analyses of the classroom discussion, students' written responses to the questions posed, and field notes reveal the ways the students grappled with three sets of intersecting challenges: (1) accessing prior knowledge *and* identifying gaps in their own understandings; (2) determining the reliability and strength of evidence *and* acknowledging being "overwhelmed" with the information; and (3) considering internal and external credibility. Cutting across these issues was a key finding— the significant role of images in students' determinations of credibility.

Accessing Prior Knowledge and Identifying Gaps

When asked to explain "How do you know?" (if the video is believable or not), students referred to their prior knowledge by noting the general climate of distrust surrounding the Bush administration, a distrust that many students shared. They also discussed how they had seen "similar video clips on the news," that some of the claims "made sense," and that they had "similar thoughts" about what had happened during the 9/11 attacks. In general, a majority of students felt that many aspects of the film "fit" with what they already knew or what they had heard about 9/11.

Others noted that although much of the evidence used in the movie is available to the public, their own lack of knowledge was a factor that interfered in deciding whether the video was believable. For example, one student said she didn't understand the references made at the beginning of the movie to Cuba (the proposed plan during the Cuban Missile Crisis in 1962 to stage fake terrorist attacks as a pretext for invading Cuba). Another student noted, "this clip seems very believable, maybe because of our lack of knowledge . . . it is easier to believe." Students also noted that much of the scientific and historical material presented in the film gave the video an air of authority, but it was information they were unable to adequately assess which interfered with their ability to determine the credibility of information in the video. Some students also noted a lack of background knowledge that would enable them to detect counterfeit documents and artifacts used to support assertions in the movie and resolve conflicting interpretations of evidence, such as those presented by the U.S. government and the maker of the video.

Determining Reliability of Evidence and Acknowledging Being Overwhelmed

In response to the question "What is believable about this text?," students referred to the different types of evidence they encountered. Most students noted the variety of sources used to support assertions, such as video clips, news articles, photos, quotes, and three-dimensional models, which led them to conclude that these multimodal forms provided "strong" evidence and good detail and description that made claims believable. Some students specified certain multimodal qualities such the narrator's tone and "firm voice," interviews with experts, and detailed visual models and explanations using scientific evidence or "scientific proof." The amount of evidence also seemed to be a credibility factor with many students commenting on the amount of facts and information used. The cumulative effect of multiple representations ("the heroic striving for evidence" suggested by Hofstadter) led to favorable assessments of credibility from students.

Students did question the reliability of specific types of evidence, such as the eyewitness accounts and bystander testimony used throughout the video. One student noted, "People saw different things that hit the Pentagon. Some said it was a helicopter, small jet, an airplane. It is hard to believe what it actually was," while others commented, "The people that were there and saw it said different things," there "were too many different views," and "eyewitness reports could be very wrong." During the discussion, one student noted that "during panicky times, your memory isn't reliable." Students seemed to discredit eyewitness testimony because they produced differing accounts, including reports that could be inaccurate.

While students deemed much of the evidence used to support the authors' assertion to be "strong," many students also expressed feeling "overwhelmed" by the "tons of information" used in the video. Because the genres, claims, and types of evidence overlapped and intersected in myriad ways, yielding a somewhat disorienting cumulative effect, it was challenging to read and evaluate the video. Students spoke specifically about grappling with the multitude of images of print documents, video footage, animation, interviews, photo images, reconstructions, sound effects, charts and graphs, and mathematical equations— all used as evidence for assertions.

Internal and External Credibility

Students struggled in assessing internal and external aspects of credibility. They tried to determine the credibility of evidence used *within the video* to support claims and evaluate the video's internal logic (whether linear or spatial). Most students acknowledged how persuasive the video was, yet several problematized how the Web works as a "self-sustaining reference system" (Burbules, 2001) where many of the news articles and documents presented as evidence were other Web sources of information; these students believed this made the claims and evidence less credible. In other words, some students deemed the intertextual references provided within the video and on the Web site to be insufficient for helping them evaluate the information in the video. While there were some students who raised these kinds of concerns about internal credibility, most students believed the cumulative effect of the multiple representations supported the internal consistency of the video. Generally, most students thought the video was well produced and effectively combined different modalities to create a compelling narrative.

In terms of external criteria for assessing credibility, students considered issues of authorship and referred to intertextual and contextual information to evaluate the video. Students wanted to know about the experiences or qualifications of the creators of the video. For example, one student commented that "these guys are like, what, students? And they sure bent over backwards to find all this info and they sure knew what they were looking for." Other comments from students included "We don't know if the creator is credible," "The creator may only show one side of the story," "There are gaps he leaves unfilled," and "I have no idea who the narrator is (I need background information)." Another student noted, "The author makes claims and he sounds like some sort of expert even though he most likely isn't. A lot of his claims about the crash into the Pentagon could be bad physics." Others noted that the creators were obviously biased.

The fact that the movie was not released theatrically also seemed to be an issue. One student commented, "It's just a Google video," while another thought the video would be more believable if it "was published."

Students' knowledge of the larger contexts surrounding 9/11 also served as evaluative criteria for many claims and evidence in the video. Most students were already familiar with many basic claims made in the movie—that the U.S. government covered up certain facts about what happened, that the Bush administration had information about the impending attacks, that the World Trade Center towers were brought down by controlled demolition explosions, and that military buildup and the war on terror have benefited some Americans financially and politically. However, students also referred to what was absent—counterarguments, contradictory evidence, and other theories and claims about what happened. The lack of alternative intertextual referents remained a concern with several students indicating that they wanted to see more perspectives or hear different stories about what happened. They wanted to know more about other theories and claims made about the 9/11 attacks. For example, during the class discussion, one student noted that claims weren't consistent with what he had seen on the Discovery Channel about the collapse of the buildings. He also added that people are often too willing to accept conspiracy theories when they don't understand something. To support his point, he cited the moon landings and the story that alternative energy source cars have been blocked by the auto and oil industries as examples of other conspiracy theories.

Power of the Visual

Students generally placed their greatest trust in images, such as photos, diagrams, models, and video clips. In terms of reliability, visual representations had greater currency than explanations (e.g., from eyewitness accounts or interviews) or print materials that were presented as evidence. One student noted that "the pictures proving the evidence makes it very believable," while another said that "diagrams make it believable." Referring to the video and photo clips used in the movie, one student noted, "The clips have genuine traits that when you see it you know it is real." Another noted that visual comparisons made the video believable: "e.g., this is what a normal plane crash should look like, this is what the scene at the Pentagon looked like," while another student commented on what would make the video more believable, saying "more pictures from 'different' angles" would support some claims.

Like eyewitness accounts, video and photo representations claim a direct connection to events. However, students didn't question whether images had been taken out of context and rearranged in new combinations to produce "reality" (Lasch, 1984). Several students wanted corroborating evidence or explanation to support eyewitness accounts but seldom challenged visual evidence. We believe this supports Kress's (2003) notions about print being supplanted by images in the new media age and the corresponding need for greater attention to issues of visual literacy as a core component of multimodal literacy education.

Summary: Need for "Lateral Cognitive Mobility" and "Meta-Knowledge"

The challenges students identified in their efforts to assess the video's credibility are related to issues of multimodality, intertextuality, and contextualization. Describing the intertextual and "interdiscursive hybridity" of texts, Fairclough (2005) argues that texts contain multiple and diverse features. Multimodal texts, such as video texts, consist of different genres, discourses, and styles; intertextual allusions; various assumptions, implications, contradictions, and rhetorical and persuasive features; and numerous linguistic features. A video, like *Loose Change*, combines several modalities and texts that

18

work together (or sometimes against each other) to produce a synergistic effect. It requires viewers to read and evaluate multiple texts and modalities *and* the multimodal text as a whole as they consider credibility.

Put another way, *Loose Change* complicates discernments of credibility in two ways: (1) there is a dynamic intertextuality among the different modes and texts within the video (what Sipe refers to as requiring transmediation) and (2) there is intertextuality between the video as a whole and other texts and discourses (existing outside of the video text). In terms of credibility, transmediation and intertextual work is important because students have to consider claims and authorship in terms of what other texts say and how well supported claims were with evidence within the text (along with their internal logic). Since claims and evidence were represented in multiple ways, readers/viewers have go back and forth in "a potentially endless process [in which] reviewing and rereading will produce ever-new insights as we construct new connections and make modifications of our previous interpretations" (Sipe, 1998, p. 106). Luke (2003) refers to the need for "critical understandings of the *relations* among ideas, their sources and histories, intertextual referents and consequences" (p. 400; italics original) and "*connection codes*" that can help students think laterally across associations and modalities. In other words, their ability to corroborate claims and evidence (Wineburg, 2001), an essentially intertextual practice of comparing one text against another and evaluating credibility in relationship to or in terms of other texts, depends upon their ability to make connections to other texts and information.

The students in this study tried to contextualize claims and evidence in *Loose Change* by situating authorship, information, claims, evidence, and texts in broader contexts. They tried to contextualize by drawing on their own prior knowledge and stances, by noting their familiarity with certain information, images, news clips, and theories, and by referring to certain contexts, such as the general climate of distrust of the Bush administration. However, to more deeply understand and critically evaluate this video (and its claims) requires an understanding of broader contexts that help us understand the prevalence of conspiracy theories, widespread distrust of the U.S. government (especially the Bush administration), the difficulties of discerning "truth" and the postmodern incredulity of truth claims, the challenges of making sense of the overwhelming amount of information we have access to in an "information society," the widespread use of "spin" and propaganda techniques, different genres and discourses, and so on. All of these contexts seem to factor into how we make sense of this video, whether it resonates with us, and how it activates certain frames, mental schema, and/or emotions. Luke (2003) refers to this widespread knowledge as "a meta-knowledge of traditional and newly blended genres or representational conventions, cultural and symbolic codes, and linguistically coded and software-driven meanings" requiring "lateral cognitive mobility across disciplines, genres, modalities, and, indeed, cultural zones" (p. 401).

MAKING "HOW DO WE KNOW?" THE MAIN FOCUS OF EDUCATIONAL PRACTICE

Examining the students' responses to *Loose Change* sheds some light on their meaning-making with this multimodal text. Yet much more needs to be done. Due to time restrictions with this study (data were collected on the last day of the school year), we were not able to more deeply investigate important issues, such as the effects of readers' different reading styles on their meaning-making or reasons for their differences in textual interpretation. More sustained studies that document and examine closely the sense-making of individual and groups of readers over time, especially with texts like *Loose Change*, and with a broader repertoire of research methods (e.g., using think-aloud protocols as readers engage with Internet texts [Coiro & Dobler, 2007]) are a key next step. In this sense, findings from this study point to the need for greater attention given to the "epistemology of text" (Wineburg, 2001) and the epistemological dimensions of literacy and inquiry practices with multimodal texts. As Delandshire (2002) suggests, emphasizing the epistemological dimensions of classroom practice means that we should ask what it means to know and *how* knowing takes place, instead of asking *what* students know. Findings from this study highlight the need for continuing dialogue with students about issues of credibility—to, for example, discuss how the video was constructed, the effects on them as viewers or readers, the quality of the information presented in video, and broader contexts that help us understand the video and the claims it makes. The findings also point to the need for new or revised criteria, tools, and practices that can help students assess the credibility of multimodal texts. For example, many students made multimodal judgments based on how the video was constructed and whether modes supported each other to provide a convincing account. Some focused on qualities that have been described by others (Warnick, 2003) as superficial aspects (such as production quality and the mix of modal elements), but we need to question whether these are superficial qualities in multimodal texts. Perhaps it is the identification and analysis of these "superficial" qualities that will help students get beneath surface impressions and explore deeper meanings of certain techniques and production processes. Perhaps more aesthetic judgments are necessary inroads for more engaged critical analysis of multimodal texts.

In terms of how teachers might best guide students to engage critically with multimodal texts, the New London Group (2000) suggests a "complex integration" of approaches comprised of four components: situated practice, overt instruction, critical framing, and transformed practice (p. 31). Intended to be interactive rather than linear or lock-step, when teachers enact these four components—immersing students in meaningful practices (situated practice); providing explicit scaffolding of key learning activities (overt instruction); helping students understand relationships between historical, political, and ideological systems of knowledge and particular social practices (critical framing); and leading students to revise and apply what they have learned to other contexts (transformed practice)—they help students develop a "meta-language" of design "for talking about language, images, texts and meaning-making interactions" (pp. 23–24). This meta-language focuses on describing meanings in various realms, including "the textual and the visual, as well as the multimodal relations between the different meaning-making processes that are now so critical in media texts and the texts of electronic media" (p. 24).

In terms of tools to guide students in developing this "meta-language" and in making reasoned judgments about credibility, there are some resources available for educators. These tools include lists of questions and suggestions provided by university or college libraries (e.g., criteria for Web page evaluation by Cornell University, http://www.library.cornell.edu/olinuris/ref/webcrit.html) as well as checklists and surveys more specifically for K–12 contexts, such as "critical evaluation surveys" for elementary, middle, and secondary school students. One particular set of surveys centers upon the technical and visual aspects of a Web page, content, and authority. These surveys also prompt students to answer a series of yes–no questions as well as write a narrative evaluation of a site (http://school.discoveryeducation.com/schrockguide/eval.html). With more explicit attention to design aspects of Web credibility, the Stanford Persuasive Technology Lab (http://captology.stanford.edu/) promotes meta-level understandings about design with 10 guidelines for creating and evaluating credible Web sites. These guidelines include making it easy to verify accuracy of site information, highlighting the expertise of the organization operating the site, and consistently updating the site's information (http://credibility.stanford.edu/guidelines/index.html).

In our own work, we have drawn on a three-dimensional model of literacy (Green, 1988; Durrant & Green, 2001) to develop critical reading and writing tools to guide students' work with Web sites (Damico, Baildon, & Campano, 2005; Damico & Baildon, 2007). This set of tools takes any Web site, places it within a frame, and then provides "lenses" which include guiding questions, models, and suggestions that readers use as they engage with the Web site. The four primary lenses are a *descriptive lens* to help readers determine the relevance and reliability of texts and links on a Web site; an *academic lens* to help readers examine claims and evidence on a site; a *critical lens* to help readers identify included and omitted perspectives on a site and evaluate how authors and Web creators attempt to influence them (e.g., use of loaded words, provocative images, links); and a *reflexive lens* to help readers examine how their own beliefs, values, and experiences affect their reading. A writing tool is also embedded within the frame where students record and save all their work with each Web site (i.e., their analyses, interpretations, and questions). With easy access to this work, teachers can assess their students' learning to inform their instruction.

Although these tools have proven successful in guiding students' work with Web sources of information (Damico & Baildon, 2007), a crucial next step is to modify these tools or create new tools to engage specifically with complex multimodal texts, such as *Loose Change*. These tools could guide students to identify and sort modalities and texts in a video, choose whether to stop the video to isolate and examine specific components, identify techniques used in video production, as well as help readers examine their own responses to the texts (e.g., their emotions and assumptions, familiarity with different genres, understanding of the content, etc.).

CONCLUDING THOUGHTS

Reading complicated multimodal texts involves situating these texts through broader processes of their production and reception, such as the way conspiracy theories shape readers' responses. The historian, Christopher Lasch (1984), although writing before the 9/11 attacks, described why this is so important: "More and more, our impressions of the world derive not from the observations we make both as individuals and as members of a wider community but from elaborate systems of communication, which spew out information, much of it unbelievable, about events of which we seldom have any direct knowledge" (p. 133). As a result, people can see themselves "as victims of policies over which they have no control. They see themselves as victims not only of bureaucracy, big government, and unpredictable technologies, but also, in many cases, of high-level plots and conspiracies" (p. 44). Because people can feel like forces beyond their control dictate their lives and mass media work to tell people what to buy, what to believe, and increasingly shape perceptions, "the technology of modern communications keeps people in line by making it easy for them to accept the unacceptable" (p. 141).

It also bears mentioning that determinations of credibility shouldn't be considered a perfectionist endeavor; "they inevitably entail judgments about *how much* credibility one needs to support action or belief based on a particular claim, and this degree will generally vary depending on the seriousness of the consequences for that person of an error" (Burbules, 2001, p. 446; italics original). The greatest danger, for Burbules, is "that one will simply choose to accept information that plausibly confirms one's prior beliefs or what one wishes were true. None of us can be entirely immune to this weakness but, to the extent that credibility judgments are recognized as having an ethical element, the consequences of doing so, for ourselves and for others, can at least be brought to the surface" (p. 452). What is required, then, is that these epistemological issues be surfaced, made explicit, and kept in the foreground of educational practice. We need to reconsider the tools, practices, and approaches that can take into account the complex and dynamic interactions among different modalities, viewers, and contexts as well as develop new research approaches that can help us understand multimodal literacy practices.

Findings from this study offer empirical grounds for this ongoing conceptualizing (and reconceptualizing) work. Dimitriadis and McCarthy (2001), for example, propose "a new model for postdisciplinary conversation, an intellectual practice not concerned with sustaining knowledge and genre stratification, nor with scaffolding institutional imperatives, but with transformative and reflective, public intellectual activity" (p. 37). Careful analysis of readers' engagements with multimodal texts like *Loose Change* offers rich opportunities for postdisciplinary conversation and inquiry where blending literacy and inquiry practices within a sociocultural framework can open up spaces for students to be creators of meaning. We believe the ability to look at the world for one-self is learned through participation with tools and within communities that can support people in asking questions that they wouldn't normally ask and reading texts, such as multimodal works. These "participatory events" (Dimitriadis & McCarthy, 2001) can involve readers of all ages in collaborative and critical investigations about core issues, such as credibility, which remain central to living in a democratic society.

REFERENCES

Allen, T. J. (2006). The 9/11 faith movement. *Alternet*. Retrieved July 29, 2006, from http://www.alternet.org/story/37647/

Appadurai, A. (1996). *Modernity at large: Cultural dimensions of globalization*. Minneapolis: University of Minnesota Press.

Bakhtin, M. (1973). *Problems of Dostoevsky's poetics* (R.W. Rotsel, Trans.). Ann Arbor, MI: Ardis.

Baldry, A., & Thibault, P. J. (2006). *Multimodal transcription and text analysis: A multimedia toolkit and coursebook*. London: Equinox.

Barthes, R. (1977). *Image-music-text*. New York: Noonday Press.

Burbules, N. C. (2001). Paradoxes of the Web: The ethical dimensions of credibility. *Library Trends, 49*(3), 441–453.

Burbules, N. C., & Callister, T. A. (2000). *Watch IT: The risks and promises of information technologies for education*. Boulder, CO: Westview.

Coiro, J. (2003). Reading comprehension on the Internet: Expanding our understanding of reading comprehension to encompass new literacies. *Reading Teacher, 56*(5), 458–464.

Coiro, J., & Dobler, B. (2007). Exploring the online reading comprehension strategies used by sixth-grade skilled readers to search for and locate information on the Internet. *Reading Research Quarterly, 42*(2), 214–257.

Damico, J. S., & Baildon, M. (2007). Reading Web sites in an inquiry-based literacy and social studies classroom. In D. Rowe & R. T. Jimenez (Eds.), *National Reading Conference yearbook* (pp. 204–217). Oak Creek, WI: National Reading Conference.

Damico, J., Baildon, M., & Campano, G. (2005). Integrating literacy, technology and disciplined inquiry in social studies: The development and application of a conceptual model. *T.H.E.N.* (Journal about Technology, Humanities, Education, & Narrative), *2*. Retrieved December 30, 2008, from http://thenjournal.orgAsfeature/92/

Delandshire, G. (2002). Assessment as inquiry. *Teachers College Record, 104*(7), 1461–1484.

Derrida, J. (1974). *Of grammatology*. Baltimore: Johns Hopkins University Press.

Dimitriadis, G., & McCarthy, G. (2001). *Reading and teaching the postcolonial: From Baldwin to Basquiat and beyond*. New York: Teachers College Press.

Durrant, C., & Green, B. (2001). Literacy and the new technologies in school education: Meeting the l(IT)eracy challenge. In H. Fehring & P. Green (Eds.), *Critical literacy: A collection of articles from the Australia Literacy Educators' Association* (pp. 142–164). Newark, DE: International Reading Association.

Fairclough, N. (1989). *Language and power*. Harlow, UK: Pearson Education.

Fairclough, N. (1995). *Media discourse*. London: Edward Arnold.

Fairclough, N. (2005). Critical discourse analysis. *Marges Linguistiques, 9*, 76–94. Retrieved February 7, 2007, from http://www.ling.lancs.ac.uk/profiles/263

Green, B. (1988). Subject-specific literacy and school learning: A focus on writing. *Australian Journal of Education, 32*(2), 156–179.

Hartman, D. K. (1995). Eight readers reading: The intertextual links of proficient readers using multiple passages. *Reading Research Quarterly, 30*(3), 520–561.

Hodge, R., & Kress, G. (1988). *Social semiotics*. Ithaca, NY: Cornell University Press.

Hofstadter, R. (1964, November). The paranoid style in American politics. *Harper's Magazine*, pp. 77–86. Retrieved March 27, 2005, from http://karws.gso.uri.edu/JFK/conspiracy_theory/the_paranoid_mentality/The_paranoid_style.html

Hull, G. A., & Nelson, M. E. (2005). Locating the semiotic power of multimodality. *Written Communications, 22*(2), 224–261.

Kress, G. (2003). *Literacy in the new media age*. New York: Routledge.

Kristeva, J. (1980). *Desire in language: A semiotic approach to literature and art*. New York: Columbia University Press.

Lankshear, C., Peters, M., & Knobel, M. (2000). Information, knowledge, and learning: Some issues facing epistemology and education in a digital age. *Journal of Philosophy of Education, 34*(1), 17–39.

Lasch, C. (1984). *The minimal self: Psychic survival in troubled times*. New York: Norton.

Levstik, L., & Barton, K. (2001). *Doing history: Investigating with children in elementary and middle schools*. Mahwah, NJ: Lawrence Erlbaum.

Lincoln, Y. S., & Guba, E. G. (1985). *Naturalistic inquiry*. Newbury Park, CA: Sage.

Luke, C. (2003). Pedagogy, connectivity, multimodality, and interdisciplinarity. *Reading Research Quarterly, 38*(3), 397–403.

New London Group. (2000). A pedagogy of multiliteracies. In B. Cope & M. Kalantzis (Eds.), *Multiliteracies: Literacy learning and the design of social futures* (pp. 9–37). London: Routledge.

Nixon, H. (2003). New research literacies for contemporary research into literacy and new media? *Reading Research Quarterly, 38*(3), 386–413. Sales, N. J. (2006). Click here for conspiracy. *Vanity Fair*. Retrieved December 28, 2006, from http://www.vanityfair.com/commentary/content/pr intables/060717roco02?print=true

Segall, A. (1999). Critical history: Implications for history/social studies education. *Theory and Research in Social Education, 27*, 358–374.

Sipe, L. (1998). How picture books work: A semiotically framed theory of textpicture relationships. *Children's Literature in Education, 29*(2), 97–108.

Sonesson, G. (2002). The varieties of interpretation: A view from semiotics. *Revista Galáxia*, 2(4). Retrieved January 12, 2007, from http://www.text-semiotics.org/english3.html

Stake, R. (1994). Case studies. In N. K. Denzin & Y. S. Lincoln (Eds.), *Handbook of qualitative research* (pp. 246–247). Newbury Park, CA: Sage.

Stone, M., & Parker, T. (2006, October 11). *South Park: Mystery of the urinal deuce* [Television series episode]. Retrieved January 12, 2007, from www.vidpeek.com

Strauss, A., & Corbin, J. (1990). *Basics of qualitative research: Grounded theory procedures and techniques.* Newbury Park, CA: Sage.

Warnick, B. (2003, October). *Online ethos: Source credibility in an "authorless"environment.* Paper presented at the Association of Internet Researchers Conference, Toronto, ON. Retrieved June 27, 2006, from http://faculty.washington.edu/barbwarn/Ethospaper1.htm

Werner, W. (2002). Reading visual texts. *Theory and Research in Social Education, 30*(3), 401–428.

Wiggins, G., & McTighe, J. (1998). *Understanding by design.* Alexandria, VA: Association for Supervision and Curriculum Development.

Wineburg, S. (2001). *Historical thinking and other unnatural acts: Charting the future of teaching the past.* Philadelphia: Temple University Press.

THE RHETORICAL SITUATION

LLOYD F. BITZER

CONSIDER AS YOU ARE READING:

Bitzer's definition of the "rhetorical situation" has become a cornerstone of the field of rhetoric and composition. Bitzer claims that rhetorical discourse exists as a result of a particular situation that demands a response. Hence, we must understand the "exigence" of the situation in order to develop a powerful and useful rhetorical response. Understanding the exigence of a rhetorical situation leads to greater insight into other rhetorical issues, such as the purpose of communication and the kinds of appeals that best address audiences' needs and values. While some aspects of this definition have been challenged since the publication of this essay in 1980, the ideas here have been the starting point for many conversations about rhetoric and writing.

1. *What does Bitzer mean by "exigence"? Why is exigence so important for a theory of rhetoric? For writers?*

2. *Think of the last significant piece of writing you authored. To what rhetorical situation or situations where you responding? What was the exigence for your writing?*

3. *Review Vatz's article, "The Myth of the Rhetorical Situation," in this volume. Vatz argues that, rather than entering into a rhetorical situation (as Bitzer suggests), humans create rhetorical situations. Where do you stand in this debate?*

If someone says, "That is a dangerous situation," his words suggest the presence of events, persons, or objects which threaten him, someone else, or something of value. If someone remarks, "I find myself in an embarrassing situation," again the statement implies certain situational characteristics. If someone remarks that he found himself in an ethical situation, we understand that he probably either contemplated or made some choice of action from a sense of duty or obligation or with a view to the Good. In other words, there are circumstances of this or that kind of structure which are recognized as ethical, dangerous, or embarrassing. What characteristics, then, are implied when one refers to "the rhetorical situation"—the context in which speakers or writers create rhetorical discourse? Perhaps this question is puzzling because "situation," is not a standard term in the vocabulary of rhetorical theory. "Audience" is standard; so also are "speaker," "subject," "occasion," and "speech." If I were to ask, "What is a rhetorical audience?" or "What is a rhetorical subject?"—the reader would catch the meaning of my question.

When I ask, What is a rhetorical situation? I want to know the nature of those contexts in which speakers or writers create rhetorical discourse: How should they be described? What are their characteristics? Why and how do they result in the creation of rhetoric? By analogy, a theorist of science might well ask, "What are the characteristics of situations which inspire scientific thought?" A philosopher might ask, "What is the nature of the situation in which a philosopher 'does philosophy'?" And a theorist of poetry might ask, "How shall we describe the context in which poetry comes into existence?"

The presence of rhetorical discourse obviously indicates the presence of a rhetorical situation. The Declaration of Independence, Lincoln's Gettysburg Address, Churchill's Address on Dunkirk, John F. Kennedy's Inaugural Address— each is a clear instance of rhetoric and each indicates the presence of a situation. While the existence of a rhetorical address is a reliable sign of the existence of situation, it does not follow that a situation exists only when the discourse exists. Each reader probably can recall a specific time and place when there was opportunity to speak on some urgent matter, and after the opportunity was gone, he created in private thought the speech he should have uttered earlier in the situation. It is clear that situations are not always accompanied by discourse. Nor should we assume that a rhetorical address gives existence to the situation; on the contrary, it is the situation which calls the discourse into existence. Clement Attlee once said that Winston Churchill went around looking for "finest hours." The point to observe is that Churchill found them—the crisis situations—and spoke in response to them.

No major theorist has treated rhetorical situation thoroughly as a distinct subject in rhetorical theory; many ignore it. Those rhetoricians who discuss situation do so indirectly—as does Aristotle, for example, who is led to consider situation when he treats types of discourse. None, to my knowledge, has asked the nature of rhetorical situation. Instead rhetoricians have asked: What is the process by which the orator creates and presents discourse? What is the nature of rhetorical discourse? What sorts of interaction occur between speaker, audience, subject, and occasion? Typically the questions which trigger theories of rhetoric focus upon the orator's method or upon the discourse itself, rather than upon the situation which invites the orator's application of his method and the creation of discourse. Thus rhetoricians distinguish among and characterize the types of Speeches (forensic, deliberative, epideictic) they treat issues, types of proof, lines of argument, strategies of ethical and emotional persuasion, the parts of a discourse and the functions of these parts, qualities of styles, figures of speech. They cover approximately the same materials, (the formal aspects of rhetorical method and discourse) whether focusing upon method, product or process; while conceptions of situation are implicit in some theories of rhetoric, none explicitly treat the formal aspects of situation.

I hope that enough has been said to show that the question— What is a rhetorical situation?—is not an idle one. I propose in what follows to set forth part of a theory of situation. This essay, therefore, should be understood as an attempt to revive the notion of rhetorical situation, to provide at least the outline of an adequate conception of it, and to establish it as a controlling and fundamental concern of rhetorical theory.

I

It seems clear that rhetoric is situational. In saying this, I do not mean merely that understanding a speech hinges upon understanding the context of meaning in which the speech is located. Virtually no utterance is fully intelligible unless meaning-context and utterance are understood; this is true of rhetorical and non-rhetorical discourse. Meaning-context is a general condition of human communication and is not synonymous with rhetorical situation. Nor do I mean merely that rhetoric occurs in a setting which involves interaction of speaker, audience, subject, and communicative purpose. This is too general, since many types of utterances—philosophical, scientific, poetic, and rhetorical—occur in such settings. Nor would I equate rhetorical situation with persuasive situation, which exists whenever an audience can be changed in belief or action by means of speech. Every audience at any moment is capable of being changed in some way by speech; persuasive situation is altogether general.

Finally, I do not mean that a rhetorical discourse must be embedded in historic context in the sense that a living tree must be rooted in soil. A tree does not obtain its character-as-tree from the soil, but rhetorical discourse, I shall argue, does obtain its character-as-rhetorical from the situation which generates it. Rhetorical works belong to the class of things which obtain their character from the circumstances of the historic context in which they occur. A rhetorical work is analogous to a moral action rather than to a tree. An act is moral because it is an act performed in a situation of a certain kind; similarly, a work is rhetorical because it is a response to a situation of a certain kind.

In order to clarify rhetoric-as-essentially-related-to-situation, we should acknowledge a viewpoint that is commonplace but fundamental: a work of rhetoric is pragmatic; it comes into existence for the sake of something beyond itself; it functions ultimately to produce action or change in the world; it performs some task. In short, rhetoric is a mode of altering reality, not by the direct application of energy to objects, but by the creation of discourse which changes reality through the mediation of thought and action. The rhetor alters reality by bringing into existence a discourse of such a character that the audience, in thought and action, is so engaged that it becomes mediator of change. In this sense, rhetoric is always persuasive.

To say that rhetorical discourse comes into being in order to effect change is altogether general. We need to understand that a particular discourse comes into existence because of some specific condition or situation which invites utterance. Bronislaw Malinowski refers to just this sort of situation in his discussion of primitive language, which he finds to be essentially pragmatic and "embedded in situation." He describes a party of fishermen in the Trobriand Islands whose functional speech occurs in a "context of situation."

> The canoes glide slowly and noiselessly, punted by men especially good at this task and always used for it. Other experts who know the bottom of the lagoon . . . are on the lookout for fish. . . . Customary signs, or sounds or words are uttered. Sometimes a sentence full of technical references to the Channels or patches on the lagoon has to be spoken; sometimes ... a conventional cry is uttered. . . . Again, a word of command is passed here and there, a technical expression or explanation which serves to harmonize their behavior towards other men. . . . An animated scene, full of movement, follows, and now that the fish are in their power the fishermen speak loudly, and give vent to their feelings. Short, telling exclamations fly about, which might be rendered by such words as: "Pull in," "Let go," "Shift further," "Lift the net."

In this whole scene, "each utterance is essentially bound up with the context of situation and with the aim of the pursuit. . . The structure of all this linguistic material is inextricably mixed up with, and dependent upon, the course of the activity in which the utterances are embedded." Later the observer remarks: "In its primitive uses, language functions as a link in concerted human activity, as a piece of human behavior. It is a mode of action and not an instrument of reflection."[1]

These statements about primitive language and the "context of situation" provide for us a preliminary model of rhetorical situation. Let us regard rhetorical situation as a natural context of persons, events, objects, relations, and an exigence which strongly invites utterance; this invited utterance participates naturally in the situation, is in many instances necessary to the completion of situational activity, and by means of its participation with situation obtains its meaning and its rhetorical character. In Malinowski's example, the situation is the fishing expedition—consisting of objects, persons, events, and relations—and the ruling exigence, the success of the hunt. The situation dictates the sorts of observations to be made; it dictates the significant physical and verbal responses; and, we must admit, it constrains the words which are uttered in the same sense that it constrains the physical acts of paddling the canoes and throwing the nets. The verbal responses to the demands imposed by this situation are clearly as functional and necessary as the physical responses.

Traditional theories of rhetoric have dealt, of course, not with the sorts of primitive utterances described by Malinowski— "stop here," "throw the nets," "move closer"—but with larger units of speech which come more readily under the guidance of artistic principle and method. The difference between oratory and primitive utterance, however, is not a difference in function; the clear instances of rhetorical discourse and the fishermen's utterances are similarly functional and similarly situational. Observing both the traditions of the expedition and the facts before him, the leader of the fishermen finds himself *obliged* to speak at a given moment—to command, to supply information, to praise or blame—to respond appropriately to the situation. Clear instances of artistic rhetoric exhibit the same character: Cicero's speeches against Cataline were called forth by a specific union of persons, events, objects, and relations, and by an exigence which amounted to an imperative stimulus; the speeches in the Senate rotunda three days after the assassination of the President of the United States were actually required by the situation. So controlling is situation that we should consider it the very ground of rhetorical activity, whether that activity is primitive and productive of a simple utterance or artistic and productive of the Gettysburg Address.

Hence, to say that rhetoric is situational means:

1. rhetorical discourse comes into existence as a response to situation, in the same sense that an answer comes into existence in response to a question, or a solution in response to a problem;

2. a speech is given rhetorical significance by the situation, just as a unit of discourse is given significance as answer or as solution by the question or problem;

3. a rhetorical situation must exist as a necessary condition of rhetorical discourse, just as a question must exist as a necessary condition of an answer;

4. many questions go unanswered and many problems remain unsolved; similarly, many rhetorical situations mature and decay without giving birth to rhetorical utterance;

5. a situation is rhetorical insofar as it needs and invites discourse capable of participating with situation and thereby altering its reality;

6. discourse is rhetorical insofar as it functions (or seeks to function) as a fitting response to a situation which needs and invites it;

7. Finally, the situation controls the rhetorical response in the same sense that the question controls the answer and the problem controls the solution. Not the rhetor and not persuasive intent, but the situation is the source and ground of rhetorical activity—and, I should add, of rhetorical criticism.

II

Let us now amplify the nature of situation by providing a formal definition and examining constituents. Rhetorical situation may be defined as a complex of persons, events, objects, and relations presenting an actual or potential exigence which can be completely or partially removed if discourse, introduced into the situation, can so constrain human decision or action as to bring about the significant modification of the exigence. Prior to the creation and presentation of discourse, there are three constituents of any rhetorical situation: the first is the exigence;

the second and third are elements of the complex, namely the audience to be constrained in decision and action, and the constraints which influence the rhetor and can be brought to bear upon the audience.

Any exigence is an imperfection marked by urgency; it is a defect, an obstacle, something waiting to be done, a thing which is other than it should be. In almost any sort of context, there will be numerous exigences, but not all are elements of a rhetorical situation—not all are rhetorical exigences. An exigence which cannot be modified is not rhetorical; thus, whatever comes about of necessity and cannot be changed—death, winter, and some natural disasters, for instance—are exigences to be sure, but they are not rhetorical. Further, an exigence which can be modified only by means other than discourse is not rhetorical; thus, an exigence is not rhetorical when its modification requires merely one's own action or the application of a tool, but neither requires nor invites the assistance of discourse. An exigence is rhetorical when it is capable of positive modification and when positive modification requires discourse or can be assisted by discourse. For example, suppose that a man's acts are injurious to others and that the quality of his acts can be changed only if discourse is addressed to him; the exigence—his injurious acts—is then unmistakably rhetorical. The pollution of our air is also a rhetorical exigence because its positive modification—reduction of pollution—strongly invites the assistance of discourse producing public awareness, indignation, and action of the right kind. Frequently, rhetors encounter exigences which defy easy classification because of the absence of information enabling precise analysis and certain judgment—they may or may not be rhetorical. An attorney whose client has been convicted may strongly believe that a higher court would reject his appeal to have the verdict overturned, but because the matter is uncertain—because the exigence might be rhetorical—he elects to appeal. In this and similar instances of indeterminate exigences the rhetor's decision to speak is based mainly upon the urgency of the exigence and the probability that the exigence is rhetorical.

In any rhetorical situation, there will be at least one controlling exigence which functions as the organizing principle: it specifies the audience to be addressed and the change to be effected. The exigence may or may not be perceived clearly by the rhetor or other persons in the situation; it may be strong or weak depending upon the clarity of their perception and the degree of their interest in it; it may be real or unreal depending on the facts of the case; it may be important or trivial; it may be such that discourse can completely remove it, or it may persist in spite of repeated modifications; it may be completely familiar—one of a type of exigences occurring frequently in our experience— or it may be totally new, unique. When it is perceived and when it is strong and important, then it constrains the thought and action of the perceiver who may respond rhetorically if he is in a position to do so.

The second constituent is the audience. Since rhetorical discourse produces change by influencing the decision and action of persons who function as mediators of change, it follows that rhetoric always requires an audience—even in those cases when a person engages himself or ideal mind as audience. It is clear also that a rhetorical audience must be distinguished from a body of mere hearers or readers: properly speaking, a rhetorical audience consists only of those persons who are capable of being influenced by discourse and of being mediators of change.

Neither scientific nor poetic discourse requires an audience in the same sense. Indeed, neither requires an audience in order to produce its end; the scientist can produce a discourse expressive or generative of knowledge without engaging another mind and the poet's creative purpose is accomplished when the work is composed. It is true, of course, that scientists and poets present their works to audiences, but their audiences are not necessarily rhetorical. The scientific audience consists of persons capable of receiving knowledge, and the poetic audience, of persons capable of participating in aesthetic experiences induced by the poetry. But the rhetorical audience must be capable of serving as mediator of the change which the discourse functions to produce.

Besides exigence and audience, every rhetorical situation contains a set of constraints made up of persons, events, objects, and relations which are parts of the situation because they have the power to constrain decision and action needed to modify the exigence. Standard sources of constraint include beliefs, attitudes, documents, facts, traditions, images, interests, motives and the like; and when the orator enters the situation, his discourse not only harnesses constraints given by situation but provides additional important constraints—for example his personal character, his logical proofs, and his style. There are two main classes of constraints: (1) those originated or managed by the rhetor and his method (Aristotle called these "artistic proofs"), and (2) those other constraints, in the situation, which may be operative (Aristotle's "inartistic proofs"). Both classes must be divided so as to separate those constraints that are proper from those that are improper.

These three constituents—exigence, audience, constraints—comprise everything relevant in a rhetorical situation. When the orator, invited by situation, enters it and creates and presents discourse, then both he and his speech are additional constituents.

III

I have broadly sketched a conception of rhetorical situation and discussed constituents. The following are general characteristics or features.

1. Rhetorical discourse is called into existence by situation; the situation which the rhetor perceives amounts to an invitation to create and present discourse. The clearest instances of rhetorical speaking and writing are strongly invited—often required. The situation generated by the assassination of President Kennedy was so highly structured and compelling that one could predict with near certainty the types and themes of forthcoming discourse. With the first reports of the assassination, there immediately developed a most urgent need for information; in response, reporters created hundreds of messages. Later as the situation altered, other exigences arose: the fantastic events in Dallas had to be explained; it was necessary to eulogize the dead President; the public needed to be assured that the transfer of government to new hands would be orderly. These messages were

not idle performances. The historic situation was so compelling and clear that the responses were created almost out of necessity. The responses—news reports, explanations, eulogies—participated with the situation and positively modified the several exigences. Surely the power of situation is evident when one can predict that such discourse will be uttered. How else explain the phenomenon? One cannot say that the situation is the function of the speaker's intention, for in this case the speakers' intentions were determined by the Situation. One cannot say that the rhetorical transaction is simply a response of the speaker to the demands or expectations of an audience, for the expectations of the audience were themselves keyed to a tragic historic fact. Also, we must recognize that there came into existence countless eulogies to John F. Kennedy that never reached a public; they were filed, entered in diaries, or created in thought.

In contrast, imagine a person spending his time writing eulogies of men and women who never existed: his speeches meet no rhetorical situations; they are summoned into existence not by real events, but by his own imagination. They may exhibit formal features which we consider rhetorical—such as ethical and emotional appeals, and stylistic patterns; conceivably one of these fictive eulogies is even persuasive to someone; yet all remain unrhetorical unless, through the oddest of circumstances, one of them by chance should fit a situation. Neither the presence of formal features in the discourse nor persuasive effect in a reader or hearer can be regarded as reliable marks of rhetorical discourse: A speech will be rhetorical when it is a response to the kind of situation which is rhetorical.

2. Although rhetorical situation invites response, it obviously does not invite just any response. Thus the second characteristic of rhetorical situation is that it invites a fitting response, a response that fits the situation. Lincoln's Gettysburg Address was a most fitting response to the relevant features of the historic context which invited its existence and gave it rhetorical significance. Imagine for a moment the Gettysburg Address entirely separated

from its situation and existing for us independent of any rhetorical context: as a discourse which does not "fit" any rhetorical situation, it becomes either poetry or declamation, without rhetorical significance. In reality, however, the address continues to have profound rhetorical value precisely because some features of the Gettysburg situation persist; and the Gettysburg Address continues to participate with situation and to alter it.

Consider another instance. During one week of the 1964 presidential campaign, three events of national and international significance all but obscured the campaign: Krushchev was suddenly deposed, China exploded an atomic bomb, and in England the Conservative Party was defeated by Labor. Any student of rhetoric could have given odds that President Johnson, in a major address, would speak to the significance of these events, and he did; his response to the situation generated by the events was fitting. Suppose that the President had treated not these events and their significance but the national budget, or imagine that he had reminisced about his childhood on a Texas farm. The critic of rhetoric would have said rightly, "He missed the mark; his speech did not fit; he did not speak to the pressing issues—the rhetorical situation shaped by the three crucial events of the week demanded a response, and he failed to provide the proper one."

3. If it makes sense to say that situation invites a "fitting" response, then situation must somehow prescribe the response which fits. To say that a rhetorical response fits a situation is to say that it meets the requirements established by the situation. A situation which is strong and clear dictates the purpose, theme, matter, and style of the response. Normally, the inauguration of a President of the United States demands an address which speaks to the nation's purposes, the central national and international problems, the unity of contesting parties; it demands speech style marked by dignity. What is evidenced on this occasion is the power of situation to constrain a fitting response. One might say metaphorically that every situation prescribes its

fitting response; the rhetor may or may not read the prescription accurately.

4. The exigence and the complex of persons, objects, events and relations which generate rhetorical discourse are located in reality, are objective and publicly observable historic facts in the world we experience, are therefore available for scrutiny by an observer or critic who attends to them. To say the situation is objective, publicly observable, and historic means that it is real or genuine—that our critical examination will certify its existence. Real situations are to be distinguished from sophistic ones in which, for example, a contrived exigence is asserted to be real; from spurious situations in which the existence or alleged existence of constituents is the result of error or ignorance; and from fantasy in which exigence, audience, and constraints may all be the imaginary objects of a mind at play.

The rhetorical situation as real is to be distinguished also from a fictive rhetorical situation. The speech of a character in a novel or play may be clearly required by a fictive rhetorical situation—a situation established by the story itself; but the speech is not genuinely rhetorical, even though, considered in itself, it looks exactly like a courtroom address or a senate speech. It is realistic, made so by fictive context. But the situation is not real, not grounded in history; neither the fictive situation nor the discourse generated by it is rhetorical. We should note, however, that the fictive rhetorical discourse within a play or novel may become genuinely rhetorical outside fictive context—if there is a real situation for which the discourse is a rhetorical response. Also, of course, the play or novel itself may be understood as a rhetorical response having poetic form.

5. Rhetorical situations exhibit structures which are simple or complex, and more or less organized. A situation's structure is simple when there are relatively few elements which must be made to interact; the fishing expedition is a case in point—there is a clear and easy relationship among utterances, the audiences, constraints, and

exigence. Franklin D. Roosevelt's brief Declaration of War speech is another example: the message exists as a response to one clear exigence easily perceived by one major audience and the one overpowering constraint is the necessity of war. On the other hand, the structure of a situation is complex when many elements must be made to interact: practically any presidential political campaign provides numerous complex rhetorical situations.

A situation, whether simple or complex, will be highly structured or loosely structured. It is highly structured when all of its elements are located and readied for the task to be performed. Malinowski's example, the fishing expedition, is a situation which is relatively simple and highly structured; everything is ordered to the task to be performed. The usual courtroom case is a good example of situation which is complex and highly structured. The jury is not a random and scattered audience but a selected and concentrated one; it knows its relation to judge, law, defendant, counsels; it is instructed in what to observe and what to disregard. The judge is located and prepared; he knows exactly his relation to jury, law, counsels, defendant. The counsels know the ultimate object of their case; they know what they must prove; they know the audience and can easily reach it. This situation will be even more highly structured if the issue of the case is sharp, the evidence decisive, and the law clear. On the other hand, consider a complex but loosely structured situation, William Lloyd Garrison preaching abolition from town to town. He is actually looking for an audience and for constraints; even when he finds an audience, he does not know that it is a genuinely rhetorical audience—one able to be mediator of change. Or consider the plight of many contemporary civil rights advocates who, failing to locate compelling constraints and rhetorical audiences, abandon rhetorical discourse in favor of physical action.

Situations may become weakened in structure due to complexity or disconnectedness. A list of causes includes these: (a) a single situation may involve numerous exigences; (b) exigences in the same situation may be incompatible; (c) two or more simultaneous rhetorical situations may compete for our attention, as in some parliamentary debates; (d) at a given moment, persons comprising the audience of situation A may also be the audience of situations B, C, and D; (e) the rhetorical audience may be scattered, uneducated regarding its duties and powers, or it may dissipate; (f) constraints may be limited in number and force, and they may be incompatible. This is enough to suggest the sorts of things which weaken the structure of situations.

6. Finally, rhetorical situations come into existence, then either mature or decay or mature and persist— conceivably some persist indefinitely. In any case, situations grow and come to maturity; they evolve to just the time when a rhetorical discourse would be most fitting. In Malinowski's example, there comes a time in the situation when the leader of the fisherman should say, "Throw the nets." In the situation generated by the assassination of the President, here was a time for giving descriptive accounts of the scene in Dallas, later a time for giving eulogies. In a political campaign, there is a time for generating an issue and a time for answering a charge. Every rhetorical situation in principle evolves to a propitious moment for the fitting rhetorical response. After this moment, most situations decay; we all have the experience of creating a rhetorical response when it is too late to make it public.

Some situations, on the other hand, persist; this is why it is possible to have a body of truly rhetorical literature. The Gettysburg Address, Burke's Speech to the Electors of Bristol, Socrates' Apology—these are more than historical documents, more than specimens for stylistic or logical analysis. They exist as rhetorical responses for us precisely because they speak to situations which persist—which are in some measure universal.

Due to either the nature of things or convention, or both, some situations recur. The courtroom is the locus for several kinds of situations generating the speech of accusation, the speech of defense, the charge to the jury. From day to day, year to year, comparable situations occur, prompting comparable responses; hence rhetorical forms are born and a special vocabulary, grammar, and style are established. This is true also of the situation which invites the inaugural address of a President. The situation recurs and, because we experience situations and the rhetorical responses to them, a form of discourse is not only established but comes to have a power of its own—the tradition itself tends to function as a constraint upon any new response in the form.

IV

In the best of all possible worlds, there would be communication perhaps, but no rhetoric—since exigences would not arise. In our real world, however, rhetorical exigences abound; the world really invites change—change conceived and effected by human agents who quite properly address a mediating audience. The practical justification of rhetoric is analogous to that of scientific inquiry: the world presents objects to be known, puzzles to be resolved, complexities to be understood—hence the practical need for scientific inquiry and discourse; similarly, the world presents imperfections to be modified by means of discourse—hence the practical need for rhetorical investigation and discourse. As a discipline, scientific method is justified philosophically insofar as it provides principles, concepts, and procedures by which we come to know reality; similarly, rhetoric as a discipline is justified philosophically insofar as it provides principles, concepts, and procedures by which we effect valuable changes in reality. Thus rhetoric is distinguished from the mere craft of persuasion which, although it is a legitimate object of scientific investigation, lacks philosophical warrant as a practical discipline.

ENDNOTE

1. "The Problem of Meaning in Primitive Languages," sections III and IV. This essay appears as a supplement in Ogden and Richards' *The Meaning of Meaning*.

THE POSSIBILITY AND ACTUALITY OF VISUAL ARGUMENTS

J. ANTHONY BLAIR

CONSIDER AS YOU ARE READING:

Anthony Blair's essay is often cited as an early example of a theorist working through a basic explanation of the rhetorical features that all visual arguments involve. Blair examines definitions of "visual" and of "argument" to explain how visual rhetorics operate and to develop criteria for determining how visual arguments persuade audiences of specific claims. Blair's essay provides an important opportunity to examine basic principles of visual arguments—a vital endeavor as more of our writing engages multimodal forms of expression.

1. *What components, according to Blair, are necessary for a visual text to be considered an "argument"?*

2. *Make a list of three visual arguments that you encountered today. Would Blair agree with your assessment that each of these makes an argument? Why or why not?*

3. *Do you agree with the way that Blair characterizes the strengths and weaknesses of visual arguments? Explain your position.*

For the last 30 years, the very concept of argument has come under fairly intense examination by the speech communication community (see Gronbeck, 1980, for the early years). Sometimes the focus has been inward, upon its central features (Brockriede, 1975; O'Keefe, 1977, 1982; Trapp, 1983; Hample, 1985). More recently, its more global features have been scrutinized (Willard, 1983, 1989; van Eemeren & Grootendorst, 1984). The present paper is intended as a contribution to the investigation of the extension of argument into a realm hitherto given scant attention. The study of argument since Aristotle has assumed it to be paradigmatically verbal, if not essentially and exclusively so. At a time when technological and cultural developments are increasingly enhancing visual communication, it behooves us to consider whether argument can partake of visual expression.

There is no doubt that images can be influential in affecting attitudes and beliefs. A single visual image can probably be more powerful than a single verbal assertion, other things being equal, although broader claims should be made with caution: probably nothing in history has been more influential than the great verbal religious works, such as the Bible and the Koran. However, it is obvious that paintings and sculpture, and the visual component of movies, television programs and commercial and political advertising, are enormously powerful influences on attitudes and beliefs. Still, from the fact that images influence beliefs and attitudes; it does not follow that such images are arguments, for there is any number of other ways of influencing attitudes and beliefs besides arguing.

Indeed, it would be a mistake to assimilate all means of cognitive and affective influence to argument, or even to assimilate all persuasion to argument. In that case, shock therapy becomes indistinguishable from a syllogism; crown mania merges with a carefully crafted case for a conclusion; and fear-mongering or appeals to blind loyalty cannot be separated from clear-eyed appeals to interests or to evidence. There is no pedantry, no hairsplitting, in recognizing that a loss of clarity and understanding attends such blurring of conceptual boundaries. So we should at the outset investigate whether there can be visual arguments, not just take it for granted that they exist.

To determine whether they exist, we need to know what a visual argument would look like if we encountered one. How, if at all, are visual and verbal arguments related? An account of a concept of visual argument serves to establish the possibility that they exist. By analogy, knowing what a symphony is tells us that symphonies are auditory, not visual; so a "visual symphony" must be a metaphor. Are visual arguments like visual symphonies? If they are possible in a non-metaphorical way, are there any visual arguments? By analogy, an adult person who is totally free of self-deception is surely possible; but has any such person lived yet? Are all the things that look as though they might be visual arguments the genuine article? These are the questions addressed in this paper.

1. PROPERTIES OF VISUAL ARGUMENTS

Let us turn first, then, to what would count as a visual argument. We are exploring new territory: little has been written about visual arguments (see Groarke, in press). Like the Norse adventurers, who are said to have kept a landfall in sight behind them when they sailed the North Atlantic,[1] it would be best to keep in mind a clear conception of argument and a clear conception of what "visual" means here, when we investigate the terra relatively incognita of visual argument. That approach sounds a prioristic, which can be a Bad Thing. But the preferred method, starting the analysis from clear and indisputable cases of visual arguments and observing their salient properties, is unavailable here because it would beg the question: the issue before us is precisely whether the paradigm of verbal arguments has room for, or can be extended to include, visual argument. And the only other alternative seems to be to list all sorts of "examples," or candidates for membership in this class, without any way of deciding which ones really belong and which ones don't. So let us begin by settling, first, what counts as an argument and, second, what counts as visual.

A. Argument

For the purpose of the present investigation, O'Keefe's concept of argument$_1$ serves admirably. O'Keefe describes the paradigm case of argument$_1$ as involving "a linguistically explicable claim and one or more linguistically explicable reasons" (O'Keefe, 1982, p. 17). Let it be clear that O'Keefe's argument$_1$ is not the logician's abstraction. Such arguments are made and used. O'Keefe suggests that, "a paradigm case of making an argument$_1$

---

1   According to Mowat (1965, see pp. 356-57), that was one of the navigational methods they used in sailing first from the Outer Islands to Iceland, and later thence to Greenland, and thence to Labrador and Newfoundland.

involves the communication of both (1) a linguistically explicable claim and (2) one or more overtly expressed reasons which are linguistically explicit."

I use O'Keefe's argument$_1$ because if anything is an argument, then arguments$_1$ are. And I use his concept of argument$_1$ rather than his concept of argument$_2$ (argument as "overt disagreement...between interactants" [1982, p. 11]), because visual arguments are more plausibly akin to reasons for claims (arguments$_1$) than to open disagreements between interacting parties (arguments$_2$).

The explicit properties of arguments$_1$ are the following:

1. there is a claim; that is, the assertion has been made that something has to be believed, or chosen, or done;

2. there is a reason or there are reasons for the claim; that is, the assertion has been made of something supporting what is to be believed, chosen or done;

3. the reason(s) is (are) linguistically explicable and overtly expressed;

4. the claim is linguistically explicable;

5. there is an attempt to communicate the claim and reason(s).

These explicit properties entail the following implicit properties of arguments$_1$:

6. there is some person who uses the claim and its reason(s) (this person may, but need not be, its author);

7. there is some intended recipient audience or interlocutor(s) to whom the claim and reason(s) are addressed.

Although not entailed by O'Keefe's descriptions of the paradigms of argument$_1$ and of making arguments$_1$, I think it is in the spirit of his account that one further property be included:

8. it is the intention of the "user" to bring the recipient to accept the claim on the basis of the reason(s) offered.

The concept of argument$_1$ has two implications of importance to the present discussion.

One is that such arguments are "propositional." Arguments$_1$ are propositional because claims and reasons making them up have propositional content, using "propositional content" in a broad way, so as to include as propositions value judgments and action prescriptions as well as descriptions, predictions, and so on. An expression has propositional content in the sense used here if it has a truth value, or (and this is a weaker but broader requirement) if it can be affirmed or rejected. Thus, "The economy is in a recession," "It is unfortunate that the economy is in a recession," and "Steps should be taken to get the economy out of the recession" all count here as expressing propositions.

The second implication of the concept of argument$_1$ that is important for present purposes is that arguments$_1$ are not necessarily linguistic or verbal arguments. All that is required by O'Keefe's account for something to qualify as an argument$_1$ is that reasons be *overtly expressed,* and that reasons and claim be linguistically *explicable.* That means we have to be able to state or restate them in language, not that they have to be expressed in language in the first place. Thus O'Keefe's concept of argument$_1$ is not inimical to the possibility of visual arguments.

What these two further implications add up to is that for something to count as an argument$_1$ we have to be able to say what the claim is and what the reasons are, and we have to be able to say so clearly enough that the claims or reasons can be accepted or rejected. (You cannot accept or reject "Yuck!"; you can accept or reject the claim, "This steak tastes like shoe leather!")

B. Visual

When we are interested in visual argument as a distinct and distinctive species, I take it that we mean to emphasize the contrast between the visual and the verbal. To be sure, verbal communications can be transmitted visually, by print or writing, but what is essential to it is the use of words and a language. Visual communication, when understood in contradistinction to verbal communication, occurs without the mediation of words or language in the literal sense. It is true that what is communicated visually can be described verbally, or translated into verbal communication. (Whether such descriptions or translations can be complete or fully adequate is a separate question.) However, such description or translation is not a *reduction* of the visual verbal. The visual communication stands on its own feet.

Visual communication may entail the use of conventions, as exemplified by the rich visual symbolism to be found in medieval church sculpture and stained glass images, and medieval and renaissance paintings (Ferguson, 1954); however, these conventions are not a language in the literal sense. There is no grammar, just signs and symbols: conventionalized images. Communication through visual imagery is not verbal.

It is also true that we now know that certain causal properties are supervenient on certain visual properties, which thus affect their viewers in predictable ways. For example, colors invoke feelings of warmth (reds, oranges) or coolness (blues, greens); photographs of young animals (puppies, kittens, children) evoke tender-heartedness; photographs of adults in different garb or uniform (physician, police officer, teenager) evoke standard responses according to stereotypes; and certain scenery (the open desert, the mountains, the seashore, hills and forests) evoke feelings of freedom and escape in their viewers. However, once again, while such properties can be and are exploited effectively to cause feelings and attitudes and to evoke responses (for example, in advertising), that does not imply that the visual images to which they attach are languages in any literal sense, for they are not verbal, and so such communication is not verbal communication.

I have been arguing that the fact and the effectiveness of visual communication do not reduce it to verbal communication. What would visual communication have to be like in order to count as arguments$_1$, or else to have some claim to the title of argument by virtue of a degree of family resemblance to arguments$_1$? The answer is, first, that it would have to have all, or some, of the salient properties of arguments$_1$ and second, that it would have to be non-verbal visual communication. We have thus at least conditionally answered our question, "What would be the properties of visual arguments?"

2. THE POSSIBILITY OF VISUAL ARGUMENT

The next question is, "Are there any?" But first we must determine that they are possible in our world. There seems to be no reason in principle for thinking there cannot be visual arguments.

Visual arguments are to be understood as propositional arguments in which the propositions and their argumentative function and roles are expressed visually, for example by paintings and drawings, photographs, sculpture, film or video images, cartoons, animations, or computer-designed visuals. Is it possible to express argumentation visually?

Propositions can be expressed in any number of ways, including by silence (the standard response to, "Anybody want to take out the trash?"), but also by signs or signals (a one-way street arrow sign, a nod at an auction), or by facial and other body-language expressions (wrinkled brow: "I'm skeptical"; squirming: "I want this lecture to be over."). So already we have examples of their being expressed visually. "Is June at home?" can be answered negatively (in some cultures) by shaking one's head from side to side just as well as by saying, "No." The fact that the communicative function of some of these signs and symbols is conventional—and symbols, at least, are by definition conventions—does not make them *ipso facto* verbal. Even granting a continuum from written languages using words, through written languages using pictograms, to conventional signs (sign as traffic signs: one-way, no parking, no passing, curve ahead), and on to communication by facial expressions (such as smiles, grins, wide-open eyes and mouth), does not imply that all items on the continuum are reducible to one type, verbal language. The visual express of propositions, then, is familiar and relatively unproblematic.

All we need in addition, in order to get visual arguments from propositions expressed visually ("visual propositions"), is for it to be possible to communicate visually the functions of the propositions, so that it can be communicated that some visual propositions are intended as claims and others as reasons for those claims—or that some visual propositions are intended as reasons for unexpressed but expressible claims. Since, "X is a reason for Y," and "You should accept Y, given X" are themselves propositions, and given that propositions can be expressed visually, there is nothing in principle preventing the "reason for" or illative function from being expressible visually. As for the assertion function, which is what turns the statement of a proposition into a claim—a claim being a proposition asserted or put forward as to be accepted—we can readily do that by adopting certain visual conventions, for certainly in verbal communication we have conventions for identifying claims, when there is any doubt about it. So there seems to be no problem in principle in having visual assertions, including the assertion of illation.

In practice, however, there is in this connection the following difference between verbal and visual expression: asserting or claiming is the default function in spoken or written language. That is, to utter or write a declarative sentence is, in the absence of any counter-indication, to assert its propositional content. The same is not true for all visual expression. When we go to an art gallery or to the movies, we do not at the outset take it that what we are encountering is likely to be visual assertion. In fact, although this is an empirical question, I suspect that there is no default function for visual expression, but instead a range of possibilities which we usually must sort through on each occasion. Sometimes the context is labeled for us: an exhibition of paintings is billed as "abstract expressionist," for example. But more often we must infer what we can from the external and internal contextual cues. Thus the movie "Batman" is taken to be sheer entertainment, not argumentative; whereas the movies "Dances With Wolves" or "J.F.K." are not only given advanced billing as "making a statement," but are dramatically structured so as to leave no doubt that they express a point of view, and thereby become candidates for, or locales for possible, visual arguments. Thus there is a systematic tendency to indeterminacy about visual expression, at least in our culture, at the present time, that is absent from verbal expression.[2] To put this point more precisely, in most instances in our culture the conditions of interpretation of visual expression are indeterminate to a much greater degree than is the case with verbal expression.[3]

---

2   This fact makes visual irony more difficult to achieve, or detect, than verbal irony, since irony requires the reversal of surface assertion.

3   Thanks to David Birdsell for this formulation.

What distinguishes visual argument form verbal argument, then, are the differences in argument expression facing the arguer, and the hermeneutical differences of identification and interpretation facing the interlocutor, audience or critic. These are likely to create formidable practical problems for arguer and audience, but they do not make visual arguments impossible in principle.

3. THE OCCURRENCE OF VISUAL ARGUMENTS

Visual arguments are possible, if we are right so far, but are there any in fact? It would be nice to find some examples. That turns out to be more easily said than done. We might expect to find visual arguments in such things as dramatic paintings and sculptures, magazine and other static advertisements, television commercials and political cartoons. Consider each of these in turn.

A. Arguments in Dramatic Painting and Sculpture

It is important to keep in mind the difference between an argument and a statement, even a complex set of related statements. Many works of art that convey a message, that communicate points of view, emotions or attitudes, do not provide or constitute arguments. Expressing a proposition, even forcefully and dramatically, is not arguing for it.

Consider as examples four famous dramatic paintings. Goya's portrayal of the execution of Spanish patriots by Napoleon's troops, "The Third of May, 1808, At Madrid: The Shootings on Principe Pio Mountain" (1808), portrays human cruelty, fear, terror, hopelessness and courage; but it gives no reasons for favoring the loyalists or opposing Napoleon. Géricault's "The Raft of the Medusa" (1818-19) expresses the despair and misery of being adrift at sea after a shipwreck, and shows us the fifteen survivors of the 150 who had clung to the raft twelve days before when the Medusa foundered; but it gives no reasons for drawing any conclusions, for example about a need for life-boats, safer vessels, or less risk-taking in trans-oceanic trade, nor is it a justification of the cannibalism that allegedly took place on the raft. Picasso's "Guernica" (1937) depicts and expresses the horrors of the German bombing of women and children in the town of Guernica in the Spanish civil war; but what conclusion are we to draw? That this was a terrible, cruel, destructive act? But that is what Picasso's painting expresses; there is no argument. Munch's "The Cry" (1893) expresses anxiety and dread; but tenders no conclusion. It may render the alienation of modern life, but it isn't an argument against it.

In order to reconstruct any of these paintings as an argument, it is necessary not only to give propositional expression to it—to treat the picture as delivering a message—but also to identify and distinguish premises (reasons, evidence: grounds) from conclusions, whether asserted visually or unexpressed (and discoverable from the context). This is the main difficulty in interpreting any of these four dramatic paintings as an argument. There is no way to have confidence in any one conclusion that the painter wanted his viewers to draw. Clearly, the painters sought to communicate. At least the first three of these paintings have narrative intent: they are records of events, they tell stories. The artist in each case intended to send a message and to evoke a reaction. I think these artists are inviting us to ponder, or to agree with, their statements. They wish us to feel or identify with the terror or fear or horror their paintings convey. It does not follow that they are presenting us with arguments.

Any assertion whatever can be placed in a context which renders it the premise of an argument. Indeed, Anscombre and Ducrot (1983) see all discourse as argumentative (see 1983). Take our earlier example, "June is not at home." Imagine it uttered in circumstances when we knew that normally June would be sure to be at home. We may then be expected to infer that something out of the ordinary has happened. The utterance of "June is not at home" is then, in that situation, the assertion of an argument (or a part of one), with a conclusion expressible as, "Something (unusual? untoward?) has happened." But in the absence of such contextual information, all we have is the possibility of argument, or possible arguments. It's easy to think of an indefinite number of possible conclusions to draw from the assertion of "June is not at home" in the absence of any context: "June is at her office," "June has run off with Chris," "June has already left for the airport," and so on. The possibility of a conclusion following from it in some imaginable context does not turn an assertion into an argument.

54

In the case of the dramatic paintings in question, nothing in principle rules out an argument-creating context. My point is that, in none of these four cases is there a context that permits anything more than speculation about a range of possibilities. Perhaps Picasso meant to argue that the Nazis were vicious, but he equally might have meant to argue that war is hell; or he might not have meant to argue at all, but just to express his own horror and evoke ours. That any of these paintings might have been argument in other circumstances does not make it an argument as things stand.

Will no work of art be an argument? I haven't made that claim. Indeed, as I have argued, nothing in principle prevents a painting or other art from expressing an argument. But I think that to do so the work of art has to satisfy the condition that we are able to identify its premise(s) and its intended conclusion (whether expressed or not).

A nice example of exactly how such conditions can be met is Groarke's (in press) case that Jacques-Louis David's famous painting, "Death of Marat" (1793), was an argument for the conclusion that "Marat was, like Christ, a great moral martyr." Groarke points out that David painted in an historical context which "saw art as a vehicle for 'the edification and uplifting of mankind'" (quoting Kelder, 1976), and that "he was committed to works that encouraged high moral standards and a sense of patriotic self-sacrifice." But Groarke goes beyond showing that David might have been painting an argument, by identifying three particular statements that may be inferred from the painting[4] and showing how—in the context of the time—these are best explained as premises in an argument. Premise 1: "Marat gave his last penny to the poor" (supported by the alm on the box beside Marat's bath and the adjacent note, portrayed as written with Marat's dying hand, which reads: "You will give this assignat to this mother of five children whose husband died in defense of the fatherland" plus the widely held belief that this was Marat's total wealth when he died). Premise 2: "Marat was a benefactor of the unfortunate" (supported by the note from Marat's assassin, Charlotte de Corday, that David painted gripped in Marat's hand, which appeals to him as a benefactor of the

---

4   Groarke says these statements are made by the painting, but what the painting actually depicts is the evidence for them.

unfortunate). Premise 3: "Marat was a poor man of great dignity and composure," supported by numerous details in the painting which portray Marat in this way. Although Groarke takes these premises and the conclusion (that "Marat was, like Christ, a great moral martyr") to be expressed, not implicit, whereas it seems to me that all are unstated inferences which David, by his painting, invites the viewer to draw, nevertheless, I think Groarke makes a compelling case that this is one conclusion of the argument which David uses the painting to make. Notice that in establishing his interpretation of "The Death of Marat" as an argument, Groarke has identified the propositions expressed or implied visually and their logical roles in the argument.

Another example of argument in art are the stone sculptures of the Last Judgment which adorn the tympanums above the doorways in many Gothic cathedrals (see Mâle, 1898/1958, chap. VI). To the right of Christ the judge, and the Archangel Michael holding the scales to weigh the good actions against the sins of the resurrected souls, are dynamic, dramatic portrayals of the elect, clothed in royal garments and crowned as they enter heaven; and to the left are the condemned, being led off in chains to the burning mouth of hell. Although these sculptures are portrayals of biblical themes and contemporary theological writings, dramatized by the individual sculptures, it seems plausible to regard them at the same time as conveying the message to the illiterate populace: "Here is what will happen to you at the time of the Last Judgment if you are virtuous, and here is what will happen to you if you are a sinner." The unexpressed assumptions, "No one wants to experience everlasting tortures; everyone wants to experience everlasting joy," and the implied conclusions, "You would be well advised not to sin, but to be virtuous" are unproblematic in the context of the times.

So I certainly agree that visual arguments in art exist; I just think they are not to be conflated with visual assertions which are expressed without argument, and thus not to be found automatically in every dramatic work of art.

B. Arguments in Magazine and Other Static Visual Ads

Many magazine advertisements combine words with pictures. The case for visual arguments in advertising will be more convincing if it can be made with purely visual ads. There are plenty of them. One striking recent example was an eight-page block advertising the Benetton clothing company that appeared in the April 29 and May 6, 1996 issue of *The New Yorker* magazine (pp. 51-58). This was a special, double-issue of the magazine devoted to the theme, Black in America. I want to discuss the Benetton ad in some detail because it seems to be a strong candidate for purely visual argument in an ad.

Figure 1

The Benetton block began with a blank all-black right-hand page. The following six pages consisted of three full two-page spreads, in color, reproduced here as Figures 1-3 in order in which they appeared in *The New Yorker*.[5] On each set, the tag "united colors of Benetton" was in white print on a bright green background; the other colors appeared natural, undoctored. The page after the Figure 3. picture, a left-hand page, was blank, all-white.

The overt messages are richly evocative. (1) The three hearts (see Figure 1) suggest: we're all humans, with hearts (and all that they symbolize) under our skin; skin color of donor and recipient is irrelevant to a heart transplant; the distinctions of

5   Figure 1., "Hearts," United Colors of Benetton, Concept: O. Toscani, Spring, 1996; Figure 2., "Angel/Devil,"United Colors of Benetton, Concept: O. Toscani, Fall/Winter, 1991/92; Figure 3., "Handcuffs" United Colors of Benetton, Concept: O. Toscani, Fall/Winter 1989/90.

color are just labels put onto us (by others); and much more. (2) The little girls (see Figure 2) suggest: innocent children have no racial prejudices; those come from adults; and adult racist attitudes destroy possibilities children represent for interracial harmony (a kind of Rousseauian thesis); and much more. (3) The manacled hands (see Figure 3) suggest: we are locked together, whites and blacks; there is no escaping our condition of whites-and-blacks together in the country and the world; we are the prisoners of our own prejudices. The identical clothing suggests equality. It is possible to find in the photo a reminder of Hegel's master-slave commentary: the uninformativeness of the picture as to which man is the controller and which is the controlled (if either) reminds us of Hegel's point that the master is controlled by the relationship by which he supposedly exerts control, and the slave has a measure of control in the relationship whereby he supposedly is denied any control, and that thus freedom for either one entails freedom for the other.

Figure 2

The three two-page spreads are brilliant in their suggestiveness, but are they an argument (or a set of arguments)? It is easy to supply further claims that are supported by the propositions suggested by the photographs, especially in the context of the ad's appearing in the special issue of *The New Yorker* on Black in America in 1996: racism is unjustified, harmful; we should be rid of it.[6] It is plausible, therefore, to interpret these photographs as a set of visual arguments against racism. Premise 1 (see Figure 1): we are all the same under our skin; we are biologically the same species, and we are all human. Premise 2 (see Figure 2): racism is a construct, not an inborn attitude; adults impose its ugliness on the innocence of children. Premise 3 (see Figure 3): we are joined together, black and white, inescapably; we are prisoners of our attitudes. Conclusion: racism is unjustified and should be ended.

Let us not forget, however, that this is a very expensive advertisement by the Benetton clothing company. How does it sell Benetton clothes? Virtually no clothing, and nothing distinctive, is shown. Factor in the Black in America theme and the fact that the readership of *The New Yorker* is predominately upper middle class and wealthy, mostly white, liberals, judging by the advertisements typically found in its pages and its standard editorial content. What the ad does is identify Benetton with the self-image of their racial attitudes held by *The New Yorker* readers. One thing that is going on is that through the ad, Benetton is conveying the message, "We share your color-blind ideals, your opposition to racism, and your recognition of the problems facing the ideal of blacks and whites living in harmony and your desire to see them overcome." And it does so with powerful images and symbols. The Benetton ad is a paradigm case of the classical advertising ploy: create an ad that the viewer feels good about or identifies with and the viewer will transfer those feelings and that identification to your company or product(s). One particular concrete way the identification in this case might transfer to the act of purchasing is that the consumer who makes it will want to act on his or her solidarity with Benetton's powerful anti-racism message by buying Benetton: "I support your stand, and I want to put my money where my mouth is—I'll take a couple of those shirts."[7]

6   Even though the three photos were not initially conceived as a unit, but on different occasions over the past seven years, their grouping here in this special issue of *The New Yorker* supplies a new context.

7   This last point is due to David Birdsell. He recalled a discussion of the effectiveness of Nike's ads with kids. The point made was that kids didn't think about buying Nikes would transform them into Michael Jordans, but they wanted to declare their allegiance. I believe one such discussion occurred in an article devoted to the agency responsible for those Nike ads that appeared in *The New Yorker* a few years ago.

But is the ad an argument for buying Benetton clothes? My contention is that the way this and similar visual ads work is precisely by NOT being arguments designed to persuade or convince us to buy the product or patronize the company. They do not engage our intellects in critical thinking about purchasing or product choices; they supply no reasons for buying the product or patronizing the company. They sell precisely by creating and trading on unconscious, unexamined identifications. In the case of the Benetton ad, just as soon as the viewer realizes what these ads are doing, she or he will see that they constitute a clever, perhaps even a cynical, attempt to trade on her or his attitudes. The now more fully aware viewer might very well reason as follows: "Benetton is a company that sells clothing. Its purpose is paying a lot of money for the creation of this ad and its placement here is to sell Benetton in order to sell Benetton clothes. Hence, its evocation of my feelings and attitudes is self-serving manipulation. I don't want to give my business to a company that tries to do that to me." In other words, the moment the viewer's focus escapes from the overt message and his or her reasoning becomes engaged, the selling power of the ad begins to weaken. (To be sure, the unconscious identifications may be more powerful than the conscious rejection of the manipulation, so exposing the manipulation may not defuse the effectiveness of the identifications.) The ad works best by being an argument at the superficial level, but above all by *not* being an argument at the deeper, affective level. In fact, the stark, spare simplicity of the Benetton ad is extremely clever as a means of avoiding reminding the viewer that this is an ad to sell clothing, while the green tag keeps the company name identification prominent.[8]

Let me sum up my theses about the Benetton ad. First, the ad presents a powerful, multi-premise, visual argument against racism. Second, the ad presents no argument, visual or otherwise, for buying from Benetton. Third, the way (or at least one principle way) that the ad is likely to contribute to an increase in Benetton sales is through the unconscious effect on viewers of the statement about Benetton that the visual argument of the ad presents. Fourth, while this effect can take various forms (simultaneously), essential to them all is

8   This general position on advertising is developed more fully in Johnson and Blair, 1994, chap. 11.

the identification of the viewer with the values expressed by the argument, and the transfer of that identification to Benetton as a company and to Benetton products.

Figure 3

Many print ads that combine texts with photographs or other pictures use the text to convey an overt argument, thereby disguising the fact that the visuals serve up the affective, psychological identification, and thus do the real selling job. It's a clever shell game: suspicious of a non-rational sell, which disarms us, thus leaving us vulnerable to the covert non-rational sell. Of course, if the argument (verbal or visual) sells by itself, or reinforces the non-argumentative identifications of the pictures, so much the better.

The interaction between text and visuals in advertising and elsewhere (in television news, and in documentary reporting like "60 Minutes," for instance) is extremely important, and deserves careful study that is beyond the scope of this paper. I speculate, however, that such study will not reveal arguments to play more than a disguising role in effective visual advertising. Recall, for example, the old STP ad that *showed* someone with STP-slicked fingers unable to hold onto a screwdriver by the tip.

The voice-over *said*, "STP reduces friction in your engine." Was the ad an argument for analogy: "The friction between fingers and a screwdriver tip is like that between a piston and a cylinder; as you can see, STP reduces the former friction; therefore it will reduce the latter?" I don't think so. Seeing the ad in terms of an argument from analogy made explicit provides the viewer with hooks on which to hang critical questions, such as, "*Are* the two kinds of friction at all comparable?" Much more likely, I suspect, is the hope that the viewer will think, "Wow! Look how slippery that stuff is: the voice-over claim is true." In any case, there is a fruitful field for case studies here.

C. Television Commercials

What has just been said about print ads goes in spades for TV commercials. The latter have enormously powerful means of evoking identifications that are independent of the text. They have music, which in a few seconds can create a mood. A familiar tune can flash us back to earlier experiences, evoking floods of feelings. The dynamics that TV images provide mean that, instead of giving us just a snapshot to identify with, we can get an entire drama, with plot and character development, structure of crisis, climax and dénouement, all in thirty seconds.

It is easier with TV than print to use humor, which is disarming and misdirecting. Many more evocative symbols (such as children, animals, nature, family, mother, doctor or scientist) can be packed into a thirty-second clip than into a static one-page magazine ad. It is also easy to use the overt, surface, verbal argumentation of the spoken script to mask the manipulation of feelings by the music, the drama, and the visuals.

Again, I am not at all saying that TV ads never use visual arguments directly to sell a product or a brand. But I would hypothesize that the effective ones either don't use arguments at all, or else they get their efficacy not directly from any arguments they proffer, but from the underlying and hidden identifications and feelings they evoke. Should we call such manipulation "persuasion," if not argument? That is a question taken up in Section 5, below.

D. Arguments in (Political) Cartoons

A good case can be made that political cartoons can and do present us with arguments. (Notice how cartoon-like are the medieval cathedral sculptures of the Last Judgment.) Groarke has found an excellent example in a 1938 David Low cartoon. In it, a man is shown sitting on a steep hillside reading a newspaper, with his back to a pile of big boulders poised above him, all prevented from tumbling down on him by one key boulder, labeled "Czechoslovakia." The boulders above it are labeled, "Poland," "Romania," "French Alliances" and "Anglo-French Security." The man is saying "What's Czechoslovakia to me anyway?" Low's visual argument was clearly that anyone who thought the Nazi psychological war against Czechoslovakia did not matter to England was wrong, because if it fell (to Hitler's bullying), then Poland and Romania would be next, followed by the French alliances, and finally the Anglo-French security pact would come crashing down. As Groarke points out, this is an obvious example of a slippery-slope argument.

Not all political cartoons present arguments; many simply make statements. What is the difference? Again, as with paintings and advertisements, enough information has to be provided visually to permit an unambiguous verbal reconstruction of the propositions expressed, so that, combining that with contextual information, it is possible to reconstruct a plausible premise-and-conclusion combination intended by the cartoonist.

Let me sum up this part of the discussion. While visual arguments are possible, they seem not to be widespread. More significantly, they seem not to constitute a radically different kind of argument from verbal ones. What makes visual messages influential, taking television advertisements as the most striking examples, is not any argumentative function they may perform, but the unconscious identifications they invoke. There is no reason to ignore or overlook visual arguments. However, their existence presents no theoretical challenge to the standard sorts of verbal argument analysis. They are easily assimilated to the paradigm model of verbal argument characterized by O'Keefe's concept of argument$_1$. The difficulties they do present are practical ones of exegesis or interpretation. Moreover, we have to translate them into verbal arguments in order to analyze and criticize them. So verbal arguments retain their position of primacy.

In the process of answering the question, "Are there any instances of visual arguments?" (Answer: Yes), we have answered the further question, "Are visual arguments significantly different from verbal arguments?" (Answer: No).

NON-PROPOSITIONAL ARGUMENT

For visual argument to represent a radically different kind of argument, it would have to be non-propositional. But what kind of argument could that conceivably be? Let us consider some candidates.

There is a use of "argument" which counts states of affairs and complex entities as arguments. "The way those two dress is an argument that opposites attract," "*All Quiet on the Western Front* is an argument against war," "Some critics think that Mailer's oeuvre (*malgré lui*) is an argument for authorial absence," or "The horrible final six months of Zoë's cancer-racked life is an argument for legalizing euthanasia." But the use of "argument" exemplified by such cases is a handy shorthand for, or summation of, an extended case consisting of verbally expressible propositions. In each case, someone can ask, "What do you mean?" and would, and should, expect in answer a fuller account showing how a propositional argument making the case would run.

We also naturally speak of narratives as arguments, or at least as having an argumentative or else at least a persuasive function. Striking examples are the great religious narratives, or the historical stories in terms of which we justify national policies, both domestic and foreign (for example, "The Opening Up of the West," or "The Cold War"). Certainly narratives can be powerfully persuasive; they may be the most persuasive kinds of discourse that exists. Yet, on the one hand, they too are propositional, however complex their propositional structure may be; and on the other hand, they accomplish their influence not by argument in any traditional sense, but by connecting our beliefs and experience into meaningful stories which we adopt as elements of our personal or collective worldviews.

Metaphors are another powerfully persuasive force. Lakoff and Johnson (1980) have shown how pervasively they shape our conceptual schemes, and hence the perceptions, interpretations and choices in terms of which we construct our lives. However, (a) metaphors can function independently of argument; but in any case, (b) metaphors too are propositional.

As we review the various extended concepts or kinds of argument or persuasion, we discover that what distinguishes them from the paradigm is not that the paradigm is propositional whereas they are not. They turn out either to be propositional, or else not arguments.

5. REPROGRAMMING, PERSUASION, ARGUMENT AND RHETORIC

Various ways of influencing beliefs, attitudes and behavior can be placed along a continuum. A course of treatments consisting of electrical impulses delivered to key locations in the brain that causes a pedophile to lose his sexual interest in children is not an example of argument or persuasion. A physical seduction (kissing, stroking, licking, nibbling) which causes someone to act very much against his or her better judgment is persuasion of one sort, but it cannot be classified as argument in any sense. The offer of a cigarette to a smoker trying to quit, or the dessert tray shown to a struggling dieter, may persuade the person (even if not persuasive in intent and made in ignorance of the interlocutors' conditions); but again, there is no argument involved. We come to a case bordering on argument with the example of the robber who points a gun at you and demands your wallet or purse.

The significant variable in all these cases is the nature and degree of mediation by the agent. Imagine a mediation mechanism that has a beep function that sounds to alert us when we have a choice to make (think of the loud warning klaxon activated when commercial vehicles are in reverse gear), and a "Yes" and "No" pair of buttons we can press to make the choice. With the brain implant treatment, the choice mechanism is bypassed: the beep does not even go off. With the seduction, the static from the stimulation of our erogenous zones interferes with our hearing the beep. (The real possibility that we make a prior choice to allow the interference to mask the choice beep is what leads us to suspect self-deception in the case of "seduction.") The habits, perhaps the addiction, in the smoking or overeating examples, seem not to camouflage the choice beep (it sounds loud and clear), but to draw us inexorably to push the "Yes" button. Most of us know first-hand the phenomenology of temptation: the sense of being pulled by a force-field to say "Yes," while the faint voice that urges us to say "No" is overwhelmed by another more powerful and seemingly by another more powerful and seemingly reasonable one, citing ever-so-good reasons for making an exception this time. What makes the robbery case different is that, at least on some occasions, for a moment we clearly experience the opportunity to choose and the choice seems open: we do a quick cost-benefit analysis (which normally makes it clear that refusal to comply is not worth the risk).

The paradigm for persuasion is verbal persuasion, as it is for its subspecies, argument. As a result, we are more comfortable identifying as persuasion those cases of belief/attitude/behavior influence in which speech is involved, even if we admit that it can be other factors than the speaker's arguments, such as her ethos or the figures she used, which are persuasive. Still, we do permit locutions like, "The mouth-watering aroma of its sauce persuaded me to try the fish," which implies that verbal factors are not necessary to persuasion. According to the Oxford English Dictionary, almost all definitions of the word "persuade" focus on the result produced. The only reference to the means used identifies persuasion with "inducing" to (believe, act, and so on). Now, to *induce* someone to believe or act is to act upon their will, which brings us back to the factor of the agent's mediation which distinguishes the brain surgery from the other cases in our examples above.

We refuse the label "persuasion" to behavior modification through brain surgery, because the agent has no mediating role to play: nothing acts on his will. We classify the cases of seduction and the temptations of smoking and dessert as persuasion precisely because the agent knew there was a choice, and could and did in some sense make a choice. The distraught cuckold or the disappointed dietitian would be entirely right to counter our protestations with: "Nonsense! You had a choice and you made it!" The salient difference between these two cases and the robbery case is phenomenological—namely the experience of having a choice that accompanies the latter more than the former. That is what, to my mind, associates the robber's threat with argument, for in the cases of argument the agent's mediation is essential: the audience of interlocutor must identify the premise and conclusion propositions and make a determination about the degree of the support the former lends to the latter.

Some might want to assimilate the offer of dessert or a cigarette to argument, too. In most restaurants that show a dessert tray, the point is either to inform the diner (visually) of what is available, or to tempt the diner, or both. The person offering a cigarette is normally just being polite, or (sometimes) mean. It strikes me as forced to view these as attempts to get someone to accept a proposition on the basis of reasons offered. However, admittedly, I have not offered a formal analysis of the difference between argumentative and non-argumentative persuasion.

To the extent that visual communication causes us to change our beliefs or attitudes, or to act, without engaging our choice buttons, it is assimilable neither to persuasion nor argument. Once the choice light flashes, persuasion is occurring. And once we have identified expressible reasons that are provided for pressing one button rather than the other, we are being persuaded by argument. In sum, the act of argument is a species of persuasion, and both entail the attempt to engage the agent as mediator in a decision to act or to change an attitude or belief. (We can be persuaded against our better judgment, but not against our will.) Persuasion by argument entails the making explicit of propositions and their alleged illative relations.

If all this is right, then the psychological sell of the advertiser who manipulates our unconscious identification can be classified neither as argument nor as non-argumentative persuasion, visual or otherwise: we don't get to choose or decide. If we reach or ask for a Coke or a Coors instead of a Pepsi or a Bud, most of us don't really know why. Many ads provide no reasons whatever for preferring one brand to the other, or one type of product to alternatives; the "reasons" others supply often cannot withstand even cursory critical analysis. Yet we claim to have preferences, and since the principle differences are between the ads, not the products, presumably somehow the ads get to us. How exactly they do so is a question eminently worthy of study. The hypothesis that I have ventured, namely manipulation of unconscious ego-identification, is undeveloped and may turn out to be untestable or false, but the idea that these ads work by persuading us with visual arguments is barking up the wrong tree, and even the hypothesis that they persuade us (perhaps non-rationally), is not plausible either, unless the concept of persuasion is stretched to include casually efficacious influence in general. Such an extension of the concept then runs into the difficulty of distinguishing that kind of persuasion from behavior modification by brain surgery.

At this point one may well ask: Where is rhetoric on this map? Even mentioning rhetoric opens a Pandora's Box, yet failing to do so in the present discussion would be culpable, so I will timorously and briefly venture a proposal. Reboul (1991, p. 4) notes a range of definitions of rhetoric, and states his own preference to be "the art of persuading by speech [*l'art de persuader par le discourse,"]* thereby agreeing, in general, with Foss, Foss and Trapp (1985, p. 12), who say, "the paradigm case of rhetoric is the use of the spoken word to persuade an audience." If these authorities are right, and if the above points about persuasion are correct, then (a) the study of rhetoric includes the study of argument, (b) the concept of visual argument is an extension of rhetoric's paradigm into a new domain. Whether the realm of rhetoric is identical to that of persuasion, or instead just partially overlaps it, depends on how tightly the concept of rhetoric is tied to that of persuasion. If rhetoric in a broader sense is the use of symbols to communicate (see Foss, Foss & Trapp, 1985, p. 11), so that symbolic communication rather than persuasion is its fundamental property, then some but not all rhetoric will be persuasive in intent and some but not all persuasion will be rhetorical in nature; there will be non-persuasion-oriented rhetoric and non-rhetorical persuasion. On the other hand, if the persuasive function lies at the heart of rhetoric, then any form of persuasion, including visual persuasion, belongs within rhetoric's province.

6. THE IMPORTANCE OF VISUAL ARGUMENT

What is lost by forgoing or overlooking visual argument? The question asks what can be accomplished only or best by using visual arguments. And what are the disadvantages of visual arguments? Like much else, visual arguments have correlative virtues and vices.

The incredibly evocative power of a movie (even more than a novel) can bring us as close to actual experiential knowledge as it is possible to get, short of living the experience. Thus movies can make the truth of premises more "real" than can any assemblage of evidence in, say, a legal brief. For example, by getting us to feel what it is like to be exploited or discriminated against, they can provide enormously powerful arguments against these treatments and the attitudes and systems that foster them. Of course, the same power can be used to distort or misrepresent, and thus to argue falsely. Movies can bring us to experience the panoply of emotions—impatience, fear, disappointment, joy, rage, frustration, contentment—but the reality of those feelings does not vouch for their legitimacy. People can be furious when they should be understanding, complacent when they should be angry; and so on. By creating false experiences, movies can convince us of conclusions that should not be drawn.

To be sure, with argument-containing films, and plays too, we have a hybrid of the visual and the verbal, not purely visual argument. It is therefore hard to extract the argumentative force of just the visual dimension of the communication. However, the dramatic difference in effect between reading a film script or a play and watching the movie or the play in the theater is familiar to us all. The nature of the visual contribution may be difficult to describe, but its force is undeniable. (The relation between the textual, the visual and the auditory dimension of film deserves study.)

The power of the visual granted, visual arguments tend to be one-dimensional: they present the case for one side only, without including the arguments against it, or without doing so sympathetically, and without representing alternative standpoints and their merits and defects. The demands of the movie or TV dramatic form include pressures for simplicity and for closure. Painting or sculpture are even more limited in this regard. Visual arguments, then, must always be suspect in this respect, and their power countered by a degree of skepticism and a range of critical questions: "Is that the whole story?" "Are there other points of view?" "Is the real picture so black and white?" Visual argument will tend to be one-sided, unidimensional argument.

While visual communication can be concrete and particular, it can also, even simultaneously, be vague or ambiguous. If suggestiveness is the aim, this is a virtue; where clarity or precision are desiderata, it is a disadvantage. The sender of the message lacks the power to have his or her intentions well understood, since the receiver is free to interpret in various ways. To be sure, this is a problem with written and spoken argument too, but less so than with visual argument. So visual argument has both the strength and the weakness of its form.

In sum, while there can be no doubt that visual argument is important by virtue of its ability to be powerfully influential, its responsible deployment calls for great skill and integrity, and its responsible consumption requires alert critical interaction.

7. CONCLUSION

The main point that I draw from these reflections is that visual arguments are not distinct in essence from verbal arguments. The argument is always a propositional entity, merely expressed differently in the two cases. Therefore visual arguments are not a particularly exciting conceptual novelty; they do not constitute a radically different realm of argumentation. The need to give visual arguments premise-conclusion propositional embodiment has the consequence that plenty of dramatic visual statements fall short of being arguments. And the non-propositional character of the truly effective psychological manipulation in much advertising has the implication that such powerful visual persuasion comes no closer to argument than the decoys or facades of argument that, by disguising the manipulation, enhance it. The attempt to conceive of the possibility of non-propositional argument (as distinct from non-propositional persuasion) comes up empty. Finally, the great advantages of visual argument, namely its power and its suggestiveness, are gained at the cost of a loss of clarity and precision, which may not always be a price worth paying.

While the preceding contentions downplay the theoretical distinctness of visual arguments, they are not meant to understate the differences inherent in its medium of communication. Just how visual images and visual forms in general can and do communicate propositions, just how the important ancillary concept of context is to be understood and how in practice context is to be interpreted and combined with the visual, and just how text and visuals (and sound) interact to produce meaning are all questions which strike me as important, difficult and unanswered by the present paper.[9]

REFERENCES

Anscombre, J. & Ducrot, O. (1983). *L'árgumentation dons la langue*. Liège: Pierre Mardaga.

Brockriede, W. (1975). Where is argument? *Journal of the American Forensic Association,* 11, 179-182.

Eemeren, F.H., van, & Grootendorst, R. (1984). *Speech acts in argumentative discussions: A theoretical model for the analysis of discussions directed towards solving conflicts of opinion.* Dordrecht: Foris.

Ferguson, G. (1954). *Signs & symbols in Christian art.* Oxford: Oxford UP.

Foss, S.K., Foss, K.A., & Trapp, R. (1985). *Contemporary perspectives on rhetoric.* Prospect Heights, IL: Waveland Press.

Groark, L. (in press). Logic, art and argument. *Informal Logic.*

Gronbeck, B. (1980). From argument to argumentation: Fifteen years of identity crisis. In J. Rhodes & S. Newell (Eds.), *Proceedings of the Summer Conference on Argumentation* (pp. 8-19). Annandale, VA: Speech Communication Association.

Hample, D. (1985). A third perspective on argument. *Philosophy and Rhetoric,* 18, 1-22.

---

9   I wish to thank an anonymous referee, Leo Groarke and David Birdsell for numerous corrections, constructive criticisms, and suggestions, all of which I have tried to respond to in revising the paper and which have much improved it.

Johnson, R.H. & Blair, J.A. (1994) *Logical self-defense* (U.S. ed.) New York: McGraw-Hill.

Kelder, D. (1976). *Aspects of "official" painting and philosophic art, 1789-1799.* New York: Garland.

Lakoff, G. & Johnson, M. (1980). *Metaphors we live by.* Chicago: U of Chicago P.

Mâle, E. (1958). *The Gothic image: Religious art in France of the thirteenth century.* (D. Nussey, Trans.). New York: Harper & Row. (Original work published in 1898).

Mowat, F. (1965). *Vestviking: The ancient Norse In Greenland and North America.* Toronto: McClelland & Stewart.

O'Keefe, D.J. (1977). Two concepts of argument. *Journal of the American Forensic Association,* 13, 121-128.

O'Keefe, D.J. (1982). The concepts of argument and arguing. In J.R. Cox and C.A. Willard (Eds.), *Advances in argumentation theory and research* (pp. 3-23). Carbondale, IL. Southern Illinois UP.

Reboul, O. (1991). *Introduction á la rhetoric.* Paris: Presses Universitaires de France.

Trapp, R. (1983). Generic characteristics of argumentation in everyday discourse. In D. Zerefsky, M.O. Sillars & J. Rhodes (Eds.), *Argument in transition: Proceedings of the third summer conference on argumentation* (pp. 516-530). Annandale, VA: Speech Communication Association.

Willard, C.A. (1983). *Argumentation and the social grounds of knowledge.* Tuscaloosa, AL: U. of Alabama P.

Willard, C.A. (1989). *A theory of argumentation.* Tuscaloosa, AL: U. of Alabama P.

Reconceiving Ethos in Relation to the Personal: Strategies of Placement in Pioneer Women's Writing

Julie Nelson Christoph

CONSIDER AS YOU ARE READING:

Too often, Christoph claims, "personal writing" is characterized exclusively as autobiographical writing. Christoph sets out to challenge that characterization and to show how personal writing can be ethically and effectively integrated into academic writing and scholarship. After examining both Aristotelian and postmodern concepts of ethos, Christoph analyzes letters produced by nineteenth-century American pioneer women. She determines that these writers use "strategies of placement" to explain how ethos circulates in these "personal" writings. This essay is a great example of the complex re-workings of traditional concepts, such as ethos, that can add sophistication and nuance to our reading and composing practices.

1. *Explain Christoph's claim that the "self" is an "historically embedded site… a network or crossroads of multiply situated knowledges," rather than a stable identity.*

2. *When is it appropriate to bring the personal into academic writing or a research project?*

3. *How effective is Christoph's choice to use letters from nineteenth-century American pioneer women for this project? Do the "strategies of placement" that Christoph identifies in pioneer women's letters also circulate in contemporary writing?*

College English's September, 2001 "Special Focus: Personal Writing" and the upcoming special-topic issue, "The Personal in Academic Writing," are only the two most recent demonstrations of the widespread interest in the role of "the personal" in the field of composition and rhetoric. As in many other disciplines, theorists in composition have experimented with writing in more explicitly personal ways, and over the past decade, several composition journals have dedicated issues to academic writing that demonstrates use of the personal.

Discussions of the personal in our field have frequently treated it as if it were something to be imported (or not) into one's academic writing—even as these discussions have reminded us that writing is *always* to some degree a subjective enterprise, grounded as it is in individual writers' perspectives on the world. "Personal writing," then, is typically understood to involve combing autobiographical and theoretical content into a new genre that has been demonstrated in such varied works as Nancy Miller's *Getting Personal: Feminist Occasions and Other Autobiographical Acts;* Victor Villanueva's *Bootstraps: From an American Academic of Color;* and Ruth Behar's *The Vulnerable Observer: Anthropology that Breaks Your Heart.* This kind of writing has been valuable to our field in the many ways that it has made us more aware and critical of how our personal and professional lives intersect in our researching, writing, and teaching.

Nonetheless, in limiting our explorations of the personal to explicitly autobiographical scholarly writing, we have missed many of the potential ways and settings in which writers invoke the personal. Most of our work on the personal has paralleled that in fields that are less interested in the composition process as a subject of inquiry; like other disciplines, we have been primarily interested in the ethics and propriety of using "the personal" in scholarly writing, and more recently, in defining what we mean by "the personal." Consequently, we have not given sufficient attention to other, more subtle ways in which the person enters into composition processes and written texts.

At the same time as we continue thinking about the possibilities for using autobiographical narrative ethically and effectively in academic writing and research, we also need to ask how the personal affects writing that is less clearly personal. While most in composition and rhetoric would agree that positivist attempts at absolute knowledge are doomed to fail, theorists within our field continue to write using a range of approaches to the personal. As Gesa Kirsch and Min-Zhan Lu write, "diverse members of the profession have responded differently to current professional pressures/invitations to live and narrate the personal within the norms of personal narrative" (Symposium collective 42). There are diverse reasons for these different responses, and there should be room in our field for diverse kinds of writing. However, we need to expand our ways of thinking about the personal to better write and read work that is not explicitly autobiographical. How do the apparently private experiences of a writer, separate from his or her work, affect writing that does not appear personal? How does the material context of a writer's life enter into his or her writing? These questions matter for much the same reasons as questions concerning autobiographical academic writing matter: regardless of one's stance toward the personal, one cannot be an informed writer or reader without considering how one's subjectivity informs one's ways of knowing.

While theorizing the personal is a relatively recent concern in the academy, it is connected to the much older question of how a writer's or speaker's character is related to his or her ability to communicate. Aristotle was among the first to theorize this relationship, and he discusses the importance of character as what he calls *ethos*—one of the triumvirate of approaches to persuasion outlined in the *Rhetoric*. Of course, Aristotle was writing from a very different, pre-Enlightenment conception of subjectivity. His idea of character was more artificial than personal, in the sense that an *appearance* of character was meant to be created specifically for a particular rhetorical situation, rather than to reflect any qualities inherent to the speaker. Despite this important distinction, Aristotle's theory of *ethos* is salient to modern discussions of the personal, in that he was the first to discuss the relevance of connections between speaker and message, and to offer a theory of composition that considers how to present character in a way that appeals to a particular audience. Aristotle reminds us that while a sense of character in a text need not involve autobiography or narrative, the personal—or at least the appearance of it—is always already a component of the persuasive capabilities of a text.

Despite the usefulness of Aristotle's concept of *ethos* to modern debates concerning the personal, its conception of the speaker as sovereign individual is problematic in light of poststructuralist and multiculturalist awareness of the limitations and constraints on subjects in modern culture. In place of Aristotle's speaker, who consciously constructs and controls his *ethos* in different contexts, recent theories have posited a much more fluid and situational kind of identity, one that is variably shaped by encounters with the shifting dynamics of gender, race, and class positions at specific points in time—in ways that writers cannot fully control or even understand. This position, too, is problematic, for as Paul Smith has noted, "current [poststructuralist] conceptions of the 'subject' have tended to produce a purely *theoretical* 'subject,' removed almost entirely from the political and ethical realities in which human agents live" (xxix).

What is lacking among discussions of the personal, Aristotelian *ethos*, and poststructuralist theories of subjectivity is a theory of how individual writers compose and present versions of themselves as living people within the texts they write. How does a writer call upon lived personal experience in depicting himself or herself as what Aristotle calls a "certain kind of person?" How do subject positions enter into this depiction? How does the material context of a writer's life infuse his or her writing?

We need to look broadly at many kinds of texts written in many kinds of contexts in order to respond to these questions and better understand the personal. To begin, though, I have chosen to examine texts that, while argumentative, would be classified by most as autobiographies. These texts, by nineteenth-century American pioneer women, rely almost exclusively on *ethos* for their persuasive qualities because these pioneer women did not have access to the political and economic evidence that middle-class men used and tracing the local and material influences on these texts, I propose that, at least in these women's texts, *ethos* is conveyed through "strategies of placement." These strategies may offer a way of updating Aristotelian *ethos* with an awareness of how the personal is affected by writers' personal histories.

"A CERTAIN KIND OF PERSON" SPEAKING TO "A CERTAIN KIND OF AUDIENCE"

The term *ethos* was used first by Aristotle as one of the three *pisteis*, or kinds of proof, listed in the *Rhetoric*. The three *pisteis* are *logos* (appeal to reason), *pathos* (appeal to emotion about the topic of discussion), and *ethos* (appeal to the audience's trust in the speaker's character). Although Aristotle presents these three as being coequal, he is aware that not all of his contemporaries would agree, and to refute certain unnamed handbook writers' belief that *ethos* is unimportant, he states after introducing the *pisteis* that "character is almost, so to speak, the controlling factor in persuasion" (1.2.4 1356a). This statement promotes *ethos* more strongly than elsewhere in the *Rhetoric* and may be overstated to match the overstatements of the handbook writers (Fortenbaugh 155); however, it is clear that Aristotle sees character as a crucial element for rhetors to consider.

Although Aristotle emphasizes the importance of character, he is not—as Plato and Cicero are—interested in a transcultural model of absolute character. Nor is he primarily concerned with attempting to represent the speaker's own character, which complicates any effort to link *ethos* with "the personal." For Aristotle, *ethos* is inherently situational, as it is grounded within a public setting in which character traits only have meaning in relation to the values of the audience. He writes that an audience's conception of the speaker's *ethos* "should result from the speech, not from a previous opinion that the speaker is a certain kind of person" (1.2.4 1356a).

As James Kinneavy and Catherine Eskin have shown, this insistence that *ethos* should be apparent *in the speech itself* demonstrates a strong reliance on *kairos*, or the right timing of a thing. Aristotle advises that adapting *ethos* to the rhetorical situation requires awareness of the disposition of the audience as well as of their understanding of the speaker's character and of his disposition toward them:

> since rhetoric is concerned with making a judgment,
> [. . .] it is necessary not only to look to the argument,
> that it may be demonstrative and persuasive, but
> also [for the speaker] to construct a view of himself

> as a certain kind of person [. . .] for it makes much difference in regard to persuasion (especially in deliberations, but also in trials) that the speaker seem to be a certain kind of person and that his hearers suppose him to be disposed toward them in a certain way and in addition if they, too, happen to be disposed in a certain way. (2.1.2-3 1377b)

Because the Aristotelian speaker must attend to all of these factors in constructing a view of himself, the value of his (and I use the masculine pronoun deliberately) *ethos* is contingent on the cooperation and receptiveness of the audience. William M.A. Grimaldi has argued that the auditors' own sense of *ethos* is sufficiently important that it must be considered essential to the heuristic process: "[T]he auditors' ηθος [*ethos*] cannot be anything but an entechnic [artistic] pisteis, for it must be understood and addressed by the speaker to ensure the credibility of his own ηθος with the auditors" (Auditors 74).

The interactive nature of the *ethos* that the Aristotelian speaker constructs in the speech is such that the *ethos* is more a testament to communal values than to any privately held values of the speaker, for as S. Michael Halloran notes, Aristotle's vision of *ethos* emphasizes the conventional rather than the idiosyncratic, the public rather than the private" (60). So while the speaker *appears* to hold the values he conveys, these values may or may not be the values he had prior to the speech. I say "prior to the speech" because Aristotle conceives of character in the *Rhetoric* and in the *Nichomachean Ethics* as developed, in part at least, through a process of habitation (Grimaldi, *Aristotle* 186-87). There is some possibility, then, that a speaker might, through speaking *as if* he had a certain character, develop the habits associated with that character and eventually possess that character.

What is clear in Aristotle, though, is that the *ethos* of a speaker does not necessarily correspond with personal aspects of the speaker in any straightforward way. The Aristotelian speaker is addressing audiences composed of people who do not know him personally, and Aristotle suggests that this lack of knowledge gives the speaker a clean slate on which to depict himself as a certain kind of person; the speaker's personal traits are completely beside the issue of how to construct character in a speech. For *ethos* to be useful in theorizing the personal, though, we must consider whether and how a rhetor might use personal traits in co-creating *ethos* with an audience.

Where Aristotle does concern himself with the individual is through the actions of the speaker, and these are likewise problematic from a modern standpoint, for the speaker can only be persuasive if he is able to accurately analyze the situation and then choose and determine all aspects of his *ethos*. For Aristotle, constructing *ethos* is a matter of clear and deliberate choice— which is problematic in light of more recent understandings of constraints on individual agency.

Aristotle's primary advice concerning how to construct *ethos* is to "guess what sort of assumptions people have and then speak in general terms consistent with these views" (2.21.15 1395b). His advice on adapting *ethos* to particular audiences is concentrated in Book 2, Chapters 12-to 17 of the *Rhetoric*, which include catalogues of several kinds of people and the character traits by which a rhetor can recognize them and, presumably, tailor his speech. To demonstrate the kind of broad stereotypes Aristotle depicts, here are a few key points from what he says about the character of the young: "In terms of their character, the young are prone to desire and inclined to follow up on their anger. [. . . T]hey are impulsive and quick-tempered and inclined to follow up on their anger. [. . .T]hey are not cynical, but guileless, because of not yet having seem much wickedness" (2.12.3-7 1389a).

This picture of the young is reassuringly clear. While Aristotle's general representation of the rhetorical situation is complex and suggests that a rhetor must be highly attuned to the needs of the audience, his descriptions of kinds of people offer no guidance for how a rhetor might sort out contradictions in the composition of an audience. His suggestion is that, while audiences on different occasions might differ, individual character types are relatively straightforward and consistent.

Furthermore, his instruction on how to adapt *ethos* to an audience depends heavily on the ability of the rhetor to deliberately control all aspects of his *ethos*. Twice in the *Rhetoric*, he refers to character as something that is developed deliberately by the rhetor: "[C]haracters become clear by deliberate choice, and deliberate choice is directed to an 'end'" (1.8.6 1366a), and later, "Speeches have character insofar as deliberate choice is clear" (2.21.16 1395b).

Poststructuralist theorists from all areas—and particularly identity and autobiography studies—have challenged this purely performative understanding of subjectivity and have pointed out the ways in which social forces interpellate subjects and complicate agency. If, as Aristotle argues, "Speeches have character insofar as deliberate choice is clear," then character is impossible when cultural, linguistic, and psychic forces that are beyond a rhetor's conscious control affect what he or she is able to say.

POSTSTRUCTURALIST IDENTITY AND THE CHALLENGE TO ARISTOTELIAN *ETHOS*

For a theory of *ethos* to function in modern writing theory, it needs to incorporate contemporary conceptions of identity, which are much less stable than those that Aristotle presents—and much less under the control of the individual. According to recent theory, identity is radically contingent, and emerges through encounters with the shifting dynamics of social and cultural conditions. Susan Stanford Friedman has aptly characterized this new conception of identity as the "geographics of identity," which, in her words,

> involves a move from the allegorization of the self in terms of organicism, stable centers, cores, and wholeness to a discourse of spatialized identities constantly on the move. [. . .] Instead of the individualistic telos of developmental models, the new geographics figures identity as a historically embedded site, a positionality, a location, a standpoint, a terrain, an intersection, a network, a crossroads of multiply situated knowledges. (19)

These geographics of identity all involve greater awareness of how gender, race, class, sexual orientation, and (to a lesser degree) characteristics such as nationality, religion, and marital status interact in a person's life. Unlike conceptions of identity in the 1970s and 1980s, these geographics do not privilege any single subject position as the determiner of identity. So, whereas feminist critics in the 1980s wrote about texts as exemplary of women's issues, current theorists using the geographics of identity strive to de-essentialize traits like gender by examining how, say, gender is differently important to a writer's identity, depending on the social context.

Unlike Aristotle's rhetor, who has no preexisting character and can pick and choose how he represents himself on any given occasion, the poststructuralist writer is limited by political, cultural, and psychological constraints that restrict his or her ability to choose any option for self-representation. This is not to say that a poststructuralist writer has no freedom, but rather to say that this freedom is limited by more than the audience's *ethos*. For poststructuralist writers, who live within power relations and are affected by subconscious influences that they understand imperfectly, completely controlling one's *ethos* is not possible.

While poststructuralism has usefully pointed out the impossibility of sovereign individuality, it has primarily done so through analyzing matrices of subject positions, through identifying how subject positions are differentially important in a writer's life and writing. Although this kind of treatment provides a basis for comparing the work of different writers and even for comparing works from different points in a single writer's career, subject positions alone do not provide precise enough tools for examining in depth how the personal functions in any particular text. Any re-conception of *ethos* needs to address this limitation.

Julia Watson's reading of Audre Lorde's *Zami,* in her essay "Unspeakable Differences: The Politics of Gender in Lesbian and Heterosexual Women's Autobiographies," provides a good example of how critics have used the geographics of identity to read texts—and of how such readings are unnecessarily restricted. In her essay, Watson attempts to demonstrate how reading lesbian autobiographies against heterosexual women's autobiographies highlights the "unspeakability" of sexual identity, and writes that

> Lorde, a black lesbian feminist of Grenadian ancestry who grew up in the 1950s in New York, does not write autobiographical difference simply. [. .] Voicing multiple specificities, [she] names her unspeakability as that which is suppressed at any intersection of racism, sexism, and homophobia. [. . T]he mystic space in which women can build a utopian community that Lorde's work proposes [is] not a "decolonized" territory, but a vision of possibility that reorients the political and personal relationships of this world. (152-53)

Throughout her reading of *Zami*, Watson attends carefully to the ways in which motifs from what Lorde calls her "biomythography" contribute to Lorde's vision of a utopian community. These motifs—Lorde's mother's toughness and her insistence that Lorde conform to middle-class American social decorum, the problems with mythic spaces that both do and do not exist, Lorde's preoccupation with the odors of food and sexuality, the restrictiveness of McCarthyite politics—all contribute to Watson's largely persuasive reading of the political project Lorde attempts in *Zami*. It is Watson's discussion of the particularities of Lorde's text, rather than the mere identification of Lorde's imbricated subject positions, that make Watson's argument compelling; however, Watson concludes less strongly than she might, that "[f]or Lorde, the *multiple differences of being a black Grenadian-American lesbian* define her as outside all available systems of naming" (164; emphasis added).

In the end, Watson's lists of subject positions as markers of subjectivity are not a very satisfying answer to the problem she identifies at the beginning of her essay, saying

> [i]f in my own life these categories [of "lesbian" and "feminist"] have seemed inadequate to describe the complexities of experience, if the formulas of sexual and identity politics and the fixities of gender have seemed insufficiently articulated for the particulars of relationships, perhaps the polarized discourse of gender itself needs to be renegotiated through the specifics of person affiliation. (141)

If the "specifics of personal affiliation" are what Watson finds compelling in her own life and what she demonstrates are compelling in Lorde's biomythography, then it seems a more logical step to look to these specifics rather than primarily to the broad categories of gender, race, class, and sexual orientation. Although these subject positions are significant, they fail to highlight the historical specificity of identity and can serve to create an impression of stable selfhood—after all, in any individual life, gender, race, and class positions remain relatively fixed. Because of this fixity, subject positions are rather blunt tools for looking carefully at texts. It is true that most theorists, like Watson, do go beyond mere lists of subject positions to look carefully at the particularities of texts; however, these particularities drop out in most theses, leaving us with lists that fail to do much to distinguish between Audre Lorde and, say, Gloria Anzaldúa—both lesbian women of color who write feminist theory and literature.

Theorizing subjectivity at a more specific, particular level is important not only as a theoretical project but also as a political one. As Susan Jarratt and Nedra Reynolds have cogently argued, "A theory that reduces all discourse to the play of difference cannot adequately serve the feminist goal of articulating specifically gendered subjectivities in their own historical moments" (38). Similarly, Toril Moi has argued that "in deconstructing patriarchal metaphysics, we also risk deconstructing the very logic that sustains" the feminist projects that have brought about social and political changes for women (6). I believe the same could be argued of queer theory, multicultural theory, and other theoretical projects that have ties to material and political conditions.

TOWARD A WORKABLE THEORY OF SUBJECTIVITY IN WRITING

So while both Aristotelian rhetoric and recent theories of identity offer useful places to begin theorizing the personal, it is necessary to move beyond them. *Ethos* rightly affirms the importance of the character in argument, but its conception of character is disconnected from the personal qualities of the rhetor. In addition, Aristotle's advice on constructing *ethos* depends too strongly on the complete control of the rhetor to mesh well with recent critical theory. In contrast, poststructuralism gives due consideration to the forces beyond the rhetor's conscious control in constructing *ethos*, but in describing how these social forces operate it gives insufficient attention to the rich particularities that are at the heart of what makes an individual writer's work compelling.

By way of a solution to these problems, Nedra Reynolds suggests a constructive next step in her call for "studies of *ethos* in written discourse that extend outward to include multiple texts as well as the historical and political context for those texts" (334). Reynolds argues that

> [l]ocating *ethos* in written texts requires attention to the mediation or negotiation that goes on in the spaces between writers and their locations, in "the tension between the speaker's private and public self" (Ronald 39). *Ethos*, in fact, occurs in the "between" (LeFevre) as writers struggle to identify their own positions at the intersections of various communities and attempt to establish authority for themselves and their claims. By emphasizing where and how texts and their writers are *located*—their intersections with others and the places they diverge, how they occupy positions and move in the between—we can retain the spatial metaphors of *ethos* without limiting it to arenas of spoken discourse and without assuming that those gathering places are harmonious or conflict-free. (333)

Reynolds wonders "How might this idea of 'the betweens' work in practice?" and goes on to suggest that "it means attending to the rhetorical strategies writers use to locate themselves, their texts, and the particular discursive communities they are mediating within and between" (333-34). Like Reynolds, I believe that to better understand how *ethos* and the personal function in arguments, it is crucial to look closely at the particular ways in which writers establish authority for themselves through defining and redefining their evolving positions in particular communities—that we look not only at *texts* but also at material, social, and political *con*texts.

Any text could demonstrate these kinds of complexities in how writers construct *ethos* because *ethos* is a component of any argument. However, identifying how and where *ethos* exists is complicated when the personal does not appear in the explicit ways that we have seen in recent "personal" scholarly work. An added complication is that we are accustomed to reading in any systematic way for *ethos*. We have been trained to see *logos* as the true measure of an argument, and our ways of reading are profoundly affected by this prejudice.

Given these difficulties, I believe that the most effective way to theorize uses of the personal is to isolate *ethos* by examining texts that depend primarily on *ethos* rather than *logos* for their persuasive force. When it is not possible for a writer to rely primarily on logic, establishing a credible *ethos* in these kinds of texts is more clear, then it will be possible to test these strategies against texts in which *ethos* is but one of the means of persuasion.

I have begun the project of reconceiving *ethos* through analyzing narratives written and published by women who participated in and commented on westward expansion in the late nineteenth and early twentieth centuries in the United States. As disenfranchised women, these writers did not have the educational background or access to information necessary to participate in public debates about westward expansion on an equal basis with men. However, their personal experiences on the frontier gave them a measure of authority, which they were able to use effectively to convey their views on westward expansion to a general audience during a time at which the merits of different phases of that expansion were being actively debated. Although these women used autobiography as their medium and sometimes made professions of ignorance regarding the masculine realm of politics, they offer clear—and often highly critical—arguments about the validity of moving west for financial or territorial gain. Because these writers base their arguments exclusively on *ethos* and personal evidence, their texts provide ample opportunity to begin theorizing how writers use self-representation in arguing a position.

In reading the ways in which these writers use *ethos*, I wanted to be open to the complex possibilities through which the writers depicted themselves and not to be limited by the a priori categories through which I might otherwise read. Keeping in mind Reynolds's call to be attentive to "the particular discursive communities" that these writers "are mediating within and between" (333), I first read the autobiographies quickly to gain a sense of the large arguments they were making, and then reread much more slowly, paying close attention line by line to the details through which the larger work takes shape.

In reading, I attempted to keep in mind the choices the writers had made in deciding what events, objects, people, and places to include, and how those choices created a different kind of *ethos* than comparable elements they chose not to include. Through reading parts of the autobiographies against one another and against biographies and archival records of the women's lives, I have developed at least a partial sense of how these texts represent options from among the many kinds of *ethos* these women might have constructed from their life experiences.

Using my analysis of these autobiographical texts, I am calling the ways in which these and possibly other writers express and position themselves rhetorically as "strategies of placement." The term "strategy" is well suited to describing the contingent nature of subjectivity in that—unlike solid, stable subject positions—strategies exist within specific historical moments and may change from moment to moment. Furthermore, as strategies, these point to the rhetorical choices that writers make in any kind of writing: a writer can never simply depict herself in a way that is unequivocally and completely "true." The aspect of *placement* is significant in relation to the material constraints of a writer's physical space and geography, as well as to placement within ideological debates.

At the same time, though, the term "strategy of placement" also resonates with Michel de Certeau's use of "strategy," or the means by which individuals are "managed" by larger, bureaucratic entities, through these entities' operation from a "place," or a central locus of power that is not available to the individuals who are managed from it (35-36). In de Certeau's conception, a strategy is an art of the strong that is used to control the weak.

De Certeau's use of the term strategy confronts my characterization of strategies of placement as, in part, under the conscious control of a writer; however, there are undeniable forces that affect a writer's work that are outside his or her control. Thus, there is a productive tension between these concepts of strategy as a force through which an individual both *acts* and is *acted upon,* and I would like to hold on to both of these senses, for they illuminate the paradoxical situation writers in any circumstance face. Writing is never completely either an act of freedom or of restriction: it is always both.

My conception of strategies of placement is based in what Pierre Bourdieu calls the *habitus* in that these strategies incorporate not only subject positions and the more of communities, but also the active presence of personal history (*Logic* 54-55). As in Aristotelian *ethos,* strategies of placement are the tools of a writer in a particular situation in which she wants to "seem to be a certain kind of person" addressing an audience of people who "happen to be disposed in a certain way." Unlike Aristotelian *ethos,* these strategies are partial and imperfectly controlled. They reflect subject positions but also more minute particularities from the writers' lives.

In each strategy, the writer's assessment of an event, her depiction of her neighbors, her description of her personal possessions, and so forth, contribute to the complete picture of the "certain kind of person" she appears to be. Through the cumulative effect of the local work these strategies do within the autobiographies, each writer develops her global argument about the validity of westward expansion. Whether the perspective presented in the autobiography is effective in appealing to the reader depends on whether the strategies resonate with the reader's own values, morals, and taste.

STRATEGIES OF PLACEMENT

I have identified three major strategies of placement that these writers use more or less explicitly—and probably more or less consciously—to construct *ethos.* Some of the strategies are quite direct, and represent moments of clarity, in which these writers treat their identities as stable; others present more internal contradiction. I call the three kinds of strategies "identity statement," "moral displays," and "material associations." In the interest of space, I will briefly describe the first two here and discuss the third, which I see as most important, at greater length.

The clearest places in which these autobiographies present *ethos* appear in what I call identity statements, in which a writer explicitly refers to some facet of her self-identity as a person affiliated with a particular place or community, saying in effect, "I am a _____." However, even these seemingly straightforward statements are complex; in many cases, the identity statements at different points in the text contradict one another, so that, at one point, a writer might identify herself with a group of well-loved women friends from the East and, at another point, celebrate her newfound identity as manager of a productive farm in the West. These identity statements approach and recede from the foreground depending on the circumstances. Thus, the ties these women express to their locales and companions, both remembered and present, do not fit neatly into any conception of self-identity, and it is through the process of making these identity statements that these women express on paper who they are at the moment and who they are becoming.

Another, more subtle, kind of strategy of placement is what I call a "moral display." These kinds of displays are often used without any specific reference to group membership, but, as with Aristotelian *ethos*, they attempt to connect with the moral standards of the community and to establish trust through demonstrating similar values. Unlike identity statements, moral displays confirm writers' alliances with "particular discursive communities" by enacting the kinds of moral assessments that are part of those community practices. In short, while identity statements tell readers that a writer identifies with a particular community, moral displays show that the writer can act like a member of that community.

More than the moral displays or the identity statements, though, I believe that the references these writers chose to make to specific elements of their material and social conditions, through what I call "material associations," are particularly significant to how they convey *ethos*. These writers accomplish much of what they do through establishing themselves as women with particular kinds of tastes and cultural sensibilities, through the references they make to particular possessions, the maxims and regional terms they use, and the kinds of education they imply having experienced. Material associations are so pervasive in the lives of all speakers and writers that they receive little explicit commentary in these autobiographies. Their very invisibility makes them perhaps the most telling of all the strategies of placement, in that writers are not necessarily conscious of the extent to which certain kinds of material associations permeate their writing, what these associations say about their characters, or why they have chosen to include certain material associations rather than others from the wealth of material property that surrounded them. As Bourdieu has argued in *Distinction: A Social Critique of the Judgment of Taste,* identity

> is found in all the properties—and property—with which individuals and groups surround themselves; houses, furniture, paintings, books, cars, spirits, cigarettes, perfume, clothes, and in the practices in which they manifest their distinction, sports, games, entertainments, only because it is in the synthetic unity of the habitus, the unifying, generative principle of all practices. (173)

Like Friedman's geographics of identity, material associations are unstable and changing. Individually, they contribute little to the writer's *ethos,* but the accreted weight of them constructs an image or images of a particular kind of person.

There are, of course, thousands of references to material property in these autobiographies, but an example that demonstrates the power of this kind of material association, occurs in Annie Green's autobiography, *Sixteen Years on the Great American Desert, or the Trials and Triumphs of a Frontier Life,* in which she makes repeated references to books she has read or owns. She demonstrates her high valuation of books when, after her house is vandalized, she devotes almost an equal amount of space to describing the destruction of her small collection of books as she does to the devastation of all her other household goods combined (20-21). This disproportionately detailed description of the books serves more to establish her taste and character than to further the immediate plot.

However, what I am calling "material associations" includes not only the kinds of tangible property that Bourdieu describes, but also linguistic tools, such as uses of maxims, intertextual references, and regional language. These linguistic tools are not tangible "property" or commodities per se, but they work similarly in that speakers and writers may choose kinds of language from a wide variety of options. As with the consumer goods that Bourdieu discusses, some linguistic "goods" are more costly than others. To use any kind of material association credibly, one must have spent time and/or money to become sufficiently enculturated to use that material or linguistic property convincingly.

Maxims work as a sort of shorthand for writers, for as Aristotle notes in his discussion of them in *Rhetoric* 2.21.2, they often simply present the conclusion of a syllogism or enthymeme without context. They state truths that are assumed to need little commentary or proof because the audience understands that they have been tested through time in order to achieve their status as maxims. Pioneer woman Dr. Bethenia Owens-Adair frequently uses maxims, such as the following one: "For so tenderly our sorrows hold the germs of future joys,/That even a disappointment brings us more than it destroys" (82). Owens-Adair's narrative of her life as a divorced mother should and can have the courage to oppose the societal forces that serve to restrict frontier women to the roles of mother and wife. The maxims she uses counterpoint her pervasive statements about being a "'thorn in the flesh'" (85) of her community and serve to show her continued adherence to the speech patterns of the community in which she has spent most of her life. Although she may irritate her neighbors by challenging their restrictions on women, her use of maxims demonstrates a traditional, conservative element to her language use and her *ethos* and, presumably, makes her message more appealing to her audience.

Unlike maxims, intertextual references have fairly clear referents and demonstrate traceable cultural affiliations, in that writers typically attribute the references to such sources as popular song lyrics or written texts. Intertextual references are pervasive in these pioneer narratives, and, like references to material goods, serve to show identity through aesthetic taste. One woman who frequently uses these intertextual references

is Annie Pike Greenwood, a pioneer in the frontier Idaho of
the early 1900s. Greenwood demonstrates her taste through
intertextual references on many levels in her narrative, but
especially in presenting small, distinct aspects of her daily life.
For instance, she relates naming her god "Tylo" after reading
Maeterlinck's *Blue Bird*, stating that "at the time we were all
going around wearing enameled bluebird pins" (8-9). At
another point in her narrative, Greenwood explains the plight
of pioneer farmers and Congress's feeble efforts to help them
by referring to Conrad: "In *Lord Jim*, Conrad says that it is not
good for a man to know that he cannot make his dreams come
true" (22).

Nearly all of these pioneer women writers use both maxims and
more erudite intertextual references. Because both the lowbrow
maxims and the highbrow intertextual references usually
demonstrate associations with the East, which had most of the
printing presses and other technology needed for this kind of
cultural circulation, the material associations these writers use
demonstrate the complexity of the speech communities not only
in the West but also in the East. For these women, constructing
an *ethos* is thus more complex even than negotiating *between* the
speech communities of the East and West, since they are also
negotiating among speech communities *within* the East.

Regional language is the most specifically located kind of material
association used in these autobiographies, because either these
writers identify the regional language they use with markers,
a sin "my husband's better judgment gave way to his sand, (*as
the old Colorado settlers say*)" (Green 136; emphasis added) or the
regional word(s) originate in another language. An example of
the range of ways in which a writer can use regional language
is Mrs. D.B. Bates's use of the word "vamos" in narrating her
experiences during the California Gold Rush. Bates first uses
the word when she describes being nearly robbed as she lies ill
in her tent in California. She relates her fear of being robbed
by the man who pokes "one of the ugliest-looking faces [. . .] I
ever beheld" (146-47) into her tent. Her response is telling: "I
exclaimed, at the tip of my voice, 'Vamos! Vamos!' Knowing him
to be Spanish by his look, I addressed him in his own language"
(147). Bates here and elsewhere makes clear her dislike for
"Spanish" people, but it is interesting that she seems to have

incorporated the Spanish word "vamos" into her vocabulary and uses it as a way to connect with (and repel) the man on his own terms. Later in her narrative, instead of using the word "leave," she uses "vamos" without commenting on it as a new or regional word—"They soon found they must *vamos* from there" (161; emphasis added) and "he then vamoosed" (196; emphasis added). The changes in her use of "vamos" throughout her narrative help develop her *ethos* as someone who, like her readers, is unfamiliar with things "Spanish," but who knows California well enough to have integrated the local vernacular into her own speech, and who thus writes knowledgeably when she ultimately condemns California as a depraved society that is unfit for people of moral character.

There is, of course, a connection between class position and these writers' uses of different kinds of material associations. However, material associations do not comment solely on class, for within any class, individual members have particular tastes that other members do not share. Annie Pike Greenwood comments on the particularities of taste, saying, "I had reveled in all the current biography, philosophy, psychology, and like subjects," and "I read so much fiction in my younger years that I scarcely ever read it now" (323). Greenwood implies here that both her current and prior reading interests were appropriate to her class. However, as she demonstrates here, even tastes that exist within a particular class can be particular to an individual and furthermore can change over time. Like all strategies of placement, material associations do have ties to subject positions, but these positions are inadequate to demonstrate the specificity of the ways in which writers use the personal.

Strategies of placement—in their connections to place and community as well as in their internal contradictions—are concrete representations of the tension between private and public self. Strategies come together to create a complex *ethos* that is so particular to the writer's sense of audience and self that it cannot be predicted or theorized in any broad way through Aristotelian *ethos* or poststructuralist subject positions. Reflecting both the writer's choices and the forces outside her control, strategies of placement are the highly localized, specific materials through which the writer's *ethos* emerges.

To demonstrate the complexity of how strategies of placement work in this process of creating *ethos,* I now discuss a passage from Greenwood's *We Sagebrush Folks,* in which she describes being forced to confront the changes in self-conception that she has undergone during her passage from an urbane city-dweller in Salt Lake City to a farmer's wife in Milner, Idaho. Greenwood was initially nonplussed by Idaho, but she marks the change in her attitude when she relates her experience helping a neighbor woman, Mrs. Curry, give birth to a child in the midst of dirt and chaos. Mr. Curry asks Greenwood in the predawn hours one morning to come help him deliver his wife's baby—expecting that, as a mother, Greenwood would have instinctive knowledge of midwifery. When Greenwood arrives at the Currys' house, she is appalled by the lack of sanitary preparation for delivery: "All I had read of the horrors of childbirth on the farms came back to me. I was the *antiputrefactive woman,* and here was a dreadful example of what I had learned meant certain death" (47; emphasis added). Unwilling to act as an expert in midwifery under these conditions, she convinces Mr. Curry of the necessity of a doctor. When the frontier doctor arrives, he immediately tells Greenwood to make him some breakfast, without even greeting her first. Greenwood is appalled, saying,

> "No man had ever spoken to me in that way before in my life. I thought that if he would only look up and see what *a wonderful creature* I was, and see also, as he must, that I had only dropped in and was not really affiliated with the Currys in any way, he would have been ashamed of ordering me around" (50; emphasis added).

But the doctor is not ashamed, and Greenwood begins to learn that "out in the brush folks are not greatly impressed by either looks or breeding" (50). Nonetheless, the experience of helping Mrs. Curry with her birth is powerfully moving to Greenwood, who ends the episode by stating, "Something happened to me. I had received my initiation as *a sagebrush woman.* Until I die, I can never get away from that fact—there are great reaches of sagebrush in me" (50; emphasis added).

Through this episode, Greenwood uses several strategies of placement to help create an *ethos* for herself, to tell the story, and, most importantly, to demonstrate the complexity of life on the frontier to an audience that was unlikely to have much more than a symbolic sense of what the West was like. As in Aristotle's sense of *ethos*, Greenwood is aware here of *kairos* and the need to present herself as a person whom her audience might view as trustworthy.

Using three identity statements—"the antiputrefactive woman," "a wonderful creature," and "a sagebrush woman"—Greenwood attempts to put a label on her role in that setting. She also makes rather direct assessments of morality, through her comment that the doctor should have "been ashamed of ordering [her] around" and through her implication that if he did not appreciate breeding, then he himself was not well bred. Greenwood's choices regarding the material conditions at the Currys' also contribute to her *ethos*. Her description of the layette demonstrates her as a woman who is accustomed to certain standards of dress, but it also characterizes her as aware of and sympathetic to the effort Mrs. Curry has put into supplying clothing for the baby, despite her limited means: "On an unpainted old kitchen chair lay two folded diapers and two little slips, all made from flour-sacks. It was a large layette considering that it took four four-sacks, and some time is needed to use four sacks of flour. There were no little wool shirts and no little wool bands" (47). Greenwood's matter-of-fact mention of her easy familiarity with the Currys' stove, as she stokes it with more sagebrush and heats water, also implies that she is experienced at using this kind of stove and fuel, and is, at least in this respect, not at all dissimilar to the Currys. Her references to "[a]ll I had read of the horrors of childbirth on the farms" (presumably in publications aimed at "the antiputrefactive woman"), her labeling of the homeopath as one of "the illegitimate children born to Father Hippocrates" (49), and her description of the scene as ripe for "the specter septicemia" (47) are all examples of material associations that serve to characterize her as a woman who has knowledge of science and medicine and who has sanitary standards appropriate to a good American woman of the early 1900s. Her use of material associations also serves to characterize the other people in the scene; rather than merely relating Mr. Curry's request for help, she chooses to quote him as saying, "Kin yuh come over to my place, Mrs. Greenwood? The woman's sick"

(47), and in so doing, she calls attention to his lack of proper diction, his euphemizing of his wife's labor, and his failure to call his wife by a proper term of respect.

Could Greenwood's *ethos* in this passage be described adequately in terms of subject positions? It seems to have something to do with gender, although it is not clear whether being a "wonderful creature" and being a "sagebrush woman" are mutually exclusive—a "wonderful creature," at least, bears similarity to the white, middle-class ideal of domestic perfection. It also seems to have something to do with race, because although the Currys are white, like Greenwood, she may associate them with the unsanitary immigrants who were the target of much of early-twentieth-century rhetoric about sanitation. And Greenwood's *ethos* has a lot to do with class, in that she is constantly negotiating between her expectations of what a middle-class birth should be like and the scene at the Currys', which is so similar to "the horrors of childbirth on the [Other, essentialized, working-class] farms."

However, I believe this moment is more complicated than that. Greenwood's impressions at the moment depend in part to her familial history. The Idaho doctor was a homeopath, while Greenwood's father was an allopath who had little respect for homeopathy. Greenwood expresses similar sentiments about homeopathy, and her initial anger at the Idaho doctor had more to do with her disrespect for the kind of medicine he practiced than with any feelings about him as a person. Her assertion at the end of the episode that "I learned [. . .] to appreciate that doctor. He was not so bad—just eccentric" (50) heightens the strength of her "initiation" into sagebrush life. Her feelings about the birth itself were also historically specific, as she had two very young children at home and was just beginning to delight in fostering life in her vegetable garden. These experiences and feelings are by no means unique to Greenwood, but the complexity of that moment cannot be fully explained by subject positions alone—and neither can sagebrush womanhood.

Establishing the complexity of sagebrush womanhood is central to Greenwood's larger rhetorical project of describing the plight of the "sagebrush folks," the pioneer farmers who risked financial insolvency every year in order to feed the nation, who were praised with empty rhetoric about doing their duty for their country but who were rewarded with low market prices and ever-increasing debt. Greenwood and her husband eventually lose their farm to bankruptcy, and her project throughout the book is to show, through positioning herself as a woman of culture and education who both is and is not like her fellow Idaho farmers, that farmers deserve more than empty rhetoric and should be rewarded financially for the important work they do. Greenwood suggests that if she and her husband, Charley—both beautiful, talented, privileged people—could not prosper in frontier Idaho, then no one could. Instead of prospering, though she writes that

Charley and I succeeded as the majority of the farmers where we were. Nearly all those who tried to own their own farms lost them, and only the tenant farmers, shifting about from farm to far, were able to survive adverse conditions, and that at the expense of the city owners. If the actual value of farm products had been paid while the Baron [her pet name for her husband] and I were on the farm, we would still be there. I loved it then; I love it now; but I am not sorry to be gone. (480)

Although traditional subject positions certainly overlap with the *ethos* Greenwood creates, this *ethos* is much richer and more complicated than gender, race, or class position can explain, and grows out of the circumstances of family history, social surroundings, geographical location, and the infinite minutiae of everyday life. Although Greenwood's audience was largely white and middle-class, she could only make her case for "[us] sagebrush folks" by depicting herself as at once a poor farmer's wife and a woman of education and middle-class sensibilities.

CONCLUSION

Few would claim in the early twenty-first century that writing is ever completely impersonal or neutral. However, there is much that we still do not understand about the personal—the ways in which writers call upon the personal in making arguments or the ways in which the contingencies of writers' lives manifest themselves in writing. While Aristotle's highly abstract, international conception of *ethos* no longer resonates strongly with how we think about relationships between writers and audiences, the new, poststructuralist emphasis on subject positions cannot fully account for how the person function in texts either. As the autobiographical writings of the pioneer women in my study show, even individuals who seem to be similar along broad lines do not identify themselves identically. It is only through looking more closely at texts that we can explain how writers construct the individual differences that make "the personal" in writing truly personal.

Strategies of placement may offer a way to conceptualize the specific, grounded resources on which writers draw as they write, and also to conceptualize some of the constraints that limit the kinds of *ethos* that are possible. Being aware of these ways in which writers personalize their work is important, not only to us as critical readers and as people interested in writing, but also to us as teachers, because students, like most writers, are sensitive about the extent to which their writing reflects their identities. In being aware of how these identities might be expressed at the local level within texts, we as writing instructors can take care not to offend or alienate students unintentionally by labeling strategies of placement in their writing as wrong or inappropriate. Identity statements are relatively easy to identify as such, but moral displays and material associations are more slippery and are also more likely to be labeled as inappropriate to academic discourse. Experienced academic writers may use moral displays and material associations, but not in the ways that student writers frequently do. For instance, rather than judging the moral standards of a character in a novel or an author of an essay, as a student might, a more experienced academic writer might comment on everything from class politics in literary texts to methodological blunders in other writers' work. Both instances of assessment are kinds of moral displays. Material associations are even more common than moral displays in academic writing, for they constitute the primary way in which experienced writers justify what they write in academic prose. We cite some authors and theorists rather than others, and we use particular terms and theories that identify us as particular kinds of academic thinkers. Undergraduate students are not always fully aware of what kinds of material associations are appropriate to academic writing, but they often use the material associations of maxims (which writing teachers might call "clichés"), intertextual references (sometimes in reference to biblical texts), and regional language (which writing teachers might call "slang"). These strategies of placement help to identify students as particular kinds of people. If we are aware of strategies of placement as rhetorical moves, then instead of merely marking these uses of material associations as inappropriate, we as writing teachers can use them as starting places for talking about how writers use rhetorical strategies to appeal to their audiences.

I would predict that strategies of placement function not only in pioneer women's autobiographies, but in other kinds of texts as well. What remains to be done is to examine other kinds of texts, to see whether these strategies account for the ways in which writers of these texts draw upon the personal to make arguments. We need also to look at writings by pioneer men, contemporary academic writers, contemporary students, and many other kinds of writers. Do all of these strategies apply to other kinds of writing? Are there other ways of equal or greater importance in which writers use the personal?

Constructing *ethos* in texts involves a complex process of placing oneself within the myriad levels of context in which all writers exist. Included among these contexts are, of course, issues of gender, race, and class, as well as the more specific contexts of national policy debates, family histories, and ideological conflicts. With these multiple contexts in mind, we as theorists must move beyond thinking in overly broad ways about subjectivity in order to better conceptualize how the person functions in arguments. We must look for the more specific, more complex family, regional, moral, and microcultural placements that ultimately shape the range of option from which writers can draw to create identities in texts that are rich, fluid, and complex.

WORKS CITED

Aristotle, *Aristotle on Rhetoric: A Theory of Civic Discourse.* Trans. George Kennedy. New York: Oxford UP, 1991.

Bates, D.B. *Incidents on Land and Water, or Four Years on the Pacific Coast. Being a Narrative of the Burning of the Ships Nonantum, Hunayoon and Fanchon together with Many Startling and Interesting Adventures on Sea and Land.* Boston: Libby, 1858.

Behar, Ruth. *The Vulnerable Observer: Anthropology that Breaks Your Heart.* Boston: Beacon, 1996.

Bourdieu, Pierre. *Distinction: A Social Critique of the Judgment of Taste.* Trans. Richard Nice. Cambridge: Harvard UP, 1984.

de Certeau, Michel. *The Practice of Everyday Life.* Trans. Steven F. Randall. Berkeley: U of California P, 1984.

Fortenbaugh, William W. "Aristotle's Accounts of Persuasion through Character." *Theory, Text, Context: Issues in Greek Rhetoric and Oratory.* Ed. Christopher Lyle Johnstone. Albany: SUNY P, 1996, 147-68.

Friedman, Susan Stanford. *Mappings: Feminism and the Cultural Geographies of Encounter.* Princeton: Princeton UP, 1998.

Green, Annie M. *Sixteen Years on the Great American Desert, or the Trials and Triumphs of a Frontier Life.* Titusville: Truesdell, 1887.

Greenwood, Annie Pike. *We Sagebrush Folks.* New York: Appleton, 1934.

Grimaldi, William M.A. *Aristotle, Rhetoric II: A Commentary.* New York: Fordham UP, 1988.

————. "The Auditors' Role in Aristotelian Rhetoric." *Oral and Written Communications: Historical Approaches.* Ed. Richard Leo Enos. Newbury Park: Sage, 1990.

Halloran, S. Michael. "Aristotle's Concept of Ethos, or If Not His Somebody Else's." *Rhetoric Review I (1982): 58-63.*

Jarratt, Susan C., and Nedra Reynolds. *"The Splitting Image: Contemporary Feminisms and the Ethics of ethos."* Ethos: New Essays in Rhetorical and Critical Theory. Ed. James S. Baumlin and Tita French Baumlin. Dallas: Southern Methodist UP, 1994, 37-63.

Kinneavy, James L., and Catherine R. Eskin. "Kairos in Aristotle's Rhetoric." *Written Communication II* (1994): 131-43.

Miller, Nancy. *Getting Personal: Feminist Occasions and Other Autobiographical Acts.* New York: Routledge, 1991.

Moi, Toril. *"Feminism, Postmodernism, and Style."* Cultural Critique (1988): 3-22.

Owens-Adair, Bethenia A. *Some of Her Life Experiences.* Portland: Mann, 1906.

Reynolds, Nedra. *"Ethos* as Location: New Sites for Understanding Discursive Authority." *Rhetoric Review II (1993): 325-38.*

Smith, Paul. Discerning the Subject. Minneapolis: U of Minnesota P, 1988.

Symposium Collective. "The Politics of the Personal: Storying Our Lives against the Grain." *College English 64* (2001): 41-62.

Villanueva, Victor. *Bootstraps: From an American Academic of Color.* Urbana, IL: National Council of Teachers of English, 1993.

Watson, Julia. "Unspeakable Differences: The Politics of Gender in Lesbian and Heterosexual Women's Autobiographies." *De/Colonizing the Subject: The Politics of Gender in Women's Autobiography.* Ed. Sidonie Smith and Julia Watson. Minneapolis: U of Minnesota P, 1992, 139-68.

Audience Addressed Audience Invoked: The Role of Audience in Composition Theory and Pedagogy

Lisa Ede and Andrea Lunsford

CONSIDER AS YOU ARE READING:

How do writers conceptualize audience? In the 1980's, after an extensive review of concepts of audience that circulated in rhetorical theories, Ede and Lunsford attempted to answer this seemingly straightforward question. They determined that there were two competing formulations for comprehending audience: "audience addressed," which understands audience as an empirically real entity whose attitudes, beliefs, and expectations can and should be understood and targeted by the writer; and "audience invoked," which understands audience as a useful fiction that a writer creates by developing cues that place readers into specific roles as they read a text. Ede and Lunsford identified the strengths and weaknesses of each formulation and ultimately suggested a more complex synthesis for understanding audience—one that takes into account both formulations of audience at different moments of the drafting process. While Ede and Lunsford have since further developed their theories, this early demonstration urges writers toward a more sophisticated understanding of audience.

1. *According to Ede and Lunsford, what are the primary strengths and weaknesses of the concepts of "audience addressed" and "audience invoked"?*

2. *Think about several writing assignments that you have recently composed. Describe how you conceptualized the audience for your assignments as you wrote. Did you consider yourself invoking or addressing an audience, or did you undertake a synthesis of the two ways of understanding audience, as proposed by Ede and Lunsford?*

3. *In what ways do you think the concept of audience in this article might be complicated by multimodal rhetoric, such as communicating via blogging or Twitter?*

One important controversy currently engaging scholars and teachers of writing involves the role of audience in composition theory and pedagogy. How can we best define the audience of a written discourse? What does it mean to address an audience? To what degree should teachers stress audience in their assignments and discussions? What *is* the best way to help students recognize the significance of this critical element in any rhetorical situation?

Teachers of writing may find recent efforts to answer these questions more confusing than illuminating. Should they agree with Ruth Mitchell and Mary Taylor, who so emphasize the significance of the audience that they argue for abandoning conventional composition courses and instituting a "cooperative effort" by writing and subject instructors in adjunct courses. The cooperation and courses take two main forms. Either writing instructors can be attached to subject courses where writing is required, an organization which disperses the instructors throughout the departments participating; or the composition courses can teach students how to write the papers assigned in other concurrent courses, thus centralizing instruction but diversifying topics."[1] Or should teachers side with Russell Long, who asserts that those advocating greater attention to audience overemphasize the role of "observable physical or occupational characteristics" while ignoring the fact that most writers actually create their audiences. Long argues against the usefulness of such methods as developing hypothetical rhetorical situations as writing assignments, urging instead a more traditional emphasis on "the analysis of texts in the classroom with a very detailed examination given to the signals provided by the writer for his audience."[2]

To many teachers, the choice seems limited to a single option— to be for or against an emphasis on audience in composition courses. In the following essay, we wish to expand our understanding of the role audience plays in composition theory and pedagogy by demonstrating that the arguments advocated by each side of the current debate oversimplify the act of making meaning through written discourse. Each side, we will argue, has failed adequately to recognize 1) the fluid, dynamic character of rhetorical situations; and 2) the integrated, interdependent nature of reading and writing. After discussing the strengths and weaknesses of the two central perspectives on audience in composition—which we group under the rubrics of *audience addressed and audience invoked*[3]—we will propose an alternative formulation, one which we believe more accurately reflects the richness of "audience" as a concept.[1*]

AUDIENCE ADDRESSED

Those who envision audience as addressed emphasize the concrete reality of the writer's audience; they also share the assumption that knowledge of this audience's attitudes, beliefs, and expectations is not only possible (via observation and analysis) but essential. Questions concerning the degree to which this audience is "real" or imagined, and the ways it differs from the speaker's audience, are generally either ignored or subordinated to a sense of the audience's powerfulness. In their discussion of "A Heuristic Model for Creating a Writer's Audience," for example, Fred Pfister and Joanne Petrik attempt to recognize the ontological complexity of the writer-audience relationship by noting that "students, like all writers, must fictionalize their audience.'"[4] Even so, by encouraging students to "construct in their imagination an audience that is as nearly a replica as is possible of those many readers who actually exist in the world of reality," Pfister and Petrik implicitly privilege the concept of audience as addressed.[5]

[1*]   A number of terms might be used to characterize the two approaches to audience which dominate current theory and practice. Such pairs as identified/ envisaged, "real"/fictional, or analyzed/created all point to the same general distinction as do our terms. We chose "addressed/ invoked" because these terms most precisely represent our intended meaning. Our discussion will, we hope, clarify their significance; for the present, the following definitions must serve. The "addressed" audience refers to those actual or real-life people who read a discourse, while the "invoked" audience refers to the audience called up or imagined by the writer.

Many of those who envision audience as addressed have been influenced by the strong tradition of audience analysis in speech communication and by current research in cognitive psychology on the composing process.[6] They often see themselves as reacting against the current-traditional paradigm of composition, with its a-rhetorical, product-oriented emphasis.[7] And they also frequently encourage what is called "real-world" writing.[8]

Our purpose here is not to draw up a list of those who share this view of audience but to suggest the general outline of what most readers will recognize as a central tendency in the teaching of writing today. We would, however, like to focus on one particularly ambitious attempt to formulate a theory and pedagogy for composition based on the concept of audience as addressed: Ruth Mitchell and Mary Taylor's "The Integrating Perspective: An Audience-Response Model for Writing." We choose Mitchell and Taylor's work because of its theoretical richness and practical specificity. Despite these strengths, we wish to note several potentially significant limitations in their approach, limitations which obtain to varying degrees in much of the current work of those who envision audience as addressed.

In their article, Mitchell and Taylor analyze what they consider to be the two major existing composition models: one focusing on the writer and the other on the written product. Their evaluation of these two models seems essentially accurate. The "writer" model is limited because it defines writing as either self-expression or "fidelity to fact" (p. 255)—epistemologically naive assumptions which result in troubling pedagogical inconsistencies. And the "written product" model, which is characterized by an emphasis on "certain intrinsic features [such as a] lack of comma splices and fragments" (p. 258), is challenged by the continued inability of teachers of writing (not to mention those in other professions) to agree upon the precise intrinsic features which characterize "good" writing.

Most interesting, however, is what Mitchell and Taylor omit in their criticism of these models. Neither the writer model nor the written product model pays serious attention to invention, the term used to describe those "methods designed to aid in retrieving information, forming concepts, analyzing complex events, and solving certain kinds of problems.'"[9] Mitchell and Taylor's lapse in not noting this omission is understandable, however, for the same can be said of their own model. When these authors discuss the writing process, they stress that "our first priority for writing instruction at every level ought to be certain major tactics for structuring material because these structures are the most important in guiding the reader's comprehension and memory" (p. 271). They do not concern themselves with where "the material" comes from—its sophistication, complexity, accuracy, or rigor. Mitchell and Taylor also fail to note another omission, one which might be best described in reference to their own model (Figure 1).

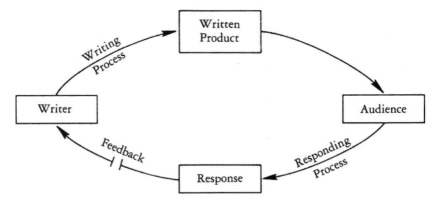

Figure 1: Mitchell and Taylor's "general model of writing." (p. 250)

This model has four components. Mitchell and Taylor use two of these, "writer" and "written product," as labels for the models they condemn. The third and fourth components, "audience" and "response," provide the title for their own "audience-response model for writing" (p. 249).

Mitchell and Taylor stress that the components in their model interact. Yet, despite their emphasis on interaction, it never seems to occur to them to note that the two other models may fail in large part because they overemphasize and isolate one of the four elements—wrenching it too greatly from its context and thus inevitably distorting the composing process. Mitchell and Taylor do not consider this possibility, we suggest, because their own model has the same weakness.

Mitchell and Taylor argue that a major limitation of the "writer" model is its emphasis on the self, the person writing, as the only potential judge of effective discourse. Ironically, however, their own emphasis on audience leads to a similar distortion. In their model, the audience has the sole power of evaluating writing, the success of which "will be judged by the audience's reaction: 'good' translates into 'effective,' 'bad' into 'ineffective.'" Mitchell and Taylor go on to note that "the audience not only judges writing; it also motivates it" (p. 250)[10] thus suggesting that the writer has less control than the audience over both evaluation and motivation.

Despite the fact that Mitchell and Taylor describe writing as "an interaction, a dynamic relationship" (p. 250), their model puts far more emphasis on the role of the audience than on that of the writer. One way to pinpoint the source of imbalance in Mitchell and Taylor's formulation is to note that they are right in emphasizing the creative role of readers who, they observe, "actively contribute to the meaning of what they read and will respond according to a complex set of expectations, preconceptions, and provocations" (p. 251), but wrong in failing to recognize the equally essential role writers play throughout the composing process not only as creators but also as readers of their own writing.

As Susan Wall observes in "In the Writer's Eye: Learning to Teach the Rereading/Revising Process," when writers read their own writing, as they do so continuously while they compose, "there are really not one but two contexts for rereading: there is the writer-as-reader's sense of what the established text is actually saying, as of this reading; and there is the reader-as-writer's judgment of what the text might say or should say ..."[12] What is missing from Mitchell and Taylor's model, and from much work done from the perspective of audience as addressed, is a recognition of the crucial importance of this internal dialogue, through which writers analyze inventional problems and conceptualize patterns of discourse. Also missing is an adequate awareness that, no matter how much feedback writers may receive after they have written something (or in breaks while they write), as they compose writers must rely in large part upon their own vision of the reader, which they create, as readers do their vision of writers, according to their own experiences and expectations.

Another major problem with Mitchell and Taylor's analysis is their apparent lack of concern for the ethics of language use. At one point, the authors ask the following important question: "Have we painted ourselves into a corner, so that the audience—response model must defend sociologese and its related styles?" (p. 265). Note first the ambiguity of their answer, which seems to us to say no and yes at the same time, and the way they try to deflect its impact:

> No. We defend only the right of audiences to set their own standards and we repudiate the ambitions of English departments to monopolize that standard-setting. If bureaucrats and scientists are happy with the way they write, then no one should interfere. But evidence is accumulating that they are not happy. (p. 265)

Here Mitchell and Taylor surely underestimate the relationship between style and substance. As those concerned with Doublespeak can attest, for example, the problem with sociologese is not simply its (to our ears) awkward, convoluted, highly nominalized style, but the way writers have in certain instances used this style to make statements otherwise unacceptable to lay persons, to "gloss over" potentially controversial facts about programs and their consequences, and thus violate the ethics of language use. Hence, although we support Mitchell and Taylor when they insist that we must better understand and respect the linguistic traditions of other disciplines and professions, we object to their assumption that style is somehow value free.

As we noted earlier, an analysis of Mitchell and Taylor's discussion clarifies weaknesses inherent in much of the theoretical and pedagogical research based on the concept of audience as addressed. One major weakness of this research lies in its narrow focus on helping students learn how to "continually modify their work with reference to their audience" (p. 251). Such a focus, which in its extreme form becomes pandering to the crowd, tends to undervalue the responsibility a writer has to a subject and to what Wayne Booth in *Modern Dogma and the*

Rhetoric of Assent calls "the art of discovering good reasons."[13] The resulting imbalance has clear ethical consequences, for rhetoric has traditionally been concerned not only with the effectiveness of a discourse, but with truthfulness as well. Much of our difficulty with the language of advertising, for example, arises out of the ad writer's powerful concept of audience as addressed divorced from a corollary ethical concept. The toothpaste ad that promises improved personality, for instance, knows too well how to address the audience. But such ads ignore ethical questions completely.

Another weakness in research done by those who envision audience as addressed suggests an oversimplified view of language. As Paul Kameen observes in "Rewording the Rhetoric of Composition," "discourse is not grounded in forms or experience or audience; it engages all of these elements simultaneously."[14] Ann Berthoff has persistently criticized our obsession with one or another of the elements of discourse, insisting that meaning arises out of their synthesis. Writing is more, then, than "a means of acting upon a receiver" (Mitchell and Taylor, p. 250); it is a means of making meaning for writer and reader.[15] Without such a unifying, balanced understanding of language use, it is easy to overemphasize one aspect of discourse, such as audience. It is also easy to forget, as Anthony Petrosky cautions us, that "reading, responding, and composing are aspects of understanding, and theories that attempt to account for them outside of their interaction with each other run the serious risk of building reductive models of human understanding."[16]

AUDIENCE INVOKED

Those who envision audience as invoked stress that the audience of a written discourse is a construction of the writer, a "created fiction" (Long, p. 225). They do not, of course, deny the physical reality of readers, but they argue that writers simply cannot know this reality in the way that speakers can. The central task of the writer, then, is not to analyze an audience and adapt discourse to meet its needs. Rather, the writer uses the semantic and syntactic resources of language to provide cues for the reader—cues which help to define the role or roles the writer wishes the reader to adopt in responding to the text. Little scholarship in composition takes this perspective; only Russell Long's article and Walter Ong's "The Writer's Audience Is Always a Fiction" focus centrally on this issue.[17] If recent conferences are any indication, however, a growing number of teachers and scholars are becoming concerned with what they see as the possible distortions and oversimplifications of the approach typified by Mitchell and Taylor's model.[18]

Russell Long's response to current efforts to teach students analysis of audience and adaptation of text to audience is typical: "I have become increasingly disturbed not only about the superficiality of the advice itself, but about the philosophy which seems to lie beneath it" (p. 221). Rather than detailing Long's argument, we wish to turn to Walter Ong's well-known study. Published in *PMLA* in 1975, "The Writer's Audience Is Always a Fiction" has had a significant impact on composition studies, despite the fact that its major emphasis is on fictional narrative rather than expository writing. An analysis of Ong's argument suggests that teachers of writing may err if they uncritically accept Ong's statement that "what has been said about fictional narrative applies ceteris paribus to all writing" (p. 17).

Ong's thesis includes two central assertions: "What do we mean by saying the audience is a fiction? Two things at least. First, that the writer must construct in his imagination, clearly or vaguely, an audience cast in some sort of role.... Second, we mean that the audience must correspondingly fictionalize itself" (p. 12). Ong emphasizes the creative power of the adept writer, who can both project and alter audiences, as well as the complexity of the reader's role. Readers, Ong observes, must learn or "know how to play the game of being a member of an audience that 'really' does not exist" (p. 12).

On the most abstract and general level, Ong is accurate. For a writer, the audience is not there in the sense that the speaker's audience, whether a single person or a large group, is present. But Ong's representative situations—the orator addressing a mass audience versus a writer alone in a room—oversimplify the potential range and diversity of both oral and written communication situations.

Ong's model of the paradigmatic act of speech communication derives from traditional rhetoric. In distinguishing the terms audience and reader, he notes that "the orator has before him an audience which is a true audience, a collectivity.... Readers do not form a collectivity, acting here and now on one another and on the speaker as members of an audience do" (p. 11). As this quotation indicates, Ong also stresses the potential for interaction among members of an audience, and between an audience and a speaker.

But how many audiences are actually collectives, with ample opportunity for interaction? In *Persuasion: Understanding, Practice, and Analysis,* Herbert Simons establishes a continuum of audiences based on opportunities for interaction.[19] Simons contrasts commercial mass media publics, which "have little or no contact with each other and certainly have no reciprocal awareness of each other as members of the same audience" with "face-to-face work groups that meet and interact continuously over an extended period of time." He goes on to note that: "Between these two extremes are such groups as the following: (1) the pedestrian audience, persons who happen to pass a soap box orator ... ; (2) the passive, occasional audience, persons who come to hear a noted lecturer in a large auditorium ... ; (3) the active, occasional audience, persons who meet only on specific occasions but actively interact when they do meet" (pp. 97-98).

Simons' discussion, in effect, questions the rigidity of Ong's distinctions between a speaker's and a writer's audience. Indeed, when one surveys a broad range of situations inviting oral communication, Ong's paradigmatic situation, in which the speaker's audience constitutes a "collectivity, acting here and now on one another and on the speaker" (p. 11), seems somewhat atypical. It is certainly possible, at any rate, to think of a number of instances where speakers confront a problem very similar to that of writers: lacking intimate knowledge of their audience, which comprises not a collectivity but a disparate, and possibly even divided, group of individuals, speakers, like writers, must construct in their imaginations "an audience cast in some sort of role."[20] When President Carter announced to Americans during a speech broadcast on television, for instance, that his program against inflation was "the moral equivalent of warfare," he was doing more than merely characterizing his economic policies. He was providing an important cue to his audience concerning the role he wished them to adopt as listeners—that of a people braced for a painful but necessary and justifiable battle. Were we to examine his speech in detail, we would find other more subtle, but equally important, semantic and syntactic signals to the audience.

We do not wish here to collapse all distinctions between oral and written communication, but rather to emphasize that speaking and writing are, after all, both rhetorical acts. There are important differences between speech and writing. And the broad distinction between speech and writing that Ong makes is both commonsensical and particularly relevant to his subject, fictional narrative. As our illustration demonstrates, however, when one turns to precise, concrete situations, the relationship between speech and writing can become far more complex than even Ong represents.

Just as Ong's distinction between speech and writing is accurate on a highly general level but breaks down (or at least becomes less clearcut) when examined closely, so too does his dictum about writers and their audiences. Every writer must indeed create a role for the reader, but the constraints on the writer and the potential sources of and possibilities for the reader's role are both more complex and diverse than Ong suggests. Ong stresses the importance of literary tradition in the creation of audience: "If the writer succeeds in writing, it is generally because he can fictionalize in his imagination an audience he has learned to know not from daily life but from earlier writers who were fictionalizing in their imagination audiences they had learned to know in still earlier writers, and so on back to the dawn of written narrative" (p. 11). And he cites a particularly (for us) germane example, a student "asked to write on the subject to which schoolteachers, jaded by summer, return compulsively every autumn: 'How I Spent My Summer Vacation'" (p. 11). In order to negotiate such an assignment successfully, the student must turn his real audience, the teacher, into someone else. He or she must, for instance, "make like Samuel Clemens and write for whomever Samuel Clemens was writing for" (p. 11).

Ong's example is, for his purposes, well-chosen. For such an assignment does indeed require the successful student to "fictionalize" his or her audience. But why is the student's decision to turn to a literary model in this instance particularly appropriate? Could one reason be that the student knows (consciously or unconsciously) that his English teacher, who is still the literal audience of his essay, appreciates literature and hence would be entertained (and here the student may intuit the assignment's actual aim as well) by such a strategy? In Ong's example, the audience—the "jaded" schoolteacher—is not only willing to accept another role but, perhaps, actually yearns for it. How else to escape the tedium of reading 25, 50, 75 student papers on the same topic? As Walter Minot notes, however, not all readers are so malleable:

> In reading a work of fiction or poetry, a reader is far more willing to suspend his beliefs and values than in a rhetorical work dealing with some current social, moral, or economic issue. The effectiveness of the created audience in a rhetorical situation is likely to depend on such constraints as the actual identity of the reader, the subject of the discourse, the identity and purpose of the writer, and many other factors in the real world.[21]

An example might help make Minot's point concrete.

Imagine another composition student faced, like Ong's, with an assignment. This student, who has been given considerably more latitude in her choice of a topic, has decided to write on an issue of concern to her at the moment, the possibility that a home for mentally-retarded adults will be built in her neighborhood. She is alarmed by the strongly negative, highly emotional reaction of most of her neighbors and wishes in her essay to persuade them that such a residence might not be the disaster they anticipate.

This student faces a different task from that described by Ong. If she is to succeed, she must think seriously about her actual readers, the neighbors to whom she wishes to send her letter. She knows the obvious demographic factors—age, race, class—so well that she probably hardly needs to consider them consciously. But other issues are more complex. How much do her neighbors know about mental retardation, intellectually or experientially? What is their image of a retarded adult? What fears does this project raise in them? What civic and religious values do they most respect? Based on this analysis—and the process may be much less sequential than we describe here—she must, of course, define a role for her audience, one congruent with her persona, arguments, the facts as she knows them, etc. She must, as Minot argues, both analyze and invent an audience.[22] In this instance, after detailed analysis of her audience and her arguments, the student decided to begin her essay by emphasizing what she felt to be the genuinely admirable qualities of her neighbors, particularly their kindness, understanding, and concern for others. In so doing, she invited her audience to see themselves as she saw them: as thoughtful, intelligent people who, if they were adequately informed, would certainly not act in a harsh manner to those less fortunate than they. In accepting this role, her readers did not have to "play the game of being a member of an audience that 'really' does not exist" (Ong, "The Writer's Audience," p. 12). But they did have to recognize in themselves the strengths the student described and to accept her implicit linking of these strengths to what she hoped would be their response to the proposed "home."

When this student enters her history class to write an examination she faces a different set of constraints. Unlike the historian who does indeed have a broad range of options in establishing the reader's role, our student has much less freedom. This is because her reader's role has already been established and formalized in a series of related academic conventions. If she is a successful student, she has so effectively internalized these conventions that she can subordinate a concern for her complex and multiple audiences to focus on the material on which she is being tested and on the single audience, the teacher, who will respond to her performance on the test.[23]

We could multiply examples. In each instance, the student writing—to friend, employer, neighbor, teacher, fellow readers of her daily newspaper—would need, as one of the many conscious and unconscious decisions required in composing, to envision and define a role for the reader. But how she defines that role—whether she relies mainly upon academic or technical writing conventions, literary models, intimate knowledge of friends or neighbors, analysis of a particular group, or some combination thereof—will vary tremendously. At times, the reader may establish a role for the reader which indeed does not "coincide[s] with his role in the rest of actual life" (Ong, p. 12). At other times, however, one of the writer's primary tasks may be that of analyzing the "real life" audience and adapting the discourse to it. One of the factors that makes writing so difficult, as we know, is that we have no recipes: each rhetorical situation is unique and thus requires the writer, catalyzed and guided by a strong sense of purpose, to reanalyze and reinvent solutions.

Despite their helpful corrective approach, then, theories which assert that the audience of a written discourse is a construction of the writer present their own dangers.[24] One of these is the tendency to overemphasize the distinction between speech and writing while undervaluing the insights of discourse theorists, such as James Moffett and James Britton, who remind us of the importance of such additional factors as distance between speaker or writer and audience and levels of abstraction in the subject. In *Teaching the Universe of Discourse*, Moffett establishes the following spectrum of discourse: recording ("the drama of what is happening"), reporting ("the narrative of what happened"), generalizing ("the exposition of what happens") and theorizing ("the argumentation of what will, may happen").[25] In an extended example, Moffett demonstrates the important points of connection between communication acts at any one level of the spectrum, whether oral or written:

> Suppose next that I tell the cafeteria experience to a friend some time later in conversation.... Of course, instead of recounting the cafeteria scene to my friend in person I could write it in a letter to an audience more removed in time and space. Informal writing is usually still rather spontaneous, directed at an audience known to the writer, and reflects the transient mood and circumstances in which the

> writing occurs. Feedback and audience influence, however, are delayed and weakened.... *Compare in turn now the changes that must occur all down the line when I write about this cafeteria experience in a discourse destined for publication and distribution to a mass, anonymous audience of present and perhaps unborn people.* I cannot allude to things and ideas that only my friends know about. I must use a vocabulary, style, logic, and rhetoric that anybody in that mass audience can understand and respond to. I must name and organize what happened during those moments in the cafeteria that day in such a way that this mythical average reader can relate what I say to some primary moments of experience of his own. (pp. 37-38; our emphasis)

Though Moffett does not say so, many of these same constraints would obtain if he decided to describe his experience in a speech to a mass audience—the viewers of a television show, for example, or the members of a graduating class. As Moffett's example illustrates, the distinction between speech and writing is important; it is, however, only one of several constraints influencing any particular discourse.

Another weakness of research based on the concept of audience as invoked is that it distorts the processes of writing and reading by overemphasizing the power of the writer and undervaluing that of the reader. Unlike Mitchell and Taylor, Ong recognizes the creative role the writer plays as reader of his or her own writing, the way the writer uses language to provide cues for the reader and tests the effectiveness of these cues during his or her own rereading of the text. But Ong fails adequately to recognize the constraints placed on the writer, in certain situations, by the audience. He fails, in other words, to acknowledge that readers' own experiences, expectations, and beliefs do play a central role in their reading of a text, and that the writer who does not consider the needs and interests of his audience risks losing that audience. To argue that the audience is a "created fiction" (Long, p. 225), to stress that the reader's role "seldom coincides with his role in the rest of actual life" (Ong, p. 12), is just as much an oversimplification, then, as to insist, as Mitchell and Taylor do, that "the audience not only judges writing, it also motivates it" (p. 250). The former view overemphasizes the writer's independence and power; the latter, that of the reader.

RHETORIC AND ITS SITUATIONS[26]

If the perspectives we have described as audience addressed and audience invoked represent incomplete conceptions of the role of audience in written discourse, do we have an alternative? How can we most accurately conceive of this essential rhetorical element? In what follows, we will sketch a tentative model and present several defining or constraining statements about this apparently slippery concept, "audience." The result will, we hope, move us closer to a full understanding of the role audience plays in written discourse.

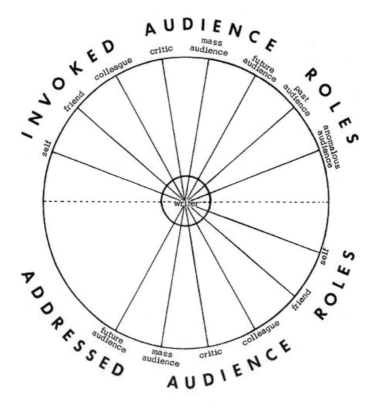

Figure 2: The Concept of Audience

Figure 2 represents our attempt to indicate the complex series of obligations, resources, needs, and constraints embodied in the writer's concept of audience. (We emphasize that our goal here is not to depict the writing process as a whole—a much more complex task—but to focus on the writer's relation to audience.) As our model indicates, we do not see the two perspectives on audience described earlier as necessarily dichotomous or contradictory. Except for past and anomalous audiences, special cases which we describe paragraphs hence, all of the audience roles we specify—self, friend, colleague, critic, mass audience, and future audience—may be invoked or addressed.[27] It is the writer who, as writer and reader of his or her own text, one guided by a sense of purpose and by the particularities of a specific rhetorical situation, establishes the range of potential roles an audience may play. (Readers may, of course, accept or reject the role or roles the writer wishes them to adopt in responding to a text.)

Writers who wish to be read must often adapt their discourse to meet the needs and expectations of an addressed audience. They may rely on past experience in addressing audiences to guide their writing, or they may engage a representative of that audience in the writing process. The latter occurs, for instance, when we ask a colleague to read an article intended for scholarly publication. Writers may also be required to respond to the intervention of others—a teacher's comments on an essay, a supervisor's suggestions for improving a report, or the insistent, catalyzing questions of an editor. Such intervention may in certain cases represent a powerful stimulus to the writer, but it is the writer who interprets the suggestions—or even commands—of others, choosing what to accept or reject. Even the conscious decision to accede to the expectations of a particular addressed audience may not always be carried out; unconscious psychological resistance, incomplete understanding, or inadequately developed ability may prevent the writer from following through with the decision—a reality confirmed by composition teachers with each new set of essays.

The addressed audience, the actual or intended readers of a discourse, exists outside of the text. Writers may analyze these readers' needs, anticipate their biases, even defer to their wishes. But it is only through the text, through language, that writers embody or give life to their conception of the reader. In so doing, they do not so much create a role for the reader—a phrase which implies that the writer somehow creates a mold to which the reader adapts—as invoke it. Rather than relying on incantations, however, writers conjure their vision—a vision which they hope readers will actively come to share as they read the text—by using all the resources of language available to them to establish a broad, and ideally coherent, range of cues for the reader. Technical writing conventions, for instance, quickly formalize any of several writer-reader relationships, such as colleague to colleague or expert to lay reader. But even comparatively local semantic decisions may play an equally essential role. In "The Writer's Audience Is Always a Fiction," Ong demonstrates how Hemingway's use of definite articles in *A Farewell to Arms* subtly cues readers that their role is to be that of a "companion in arms... a confidant" (p. 13).

Any of the roles of the addressed audience cited in our model may be invoked via the text. Writers may also invoke a past audience, as did, for instance, Ong's student writing to those Mark Twain would have been writing for. And writers can also invoke anomalous audiences, such as a fictional character— Hercule Poirot perhaps. Our model, then, confirms Douglas Park's observation that the meanings of audience, though multiple and complex, "tend to diverge in two general directions: one toward actual people external to a text, the audience whom the writer must accommodate; the other toward the text itself and the audience implied there: a set of suggested or evoked attitudes, interests, reactions, conditions of knowledge which may or may not fit with the qualities of actual readers or listeners."[28] The most complete understanding of audience thus involves a synthesis of the perspectives we have termed audience addressed, with its focus on the reader, and audience invoked, with its focus on the writer.

One illustration of this constantly shifting complex of meanings for "audience" lies in our own experiences writing this essay. One of us became interested in the concept of audience during an NEH Seminar, and her first audience was a small, close-knit seminar group to whom she addressed her work. The other came to contemplate a multiplicity of audiences while working on a textbook; the first audience in this case was herself, as she debated the ideas she was struggling to present to a group of invoked students. Following a lengthy series of conversations, our interests began to merge: we shared notes and discussed articles written by others on audience, and eventually one of us began a draft. Our long distance telephone bills and the miles we traveled up and down I-5 from Oregon to British Columbia attest most concretely to the power of a co-author's expectations and criticisms and also illustrate that one person can take on the role of several different audiences: friend, colleague, and critic.

As we began to write and rewrite the essay, now for a particular scholarly journal, the change in purpose and medium (no longer a seminar paper or a textbook) led us to new audiences. For us, the major "invoked audience" during this period was Richard Larson, editor of this journal, whose questions and criticisms we imagined and tried to anticipate. (Once this essay was accepted by *CCC*, Richard Larson became for us an addressed audience: he responded in writing with questions, criticisms, and suggestions, some of which we had, of course, failed to anticipate.) We also thought of the readers of *CCC* and those who attend the annual CCCC, most often picturing you as members of our own departments, a diverse group of individuals with widely varying degrees of interest in and knowledge of composition. Because of the generic constraints of academic writing, which limit the range of roles we may define for our readers, the audience represented by the readers of *CCC* seemed most vivid to us in two situations: 1) when we were concerned about the degree to which we needed to explain concepts or terms; and 2) when we considered central organizational decisions, such as the most effective way to introduce a discussion. Another, and for us extremely potent, audience was the authors—Mitchell and Taylor, Long, Ong, Park, and others—with whom we have seen ourselves in silent dialogue. As we read and reread their analyses and developed our responses to them, we felt a responsibility to try to understand their formulations as fully as possible, to play fair with their ideas, to make our own efforts continue to meet their high standards.

Our experience provides just one example, and even it is far from complete. (Once we finished a rough draft, one particular colleague became a potent but demanding addressed audience, listening to revision upon revision and challenging us with harder and harder questions. And after this essay is published, we may revise our understanding of audiences we thought we knew or recognize the existence of an entirely new audience. The latter would happen, for instance, if teachers of speech communication for some reason found our discussion useful.) But even this single case demonstrates that the term audience refers not just to the intended, actual, or eventual readers of a discourse, but to all those whose image, ideas, or actions influence a writer during the process of composition. One way to conceive of "audience," then, is as an over determined or unusually rich concept, one which may perhaps be best specified through the analysis of precise, concrete situations. We hope that this partial example of our own experience will illustrate how the elements represented in Figure 2 will shift and merge, depending on the particular rhetorical situation, the writer's aim, and the genre chosen. Such an understanding is critical: because of the complex reality to which the term audience refers and because of its fluid, shifting role in the composing process, any discussion of audience which isolates it from the rest of the rhetorical situation or which radically overemphasizes or underemphasizes its function in relation to other rhetorical constraints is likely to oversimplify. Note the unilateral direction of Mitchell and Taylor's model (p. 5), which is unable to represent the diverse and complex role(s) audience(s) can play in the actual writing process—in the creation of meaning. In contrast, consider the model used by Edward P. J. Corbett in his *Little Rhetoric and Handbook.*[29]

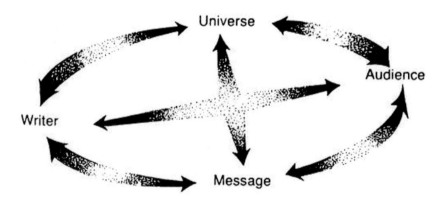

Figure 3: Corbett's model of "The Rhetorical Interrelationships" (p.5)

This representation, which allows for interaction among all the elements of rhetoric, may at first appear less elegant and predictive than Mitchell and Taylor's. But it is finally more useful since it accurately represents the diverse range of potential interrelationships in any written discourse.

We hope that our model also suggests the integrated, interdependent nature of reading and writing. Two assertions emerge from this relationship. One involves the writer as reader of his or her own work. As Donald Murray notes in "Teaching the Other Self: The Writer's First Reader," this role is critical, for "the reading writer—the map-maker and map-reader—reads the word, the line, the sentence, the paragraph, the page, the entire text. This constant back-and-forth reading monitors the multiple complex relationships between all the elements in writing."[30] To ignore or devalue such a central function is to risk distorting the writing process as a whole. But unless the writer is composing a diary or journal entry, intended only for the writer's own eyes, the writing process is not complete unless another person, someone other than the writer, reads the text also. The second assertion thus emphasizes the creative, dynamic duality of the process of reading and writing, whereby writers create readers and readers create writers. In the meeting of these two lies meaning, lies communication.

A fully elaborated view of audience, then, must balance the creativity of the writer with the different, but equally important, creativity of the reader. It must account for a wide and shifting range of roles for both addressed and invoked audiences. And, finally, it must relate the matrix created by the intricate relationship of writer and audience to all elements in the rhetorical situation. Such an enriched conception of audience can help us better understand the complex act we call composing.

ENDNOTES

1. Ruth Mitchell and Mary Taylor, "The Integrating Perspective: An Audience-Response Model for Writing," *CE*, 41 (November, 1979), 267. Subsequent references to this article will be cited in the text.

2. Russell C. Long, "Writer-Audience Relationships: Analysis or Invention," *CCC*, 31 (May, 1980), 223 and 225. Subsequent references to this article will be cited in the text.

3. For these terms we are indebted to Henry W. Johnstone, Jr., who refers to them in his analysis of Chaim Perelman's universal audience in *Validity and Rhetoric in Philosophical Argument: An Outlook in Transition* (University Park, PA: The Dialogue Press of Man & World, 1978), p. 105.

4. Fred R. Pfister and Joanne F. Petrik, "A Heuristic Model for Creating a Writer's Audience," *CCC*, 31 (May, 1980), 213.

5. Pfister and Petrik, 214; our emphasis.

6. See, for example, Lisa S. Ede, "On Audience and Composition," *CCC*, 30 (October, 1979), 291-295.

7. See, for example, David Tedlock, "The Case Approach to Composition," *CCC*, 32 (October, 1981), 253-261.

8. See, for example, Linda Flower's *Problem-Solving Strategies for Writers* (New York: Harcourt Brace Jovanovich, 1981) and John P. Field and Robert H. Weiss' *Cases for Composition* (Boston: Little Brown, 1979).

9. Richard E. Young, "Paradigms and Problems: Needed Research in Rhetorical Invention," in *Research on Composing: Points of Departure*, ed. Charles R. Cooper and Lee Odell (Urbana, IL: National Council of Teachers of English, 1978), p. 32 (footnote # 3).

10. Mitchell and Taylor do recognize that internal psychological needs ("unconscious challenges") may play a role in the writing process, but they cite such instances as an "extreme case (often that of the creative writer)" (p. 251). For a discussion of the importance of self-evaluation in the composing process.

11. Susan Miller, "How Writers Evaluate Their Own Writing," *CCC*, 33 (May, 1982), 176-183.

12. Susan Wall, "In the Writer's Eye: Learning to Teach the Rereading/ Revising Process," *English Education*, 14 (February, 1982), 12.

13. Wayne Booth, *Modern Dogma and the Rhetoric of Assent* (Chicago: The University of Chicago Press, 1974), p. xiv.

14. Paul Kameen, "Rewording the Rhetoric of Composition," *Pre/Text*, 1 (Spring-Fall, 1980), 82.

15. Mitchell and Taylor's arguments in favor of adjunct classes seem to indicate that they see writing instruction, wherever it occurs, as a skills course, one instructing students in the proper use of a tool.

16. Anthony R. Petrosky, "From Story to Essay: Reading and Writing," *CCC*, 33 (February, 1982), 20.

17. Walter J. Ong, S. J., "The Writer's Audience Is Always a Fiction," *PMLA*, 90 (January, 1975), 9-21. Subsequent references to this article will be cited in the text.

18. See, for example, William Irmscher, "Sense of Audience: An Intuitive Concept," unpublished paper delivered at the CCCC in 1981; Douglas B. Park, "The Meanings of Audience: Pedagogical Implications," unpublished paper delivered at the CCCC in 1981; and Luke M. Reinsma, "Writing to an Audience: Scheme or Strategy?" unpublished paper delivered at the CCCC in 1982.

19. Herbert W. Simons, *Persuasion: Understanding, Practice, and Analysis* (Reading, MA: Addison-Wesley, 1976).

20. Ong, p. 12. Ong recognizes that oral communication also involves role-playing, but he stresses that it "has within it a momentum that works for the removal of masks" (p. 20). This may be true in certain instances, such as dialogue, but does not, we believe, obtain broadly.

21. Walter S. Minot, "Response to Russell C. Long," *CCC*, 32 (October, 1981), 337.

22. We are aware that the student actually has two audiences, her neighbors and her teacher, and that this situation poses an extra constraint for the writer. Not all students can manage such a complex series of audience constraints, but it is important to note that writers in a variety of situations often write for more than a single audience.

23. In their paper on "Student and Professional Syntax in Four Disciplines" (unpublished paper delivered at the CCCC in 1981), Ian Pringle and Aviva Freedman provide a good example of what can happen when a student creates an aberrant role

for an academic reader. They cite an excerpt from a third year history assignment, the tone of which "is essentially the tone of the opening of a television travelogue commentary" and which thus asks the reader, a history professor, to assume the role of the viewer of such a show. The result is as might be expected: "Although the content of the paper does not seem significantly more abysmal than other papers in the same set, this one was awarded a disproportionately low grade" (p. 2).

24. One danger which should be noted is a tendency to foster a questionable image of classical rhetoric. The agonistic speaker-audience relationship which Long cites as an essential characteristic of classical rhetoric is actually a central point of debate among those involved in historical and theoretical research in rhetoric. For further discussion, see: Lisa Ede and Andrea Lunsford, "On Distinctions Between Classical and Modern Rhetoric," in *Classical Rhetoric and Modern Discourse: Essays in Honor of Edward P. J. Corbett,* ed. Robert Connors, Lisa Ede, and Andrea Lunsford (Carbondale, IL: Southern Illinois University Press, 1984).

25. James Moffett, *Teaching the Universe of Discourse* (Boston: Houghton Mifflin, 1968), p. 47. Subsequent references will be mentioned in the text.

26. We have taken the title of this section from Scott Consigny's article of the same title, *Philosophy and Rhetoric,* 7 (Summer,1974), 175-186. Consigny's effort to mediate between two opposing views of rhetoric provided a stimulating model for our own efforts.

27. Although we believe that the range of audience roles cited in our model covers the general spectrum of options, we do not claim to have specified all possibilities. This is particularly the case since, in certain instances, these roles may merge and blend-shifting subtly in character. We might also note that other terms for the same roles might be used. In a business setting, for instance, colleague might be better termed co-worker; critic, supervisor.

28. Douglas B. Park, "The Meanings of Audience,"' *CE*, 44 (March, 1982), 249.

29. Edward P. J. Corbett, *The Little Rhetoric & Handbook*, 2nd edition (Glenview, IL: Scott, Foresman, 1982), p. 5.

30. Donald M. Murray, "Teaching the Other Self: The Writer's First Reader," *CCC*, 33 (May, 1982), 142.

"AMONG THE AUDIENCE": ON AUDIENCE IN AN AGE OF NEW LITERACIES

ANDREA A. LUNSFORD AND LISA EDE

CONSIDER AS YOU ARE READING:

Writing some twenty years after the publication of their foundational article, "Audience Addressed/Audience Invoked: The Role of Audience in Composition Theory and Pedagogy," Ede and Lunsford contemplate the impact of new literacies and electronic media on the concept of audience. They question whether "audience" is even a relevant term in a society dominated by participatory media, such as Facebook and Twitter, and they seek to understand the relationships among text, author, medium, context, and audience. In an effort to revise and expand definitions of audience to account for these new realities, Ede and Lunsford redefine the concept of the rhetorical triad to account for the manner in which the roles of writers and audience often conflate, merge, and shift. This essay is a strong reminder that scholarship is always part of an ongoing conversation that is influenced by social developments, such as technology.

1. *Explain how this version of "audience" differs from that set forth in "Audience Addressed/Audience Invoked."*

2. *Describe a situation in which you composed an essay that the authors would describe as "participatory." How did your understanding of the audience differ from a situation in which you were composing a "traditional" academic essay?*

3. *Do you find Ede and Lunsford's new model of audience to be a helpful guide in composing arguments for and in new media? Why or why not?*

With participatory media, the boundaries between audiences and creators become blurred and often invisible. In the words of David Sifry, the founder of Technorati, a search engine for blogs, one-to-many "lectures" (i.e., from media companies to their audiences) are transformed into "conversations" among "the people formerly known as the audience."

—Andreas Kluth,
"Among the Audience: A Survey of New Media."
The Economist, p. 4)

Critics argue that privacy does not matter to children who were raised in a wired celebrity culture that promises a niche audience for everyone. Why hide when you can perform? But even if young people are performing, many are clueless about the size of their audience.

—Ari Melber,
"About Facebook." *The Nation*, p. 23.

When we wrote "Audience Addressed/Audience Invoked: The Role of Audience in Composition Theory and Pedagogy" (hereafter AA/AI), which was published in *College Composition and Communication* in 1984, we little realized the life that it would have. Much has changed in the teaching of writing—and in the technologies of communication—since we published AA/AI. Much has changed, as well, in our culture and cultural awareness. So much, in fact, that we saw the need in 1996 to critique our earlier essay, calling attention to several unexamined assumptions that we wished to expose and challenge. In "Representing Audience: Successful Discourse and Disciplinary Critique," published in *College Composition and Communication* in 1996, we observed, for instance, that although we intended our essay "to invoke and address a broad range of audiences, it speaks most strongly to those whose identifications and experiences mirror our own, while turning away from the potential difficulties and costs often inherent in the effort to achieve the kind of academic 'success' that our essay takes for granted as well as from those who would wish to subvert such 'success'" (175).

More than a dozen years later still, we see the need to reflect yet again on the role of audience in composition theory and pedagogy. We are particularly interested in the role that new literacies are playing in expanding the possibilities of agency, while at the same time challenging older notions of both authorship and audience. In addition, observations of and talks with students—as well as changes in our own reading, writing, and researching practices—have alerted us to new understandings and enactments of textual production and ownership. As a result, our goal in this essay is both theoretical and pedagogical. We wish to subject the concept of audience to renewed inquiry, attempting to account for the way texts develop and work in the world in the twenty-first century. We hope, as well, that the resulting analysis will be useful in our classrooms. As we conduct this exploration, we will address the following questions.

In a world of participatory media—of FaceBook, YouTube, Wikipedia, Twitter, and Del.icio.us—what relevance does the term "audience" hold?

How can we best understand the relationships among text, author, medium, context, and audience today? How can we usefully describe the dynamic of this relationship?

To what extent do the invoked and addressed audiences that we describe in our 1984 essay need to be revised and expanded?

What other terms, metaphors, or images might prove productive?

What difference might answers to these questions make to twenty-first century teachers and students?

ON NEW MEDIA AND NEW LITERACIES[1]

Before turning to these questions, we would like to situate our discussion in the context of recent research on new media[2] and new literacies, for how we view their relationship matters a good deal to our understanding of both audience and authorship. Are new literacies "new" simply because they rely upon new media, or is the relationship more complex? This is a question that Michele Knobel and Colin Lankshear raise in the introduction to *A New Literacies Sampler*. Knobel and Lankshear argue that the latter is the case. While acknowledging that new media have certainly played an important role in the development of new literacies, they argue that what they term "paradigm cases" of new literacies have, as they put it, both "new 'technical' stuff and new 'ethos' stuff" (7). Central to the development of new literacies is the mobilization of "very different kinds of values and priorities and sensibilities than the literacies we are familiar with" (7). New literacies, they argue, are "more 'participatory,' 'collaborative,' and 'distributed' in nature than conventional literacies. That is, they are less 'published,' 'individuated,' and 'author-centric' than conventional literacies." They are also "less 'expert-dominated' than conventional literacies" (9).

Thus, new literacies involve a different kind of mindset than literacies traditionally associated with print media. In their introduction to *A New Literacies Sampler*, Knobel and Lankshear contrast what they refer to as a "physical-industrial" mindset—the mindset that the two of us certainly grew up with throughout our schooling and a good deal of our working lives—with a "cyberspatial-postindustrial mindset" (10). According to Knobel and Lankshear, those whose experience grounds them primarily in a physical-industrial mindset tend to see the individual person as "the unit of production, competence, intelligence." They also identify expertise and authority as "located in individuals and institutions" (11). Those who inhabit a "cyberspatial-postindustrial mindset," in contrast, increasingly focus on "collectives as the unit of production, competence, intelligence" and tend to view expertise, authority, and agency as "distributed and collective" (11). In a "cyberspatial-postindustrial mindset," the distinction between author and audience is much less clear than in that of the physical-industrial mindset of print literacy.

Those familiar with research in our field on new media and new literacies—research undertaken by scholars such as Cynthia Selfe, Gail Hawisher, James Porter, Anne Wysocki, Johndan Johnson-Eilola, James Gee, Heidi McKee, Christine Blair, Cheryl Ball, Danielle DeVoss, Todd Taylor, the New London Group, and others—will recognize that the distinction that Knobel and Lankshear draw has been made before. (They will recognize, as well, the value of complicating this binary, useful as it is in a general sense.) The scholarly work of media historians is particularly helpful in this regard. (See, for instance, Lisa Gitelman and Geoffrey B. Pingree's *New Media: 1740-1915.*) The insights generated by these and other scholars in our field have been enriched by research in such related areas as literacy, cultural, and internet studies. In works ranging from Gunther Kress's *Literacy in the New Media Age* to Howard Rheingold's *Smart Mobs: The Next Social Revolution,* Henry Jenkins' *Convergence Culture: Where Old and New Media Collide,* Lisa Nakamura's *Digitizing Race: Visual Cultures of the Internet,* Keith Sawyer's *Group Genius,* and Clay Shirky's *Here Comes Everybody,* those studying online and digital literacies—particularly Web 2.0 literacies—are challenging conventional understandings of both authorship and audience.[3]

As we have engaged this literature and have attempted to better understand what it means to be a reader and writer in the twenty-first century, we have come to see that what we thought of as two separate strands of our scholarly work— one on collaboration, the other on audience—have in fact become one. As writers and audiences merge and shift places in online environments, participating in both brief and extended collaborations, it is increasingly obvious that writers seldom, if ever, write alone. In short, when receivers or consumers of information become creators of content as well, it is increasingly difficult to tell when writers are collaborative writers or authors and when they are members of audiences.

The End of Audience?

In our contemporary world of digital and online literacies, it seems important to question the status and usefulness of the concept of "audience." Are the changes brought about by new media and new literacies so substantial that it is more accurate to refer to those who participate in new media writing, ranging from user-generated content and tagging to tweeting and digital remixing, as "the people formerly known as the audience," as David Sifry suggests in the first epigraph to this essay?

Even before the explosion of such social networking sites as blogs, Facebook, and Twitter, some scholars in the field of rhetoric and writing argued that the term "audience" may have outlived its usefulness. Some suggested, for instance, that the term "discourse community" better reflects social constructionist understandings of communication. This is the position that James Porter espouses in his 1992 *Audience and Rhetoric: An Archaeological Composition of the Discourse Community.* Others have wondered whether the term "public," as articulated and developed by Jürgen Habermas and explored and extended in Michael Warner's *Publics and Counterpublics*, might not be just as useful as—or more useful than—the term "audience." In *Citizen Critics: Literary Public Spheres*, for instance, Rosa Eberly argues that the term "public" is more helpful than the terms "reader" or "audience" for her study of letters to the editor about four controversial literary texts—two published early in the twentieth century, and two published later.

These and other efforts to re-examine and problematize the concept of audience reflect developments in the field over the last several decades. In the early 1980s when we were talking, thinking, and writing about audience, the need for such problematization was anything but apparent to us. To put it mildly, our context was different. At that time, we were immersed in research on the contemporary relevance of the classical rhetorical tradition, as our 1984 essay "On Distinctions between Classical and Modern Rhetoric" attests. That same year saw the publication of our co-edited *Essays on Classical Rhetoric and Modern Discourse.*

In the years since we published AA/AI, we have come to recognize the limitations, as well as the strengths, of the classical (and more broadly Western) rhetorical tradition. In our 1996 reflection on AA/AI, "Representing Audience," for example, we acknowledge the individualism inherent in this tradition. We also point out that the rhetorical tradition's commitment to *successful* communication has exacted a high hidden price, particularly in terms of efforts to address the ethics of diversity: "For how better to avoid misunderstanding and failure (and to make 'successful' communication more likely) than to exclude, to disenfranchise those who by their very presence in the arena of discourse raise increased possibilities for communicative failures" (174). The rhetorical tradition, as a consequence, risks indifference or hostility to issues of difference, to "audiences ignored, rejected, excluded, or denied" (174).

Does this mean that we wish to reject the term "audience"? No, it does not. We believe that "audience," like other terms such as "discourse community" or "public," is inevitably overdetermined, but is still (as is the case with these other terms) in many contexts both helpful and productive. Finally, terms like "audience," "reader," "discourse community," and "public" gesture toward and evoke differing concerns, traditions, and interests. The emphasis on the reader in reader response criticism, for instance, was clearly a salutary response to the emphasis on the text in formalist New Criticism.[3] In the final analysis, one of the beauties of a fluid, multiplicitous term like "audience" is its heuristic value in exploring fine distinctions and teasing out important nuances in any communicative situation.

We continue to believe, then, that the concept of audience provides a helpful theoretical and practical grounding for efforts to understand how texts (and writers and readers) work in today's world. We also believe, as we stated in AA/AI, that a productive way to conceive of audience "is as an overdetermined or unusually rich concept, one which may perhaps be best specified through the analysis of precise, concrete situations" (168). Indeed, in rereading AA/AI we are struck by the powerful role that the analysis of such situations plays in our own essay. As readers may already realize, in remaining committed to the term "audience" we remain committed to rhetoric and to the rhetorical tradition. Our understanding of the rhetorical tradition has changed and expanded since we first wrote AA/AI, but we continue to find rhetoric's emphasis on the rhetorical situation to be theoretically and pedagogically enabling.

The "Rhetorical Triangle" Revisited

In AA/AI we described our own experiences with varying audiences, arguing that "the elements [of invoked and addressed audience roles] shift and merge, depending on the particular rhetorical situation, the writer's aim, and the genre chosen (168)." Thus we embedded our discussion of audience in the classical conception of the "rhetorical triangle," the set of relationships among text, author, and audience out of which meaning grows. Twenty-five years ago, while our work attempted to complicate these sets of relationships, this basic understanding served us simply and well. Today, however, we need a more flexible and robust way of understanding these traditional elements of discourse and the dynamic at work among them.

As a result, we now use the following figure to portray the basic elements of the rhetorical situation. This figure includes speakers as well as writers, viewers, listeners, and readers.

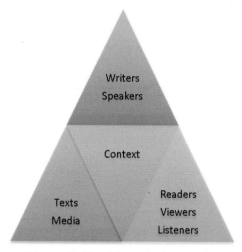

Figure 1: The Rhetorical Triangle

This figure captures more of the complexity of the rhetorical situation: it acknowledges the plurality of authorship/ readership; it includes media as a key element of thinking about texts; and it includes context as the element that touches on, connects, and shapes all angles of the triangle. This element of the rhetorical situation calls attention to the diverse and multiple factors that writers must consider when they compose—from generic or situational constraints to ideologies that make some writerly choices seem obvious and "natural," while others are "unnatural" or entirely hidden from view. As the figure suggests, the relationship among writer and message and medium (or media) is complex and full of reciprocity. In a digital world, and especially in the world of Web 2.0, speakers and audiences communicate in multiple ways and across multiple channels, often reciprocally. This momentous shift has challenged not only traditional models of communication but also the relationship between "creators" of messages and those who receive them. Today, as we have pointed out, the roles of writers and audiences often conflate, merge, and shift.

The deeply participatory nature of much new media writing provides opportunities for writerly agency,[4] even as it challenges notions of intellectual property that have held sway now for over 300 years, leading—as we have been at pains to point out in our research on collaboration and collaborative writing—both to diverse forms of multiple authorship and to the kind of mass authorship that characterizes sites such as Wikipedia, Rotten Tomatoes, or collaborative blogs. To say that the music and film industries, along with some print-based companies, are resisting such shifts in authorship is an understatement. While these entities will continue to cling to traditional intellectual property regimes of the past, it seems clear that new ways of managing the relationship among texts, "authors," media, contexts, and audiences are emerging. In this regard, consider the alternative rock group Radiohead's decision to release its seventh album, *In Rainbows*, as a digital download on the Internet. Fans of this group could purchase the music collection on the Web—for whatever price they wished to pay.[5]

In *The Economics of Attention*, Richard Lanham argues that we have moved from what he calls a "stuff economy" (one based on material goods) to a "fluff economy" (one based on immaterial information). With his typical humor and verve, Lanham shows that while in a "stuff" economy scarcity is the major economic principle at work, that principle utterly fails in a "fluff" economy, where information is anything but scarce. In fact, as Lanham points out, we are drowning in it. In such an economy, what is needed, according to Lanham, is *attention*—that is, a way of attending sensibly to the information pouring in:

In an attention economy, the center of gravity for property shifts from real property to intellectual property. This shift has plunged us into confusions about the ownership of such property . . . that it will take some time to sort out. . . . Information, unlike stuff, can be both kept and given away at the same time. As long as the means of notation were fixed in physicality as books, reports, painted images, we could gloss over this major obstacle: that "possession" means something different from a private property in stuff. Now, with information expressed on a digital screen, with its new means of dissemination, we can no longer continue this gloss. Hence the current agonies in the music and film business. They have been caught in a vise, squeezed between the macro and the micro economics of attention (259).

We too are caught between the macro and micro economies of attention, since we cannot ignore the world of "stuff." But we are clearly in what Lanham calls a "revisionist" way of thinking. "Our locus of reality has shifted," he argues:

We have not left the physical world behind and become creatures of pure attention. Neither has wealth become totally disembodied. Our view is now bi-stable. We must always be ready to move from one view of the world to another. They are always competing with each other. We are learning to live in two worlds at once. (258)

In a time of transition, some people are differentially advantaged or disadvantaged: individuals are—or are not—members of Lanham's "we," a fact which reminds us that inequalities and differing degrees of access persist in an attention economy.

As Lanham's discussion suggests, writers who want and need to shift among worlds must be able to hold flexible views of the real and potential relationships among text, context, author, medium, and audience. They must be able to negotiate distinctions between writing and reading, between author and audience that refuse to remain stable; they must also be able to sort out the competing claims of words, images, and sounds in choosing the best medium or media of communication. And they must also become comfortable with new ways of thinking about property, about ownership of the messages that are created amidst the dynamic interaction of writers, audiences, and media.

In many ways, our students are already experienced inhabitors of Lanham's two worlds, and they are increasingly comfortable with new ways of thinking about textual ownership. Such new ways began to emerge in interviews with students conducted during the Stanford Study of Writing (SSW), when researchers asked the students in the study about their views on intellectual property. These interviews, which took place between 2001 and 2006, revealed what at first felt like a hard-to-describe, nebulous change: the best the researchers could say was that something seemed to be happening to the way students thought about intellectual property and ownership. But more recent analyses of the transcripts of some 150 interviews indicate the kind of flexible shifting back and forth described above.

Perhaps one vivid example will serve to limit this potential shift in understanding and attitude toward textual ownership. One participant in the study, Mark Otuteye, wrote a poem during the early weeks of his first year at Stanford. Titled "The Admit Letter," this poem was performed by Mark later that year during Parents' Weekend; it opens with a "so-called friend" saying to Mark "Oh sure, you got into Stanford: you're Black." What follows in this spoken word poem is Mark's imagining of what his "so-called friend" thought his admit letter might have said. The two imaginary versions of the admit letter that Mark performed were biting—and very, very funny; together, they not only put the so-called friend in his place but manage to send up the University as well. On the Stanford campus, news of this poem spread like proverbial wildfire and Otuteye was called on to perform it in numerous venues. In one such venue, the poem changed significantly: now it was performed by Mark and a Chicana student, who powerfully wove together versions of their "admit letters."

"The Admit Letter" went through additional permutations during Otuteye's college career, and during one of the interviews with him, SSW researchers asked, "So is this poem yours? Do you own it?" In a lengthy conversation, Mark said that he considered the poem to be his in significant and important ways—but not *exclusively* his; in fact, he said, his work is usually written and performed collaboratively, and he sees it as part of a large poetic commons. In short, this student was already beginning to move between the information and the attention worlds, and he was comfortable writing with as well as for others, and in a range of media. For Mark, and for many other students in this study, what has seemed at times to us the perplexing fluidity and even tension among writer, text, context, medium, and audience feels like home turf. This home turf, however, is not without its potential dangers and challenges (including challenges to notions of textual ownership). As we will discuss in a later section of this essay, other problems can arise if students fail to differentiate between the constraints and opportunities inherent in their self-sponsored writing and those of the academic rhetorical situation.

Taxonomizing Audiences

When we wrote AA/AI, we literally could not have imagined the textual and material worlds we inhabit today. At that time, we were attempting to intervene in a then-contemporary debate over audience. In our effort to understand and give coherence to this debate, we grouped various scholars work on audience under two constructs, that of audience invoked (the intended audience as well as those imagined and hailed by the writer) and of audience addressed (the actual people reading a writer's work). If reprintings and references to AA/AI are any indication, others have found the constructs of audience addressed/audience invoked useful. But we are also aware that the impulse to taxonomize—to create binaries and various other sorts of categories—has disadvantages as well as advantages. Indeed, we felt the need to go beyond addressed and invoked audiences to acknowledge audiences that are "ignored, rejected, excluded, or denied" motivated our effort to look again at AA/AI when we wrote "Representing Audience" (174).

A quarter of a century after AA/AI was published; we want to look again at these two constructs to determine what relevance they hold in an age of new media and new literacies.[6] When we look at our earlier work, we continue to value the way that the constructs of audience addressed and audience invoked enable us to call attention to (1) the fluid, dynamic character of rhetorical situations; and (2) "the integrated, interdependent nature of reading and writing" (156). We value as well the extent to which they discourage overly stark binaries—such as those that posit sharp dichotomies between speaking and writing. In AA/AI we point out, for instance, that Walter Ong's representative situations (in "The Writer's Audience is Always a Fiction") of "the orator addressing a mass audience versus a writer alone in a room" will always "oversimplify the potential range and diversity of both oral and written communication situations" (161).

If this statement was true in 1984, it is even more compelling today with the proliferation of electronic and online media and social networking sites. Increasingly, for instance, students in our writing classes post messages to course discussion boards and blogs and/or contribute to wikis. When they compose academic texts, they may well insert images and sound, or provide tables or spreadsheets with supporting information. When students turn from academic writing to self-sponsored communication, the possibilities explode—including everything from instant messaging and texting to blogging, creating text and images on Facebook (and commenting on others pages), posting photos on Flickr, and sharing tags on Del.icio.us.

As we noted earlier in this essay, these kinds of participatory communications challenge conventional understandings of both authorship and audience, even as they provide an opportunity for anyone and everyone to become author and audience, writer and reader.[7] But do they invalidate the general constructs of audience addressed and audience invoked that we established in AA/AI? In the most general sense, the kinds of participatory communication that we have just described can, we believe, be encompassed within these two categories—which, we argue in AA/AI, are best understood as a dialogic pair.

Consider, in this regard, our experience writing this chapter. Rather than relying on the technologies of telephone, electric correcting typewriter, and photocopy machines (technologies essential to the composition of AA/AI), we relied on contemporary electronic technologies, particularly word processing, email, and the Web. Yet our experience composing this text still required us to negotiate both addressed and invoked audiences—from the readers we envisioned as we worked on drafts of this essay to colleagues and students who actually read and responded to it. In short, we find that the categories of invoked and addressed audiences still inform the much more complex online communicating we do today. As we post to listservs, look for videos on YouTube that we can use in our classes, or participate in a wiki devoted to developing an accreditation report for one of our institutions, we are conscious of both addressed and invoked audiences. In the case of the accreditation report, some thirty members of a task force are contributing to this document, which is addressed directly to the university's accreditation board. In a more indirect way, this document is also addressed to all members of the accreditation team and to our upper administrators as well. But to address these audiences, and especially the first one, we must invoke the accreditation board, which we have done very carefully and cautiously: a lot is at stake in our getting this particular invocation right.

Even so, we need to acknowledge that precisely because the constructs of audience addressed and audience invoked are so broad and encompassing, they can only take us so far in our understanding of audience, including contemporary online and electronic audiences.[8] A person who reads Barbara Kingsolver's *The Poisonwood Bible*, for instance, and then posts the 1497th customer review on Amazon.com no doubt has an invoked audience in mind, while the addressed audience is potentially vast and largely unknowable.[9] We are likewise fascinated by the potential relationships among the photographers who (as of our last checking) posted 66,977 photos of black labs on Flickr, tagging them so that other audiences with a similar passion for this breed of dogs can easily find them,[10] not to mention the relationship we might establish if we clicked on the profile of one of these photographers or if we commented on a photo we find particularly compelling. In these instances, we are invoking this photographer even as the photographer invokes other audiences, which may or may not include us. Further, our invocation of the photographer may lead us to address him or her directly—or not. In any case, the concepts of "addressed" and "invoked" seem to ripple out, overlap, and echo one another in provocative ways.

And such examples proliferate. When Henry Jenkins in *Fans, Bloggers, and Gamers: Exploring Participatory Culture* refers to "the interactive audience" (136), it seems clear that those communicating with such an audience must necessarily both address and invoke each other. But having said that, what more might we add? How does the technology of gaming or blogging, for example, ignore or exclude certain audiences? What ideological positions may be unspoken in such activities? And how can we avoid the utopian/dystopian ways in which audiences and members of new online communities are often framed, both in the popular press and in more serious scholarly work? In attempting to answer this last question, Jenkins observes that "the interactive audience is more than a marketing concept and less than a "semiotic democracy" (136). Jenkins's comment suggests that interactive or participatory audiences fall somewhere along a continuum, from those who consume media and content on the Web in fairly traditional ways to the full shared agency characteristic of many online communities.

We have additional issues and questions as well. In an online, participatory culture, the concerns that we articulated in "Representing Audience" about audiences "ignored, rejected, excluded, or denied" become even more salient (174).[11] As we will discuss more fully in the next section, many students easily forget that when they post something on the Web they may encounter unwanted or future audiences—such as an employer checking their Facebook entries or a researcher checking on their use of his or her scholarly work.

Although these questions suggest potential limitations of the constructs of audience addressed and audience invoked, we believe that these constructs can still usefully remind us of the rich complexity of any form of communication, written or spoken, print or online. But as we have suggested, they are too general to directly address questions such as the ones we have just articulated. These questions require the kind of "analysis of precise, concrete situations" that we call for near the end of AA/AI (168).[12] Such work is currently being done, most often in qualitative studies that require the depth and breadth of ethnography. One powerful example of such work occurs in Angela Thomas's chapter on "Blurring and Breaking through the Boundaries of Narrative, Literacy, and Identity in Adolescent Fan Fiction" in Knobel and Lankshear's *New Literacies Sampler*. In this four-year ethnographic study, Thomas explores the experiences of two adolescent females: "Tiana, aged 14 years, and Jandalf, aged 17 years, friends who met online and who have been collaboratively writing fan fiction for over a year" (139). These two young authors prove to be extraordinary in a number of ways, including the degree of self-reflexivity and flexibility that they exhibit. In characterizing their writing, both individual and collaborative, Thomas observes that Tiana and Jandalf move successfully "in and out of media type, text type, form, style and literary device with an ease and poetry of linguistic dexterity that is truly exceptional" (151). In doing so, they assume a range of audience roles for each other, taking turns for example at role playing as they develop the outlines of plots and of characters for their fan fiction. Tiana explains: "[W]hen I transcribe over, I sort of become two people—Tiana and a narrator. I make myself see things from a third person POV [point of view] while still writing as my characters" (144). In describing the many kinds of writing the pair undertake, Thomas mentions "the role playing, the out-of-character discussions occurring synchronously within the role playing, the character journals, the art work, the careful plotting out of story lines, the forum discussions, the descriptions of worlds and cultures, the invention of language, the playful spoofing, the in-role poetry, the meta-textual allusions to sound effects, movie techniques" (145).[13]

Another instructive analysis of precise, concrete situations occurs in Kevin Brooks and his student Aaron Anfinson's, study of Afinson's own capstone project as well as Brooks's response to it. The study, "Exploring Post-critical Composition: MEmorials[14] for Afghanistan and the Lost Boys of Sudan," examined co-author Anfinson's effort to meet the requirements of a senior English project while also, as Anfinson observed in an email to Brooks, writing "something different. . . I think I just wanted to do something I've never done and to truly learn something and have fun while doing it—quite a challenge caught up in the sometimes-captive atmosphere of the classroom" (78). As an active member of the National Guard who could be deployed at any time, Anfinson wanted to raise political issues and questions about the war in Afghanistan but was "reluctant to divulge much personal information" (85). In Anfinson's written reflections on his experience and in his discussions with Brooks, Anfinson did not focus extensively on audience. This choice was in part the result of his gradual decision to create what Gregory Ulmer terms "electronic monuments." Such monuments encourage writers to emphasize their own preferences over the interests and needs of readers and encourage such strategies as borrowing, collage, and intentional minimalism. In his only reflection on audience, Anfinson comments on how he drew upon his own inclinations in making decisions, even those related to his readers: "I think the idea for videos came actually from a bit of laziness. Rather than entertain, I wanted to be entertained. . . I enjoy finding videos. . . I too thought that a reader who is not so academically inclined would sit through a video or two, but would never read a huge block of text" (83). This example demonstrates how the role of audience can shift depending on the author's context, sense of agency, and personal inclinations.

In the case of Anfinson's capstone project, "A MEmorial for Afghanistan," genre played a more important role than audience. In Brooks' view, the MEmorial was an effective genre for Anfinson, who focused his self-evaluation on the role it played in increasing his own knowledge. In a reflective paper he submitted with his MEmorial, Anfinsin observed that "Overall, in my MEmorial, I think I learned a lot. If nothing else, due to my "public participation in monumentality... [and] deconsultancy,"[16] I learned what I truly think about an issue that I have been inactive in directly confronting" (86). In commenting on the power of Anfinson's project, Brooks observes that it inspired him to undertake a similar effort, "A MEmorial for the Lost Boys of Sudan." His own project is, he believes, "not as visually interesting as Aaron's and I have not been able to emulate his textual minimalism, but I have tried to learn from his various strategies of composing with others' videos (appropriation), and arranging video, text, and still images in various patterns on the screen (collage)" (86). Thus does the teacher learn from the student.

As the examples from Thomas and from Brooks and Anfinson demonstrate, understanding the complexity of writing processes, audience awareness, and collaboration calls for specific, grounded, and nuanced analysis that goes well beyond the analytic binary of addressed and invoked audiences. Issues of authority may play a particularly key role here. Tiana and Jandalf had a good deal of authority and autonomy in their self-sponsored writing. As Anfinson's teacher, Brooks also granted him considerable flexibility and authority.

Teaching Audience in the Twenty-first Century

Imagine this: a student in a required writing class composes a research-based argument and then presents an oral version of the argument as part of a panel at an in-class "conference" held at the end of the term. The teacher of the class creates a Website and posts all of the student arguments on it, inviting response from the students as well as other audiences. Two years later, the teacher gets a response from a professor at another university, pointing out that the student's argument drew on the professor's work, citing that work but often failing to enclose directly quoted passages within quotation marks. The professor demands that the student's argument be taken off the Website, accusing the student of sloppy habits at best, plagiarism at worst. Notified of this turn of events, the student—now a prospective graduating senior—is completely surprised: he had not meant to plagiarize, and he certainly had not imagined that one of his sources would go to the trouble of accessing his essay.

Like many others, this student experiences the Internet and many of its sites as fairly private, when the reality is that audiences are there all the time, browsing, searching, engaging, responding, sometimes accusing. Many scholars and commentators have noted the breakdown between private and public today and on the somewhat contradictory attitudes students hold: students often say they are comfortable being in public—that a public stance comes with the territory of digital communication. But they also sometimes view sites—and especially social networking sites such as Facebook—as relatively private, away from the prying eyes of parents and other unwanted audiences. We had these students in mind when we quoted Ari Melber at the opening of this essay: "Critics argue that privacy does not matter to children who were raised in a wired celebrity culture that promises a niche audience for everyone. Why hide when you can perform? But even if young people are performing, many are clueless about the size of their audience" (23).[15]

Clearly, even though many of our students are completely at ease in the digital landscape, they nevertheless need to become more knowledgeable about the nature and complexity of the audiences for whom they perform, particularly as they shift back and forth from self-sponsored online writing to academic writing. The first lesson we draw from grappling with the questions we pose in this essay, then, is that we have a responsibility to join with our students in rich and detailed explorations of just what "audience" can mean in their writing and in their lives. Such explorations might well begin with exploring the problematics of viewing the teacher as the sole audience for student writing. As the real-life example above suggests, the teacher remains *an* audience for student texts, but by no means the only audience, especially when student writing is posted on the Web. Even if it is not posted, student writing often invokes and addresses audiences well beyond the teacher (who is also, often, both addressed and invoked).

Beyond unpacking the concept of teacher as audience, teachers can help students understand the contemporary complexities of audience by providing case studies that exemplify various kinds of audiences. The participatory audience of peer review, for instance, can be theorized and interrogated by students in their composition classes: that is, rather than simply responding to one another's texts, students can take time to get to know these real-life audiences, along with their assumptions and values, literally examining where these members of the audience are coming from. Or students can create a genealogy of audiences for a particular social networking site, exploring the many diverse individuals and groups that have access to the site and asking which audiences the site invokes and which it seems to address. Students could examine the many issues raised, for instance, by various Pro Ana (pro anorexia) sites on the Web. Who are the sponsors of these sites? What kinds of collaborative relationships are being invoked and addressed by those who post to and read this site?

As we have noted in this essay, what began for us as two different strands of research—one on audience, another on collaboration—have all but merged during the last couple of years as we have seen how frequently writers become audiences and vice versa. Yet more often than not, students resist collaboration in their schoolwork even as they collaborate constantly in their out-of-class online writing. There are reasons for this seeming contradiction or tension: school writing is part of a deeply individualistic system that rewards individual students through a system of grades and points that values the individual GPA, and working collaboratively runs counter to that system. Scholars and teachers need to challenge the hyper-individualistic base of higher education in the United States; we need also to engage students in substantial discussions of this issue. As we have been arguing for some time, we know that most of the innovative work that gets done in the world today gets done in collaborative groups (see Sawyer, Tapscott and Williams, Sunstein, Ede and Lunsford)—including, increasingly, teams that work primarily online. And we know that colleges and universities, for reasons mentioned above, are doing very little to prepare students to thrive in such an environment (see Bok, Light). We need to do more, then, than *assign* collaborative projects: we need to provide a theoretical rationale for such projects along with data to support it. In addition, we need to craft collaborative projects that will work hard to engage every member of the group and guide the group in analyzing their work together from beginning to end. And we need to join with students in exploring the use of free collaborative writing tools such as Google Docs, Zoho, and Writeboard.

We also need to consider the impact that new literacies are having—and should have—in our teaching. Such literacies often call for producing new texts, often referred to as "new media" texts. The question of whether and how to teach such new media writing pose significant challenges to teachers of writing today. Thanks to the work of Anne Wysocki, Johndan Johnson Eilola, Cynthia Selfe, Geoffrey Sirc, their collaborative *Writing New Media* paints a rich picture of the kinds of writing students are increasingly doing today, both inside and outside of the classroom. In one chapter in this study, Cynthia Selfe points out the double-edged sword that comes along with new media texts, as she tells the story of David, a young man who teaches himself to produce effective new media texts only to fail his college classes because of his inability to create acceptable traditional print texts. The point Selfe makes is one all teachers of writing need to heed: we must help our students to learn to conceive and produce a repertoire of texts, from the convincing academic argument to the compelling Website or memorable radio essay. (Selfe has also recently published a helpful guide for teachers, *Multimodal Composition: Resources for Teachers,* as well as a passionate call for moving teacherly attention well beyond print literacy in "Aurality and Multimodal Composing").

It is important to acknowledge the difficulties inherent in taking on such a task. At Stanford, when the Faculty Senate mandated that the Program in Writing and Rhetoric (PWR) develop a new second-level course that would go beyond academic writing to embrace oral presentations with multimedia support, the PWR teaching staff responded with great enthusiasm. By the time they began piloting courses to equally enthusiastic students, the sky seemed to be the limit: students wanted to write and produce hour-long documentaries; to produce NPR-quality audio essays; to design, write, and produce online magazines; not to mention creating other new media texts to be performed in a wide range of settings. By the end of the second quarter of the pilot, however, both teachers and students realized that their reach had clearly exceeded their grasp. Most notably, the writing that students were doing as they worked their way toward new media or multimodal texts was declining in quality. Both students and teachers recognized that time spent on perfecting visual design and enriching texts with multimedia was time—given the constraints of the ten-week academic term—that students could no longer spend on their written texts. As a result, before the new course was fully implemented, the teaching staff, working in conjunction with the Undergraduate Advisory Board, pulled back from some of their ambitions, focusing the course first on producing a research-based argument and then working the rest of the term to "translate" that argument into various genre and media. As the Stanford teachers continued to refine this new course and its assignment sequence, they were able to inch a bit back toward those earlier ambitions. But it is instructive to note the power of tradition in the face of challenging new ways of composing. It is even more instructive to note that the response of the upper administration to this new course, even though mandated by the Faculty Senate, was less than supportive: "Are you teaching 'real writing?' they asked. The response to that question was, emphatically "yes," but even an extensive rationale for the answer failed to convince some colleagues and administrators.

As this discussion has suggested, universities and the culture at large seem not to have arrived at a consensus on what "writing" is and can be in this age of new literacies. In short, we don't yet know how best to balance our obligation to open opportunities for students to engage new media fully in their writing with our obligation to honor university mandates to strengthen and expand students' grasp of traditional print academic discourse. The way forward is neither easy nor obvious, but scholars, teachers, and students need to work together to explore and experiment with both theories and practices that can help guide us. In this section of our essay, we have explored several important implications for teaching the concept of audience in the twenty-first century, the most important of which is to engage our students in analyzing and theorizing the new literacies and new media themselves, especially as these practices call for collaboration, for new understandings of audience, and for a robust ethics of communication. Exploring new literacies and new media with students means crafting syllabi that leave time for such interrogations and for the experimentation they will demand. In addition to working closely with our students, we can revisit our assignments, looking in our required composition courses for ways to stretch the boundaries of academic discourse and to allow students collaborative opportunities for engaging with new media and new audiences. And we can offer advanced elective courses that move well beyond print literacy, calling on students to create innovative new media texts and to analyze them in the context of their audiences. Michigan State's program in professional writing offers a range of exciting courses on Web authoring and multimedia writing, and other examples of such classes abound.[16] These sites offer, we believe, fertile ground for detailed ethnographic explorations of writerly agency and of audiences, including those invoked and addressed.

Ethics and Participatory Literacies

As we have worked on this essay, we have found ourselves meditating on audiences across the millennia—from audiences who gathered before the ancient Greek rhapsodes, who "read" the scriptures along with literate scribes in the medieval period, who sat among the groundlings at the Globe and other Elizabethan theatres, who waited in rapt anticipation for the next issue of the latest Dickens novel, who gathered at whistle stops throughout the United States to engage with political hopefuls, and who today log on to check in with Facebook friends or read and comment on their favorite blog. In some ways, there has always been a relational or participatory quality to audiences. Yet it seems clear that changes in technology and other material conditions that have brought us to the present moment have opened avenues for audiences to take on agency and to become participants and creators/shapers of discourse

146

in more profound ways than ever before. While nineteenth-century audience members could meet in salons or coffeehouses to discuss the latest installment of *Great Expectations,* think of the possibilities for enhanced agency and participation that blogging or the ability to post comments online (to take just two examples) offers today.

In noting the opportunity for enhanced agency and participation in online writing, we do not intend to join those who characterize the Web and social-networking sites in utopian terms. If we have learned anything from our study of the rhetorical tradition, it is that the nature and consequence of any act of communication can never be determined in advance and that inquiry into issues such as these requires a deeply situated, finely tuned analysis. When consumers post reviews to Amazon.com, for instance, are they expanding their possibilities for agency and for collaborations with others or are they serving as unpaid volunteer workers for this ever-expanding company? There are no simple, decontextualized answers to questions such as these.

Our engagement with the rhetorical tradition, as well as our study of the history of communicative technologies, thus reminds us that both utopian and dystopian views of our current moment are likely to oversimply. They also remind us of how difficult it is to predict how various communication technologies will be employed. The earliest graphic symbols, it is good to remember, were used for accounting, not writing. We might consider in this regard Twitter, the social networking and microblogging service that allows users to publicly post 140-character "tweets" or send private 140-character "direct messages" to each other. "Tweets" are used by restaurants, clubs, bands, and stores—as well as individuals—to promote and inform, and many users use Twitter as a source of personalized breaking news. Who would have expected, then, that some users of Twitter would decide that it provides the perfect online space to write haiku, much less that the haiku created on Twitter would invoke an avid audience? Just how much interest is there in the world today in Twitter haiku? We can't know for sure, but a quick check on Google instantly pulled up 1,750,000 hits. In searching the Web, we have also found numerous references to Twitter contests. One frequent challenge invites writers to compose microessays and microstories limited to Twitter's 140 characters. In case you're interested, a search on Google using the term "Twitter contests" generated 136,000,000 hits.[17] Here's what one Twitter user, Calvin Jones, posted to his Web site Digital Marketing Success about his fascination with Twitter:

I love the way Twitter makes you condense your writing, squeezing the maximum out of every character. Here's my swiftly penned missive:

She paused, shivering involuntarily; the wave of adrenalin surged through her, leaving her giddy and disoriented. It was quiet. He was gone!

Twitter was released to the public in October 2006, and we conducted these Google searches in late July, 2010. Thus does a software program evolve in lightning speed on the Web, making a space for readers to become writers who then become invoked and addressed audience members for still other writer/readers.

What if a friend or family member prefers not to know what someone close (or not so close) to them is doing throughout the day? Twitter.com addresses this issue by requiring users to sign up for Twitter to receive tweets and by allowing for privacy settings. But surely ethical issues remain. Twitter can be used to help groups gather quickly, whether for positive purposes (engaging in civic discussion or action) or negative. How can those interested in participating in this social networking and micro-blogging site best understand their responsibilities as writers and audiences for others? In this regard, we have been interested in the use of Twitter to call for and promote protests during the summer 2009 Iranian election. Of particular note during these demonstrations were the many signs protesting the validity of the elections written in English, both addressing and invoking audiences rejected by the official regime, which refused to allow Western reporters into the country. In response to this prohibition, protesters used their cell phones and hand-held cameras to document and share these signs and images with the rest of the world.

At its strongest and most productive moments, the rhetorical tradition has acknowledged the potentially powerful ethical implications inherent in any act of communication. As we

148

conclude this discussion of audience in an age of new literacies, then, we turn to several other ethical questions that seem compelling to us as teachers and scholars. Perhaps most importantly, in a world of participatory media, it seems essential for teachers and students to consider the multiple reciprocal responsibilities entailed in writer-audience relationships. What does a student writer posting to Facebook owe to all the potential audiences of that post, from a former partner to a potential employer? And what responsibilities do audiences have toward those whose messages they receive, seek, reject, or encounter? One goal of future research on audience must surely be to explore the ethical dimensions of such relationships, following the lead of social media researcher and Berkman Center for Internet and Society Fellow danah boyd and others.

It seems equally important for scholars, teachers, and students to explore collaboratively the increasingly complex issue of plagiarism/patchwriting in an online world.[18] As the example of the professor who found his work used without proper attribution in a student essay on a class Website demonstrates, the ease of cutting and pasting and the wide availability of sources make holding to traditional norms of scholarly citation increasingly difficult. While students we know roundly condemn buying or downloading a paper wholesale from a Web site as unacceptable cheating, they are much more ambivalent about using a form of sampling in their writing, and they are downright resistant to the need for what they often think of as excessive (or even obsessive) citation: if you go to the Web with a question and get thousands of "hits" in answer to it, they say, shouldn't that answer be considered as common knowledge that doesn't need to be cited? We're inclined to answer "yes" to this question, but if we answer "no," which one of the thousands of sources should be *the* one to be cited? These questions and the issues they raise suggest that we must continue not only to explore students' understandings of intellectual property but also to engage them in a full discussion of where academic citation practices came from, why they have been so deeply valued, and what is at stake in developing alternative practices—such as a much broader definition of "common knowledge" as well as alternative forms of attribution.

If plagiarism and potential misuse of sources represents one ethical problem that contemporary audiences must address, another problem has quite diverse origins and implications. What are the consequences for civic discourse in a world where those interested in a specific topic or audience can, if they have internet access, easily find sites where they can communicate with like-minded individuals, where our culture seems to promise, as Ari Melbur observes, "a niche audience for everyone" (23)[19]. Is our culture likely to fragment into what legal scholar Cass R. Sunstein refers to as "information cocoons"? (9) And how can we best understand and enact an appropriate relationship between privacy and free speech on the Web? One place to turn in exploring this set of ethical issues is the extensive work on public discourse being pursued by many scholars in rhetoric and communication studies.[20] Most generally, our goal as teachers should be to encourage (even inspire) students to build bridges between the seemingly private voices they inhabit online and the public ones they can establish as students, workers, and citizens.

In his 2007 "Vision of the Future," Howard Rheingold notes the need for students who use the Web to take responsibility for determining the accuracy of what they find there and for parents and students alike to take responsibility for the ethical and moral choices they make in reading and writing online. (Rheingold cites, for example, the responsibility of parents in establishing rules for access that would protect their children from pornographic sites.) But in this talk, Rheingold is primarily interested in how young people can get beyond the small niches of the Web to participate most effectively in online settings. Noting that while students today are "naturals" when it comes to point-and-click explorations, "there's nothing innate about knowing how to apply their skills to the processes of democracy" (4), Rheingold calls on teachers to help students make connections "between the literacies students pick up simply by being young in the 21st century and those best learned through reading and discussing texts" (5). We can help students make such connections, Rheingold argues, by allowing them to move "from a private to a public voice" that will help them "turn their self-expression into a form of public participation" (5). Public voice, Rheingold insists, is "learnable, a matter of consciously engaging with an active pubic rather than broadcasting to a passive audience" (5).

Thus while Rheingold recognizes the potential for fragmentation, for performing only for small niche audiences, and for existing "information cocoons," he also sees the potential for developing participatory public opinion that can "be an essential instrument of democratic self-governance" (5). We believe that Rheingold is right to argue that if we want such public voices to arise, we must teach to and for them. And along with Rheingold, we recognize that teaching to and for new publics and public voices calls for "a whole new way of looking at learning and teaching" that will, we believe, require close attention to the ethical issues raised by new literacies and new media (7). It will also call for resisting the dichotomy between those who dream utopian dreams of a vast collective and participatory democracy enabled by Web 2.0 and those who bemoan a collapse into fragmentation and solipsism that can come from talking only with those who already think just as you do. Limiting an audience to or collaborating only with like thinkers will almost surely fail to develop a "whole new way of looking at learning and teaching" or addressing the ethical issues we have raised.

At its best, the Western rhetorical tradition, however flawed, has encouraged both writers and teachers of writing to take a deeply situated perspective on communication—and thus to challenge the kind of binaries that we have just described. Whenever we write, read, speak, or (as Krista Ratcliffe has so eloquently reminded us) listen, there are no guarantees that either the process or outcome will be ethical. This is an understanding that we can—and should—bring with us when we enter our classrooms, especially our first-year writing classrooms. For there we have the opportunity to help our students experience the intellectual stimulation and excitement, as well as responsibility, of engaging and collaborating with multiple audiences, from peers to professors to addressed and invoked audiences of all kinds.

ENDNOTES

1   We are keenly aware of the irony inherent in this essay on new media and new literacies, composed as it is almost entirely of words and published in print. At least one reason for this irony is practical: we wrote this essay in response to an invitation to contribute to a print book, *Engaging Audience: Writing in an Age of New Literacies*, edited by M. Elizabeth Weiser, Brian M. Fehler, and Angela M. González. The essay has been revised since this publication.

2   We use the term "Web 2.0" here and elsewhere recognizing that some have argued that this term is inaccurate and/or hyperbolic. In an interview posted on IBM's developer Works site, for instance, Tim Berners-Lee argues that Web 2.0 is "a piece of jargon, nobody even knows what it means. If Web 2.0 for you is blogs and wikis, then that is people to people [as opposed to Web 1, which is sometimes described as computer to computer]. . . But that was what the Web was supposed to be all along." Berner-Lee prefers to use the term "Semantic Web" rather than Web 2.0 (Laningham).

3   Two recent monographs helpfully remind us of the differing concerns, traditions, and interests that scholars have brought to the concept of audience. The first study, Mary Jo Rieff's 1994 *Approaches to Audience: An Overview of the Major Perspectives*, chronicles the development of research on audience within English studies in general and rhetoric and writing in particular. The second study, Denis McQuail's 1997 monograph *Audience Analysis*, is written from the perspective of communication studies, particularly mass communication and cultural studies.

4   Recent work on gaming and gamers sometimes explores agency in such venues. See the special issue of *Computers and Composition* devoted to Reading Games: Composition, Literacy, and Video Gaming and particularly the articles by John Alberti and Matthew S.S. Johnson.

5   After making their album available on the Web, Radiohead also released their music as a conventional CD.

6   Other scholars have also examined these constructs in helpful ways. We would particularly like to call attention to Robert Johnson's "Audience Involved: Toward a Participatory Model of Writing," Jack Selzer's "More Meanings of Audience," Rosa Eberly's "From Writers, Audiences, and Communities to Publics: Writing Classrooms as Protopublic Spaces," Mary Jo Reiff's "Rereading „Invoked and „Addressed Readers Through a Social Lens: Toward a Recognition of Multiple Audiences," and the essays published in Gesa Kirsch and Duane H. Roen's edited collection *A Sense of Audience in Written Communication*. Though space limitations do not allow us to discuss

these studies, we have benefited from these authors' analyses and critiques.

7   In "Agency and Authority in Role-Playing texts," Jessica Hammer identifies three kinds of authorship in video games: primary, secondary, and tertiary. As Hammer notes, "The primary author develops a world and a set of rules," while "the secondary author takes the work of the primary author and uses it to construct a specific situation or scenario. . . . The tertiary authors, then, 'write' the text of the game in play" (71).

8   In *Audience Analysis,* for instance, Denis McQuail helpfully identifies the following dimensions of audience: "degree of activity or passivity; degree of interactivity and interchangeability; size and duration; locatedness in space; group character (social/cultural identity); simultaneity of contact with source; heterogeneity of composition; social relations between sender and receiver; message versus social/ behavioral definition of situation; degree of 'social presence;' sociability of context of use" (150).

9   As of July 25, 2010, this was the number of customer reviews of the Harper Perennial Modern Classic paperback edition of Kingsolver's novel on Amazon.com.

10 This search of Flickr was also conducted on July 25, 2010.

11 In *Rhetorical Refusals: Defying Audiences' Expectations*, John Schilb examines cases in which speakers and writers intentionally defy audience expectations.

12 Scholars in such areas as media and cultural studies, communication, sociology, and anthropology have undertaken research in media reception and audience ethnography. For an introduction to this interdisciplinary body of work, see Pertti Alasuutari's *Rethinking the Media Audience: The New Agenda.* Representative studies include Virginia Nightingale's *Studying Audiences: The Shock of the Real,* S. Elizabeth Bird's *The Audience in Everyday Life: Living in a Media World,* and Will Brooker and Deborah Jermyn's *The Audience Studies Reader.*

13 Thomas goes on to observe that "in addition to exploring the scope of the narrative worlds of the fan fiction, it is important to note that the girls also produce multimodal texts to enhance their fan fiction, making avatars (images to represent themselves) for role playing, making visual signatures as can be seen at the side and end of each post on the forum . . . , finding icons to reflect mood, creating music bytes, making fan fiction posters in the form of an advertisement and teaser, and creating mini movie trailers using their own spliced-together combination of existing movie clips, music, voiceovers, and

text. They also draw maps and room plans of their world, draw and paint scenery, and sketch images of their many characters. As well as hand-drawn sketches, they create digital images, digital colorizations or enhancements of their sketches, or purely digitally-created images" (150-51).

14 See Gregory Ulmer's *Electronic Monuments* for a discussion of this concept.

15 Internet studies scholar danah boyd has done considerable research on this topic. See, for instance, her "Social Network Sites: Public, Private, or What?" Here boyd argues that "[n]ew social technologies have altered the underlying architecture of social interaction and information distribution" and that today's teenagers ". . .are embracing this change, albeit often with the clumsy candor of an elephant in a china shop."

16 Readers will know of many similar efforts, such as Advanced Studies in Digital Rhetoric and Writing in Digital Environments at the University of Texas, Austin; or the digital media writing courses in MIT's Department of Writing and Humanistic Studies; or Ohio State's Digital Media Studies Program. At the Bread Loaf School of English last summer, Andrea's students used WordPress to build a class blog that allowed for tagging, searching, linking, and multiple forms of interaction as well as opportunities for experimental writing that fell outside the bounds of what colleges usually call "academic discourse," including graphic memoirs and visual/audio narratives. Students in another class filmed documentary essays aimed at changing one or more policies at the schools where they teach during the regular academic year.

17 Both searches were conducted on July 25, 2010.

18 Rebecca Howard has written extensively and compellingly about the developmental nature of what she calls "patchwriting" as well as about the ways in which students and teachers understand (and often misunderstand) plagiarism.

19 In 2009, 1.8 billion people—more than a quarter of the world's population—had internet access, according to the International Communication Union. The possibilities for audience, then, are larger than ever before.

20 Several essays in Section IV of *The Sage Handbook of Rhetorical Studies* explore such issues; see, especially, Gurak and Antonijevic and Beasley.

WORKS CITED

Alasuutari, Pertti, ed. *Rethinking the Media Audience: The New Agenda*. London: Sage, 1999. Print.

Alberti, John. "The Game of Reading and Writing: How Video Games Reframe Our Understanding of Literacy." *Computers and Composition* 25 (2008): 258-269. Print.

Ang, Ien. *Livingroom Wars: Rethinking Audiences for a Postmodern World*. New York: Routledge, 1995. Print.

Ball, Cheryl and James Kalmbach. *RAW: Reading and Writing New Media*. Cresskill, NJ: Hampton Press, forthcoming. Print.

Beasley, Vanessa. "Between Touchstones and Touchscreens: What Counts as Contemporary Political Rhetoric." *The Sage Handbook of Rhetorical Studies*. Ed. Andrea A. Lunsford, Kirt Wilson, and Rosa Eberly. Thousand Oaks, CA: Sage P, 2009. Print.

Bird, S. Elizabeth. *The Audience in Everyday Life: Living in a Media World*. New York: Routledge, 2003. Print.

Bok, Derek. *Our Underachieving Colleges*. Princeton: Princeton UP, 2006. Print.

boyd, danah. "Social Network Sites: Public, Private, or What?" *Knowledge Tree* 13. Australian Flexible Learning Network, May 2007. Web. 24 Aug. 2010.

_____. "Viewing American Class Divisions through Facebook and MySpace." *Apophenia*. danah boyd Weblog, 24 June 2007. Web. 24 Aug. 2010.

Brooker,Will and Deborah Jermyn, eds. *The Audience Studies Reader*. London: Routledge, 2003. Print.

Brooks, Kevin and Aaron Anfinson. "Exploring Post-critical Composition MEmorials for Afghanistan and the Lost Boys of Sudan." *Computers and Composition* 26 (2009): 78-91. Print.

DeVoss, Danielle N., Gail E. Hawisher, Charles Jackson, Joseph Johansen, Brittney Moraski, and Cynthia L. Selfe. "The Future of Literacy." *Literate Lives in the Information Age: Narratives of Literacy from the United States.* Eds. Cynthia L. Selfe and Gail E. Hawisher. Mahwah, NJ: Lawrence Erlbaum, 2004: 183-210. Print.

Eberly, Rosa. *Citizen Critics: Literary Public Spheres.* Urbana: U Illinois P, 2000. Print.

_____. "From Writers, Audiences, and Communities to Publics: Writing Classrooms as Protopublic Spaces." *Rhetoric Review* 18 (1999): 165-78. Print.

Ede, Lisa and Andrea Lunsford. "Audience Addressed/Audience Invoked: The Role of Audience in Composition Theory and Pedagogy." *College Composition and Communication* 35 (1984): 155-73. Print.

_____. *Singular Texts / Plural Authors: Perspectives on Collaborative Writing.* Carbondale: Southern Illinois UP, 2000. Print.

Gee, James. *What Videogames Have to Teach Us about Learning and Literacy.* New York: Palgrave/Macmillan, 2004. Print.

Gitelman, Lisa and Geoffrey B. Pingree, eds. *New Media: 1740-1915.* Cambridge: MIT P, 2003. Print.

"Global number of Internet users by development status, 2003 compared to 2009." *International Telecommunication Union.* United Nations, n.d. Web. 24 Aug. 2010.

Gurak, Laura and Smiljana Antonijevic. "Digital Rhetoric and Public Discourse." *The Sage Handbook of Rhetorical Studies.* Ed. Andrea A. Lunsford, Kirt Wilson, and Rosa Eberly. Thousand Oaks, CA: Sage P, 2009. Print.

Hammer, Jessica. "Agency and Authority in Role-Playing Texts." *A New Literacies Sampler.* Ed. Michele Knobel and Colin Lankshear. New York: Peter Lang, 2007. 67-94. Print.

Howard, Rebecca Moore. *Standing in the Shadow of Giants: Plagiarists, Authors, Collaborators.* Stamford, CT: Ablex, 1999. Print.

Johnson, Matthew S. S. "Public Writing in Gaming Spaces." *Computers and Composition* 25 (2008): 270-283. Print.

Johnson, Robert. "Audience Involved: Toward a Participatory Model of Writing." *Computers and Composition* 14 (1997): 361-76. Print.

Jones, Calvin. "Twitter Story Competition." Digital Marketing Success. *Digital Marketing Success,* 23 May 2008. Web. 5 June 2008.

Kirsch, Gesa and Duane Roen, eds. *A Sense of Audience in Written Communication.* Newbury Park, CA: Sage, 1990. Print.

Kluth, Andreas. "Among the Audience: A Survey of New Media." *The Economist* 22 Apr. 2006: 4. Print.

Knobel, Michele and Colin Lankshear, eds. *A New Literacies Sampler.* New York: Peter Lang, 2007. Print.

Kress, Gunther. *Literacy in the New Media Age.* New York: Routledge, 2003. Print.

Lanham, Richard A. *The Economics of Attention: Style and Substance in the Age of Information.* Chicago: U Chicago P, 2006. Print.

Laningham, Scott. "Interview with Tim Berners-Lee." Host Scott Laningham. developer Works Interviews. IBM, 22 Aug. 2006. Web. 5 June 2008

Light, Richard J. *Making the Most of College.* Cambridge: Harvard UP, 2004. Print.

Lunsford, Andrea A. and Lisa Ede. "On Distinctions between Classical and Modern Rhetoric." *Essays on Classical Rhetoric and Modern Discourse.* Eds. Robert J. Connors, Lisa S. Ede, and Andrea A. Lunsford. Carbondale: Southern Illinois UP, 1984: 37-49. Print.

_____. "Representing Audience: "Successful Discourse and Disciplinary Critique." *College Composition and Communication 47* (1996): 167-79. Print.

McKee, Heidi and James E. Porter. "The Ethics of Digital Writing Research: A Rhetorical Approach." *College Composition and Communication 59* (June 2008): 711-749. Print.

McLuhan, Marshall. *The Medium is the Massage.* New York: Bantam, 1967. Print.

McQuail, Dennis. *Audience Analysis.* Thousand Oaks, CA: Sage P, 1997. Print.

Melber, Ari. "About Facebook." *The Nation* 7/14 Jan. 2008: 23. Print.

Nightingale, Virginia. *Studying Audiences: The Shock of the Real.* London: Routledge, 1996. Print.

Ong, Walter J. "The Writer's Audience is Always a Fiction." *PMLA* 90 (1975): 9-21. Print.

Porter, James. *Audience and Rhetoric: An Archaeological Composition of the Discourse Community.* Upper Saddle River, NJ: Prentice Hall, 1992.

Radiohead. In Rainbows. Ato Records, 2008. Web and CD-ROM.

Ratcliffe, Krista. *Rhetorical Listening: Identification, Gender, Whiteness.* Carbondale: Southern Illinois UP, 2005. Print.

Reiff, Mary Jo. *Approaches to Audience: An Overview of the Major Perspectives.* Superior, WI: Parlay P, 2004. Print.

_____. "Rereading 'Invoked' and 'Addressed' Readers Through a Social Lens: Toward a Recognition of Multiple Audiences." JAC 16 (1996): 407-24. Print.

Rheingold, Howard. "Vision of the Future." Education.au Seminar. Melbourne, Australia. 2 Oct. 2007. Web. 24 Aug. 2010.

Sawyer, Keith: *Group Genius: The Creative Power of Collaboration.* New York: Basic Books, 2007. Print.

Schilb, John. *Rhetorical Refusals: Defying Audiences' Expectations.* Carbondale: Southern Illinois UP, 2007. Print.

Selfe, Cynthia. "Aurality and Multimodal Composing." *College Composition and Communication* 60 (June 2009): 616-663. Print.

_____. *Multimodal Composition: Resources for Teachers.* Cresskill, NJ: Hampton P, 2007. Print.

Selzer, Jack. "More Meanings of Audience." *A Rhetoric of Doing.* Eds. Stephen P. Witte and Neil Nakadate. Carbondale: Southern Illinois UP, 1992. 161-77. Print.

Stanford Study of Writing. Andrea Lunsford and John Bravman, Stanford U, Sept. 2001-Sept. 2006. Web. 24 Aug. 2010.

Sunstein, Cass R. *Infotopia: How Many Minds Produce Knowledge.* Oxford: Oxford UP, 2006. Print.

Tapscott, Don and Anthony D. Williams. *Wikinomics: How Mass Collaboration Changes Everything.* New York: Penguin, 2006. Print.

Taylor, Todd. "Design, Delivery, and Narcolepsy." *Delivering College Composition: The Fifth Canon.* Portsmouth, NH: Boynton/Cook, 2006: 127-140. Print.

Thomas, Angela. "Blurring and Breaking through the Boundaries of Narrative, Literacy, and Identity in Adolescent Fan Fiction." *A New Literacies Sampler.* Eds. Michele Knobel And Colin Lankshear. New York: Peter Lang, 2007. 137-66. Print.

Ulmer, Gregory. *Electronic Monuments.* Minneapolis: U Minnesota P, 2005. Print.

Warner, Michael. *Publics and Counterpublics.* New York: Zone Books, 2005. Print.

Weiser, Elizabeth M., Brian M. Fehler, and Angela M. Gonzalez, eds. *Engaging Audience:*

Writing in an Age of New Literacies. Urbana: NCTE, 2009. Print.

Wysocki, Anne, Johndan Johnson Eilola, Cynthia Selfe, and Geoffrey Sirc. *Writing New Media: Theory and Applications for Expanding the Teaching of Composition.* Logan: Utah State UP, 2004. Print.

BEYOND PERSUASION: A PROPOSAL FOR AN INVITATIONAL RHETORIC

SONJA K. FOSS AND CINDY L. GRIFFIN

CONSIDER AS YOU ARE READING:

Foss and Griffin begin with the observation that most traditional rhetorical theories reflect a patriarchal bias; the history of rhetoric is a history of speakers/writers who engage in a struggle for power over an audience, as their primary intention is to change others and persuade them to action. In an attempt to develop a non-patriarchal theory of rhetoric, Foss and Griffin seek a feminist approach that would foster relationships of equality and eliminate the dominance and control characteristic of patriarchal models. The theoretical mode that they describe is termed "Invitational Rhetoric," because it invites the audience to enter the rhetor's world and see it as the rhetor does. This occurs without denigrating or disparaging the world-view of the audience. A theoretical alternative to traditional rhetorical theories, this essay has been widely debated since its initial publication.

1. *Identify at least four features of "invitational rhetoric."*

2. *Think about the most recent argumentative essay you've written for a course other than this composition course. In what ways did that assignment reflect tenets of invitational rhetoric? In what ways did it reflect more traditional forms of persuasion and power relationships between writer and audience?*

3. *Do you agree with the authors' assessment that traditional rhetorical theory has a patriarchal bias? Why or why not?*

Most traditional rhetorical theories reflect a patriarchal bias in the positive value they accord to changing and thus dominating others. In this essay, an alternative rhetoric—invitational rhetoric—is proposed, one grounded in the feminist principles of equality, immanent value, and self-determination. Its purpose is to offer an invitation to understanding, and its communicative modes are the offering of perspectives and the creation of the external conditions of safety, value, and freedom.

Acknowledgement of the patriarchal bias that undergirds most theories of rhetoric is growing steadily in the communication discipline. As feminist scholars have begun to explicate the ways in which standard theories of rhetoric embody patriarchal perspectives, they have identified communicative modes that previously have not been recognized or theorized because they are grounded in alternative values (see, for example, Edson, 1985; Elshtain, 1982; Foss & Foss, 1991; Foss, Foss & Trapp, 1991; Foss & Griffin, 1992; Gearhart, 1979; Griffin, 1993; Kramarae, 1989; Shepherd, 1992). Attention to non-patriarchal forms of communication, feminist scholars argue, expands the scope of rhetorical theory and enhances the discipline's ability to explain diverse communicative phenomena successfully.

One manifestation of the patriarchal bias that characterizes much of rhetorical theorizing is the definition of rhetoric as persuasion. As far back as the Western discipline of rhetoric has been explored, rhetoric has been defined as the conscious intent to change others. As Shepherd (1992) notes, in humanistic, social scientific, and critical perspectives on communication, "interaction processes have typically been characterized essentially and primarily in terms of persuasion, influence, and power" (p. 204). Every communicative encounter has been viewed "as primarily an attempt at persuasion or influence or as a struggle over power" (p. 206). As natural as an equation of rhetoric with persuasion seems for scholars of rhetoric, this conception is only one perspective on rhetoric and one, we suggest, with a patriarchal bias.

Implicit in a conception of rhetoric as persuasion is the assumption that humans are on earth to alter the "environment and to influence the social affairs" of others. Rhetorical scholars "have taken as given that it is a proper and even necessary human function to attempt to change others" (Gearhart, 1979, p. 195). The desire to effect change is so pervasive that the many ways in which humans engage in activities designed for this purpose often go unnoticed:

> We conquered trees and converted them into a house, taking pride in having accomplished a difficult task. We conquered rivers and streams and converted them into lakes, marveling in ourselves at the improvement we made on nature. We tramped with our conquering spaceboots on the fine ancient dust of the Moon and we sent our well-rehearsed statements of triumph back for a waiting world to hear. (Gearhart, 1979, p. 196).

Embedded in efforts to change others is a desire for control and domination, for the act of changing another establishes the change agent over that other. In some instances, the power of the rhetor over another is overt, as it is, for example, in laws that exert control over women's bodies, such as those concerned with abortion. In securing the adherence of women to these laws, lawmakers have power over women and their lives. But even in cases where the strategies used are less coercive, rhetors who convince others to adopt their strategies viewpoints exert control over part of those others' lives. A student who tells another student that she ought to take a particular course, for example, controls or influences the nature of another's life, if only for a few minutes, if the other enrolls in the course or even considers enrolling in it. We suggest that a strikingly large part of many individuals' lives is spent in such efforts to change others, even when the desired changes have absolutely no impact on the lives of the change agents. Whether a friend enrolls in a particular course, for example, often is irrelevant to a student's own life.

The reward gained from successful efforts to make others change is a "rush of power" (Gearhart, 1979, p. 201)—a feeling of self-worth that comes from controlling people and situations. The value of the self for rhetors in this rhetorical system comes from the rhetor's ability to demonstrate superior knowledge, skills, and qualifications—in other words, authority—in order to dominate the perspectives and knowledge of those in their audiences. The value of the self, derives not from a recognition of the uniqueness and inherent value of each living being, but from gaining control over others.

The act of changing others not only establishes the power of the rhetor over others but also devalues the lives and perspectives of those others. The belief systems and behaviors others have created for living in the world are considered by rhetors to be inadequate or inappropriate and thus in need of change. The speaker's role very often "may be best described as paternalistic" (Scott, 1991, p. 205) in that the rhetor adopts a "'let me help you, let me enlighten you, let me show you the way' approach" (Gearhart, 1979, p. 195). Audience members are assumed to be naïve and less expert than the rhetor if their views differ from the rhetor's own.

Rhetorical scholars have prided themselves on the eschewal of physical force and coercion and the use, in their place, of "language and meta-language, with refined function of the mind" (Gearhart, 1979, p. 195) to influence others and produce change. Although these discursive strategies allow more choice to the audience than do the supposedly more heavy-handed strategies of physical coercion, they still infringe on others' rights to believe as they choose and to act in ways they believe are best for them. Even discursive strategies can constitute a kind of trespassing on the personal integrity of others when they convey the rhetor's belief that audience members have inadequacies that in some way can be corrected if they adhere to the viewpoint of the rhetor. Such strategies disallow, in other words, the possibility that audience members are content with the belief systems they have developed, function happily with them, and do not perceive a need to change.

The traditional conception of rhetoric, in summary, is characterized by efforts to change others and thus to gain control over them, self-worth derived from and measured by the power exerted over others, and a devaluation of the life worlds of others. This is rhetoric of patriarchy, reflecting its values of change, competition, and domination. But these are not the only values on which a rhetorical system can be constructed, and we would like to propose as one alternative a feminist rhetoric.

Although definitions of *feminism* vary, feminists generally are united by a set of basic principles. We have chosen to focus on three of these principles—equality, immanent value, and self-determination—to serve as the starting place for a new rhetoric. These principles are ones that explicitly challenge the positive value the patriarchy accords to changing and thus dominating others.

Primary among the feminist principles on which our proposed rhetoric is based is a commitment to the creation of relationships of equality and to the elimination of the dominance and elitism that characterize most human relationships. As Wood (1994) aptly summarizes this principle, "I don't accept oppression and domination as worthy human values, and I don't believe differences must be ranked on a continuum of good and bad. I believe there are better, more humane and enriching ways to live" (p. 4). Efforts to dominate and gain power over others cannot be used to develop relationships of equality, so feminists seek to replace the "alienation, completion, and dehumanization" that characterize relationships of domination with "intimacy, mutuality, and camaraderie" (Hooks, 1984, p. 34).

Yet another principle that undergirds most feminisms is a recognition of the immanent value of all living beings. The essence of this principle is that every being is a unique and necessary part of the pattern of the universe and thus has value. Immanent value derives from the simple principle that "your life is worth something . . . You need only be what you are" (Starhawk, 1987, pp. 115-116). Worth cannot be determined by positioning individuals on a hierarchy so they can be ranked and compared or by attending to emblems of external achievement, for worth cannot be "earned, acquired, or proven" (Starhawk, 1987, p. 21). Concomitant with a recognition of the immanent value of another individual's unique perspective to that held by the rhetor.

Self-determination is a third principle that typically comprises a feminist world view. Grounded in a respect for others, self-determination allows individuals to make their own decisions about how they wish to live their lives. Self-determination involves the recognition that audience members are the authorities on their own lives and accords respect to others' capacity and right to constitute their worlds as they choose. As Johnson (1991) explains, this principle involves a trust that others are doing the best they can at the moment and simply need "to be unconditionally accepted as the experts on their own lives" (p. 162). When others are seen as experts who are making competent decisions about their lives, efforts by a rhetor to change those decisions are seen as a violation of their life worlds and the expertise they have developed.

Our purpose in this essay is to propose a definition and explication of a rhetoric built on the principles of equality, immanent value, and self-determination rather than on the attempt to control others through persuasive strategies designed to effect change. Although we believe that persuasion is often necessary, we believe an alternative exists that may be used in instances when changing and controlling others is not the rhetor's goal; we call this rhetoric *invitational rhetoric*. In what follows, we offer a description of this rhetoric, beginning with a discussion of its definition and purpose and then describing the communicative options available to rhetors who wish to use it. We conclude our essay with two examples of invitational rhetoric and a discussion of some implications of invitational rhetoric for rhetorical theory.

Although invitational rhetoric is constructed largely from feminist theory, the literature in which its principles and various dimensions have been theorized most thoroughly, we are not suggesting that only feminists have dealt with and developed its various components or that only feminists adhere to the principles on which it is based. Some dimensions of this rhetoric have been explicated by traditional rhetorical theorists, and we have incorporated their ideas into our description of this rhetoric. We also do not want to suggest that the rhetoric we propose describes how all women communicate or that it is or can be used only by women. Feminism "implies an understanding of inclusion with interests beyond women" (Wood, 1993, p. 39), and its aim is not to "privilege women over men" or "to benefit solely any specific group of women" (Hooks, 1984, p. 26). The rhetoric we describe is a rhetoric used at various times by some women and some men, some feminists and some non-feminists. What makes it feminist is not its use by a particular population of rhetors, but rather the grounding of its assumptions in feminist principles and theories. Our goal in offering this theory is to expand the array of communicative options available to all rhetors and to provide an impetus for more focused and systematic efforts to describe and assess rhetoric in all of its manifestations.

DEFINITION

Invitational rhetoric is an invitation to understanding as a means to create a relationship rooted in equality, immanent value, and self-determination. Invitational rhetoric constitutes an invitation to the audience to enter the rhetor's world and to see it as the rhetor does. In presenting a particular perspective, the invitational rhetor does not judge or denigrate others' perspectives, but is open to and tries to appreciate and validate those perspectives, even if they differ dramatically from the rhetor's own. Ideally, audience members accept the invitation offered by the rhetor by listening to and trying to understand the rhetor's perspective and then presenting their own. When this happens, rhetor and audience alike contribute to the thinking about an issue so that everyone involved gains a greater understanding of the issue in its subtlety, richness, and complexity. Ultimately, though, the result of invitational rhetoric is not just a non-adversarial framework established for the interaction; an understanding of the participants themselves occurs, an understanding that engenders appreciation, value, and a sense of equality.

The stance taken by invitational rhetors toward their audiences obviously is different from that assumed by traditional rhetors. Invitational rhetors do not believe they have the right to claim that their experiences or perspectives are superior to those of their audience members and refuse to impose their perspectives on them. Rhetors view the choices selected by audience members as right for them at the particular item, based on their own abilities to make those decisions. Absent are efforts to dominate another because the goal is the understanding and appreciation of another's perspective rather than the denigration of it simply because it is different from the rhetor's own. The result of the invitational rhetor's stance toward the audience is a relationship of equality, respect, and appreciation.

Invitational rhetoric is characterized, then, by the openness with which rhetors are able to approach their audiences. Burke (1969) suggests that rhetors typically adjust their conduct to the external resistance they expect in the audience or situation: "We in effect modify our own assertion in reply to its assertion" (p. 237). In invitational rhetoric, in contrast, resistance is not anticipated, and rhetors do not adapt their communication to expected resistance in the audience. Instead, they identify possible impediments to the creation of understanding and seek to minimize or neutralize them so they do not remain impediments.

Change may be the result of invitational rhetoric, but change is not its purpose. When change does occur as a result of understanding, it is different from the kind of change that typifies the persuasive interactions of traditional rhetoric. In the traditional model, change is defined as a shift in the audience in the direction requested by the rhetor, who then has gained some measure of power and control over the audience. In invitational rhetoric, change occurs in the audience or rhetor or both as a result of new understanding and insights gained in the exchange of ideas. As rhetors and audience members offer their ideas on an issue, they allow diverse positions to be compared in a process of discovery and questioning that may lead to transformation for themselves and others. Participants even may choose to be transformed because they are persuaded by something someone in the interaction says, but the insight that is persuasive is offered by a rhetor not to support the superiority of a particular perspective, but to contribute to the understanding by all participants of the issue and of one another.

The internal processes by which transformation occurs also are different in invitational rhetoric. In traditional rhetoric, the change process often is accompanied by feelings of inadequacy, insecurity, pain, humiliation, guilt, embarrassment, or angry submission on the part of the audience as rhetors communicate the superiority of their positions and the deficiencies of those of the audience. In invitational rhetoric, on the other hand, rhetors recognize the valuable contributions audience members can make to the rhetors' own thinking and understanding, and they do not engage in strategies that may damage or sever the connection between them and their audiences. This does not mean that invitational rhetoric always is free of pain. In invitational rhetoric, there may be a wrenching loose of ideas as assumptions and positions are questioned as a result of an interaction, a process that may be uncomfortable. But because rhetors affirm the beliefs of and communicate respect for others, the changes that are made are likely to be accompanied by an appreciation for new perspectives gained and gratitude for the assistance provided by others in thinking about an issue.

COMMUNICATIVE OPTIONS

The process of engaging in invitational rhetoric assumes two primary rhetorical forms. One is offering perspectives, a mode by which rhetors put forward for consideration their perspectives; the second is the creation of external conditions that allow others to present their perspectives in an atmosphere of respect and equality.

Offering Perspectives

When rhetors do not seek to impose their positions on audience members in invitational rhetoric, the presentation and function of individual perspectives differ significantly from their nature and function in traditional rhetoric. Individual perspectives are articulated in invitational rhetoric as carefully, completely, and passionately as possible to give them full expression and to invite their careful consideration by the participants in the interaction. This articulation occurs not through persuasive argument, but through offering—the giving of expression to a perspective without advocating its support or seeking its acceptance. Offering involves not probing or invading but giving, a process "of wrapping around the givee, of being available to her/him without insisting; our giving is a *presence,* an *offering*" (Gearhart, 1982, p. 198). In offering, rhetors tell what they currently know or understand; they present their vision of the world and show how it looks and works for them.

As a rhetorical form, offering may appear to be similar to some traditional rhetorical strategies, such as the use of personal narrative as a form of support for a rhetor's position. But narrative as offering functions differently from narrative as a means of support. It is presented in offering for the purpose of articulating a viewpoint, but not as a means to increase the likelihood of the audience's adherence to that viewpoint. The offering of a personal narrative is, itself, the goal; the means and the ends are the same in offering. Offering is not based on a dichotomy of cause and effect, an action done in the present to affect the future. Instead, as Johnson (1989) explains, the "'means are the ends; . . . *how* we do something is *what* we get'" (p. 35). In this mode, then, a story is not told as a means of supporting or achieving some other end, but as an end in itself—simply offering the perspective the story represents.

A critical dimension of the offering of a perspective, in whatever form it takes, is a willingness to yield. Not unlike Buber's (1965) notion of the "I-Thou" relationship, the basic movement of a willingness to yield is a turning toward the other. It involves meeting another's position "in its uniqueness, letting it have its impact" (p. xiv). Tracy (1987) explains the connection between the meeting of another's uniqueness and a willingness to yield: "To attend to the other as other, the different as different, is also to understand the different *as* possible" (p. 20). When they assume such a stance, rhetors communicate a willingness to call into question the beliefs they consider most inviolate and to relax their grip on those beliefs. The process is not unlike the self-risk that Natanson (1965) describes as the risking

> of the self's world of feeling, attitude, and the total subtle range of its affective and conative sensitivity . . . . [W]hen I truly risk myself in arguing I open myself to the viable possibility that the consequence of an argument may be to make me *see* something of the structure of my immediate world. (p. 15)

Scott (1976) calls this self-risk "a grave risk: the risk of the self that resides in a value structure" (p. 105). Thus, the perspective presented through offering represents an initial, tentative commitment to that perspective—one subject to revision as a result of the interaction.

A few specific examples of offering may clarify the nature of this rhetorical form. Although much rarer than we would like, offering sometimes occurs in academic settings when faculty members and/or students gather to discuss a topic of mutual interest. When they enter the interaction with a goal not of converting others to their positions but of sharing what they know, extending one another's ideas, thinking critically about all the ideas offered, and coming to an understanding of the subject and of one another, they are engaged in offering. Offering also is marked by discursive forms such as "I tried this solution when that happened to me; I thought it worked well " or "What would happen if we introduced the idea of _____ into this problem?" rather than statements with forms such as "You really ought to do _____" or " Your idea is flawed because you failed to take into account _____."

Offering may occur not only in small-group settings, but also in formal presentational contexts. A rhetor who presents her ideas at an academic colloquium, for example, engages in offering when she presents her ideas as valuable yet also as tentative. She acknowledges the fact that her work is in progress; thus she is open to the ideas of others so she can continue to revise and improve it. She builds on and extends the work of others rather than tearing their ideas apart in an effort to establish the superiority of her own. In an offering mode, she provides explanations for the sources of her ideas rather than marshaling evidence to establish their superiority. Audience members, too, may engage in offering behavior. They do so when they ask questions and make comments designed not to show the stupidity or error of the perspective presented or to establish themselves as more powerful or expert than the presenter. Instead, their questions and suggestions are aimed at learning more about the presenter's ideas, understanding them more thoroughly, nurturing them, and offering additional ways of thinking about the subject for everyone involved in the interaction.

We have tried to write this essay using such features of the offering form. We present a *proposal* for an invitational rhetoric, for example, a word we chose deliberately to suggest that what we present here is only one of many equally legitimate perspectives possible. We suggest that invitational rhetoric is a viable form of interaction in many instances, but do not assert that it is the only appropriate form of rhetoric and should be used in all situations or contexts. We acknowledge the importance and usefulness of traditional theories of rhetoric even as we propose an alternative to them, and we try to build

171

on and extend the work of other theorists—both traditional and feminist—rather than characterizing their work as inaccurate or misguided. Although we are constrained somewhat by the format of a journal article, we see this essay as in progress and plan to continue to work on our ideas; the responses of some of our colleagues and the reviewers and editor of *Communication Monographs* already have helped us clarify and improve our description of this rhetoric. We have attempted, then, to model the offering of a perspective within the perimeters allowed by a framework of scholarly discourse.

Offering also may be seen in the nonverbal realm; a perspective may be offered in the clothing individuals wear, the places in which and how they live, and in all of the symbolic choices rhetors make that reveal their perspectives. This kind of offering is illustrated by Purple Saturday, sponsored by the Women's Caucus at Speech Communication Association (SCA) conventions. On Purple Saturday, the women attending the convention (and those men who wish to show their support for women) are asked to wear purple, a color of the early women's suffrage movement, to proclaim women's solidarity and presence in SCA. When women wear purple on Saturday at the convention, they are not trying to persuade others to become feminists, to accept feminist scholarship, or to value women. Instead, they are simply offering a perspective so that those who wish to learn more about feminist scholarship or to join in the celebration of feminism may do so. Although not designed to influence others to change in particular directions, such nonverbal offerings may have that effect; some who view the wearing of purple by others at a convention may choose, for example, to explore or engage in feminist research themselves.

Another form offering may take, particularly in a hostile situation or when a dominant perspective is very different from the one held by the rhetor, is re-sourcement (Gearhart, 1982). Re-sourcement is a response made by a rhetor according to a framework, assumptions, or principles other than those suggested in the precipitating message. In using re-sourcement, the rhetor deliberately draws energy from a new source—a source other than the individual or system that provided the initial frame for the issue. It is a means, then, of communicating a perspective that is different from that of the individual who produced the message to which the rhetor is responding. Re-sourcement is not unlike Burke's (1984) notion of perspective by incongruity, but in re-sourcement, the juxtaposition of two systems or frameworks is split between rhetor and audience, with one reflected in the original message, the other in the response.

Re-sourcement involves the two processes of disengagement from the framework, system, or principles embedded in the precipitating message and the creative development of a response so that the issue is framed differently. Rorty's (1986) description of the process of generating new vocabularies points to this two-part process: "The idea is to get a vocabulary which is (at the moment) incommensurable with the old in order to draw attention away from the issues stated in the old, and thereby help people to forget them" (p. 114). In Forget's (1989) words, this kind of communication is "a swerve, a leap to the other side, which lets us . . . deploy another logic or system" (p. 136).

Although a refusal to engage in conflict or interaction under the terms proposed by a rhetor sometimes is seen as a negative, ineffective form of communication because it is interpreted as disconfirmation (e.g., Veenendall & Feinstein, 1990) or as a kind of manipulation associated with passive-aggressive behavior, it can be a positive response to a situation. It allows rhetors to continue to value themselves as well as the audience because it communicates that they are not willing to allow the audience to violate their integrity. Re-sourcement also opens up possibilities for future rhetorical choices, providing more options for rhetors than were previously available. As later options, rhetors who use re-sourcement may articulate their positions through more traditional forms of offering or standard forms of persuasion.

An example of re-sourcement is provided by Starhawk (1987) in her description of an incident that followed the blockade of the Livermore Weapons Lab in California to protest its development of nuclear weapons. She and other women were arrested and held in a school gym, and during their confinement, a woman was chased into the gym by six guards. She dove into a cluster of women, and they held on to her as the guards pulled at her legs, trying to extract her from the group. The guards were on the verge of beating the women when one woman sat down and began to chant. As the other women followed suit, the guards' action changed in response:

> They look bewildered. Something they are unprepared for, unprepared even to name, has arisen in our moment of common action. They do not know what to do. And so, after a moment, they withdrew . . . In that moment in the jail, the power of domination and control met something outside its comprehension, a power rooted in another source. (p. 5)

The guards' message was framed in a context of opposition, violence, hostility, and fear; the women, in contrast, chose to respond with a message framed in terms of nonviolence and connection.

Re-sourcement in a discursive form is exemplified in a story told by Watzlawick, Weakland, and Fisch (1974) about a police officer who was

> issuing a citation for a minor traffic violation when a hostile crowd began to gather around him. By the time he had given the offender his ticket, the mood of the crowd was ugly and the sergeant was not certain he would be able to get back to the relative safety of his patrol car. It then occurred to him to announce in a loud voice: "You have just witnessed the issuance of a traffic ticket by a member of your Oakland Police Department." And while the bystanders were busy trying to fathom the deeper meaning of this all too obvious communiqué, he got into his cruiser and drove off. (pp. 108-109)

The initial message presented to the police office was framed in the context of opposition and hostility; he chose, however, to respond with a message grounded in a framework of simple explanation, cooperation, and respect. Re-sourcement, as a means of offering, allowed him to diffuse the situation and to communicate his own perspective—that he was doing the job he was hired by the crowd members, as taxpayers, to do.

External Conditions

Offering can occur whether or not an audience chooses to join with a rhetor in a process of discovery and understanding. But if invitational rhetoric is to result in *mutual* understanding of perspectives, it involves not only the offering of the rhetor's perspective, but the creation of an atmosphere in which audience members' perspectives also can be offered. We propose that to create such an environment, an invitational rhetoric must create three external conditions in the interaction between rhetors and audience members—safety, value, and freedom. These are states or prerequisites required if the possibility of mutual understanding is to exist.

The condition of *safety* involves the creation of a feeling of security and freedom from danger for the audience. Rhetoric contributes to a feeling of safety when it conveys to audience members that the ideas and feelings they share with the rhetor will be received with respect and care. When rhetoric establishes a safe context, the rhetor makes no attempt to hurt, degrade, or belittle audience members or their beliefs, and audience members do not fear rebuttal of or retribution for their most fundamental beliefs. Even in a volatile situation such as that described by Starhawk, when the guards were about to beat a woman seeking safe haven in a group of protesters, rhetoric that promotes a feeling of safety can be created. In this case, the women did nothing to endanger the guards or make them feel as though they would be hurt. They did not fight them physically or argue against the guards' use of force; neither did they engage in verbal abuse or ridicule the guards' training and beliefs about how to deal with prisoners.

Rhetoric that contributes to a feeling of safety also provides some means for audience members to order the world so it seems coherent and makes sense to them. When audience members feel their sense of order is threatened or challenged, they are more likely to cling to familiar ways of thinking and to be less open to understanding the perspectives of others. When a safe environment is created, then, audience members trust the rhetor and feel the rhetor is working with and not against them.

The condition of *value* is the acknowledgment that audience members have intrinsic or immanent worth. This value is what Benhabib (1992) calls *"the principle of universal moral respect"*—"the right of all beings capable of speech and action to be participants" in the conversation (p. 29). Barrett (1991) describes this condition as "respectfully, affirming others" while at the same time "one affirms oneself" (p. 148).

Value is created when rhetors approach audience members as "unrepeatable individuals" and eschew "distancing, depersonalizing, or paternalistic attitudes" (Walker, 1989, pp. 22, 23). As a result, audience members feel their identities are not forced upon or chosen for them by rhetors. Rhetors do not attempt to fit audience into any particular roles but face "the 'otherness of the other,' one might say to face their 'alterity,' their irreducible distinctness and difference from the self" (Benhabib, 1992, p. 167). Rhetors celebrate the unique and individual identities of audience members—what Benhabib (1992) describes as

> the actuality of my choices, namely to how I, as a finite, concrete, embodied individual, shape and fashion the circumstances of my birth and family, linguistic, cultural and gender identity into a coherent narrative that stands as my life's story. (pp. 161-162).

One way in which rhetoric may contribute to the acknowledgment and celebration of freely chosen, unique identities by audience members is through a process Gendlin (1978) calls *"absolute listening"* (p. 116), Morton (1985) describes as "hearing to speech" (p. 202), and Johnson (1987) terms "hearing into being" (p. 130). In such rhetoric, listeners do not interrupt, comfort, or insert anything of their own as others tell of their experiences. Such a stance contrasts with typical ways of listening, in which "we nearly always stop each other from getting very far inside. Our advice, reactions, encouragements, reassurances, and well-intentioned comments actually prevent people from feeling understood" (Gendlin, 1978, p. 116) and encourage them to direct their comments toward listeners' positions or orientations (Johnson, 1987). While speaking to listeners who do not insert themselves into the talk, individuals come to discover their own perspectives. Morton (1985) quotes a woman's description of her experience in the process of being heard to speak: "'You didn't smother me. You gave it [my voice] space to shape itself. You gave it time to come full circle'" (p. 205).

Value is conveyed to audience members when rhetors not only listen carefully to the perspectives of others, but try to think from those perspectives. Benhabib's (1992) notion of the "'reversibility of perspectives'" (p. 145) is relevant here; it is the capacity to reverse perspectives and to reason from the standpoint of others, "making present to oneself what the perspectives of others involved are or could be" (p. 137). When value is created in a communicative situation, audience members feel rhetors see them as significant individuals and appreciate and attend to their uniqueness. They feel rhetors care about them, understand their ideas, and allow them to contribute in significant ways to the interaction.

Freedom, the power to choose or decide, is a third condition whose presence in an environment is a prerequisite for the possibility of mutual understanding. In invitational rhetoric, rhetors do not place restrictions on an interaction. Participants can bring any and all matters to the interaction for consideration; no subject matter is off limits, and all presuppositions can be challenged. The rhetor's ideas also are not privileged over those of the audience in invitational rhetoric. All the participants in the interaction are able, in Barrett's (1991) words, to "speak up, to speak out" (p. 148). Benhabib (1992) calls this *"the principle of egalitarian reciprocity"* (p. 29); within conversations, it suggests, "each has the same symmetrical rights to various speech acts, to initiate new topics, to ask for reflection about the presuppositions of the conversation, etc." (p. 29).

Freedom also is developed when a rhetor provides opportunities for others to develop and choose options from alternatives they, themselves, have created. Rather than presenting a predetermined set of options from which individuals may choose, a rhetor who wishes to facilitate freedom allows audience members to develop the options that seem appropriate to them, allowing for the richness and complexity of their unique subjective experiences. Perspectives are articulated as a means to widen options—to generate more ideas than either rhetors or audiences had initially—in contrast to traditional rhetoric, where rhetors seek to limit the options of audiences and encourage them to select the one they advocate.

Freedom of choice is made available to audiences, as well, in that, in invitational rhetoric, the audience's lack of acceptance of or adherence to the perspective articulated by the rhetor truly makes no difference to the rhetor. Some audience members will choose to try to understand the perspective of the rhetor, but others will not. Of those who do, some will choose to accept the acceptance or rejection—which is seen as perfectly acceptable by the invitational rhetor, who is not offended, disappointed, or angry if audience members choose not to adopt a particular perspective. Should the audience choose not to accept the vision articulated by the rhetor, the connection between the rhetor and the audience remains intact, and the audience still is valued and appreciated by the rhetor. The maintenance of the connection between rhetors and audiences is not dependent on rhetors' approval of the choices made by audience members. Rogers' (1962) notion of unconditional positive regard suggests the nature of the autonomy the rhetor accords the audience; the audience has the freedom to make choices without the possibility of losing the respect of the rhetor.

ILLUSTRATIONS

Invitational rhetoric offers an invitation to understanding—to enter another's world to better understand an issue and the individual who holds a particular perspective on it. Ultimately, its purpose is to provide the basis for the creation and maintenance of relationships of equality. Its primary communicative options are offering perspectives and the creation of the external conditions of safety, value, and freedom that enable audience members to present their perspectives to the rhetor. In this section, we present two examples of invitational rhetoric to clarify its primary features.

The first example is the acceptance speech given by Adrienne Rich when she was awarded the National Book Awards' prize for poetry in 1974 (Rich, Lorde, & Walker, 1974/1994). When Rich accepted the award, she read a statement that she had prepared with Alice Walker and Audre Lorde—both of whom also had been nominated for the prize. In the statement, the three women announced that they were accepting the award together: "We, Audre Lorde, Adrienne Rich, and Alice Walker, together accept this award in the name of all the women whose voices have gone and still go unheard in a patriarchal world" (p. 148).

The statement clearly articulated the women's own position: "We believe that we can enrich ourselves more in supporting and giving to each other than by competing against each other; and that poetry—if it *is* poetry—exists in a realm beyond ranking and comparison" (p. 148). They presented no arguments in favor of their belief, however, nor did they argue against the position held by representatives of the National Book Awards. Thus, they did not seek the adherence of others to their perspective, but simply offered their own vision.

The speech illustrates re-sourcement as a form of offering in that the women communicated their differences with the hierarchical, competitive framework established by the National Book Awards simply by no communicating within the terms of that framework: "None of us could accept this money for herself" (p. 148). They chose to respond within a different framework— one based on support and cooperation—by accepting the prize in the name of all women: "We will share this prize among us, to be used as best we can for women" (p. 148).

The three external conditions of safety, value, and freedom required for others to present their perspectives were created by the speech. The rhetors communicated safety when they suggested that they regarded the perspective of the judges as a legitimate one that they would treat with respect and care. "We appreciate the good faith of the judges for this award" (p. 148), they stated.

They accorded value in very specific ways to many individuals, both those in their immediate audience and others:

> We dedicate this occasion to the struggle for self-determination of all women, of every color, identification, or derived class: the poet, the housewife, the lesbian, the mathematician, the mother, the dishwasher, the pregnant teenager,

> the teacher, the grandmother, the prostitute, the philosopher, the waitress, the women who will understand what we are doing here and those who will not understand yet.. (pp. 148-149)

They not only recognized these diverse and unique individuals, but credited them as sources for their own work, calling them "the silent women whose voices have been denied us, the articulate women who have given us strength to do our work" (p. 149).

The brevity of the speech precluded the opportunity for the extensive development of freedom for the audience, but it is evident in that Rich, Walker, and Lorde do not specify particular options for actions for women; they leave open to women whatever routes of "self-determination" (p. 148) they, themselves, choose. Nor do they suggest the kind of support women should give to each other or the particular contributions other women have made to them. Their ambiguity in these areas leaves open options for the audience and does not confine the terms of the interaction they initiated.

Feminist and animal-rights activist, Sally Miller Gearhart (1993) provides a second example of invitational rhetoric in her narration of her interaction with an anti-abortion advocate. In the interaction, Gearhart used both traditional and invitational rhetoric, so her narrative provides a useful contrast between the two and the kinds of results each tends to produce. On a trip with a friend to upstate New York, Gearhart encountered a man in the Kennedy airport "railing about all these women and abortion rights." Because of her own pro-choice beliefs, Gearhart

> took him on. As a matter fact, I took him on so loudly that we gathered a little crowd there in the Kennedy airport. I was screaming at him; I was trying to make him change. It was not successful, and it was pretty ugly, as a matter of fact . . . They didn't have to actually physically separate us, but it was close to that.

An hour later, as she was boarding the shuttle bus to take her to Plattsburg, her destination, Gearhart encountered the man again: "There was only one seat on that bus, and guess who it was next to? . . . He looked at me and I looked at him as if to say, 'Oh, my God, what are we going to do?'" Rather than continue to engage the man as she had in the airport, Gearhart decided to try something different—to engage in what we suggest was invitational rhetoric: "I decided that what I would do was to try to approach this man with something different . . . and so I began asking him about his life and about the things that he did," seeking to understand his perspective and the reasons it made sense to him. "In fact," he was a chemist, and he had experimented on animals. He had grown up as a hunter and, of course, all that is absolutely counter to the things that I believe." But rather than attempting to convince him of the error of his ways, Gearhart continued to listen to the man, and he did the same as she shared her own perspectives and experiences with him.

The invitational rhetoric in which the two engaged brought Gearhart and the man together, although neither one "had changed our original position." As the two crossed paths for the third time in the parking lot, waiting for their respective rides, they started walking toward each other. Gearhart finishes the story:

> I don't know which one of us did it first, but I guess maybe I flung open my arms and he flung open his arms and we came together in this terrific hug, both of us in tears, sobbing, crying like babies. I said, "You know, I don't know what has happened here, but my life has been totally changed after today." And he said, "My life is totally changed, too, and I don't know what's happened."

We suggest that what happened was that the two individuals had offered their perspectives and listened to and acknowledged one another's perspectives in an environment of safety, value, and freedom. Their communication thus invited understanding and brought them to a new place of awareness of and appreciation for one another. Gearhart's (1993) summary of the experience is an excellent summary of invitational rhetoric: "It's a way to disagree and at the same time not to hurt each other and to respect each other and to have, actually, something very close and tender."

We see the statement of Rich, Lorde, and Walker and Gearhart's interaction as invitational, then, in that both were rooted in the principles of equality, immanent value, and respect for others and validation of their perspectives. Rich, Lorde, and Walker offered a perspective and communicated its difference with that of the judges, but they neither sought adherence for it nor denigrated the different viewpoint of the judges. Gearhart also offered a perspective very different from that of her acquaintance and listened to one very different from her own without seeking adherence or pronouncing judgment. Each rhetor created conditions of safety, value, and freedom, contributing to an environment in which audience members were able to present their different perspectives. The result was an understanding on which relationships of equality and respect could be built.

IMPLICATIONS FOR RHETORICAL THEORY

The expansion of the notion of rhetoric to include invitational rhetoric has several implications for rhetorical theory. The introduction of invitational rhetoric into the scope of rhetorical theory challenges the presumption that has been granted to persuasion as the interactional goal in the rhetorical tradition. Identification and explication of a rhetoric not grounded in the intent to produce a desired change in others undermines the position of privilege accorded to efforts to influence in rhetoric. The existence of invitational rhetoric encourages the exploration of yet other rhetorics that do not involve this singular interactional goal.

A second implication is that invitational rhetoric may contribute to the efforts of communication scholars who are working to develop models for cooperative, non-adversarial, and ethical communication. Such a goal, for example, is espoused by Herrick (1992), in his discussion of the link between rhetoric and ethics, when he suggests "that a virtue approach to rhetorical ethics may provide the kind of flexible, yet directive, ethic needed" to maintain the democratic nature of a pluralistic social order (p. 147). Van Eemeren and Grootendorst (1992) also propose such a goal in their book on argumentation; their approach is designed to create an open and free exchange and responsible participation in cooperative, dialogic communication. The framework provided by invitational rhetoric may allow such theorists to achieve their laudatory missions more easily by contributing to a reconciliation of goals and means (Makau, in press). According to Hewrrick's and Van Eemeren and Grootendorst's definitions of rhetoric as a process in which tend to see their audiences as opponents and sometimes may be tempted to engage in questionable ethical practices to win their "battles" with them. Rules thus are required to contain the interaction that results from the use of such strategies. Invitational rhetoric may serve as a way to allow these scholars to develop models for interaction not characterized by the opposition and competition that make the achievement of their goal difficult.

The introduction of invitational rhetoric to the array of rhetorical forms available also serves a greater heuristic, inventive function than rhetoric previously has allowed. Traditional theories of rhetoric occur within pre-imposed or preconceived frameworks. In rhetoric in which the rhetor seeks to impose change on others, an idea is adapted to the audience or is presented in ways that will be most persuasive to the audience; as a result, the idea stays lodged within the confines of the rhetorical system in which it was framed. Others may challenge the idea, but only within the confines of the framework of the dispute already established. The inventive potential of rhetoric is restricted as the interaction converts the idea to the experience required by the framework.

Invitational rhetoric, on the other hand, aims at converting experience "to one of the many views which are indeterminately possible" (Holmberg, 1977, p. 237). As a result, much is open in invitational rhetorics—the potential of the audience to contribute to the generation of ideas is enhanced, the means used to present ideas are not those that limit the ideas to what is most persuasive for the audience, the view of the kind of environment that can be created in the interaction is expanded, and the ideas that can be considered multiply. The privileging of invention in invitational rhetoric allows for the development of interpretations, perspectives, courses of actions, and solutions to problems different from those allowed in traditional models of rhetoric. Rather than the discovery of how to make a case, invitational rhetoric employs invention to discover more cases, a process Daly (1984) describes as one of creating "an atmosphere in which further creativity may flourish . . . [w]e become breathers/creators of free space. We are windy, stirring the stagnant spaces with life" (p. 18).

The inclusion of an invitational rhetoric in the array of rhetorics available suggests that need to revise and expand rhetorical constructs of various kinds to take into account the nature and function of this form. Invitational rhetoric suggests, for example, that the traditional view of the audience as an opponent ought to be questioned. It challenges the traditional conception of the notion of rhetorical strategies as means to particular ends in that in invitational rhetoric, the means constitute the ends. It suggests the need for a new schema of ethics to fit interactional goals other than inducement of others to adherence to the rhetor's own beliefs.

Finally, invitational rhetoric provides a mode of communication for women and other marginalized groups to use in their efforts to transform systems of domination and oppression. At first glance, invitational rhetoric may seem to be incapable of resisting and transforming oppressive systems such as patriarchy because the most it seems able to do is to create a space in which representatives of an oppressive system understand a different—in this case, a feminist—perspective but do not adopt it. Although invitational rhetoric is not designed to create a specific change, such as the transformation of systems of oppression into ones that value and nurture individuals, it may produce such an outcome. Invitational rhetoric may resist an oppressive system simply because it models an alternative to the system by being "itself an Other way of thinking/speaking" (Daly, 1978, p. xiii)—it presents an alternative feminist vision rooted in affirmation and respect and thus shows how an alternative looks and works. Invitational rhetoric thus may transform an oppressive system precisely because it does not engage that system on its own terms, using arguments developed from the system's framework or orientation. Such arguments usually are co-opted by the dominant system (Ferguson, 1984) and provide the impetus "to strengthen, refine, and embellish the original edifice," entrenching the system further (Johnson, 1989, p.

16-17). Invitational rhetoric, in contrast, enables rhetors to disengage from the dominance and mastery so common to a system of oppression and to create a reality of equality and mutuality in its place, allowing for options and possibilities not available within the familiar, dominant framework.

Our interest in inserting invitational rhetoric into the scope of rhetorical theory is not meant to suggest that it is an ideal for which rhetors should strive or that it should or can be used in all situations. Invitational rhetoric is one of many useful and legitimate rhetorics, including persuasion, in which rhetors will want to be skilled. With the identification of the rhetorical mode of invitational rhetoric, however, rhetors will be able to recognize situations in which they seek not to persuade others, but simply to create an environment that facilitates understanding, accords value and respect to others' perspectives, and contributes to the development of relationships of equality.

REFERENCES

Barrett, H. (1991). *Rhetoric and civility: Human development, narcissism, and the good audience.* New York: State University of New York Press.

Benhabib, S. (1992). *Situating the self: Gender, community and postmodernism in contemporary ethics.* New York: Routledge.

Buber, M. (1965). *Between man and man* (R.G. Smith,Trans.). New York: Macmillan.

Burke, K. (1984). *Attitudes toward history* (3rd ed.). Berkeley: University of California Press.

Burke, K. (1969). *A grammar of motives.* Berkeley: University of California Press.

Daly, M. (1978). *Gyn/ecology: The metaethics of radical feminism.* Boston: Beacon.

Daly, M. (1984). *Pure lust: Elemental feminist philosophy.* Boston, Beacon.

Edson, B.A. (1985). Bias in social movement theory: A view from a female-systems perspective. *Women's Studies in Communication, 8,* 34-35.

Elshtain, J.B. (1982). Feminist discourse and its discontents: Language, power, and meaning. *Signs, 7,* 603-621.

Ferguson, K.E. (1984). *The feminist case against bureaucracy.* Philadelphia: Temple University Press.

Ferguson, M. (1980). *The Aquarian conspiracy: Personal and social transformation in the 1980s.* Los Angeles: J.P. Tarcher.

Forget, P. (1989). Argument(s). In D. Michelfelder & R. Palmer (Eds.), *Dialogue and deconstruction: The Gadamer-Derrida encounter* (pp. 129-149). Albany, NY: SUNY Press.

Foss, K.A., & Foss, S.K. (1991). *Women speak: The eloquence of women's lives.* Prospect Heights, IL: Waveland.

Foss, S.K., Foss, K.A., & Trapp, R. (1991). *Contemporary perspectives on rhetoric* (rev. ed.). Prospect Heights, IL: Waveland.

Gearhart, S.M. (1979). The womanization of rhetoric. *Women's Studies International Quarterly, 2,* 195-201.

Gearhart, S. (1982). Womanpower: Energy re-sourcement. In C. Spretnak (Ed.), *The politics of women's spirituality: Essays on the rise of spiritual power within the feminist movement.* (pp. 194-206). Garden City, NY: Anchor.

Gearhart, S.M. (1993, January). [Videotaped interview with Sonja K. Foss and members of the Feminist Rhetorical Theory class, Ohio State University].

Gendlin, E.T. (1978). *Focusing.* New York, Everest.

Griffin, C.L. (1993). Women as communicators: Mary Daly's hagiography as rhetoric. *Communication Monographs, 60,* 158-177.

Herrick, J.A. (1992). Rhetoric, ethics, and virtue. *Communication Studies, 43,* 133-149.

Holmberg, C. (1977). Dialectical rhetoric and rhetorical rhetoric. *Philosophy and Rhetoric,* 10, 232-243.

Hooks, B. (1984). *Feminist theory: From margin to center.* Boston: South End.

Johnson, S. (1987). *Going out of our minds: The metaphysics of liberation.* Freedom, CA: Crossing.

Johnson, S. (1989). *Wildfire: Igniting the she/volution.* Albuquerque, NM: Wildfire.

Johnson, S. (1991). *The ship that sailed into the living room: Sex and intimacy reconsidered.* Estancia, NM: Wildfire.

Kramarae, C. (1989). Feminist theories of communication. In E. Barnouw (Ed.), *International encyclopedia of communications* (Vol. 2, pp. 157-160). New York: Oxford University Press.

Makau, J.M. (in press). [Review of *Argumentation, communication and fallacies: A pragma-dialectical perspective*]. *Philosophy and Rhetoric.*

Morton, N. (1985). *The journey is home.* Boston: Beacon.

Natanson, M. (1965). The claims of immediacy. In M. Natanson & H.W. Johnstone, Jr. (Eds.), *Philosophy, rhetoric and argumentation* (pp. 10-19). University Park: Pennsylvania State University Press.

Rich, A., Lorde, A., & Walker, A. (1994). A statement for voices unheard: A challenge to the National Books Awards. In S.K. Foss & K.A. Foss, *Inviting transformation: Presentational speaking for a changing world* (pp. 148-149). Prospect Heights, IL: Waveland. (Speech presented 1974).

Rogers, C.R. (1962). The interpersonal relationship: The core of guidance. *Harvard Educational Review,* 32, 416-429.

Rorty, r. (1986). Beyond realism and anti-realism. In L. Nagl & R. Heinrick (Eds.), *Wo steht die Analytische Philosophie heute?* (pp. 103-115). Vienna, Austria: Oldenbourg.

Scott, R.L. (1976). Dialogue and rhetoric. In J. Blankenship & H. Stelzner (Eds.), *Rhetoric and communication: Studies in the University of Illinois tradition* (99-109). Urbana: University of Illinois Press.

Scott, R.L. (1991). The necessary pluralism of any future history of rhetoric. *Pre/Text,* 12, 195-209.

Shepard, G.J. (1992). Communication as influence: Definitional exclusion. *Communication Studies,* 43, 203-219.

Starhawk. (1988). *Truth or dare: Encounters with power, authority, and mystery.* San Francisco: Harper and Row.

Starhawk. (1988). *Dreaming the dark: Magic, sex and politics* (rev. ed.). Boston, Beacon.

Tracy, D. (1987). *Plurality and ambiguity: Hermeneutics, religion, hope.* San Francisco: Harper and Row.

Van Eemeren, F.H., & Grootendorst, R. (1992). *Argumentation, communication and fallacies: A pragma-dialectical perspective.* Hillsdale, NJ: Lawrence Erlbaum.

Veenendall, T.L., & Feinstein, M.C. (1990). *Let's talk about relationships.* Prospect Heights, IL: Waveland.

Walker, M.U. (1989). Moral understandings: Alternative "epistemology" for a feminist ethics. *Hypatia,* 4, 15-28.

Watzlawick, P., Weakland, J.H., & Fisch, r. (1974). *Change: Principles of problem formation and problem resolution.* New York: W.W. Norton.

Wood, J.T. (1993). Enlarging conceptual boundaries: A critique of research in interpersonal communication. In S.P. Bowen & N. Wyatt (Eds.), *Transforming visions: Feminist critiques in communication studies* (pp. 19-49). Cresskill, NJ: Hampton.

Wood, J.T. (1994). *Gendered Lives: Communication, gender, and culture.* Belmont, CA: Wadsworth.

Merck's Open Letters and the Teaching of Ethos

Frank Griffin

CONSIDER AS YOU ARE READING:

It is true: if we do not have the ability to read arguments critically, we can easily be manipulated by skillful rhetors. Griffin's analysis of how a major pharmaceutical company handled a crisis is a case in point. Using premises of Aristotelian rhetoric to analyze ethos and ethical appeals, Griffin dissects two specific communications issued by the pharmaceutical company, Merck, after a drug recall. While he avoids making any judgment about whether Merck's communication strategies were ethical, he offers insightful analysis of those strategies and invites us—as consumers of essays and as consumers of goods—to enhance our understanding of the way ethos can be constructed to both forward principled communications and to manipulate readers.

1. *Be sure you read the two communications that Merck distributed about this crisis (you'll find them at the end of the article). How do you think Merck tries to bolster its image? What are the major strengths it promotes to build its ethos in the eyes of the consumer?*

2. *As a consumer, what is your response to Merck's communications? Do you feel consoled, manipulated, or something else altogether as you read Merck's public announcements? How might your response to these communications influence a text you would write in response to a particularly difficult situation?*

3. *Griffin is very careful not to "take a side" in this essay. Comment on that approach. Why do you think he avoids taking a position about whether Merck's communications were ethical? How does his neutral stance affect his credibility?*

In fall 2004, Merck faced a significant threat to the company's public image because of the withdrawal of VIOXX, and Merck executives were forced to defend the company's actions, its motivation for those actions, and its reputation. Confronted with enormous rhetorical challenges, Merck tried to generate public goodwill toward the company by creating a personalized image of a corporate giant worthy of understanding, sympathy, and trust. Open letters released during the initial response to the VIOXX crisis rely on the intimacy of interpersonal communication and demonstrate to students of business communication arguments based on ethos. The syntax and diction of these documents are analyzed to demonstrate how they create a secondary narrative of Merck's good sense, good moral character, and goodwill. Finally, the study presents apparently contradictory narratives of this pharmaceutical giant's responsibility, narratives that summarize the arguments in the VIOXX litigation. Analysis of Merck's open letters underscores the relevance of many concepts covered in the business communications classroom.

In September 2004, Merck announced the worldwide withdrawal of its popular VIOXX drug after studies showed an increased risk of heart attacks and strokes for long-term users of the drug. One estimate was that 80 million people worldwide had taken the drug by that time (20 million of them were American); Merck's 2003 sales for VIOXX totaled $2.5 billion (Juni et al., 2004, p. 2021; Mathews & Martinez, 2004). The crisis caused by this withdrawal and Merck's public response to it offers an opportunity to introduce students of business communications to the area of crisis communication and the persuasive response to that crisis. Specifically, this study highlights Merck's attempts during the initial response phase of the crisis in late 2004 and early 2005 by applying Aristotle's precepts for the development of a positive ethos. This approach shows students how a large corporation can make an effort to personalize its communication with stakeholders and to cultivate an ethos as a responsible corporate citizen. Thus, the Merck example provides those of us in the business communications classroom a current case that makes textbook discussions of credibility in persuasion concrete and relevant (Bovée & Thill, 2006, pp. 245-246; Guffey, 2003, pp. 287, 291; Locker & Kaczmarek, 2007, p. 200; Ober, 2006, pp. 201-202).

RHETORICAL CHALLENGES

Merck faced serious rhetorical challenges in part because of the complexities of the VIOXX case. First was the perception of its causal relationship to the events. Was Merck's crisis "accidental" (Coombs, 2004)? Did Merck management, in other words, have limited control because the crisis resulted from the necessary passage of 18 months before follow-up studies of VIOXX showed a problem with increased cardiovascular events"? Or was Merck's crisis "intentional" (Coombs, 2004) because the company knowingly continued to market a product that harmed consumers? Clearly, the public's perception of these possibilities would have a tremendous effect on its perception of Merck's motivation. Although the withdrawal itself could be perceived as the protective removal of a dangerous product, the perception of a delay in acting would counter that relief with the suspicion that Merck's actions were motivated by profits.

A second rhetorical challenge is derived from Merck's attempt to demonstrate the accidental nature of the crisis. This issue allows business communications instructors to highlight key concepts related to audience analysis. When one is communicating the results of complex clinical trials to the general public, who should be the designated spokesperson for the corporation? The explanation offered by Merck President, Chairman, and CEO at the time, Raymond Gilmartin, to the United States Senate Finance Committee illustrates the rhetorical hurdle of scientific jargon: "The combined data from randomized controlled clinical trials showed no difference in confirmed cardiovascular event rates between VIOXX and placebo and VIOXX and NSAIDS other than naproxen" (Gilmartin, 2004c).

A third rhetorical challenge emerged when stories appeared in the media questioning Merck's marketing of VIOXX and its handling of the data from the various trials. Students will need to be given a summary of these events to understand the context of Merck's defense. In early November 2004, *The Lancet* published an article online (and in the December print journal; "Vioxx, the implosion of Merck," 2004) that was highly critical of Merck's response to the cumulative data collected on the risks of using VIOXX. The authors concluded that "an increased risk of myocardial infarction was evident from 2000 onwards. At the end of 2000, the effect was both substantial and unlikely to be a chance finding" (Juni et al., 2004, p. 2025).

At the same time *The Lancet* was criticizing Merck, the *Wall Street Journal* (*WSJ*) was reporting that "internal Merck e-mails and marketing materials as well as interviews with outside scientists show that the company fought forcefully for years to keep safety concerns from destroying the drug's commercial prospects" (Mathews & Martinez, 2004, p. A1). The article cited an email from Merck's research chief at the time, Edward Scolnick, on March 9, 2000 that said cardiovascular events associated with VIOXX were "clearly there." The *WSJ* article also reported that Merck's marketing of VIOXX included a 16-page document for sales representatives called "Dodge Ball VIOXX" that coached them on how to respond to questions about the drug's safety. Each of the first 12 pages presented a potential concern expressed by a physician about VIOXX and how the sales representatives should respond. The final four pages contained one word each: "DODGE!" (Mathews & Martinez, 2004, p. A1).

In addition to these internal Merck revelations, the *WSJ* article described how Merck officials had contacted academics and physicians who had publicly questioned the safety of VIOXX to complain about the criticism. Merck contacted researchers at the Stanford University Medical School, Beth Israel Deaconess Medical Center in Boston, the University of Minnesota, and the Cleveland Clinic.

Against this backdrop of public confusion and doubt, media revelations, and scientific criticism, Merck crafted responses for various audiences. Its officers appeared before a Congressional investigative committee; it created a VIOXX subsite on its Web site containing both print and video responses to the crisis; it issued almost daily press releases; and it created Open Letters designed to appear on its Web site, in newspapers, and in magazines around the world to address the general public. Before presenting students with those Open Letters, it might be helpful to provide them with an overview of Aristotle's (n.d.) discussion of ethos from his *Rhetoric*.

ARISTOTLE'S PRINCIPLES OF ETHOS

Books I and II of Aristotle's (n.d.) *Rhetoric* provide insight into the means by which a speaker cultivates the ethos that will give him credibility with an audience. To create this ethos of confidence in his character, the speaker must demonstrate good sense, good moral character, and goodwill (p. 1378a). Doing so, says Aristotle, will inspire trust in the speaker and therefore trust in the message.

Because Aristotle in the *Rhetoric* defines good sense through its opposite, Corbett's (1990) discussion of how the text itself must reveal the speaker's good sense offers students an accessible insight. Corbett says that a discourse

> must show that the speaker or writer has an adequate, if not a professionally erudite, grasp of the subject being talked about, that the speaker or writer knows and observes the principles of valid reasoning, is capable of viewing the situation in a proper perspective, has read widely, and has good taste and discriminating judgment. (p. 81)

Describing its opposite, Aristotle says that people may form false opinions because of lack of good sense or, linking good sense with good moral character, he says they form a true opinion "but because of their moral badness do not say what they really think" (p. 1378a). A third possibility he links with goodwill is the following: They may be both "sensible and upright, but not well disposed to their hearers" and may therefore "fail to recommend what they know to be the best course" (p. 1378a). In the VIOXX crisis, we see that what constitutes the evidence for forming a "true opinion" is the crux of the dispute.

Aristotle describes good moral character as the result of virtues such as justice, courage, temperance, magnanimity, and "all such qualities, as being excellences of the soul," and he links these virtues to action: "for it is by possessing these that we are in a good condition, and they tend to produce good works and good actions" (p. 1362b). Then expanding his list of "things that must be good," he offers an observation that relates directly to the Merck crisis:

> Further, health, beauty, and the like, [must be good] as being bodily excellences and productive of many other good things: for instance, health is productive both of pleasure and of life, and therefore is thought the greatest of goods, since these two things which it causes, pleasure and life, are two of the things most highly prized by ordinary people. (p. 1362b)

Other contributors to good moral character described by Aristotle relate to the VIOXX crisis: Wealth, honor, and reputation contribute to good moral character, he says, because they are "productive of many other good things" (p. 1362b).

The speaker can cultivate the audience's perception of his goodwill, says Aristotle, if he is able to convince the listeners that he wishes good things for them, preferably appearing to have no benefit for the speaker. Specifically, Aristotle says, the audience will embrace as a friend a speaker who wants to treat the audience well where money or personal safety is concerned (p. 1381a). Furthermore, the speaker can build confidence by exploiting

> a mental picture of the nearness of what keeps us safe and the absence or remoteness of what is terrible: it may be due either to the near presence of what inspires confidence or to the absence of what causes alarm. (p. 1383a)

People will face danger calmly, says Aristotle, "if they may have means to deal with it" (p. 1383a).

Aristotle's precepts for ethos, then, focus on an honest commitment to knowledge, the formation of true opinions, and the willingness to express them; they also derive from a commitment to the safety and well-being of the audience, providing the audience the means to accept and confront threats. These commitments lead to selfless, moral action. The rhetorical challenges described earlier—the argument for the accidental nature of the crisis, the explanation of how the VIOXX threat was discovered, and the rebuttal of media revelations and criticism—all hinge on the company's ability to demonstrate good sense, goodwill, and good moral character, as students will see in Merck's published "open letters."

PERSONALIZATION THROUGH OPEN LETTERS: MERCK'S SECONDARY NARRATIVE

An analysis of the "Open Letter from Merck" (Gilmartin, 2004a) shows how Merck responded to criticism by constructing an ethos of commitment to science and to patients (see Appendix A). This letter also illustrates a secondary narrative, in which a company facing a crisis counters the primary narrative of events described in the media with its own retelling of those events in a more favorable interpretation (Hart, 1993; Hay, 1995; Tenkasi & Boland, 1993; Venette, Sellnow, & Lang, 2003). Keys to the secondary narrative are its ability to define events while at the same time being "abstract enough to allow for the explanation of newly discovered failures" (Venette, Sellnow, & Lang, 2003, p. 225). The narrative that is most likely to connect with the audience's experience is a "coherent and simple discourse" (Hay, 1995, p. 65). The "Open Letter from Merck" illustrates these strategies for simplicity and coherence and thus offers another opportunity to highlight for students the importance of writing with one's audience in mind.

The first two paragraphs constitute a mini *exordium*, in which the writer attempts to create rapport with the readers by insisting that he is answering questions and correcting inaccurate information. He is answering unnamed others (the primary narrative in *The Lancet* and the *Wall Street Journal*, for example) and asking readers to consider his side of the situation (his secondary narrative).

The *confirmation*, the proof offered, employs a series of personal pronouns ("We," not "it") and active verbs, "We extensively studied," "We promptly disclosed," "We took additional steps," and "we acted promptly." Furthermore, these actions were governed by the greater good of "putting the interests of patients first." This strategy personalizes Merck while again arguing that the company was motivated by a selfless wishing of good things for consumers.

The paragraph emphasis throughout the Open Letter hammers at key points. The syntax at the ends of the paragraphs simultaneously argues for the company's integrity and presents supporting evidence:

- "answer those questions in a straightforward way"

- "set the record straight"

- "gain more clinical evidence about the medicine"

- "acted promptly and made the decision to voluntarily withdraw VIOXX"

- "controlled clinical studies"

- "scientific discipline and transparency"

- "bring new medicines to patients who need them"

The verb phrases in the first four bullets reinforce the company's good moral character as they emphasize Merck's acting with integrity. The phrases in the fifth and sixth bullets underscore its good sense. The final bullet, of course, demonstrates the company's goodwill through its commitment to the audience's personal safety.

The net effect of this secondary narrative is synecdoche in which the personal voice of Gilmartin substitutes for the impersonal corporation. The speaker demonstrates *good sense* (commitment to scientific inquiry), *good moral character* (transparency, integrity, prompt and decisive action), and *goodwill* (commitment to the interests of patients first).

A second open letter, "For 100 years, patients first" (Gilmartin, 2004b), tries to demonstrate the same good sense, good moral character, and goodwill (see Appendix B). The company's "challenging mission" means "the responsibility to conduct rigorous scientific investigation and maintain high standards of corporate behavior."

In fact, an outline of this open letter almost suggests the writer composed it with Aristotle's (n.d.) *Rhetoric* as a guide. Paragraphs 2 and 3 describe Merck's good sense as it studies its medicines "both before and after [they] are approved by regulatory authorities." Data are analyzed and made public "in scientific forums," and product labeling is "properly balanced with benefits and risks." Paragraphs 4 and 5 describe Merck's commitment to business and scientific ethical standards and its recognition as "one of the world's most ethical companies." Paragraphs 6 and 7 describe Merck's goodwill by highlighting its history of producing "life-saving benefits for countless patients." Asked to analyze this open letter's argument, students will have little difficulty seeing how it follows Aristotle's principles.

Students can also be shown how in this open letter, the writer's good sense is manifest in the straightforward syntax of active voice verbs and declarative independent clauses: "we know," "We extensively study," "we promptly disclose," "we quickly analyze, explore, and conduct," "We strive," and "We believe." His good sense is also demonstrated by the narration of scientific studies and the careful balance of "when" clauses with their corresponding actions. This use of anaphora creates a sense of building evidence; whereas anaphora is often used for creating a sense of rising emotion, here it has the opposite effect: creating a tone of rational response.

The speaker's good moral character asserted in paragraph 4 is based on ethical standards that are "at the heart of how we do business." Students might be asked to consider how this expression plays on "heart" both as a central focus but also as the traditional source of caring in a sentient being. Again, as in the first open letter, the effect is synecdoche that personalizes the corporation.

The goodwill of the speaker (and of Merck) is first expressed through an abstraction in paragraph 6, the "life-saving benefits for countless patients in numerous therapeutic areas." However, that description is followed by a concrete recounting of research into diabetes, obesity, Alzheimer's disease, and cancer, thus appealing to the readers' sense of personal safety, as Aristotle suggests. The recitation of attempts to combat these diseases recalls Aristotle's statement that people will face danger calmly "if they have means to deal with it." The writer reminds the reader that Merck represents those means.

THE CORPORATE VOICE

The rhetorical strategies employed in the construction of Merck's secondary narrative of the VIOXX crisis illustrate its fundamental conflict. Aristotle specifically mentions two means to garner the audience's trust: matters of money and of personal safety. Merck's business is predicated not just on making money but on providing people the means to deal with dangerous, life-threatening diseases. It should, as a result, have a huge reservoir of goodwill with the public. However, because it is so inextricably bound up with profit, with a health care industry whose costs often bewilder patients, and with complex scientific research, it is cast in the primary narrative as an intimidator. Its reservoir of goodwill is countered by the public's feelings of helplessness when faced not only with illness but also with medical bills. As Aristotle says, "fear is caused by whatever we feel has great power of destroying or of harming us in ways that tend to cause great pain" (p. 1382b). The synecdoche of the personalized, concerned, caring voice in the open letters highlighted here is evidence of Merck's awareness of and response to this fundamental contradiction in its relationship with the public.

The synecdoche goes deeper than the personalized speaker and the corporation, however. The primary narrative presented in the media suggested that VIOXX itself was emblematic of its parent company. The drug appeared promising not only in the treatment of severe pain but also potentially in the treatment of Alzheimer's disease, colon cancer, and prostate cancer. However, its true nature was revealed when it was found to cause a higher than expected rate of heart attacks and strokes. Merck's true nature was subsequently revealed, according to the primary narrative, when it sought to suppress damaging study results and to continue marketing the drug despite the clinical warnings. The secondary narrative presented by Merck counters by arguing not the events but their interpretation: The events surrounding VIOXX demonstrate Merck's commitment to careful scientific inquiry and follow up, its morality in the way it treated the results of that inquiry, and therefore Merck's true nature: service to "patients first." Thus in Merck's secondary narrative, VIOXX led to a crisis that allowed the corporation to demonstrate its true nature: a responsible corporate citizen imbued with good sense, the highest moral character, and the utmost goodwill toward consumers.

One narrative thus recounts how a corporation acted responsibly when it received conclusive evidence that its product had the potential to harm those it was intended to help. The other narrative describes a corporation that was aware of potentially lethal side effects of its product almost from its inception, that sought to silence critics and minimize or hide damaging research data, and that was therefore responsible for the deaths or injuries to the very patients it publicly vowed to help. In one narrative, the ethos of responsibility represents Merck's culpability. In the other, the ethos of responsibility represents Merck's prompt reaction to danger. The litigation that resulted from this crisis was largely a contest between these two narratives.

Students of business communications who reflect on this crisis are able to understand how the messages crafted by Merck exist in a complex rhetorical environment and how the writer(s) must rely on audience analysis, clarity of purpose, and applied principles of persuasive credibility. Students can also be shown how strategies to which they have been introduced, such as active voice, confident tone, direct syntax, and emphasis in sentences and paragraphs, support those persuasive principles. The Merck open letters responding to the VIOXX crisis offer students a microcosm of their business communications course and demonstrate that their course material is relevant, applicable, and dynamic.

REFERENCES

Aristotle. (n.d.). *Rhetoric*. (W. Rhys Roberts, Trans.). Retrieved June 6, 2007, from http://www2.iastate.edu/~honeyl/ Rhetoric.

Bovée, C., & Thill, J. (2006). *Business communication essentials* (2nd ed.). Upper Saddle River, NJ: Prentice Hall.

Coombs, W.T. (2004). Impact of past crises on current crisis communication: Insights from situational crisis communication theory. *Journal of Business Communication, 41*, pp.265-290.

Corbett, E. P. J. (1990). *Classical rhetoric for the modern student* (3rd ed.), New York: Oxford University Press.

Gilmartin, R. V. (2004a, November 11). Open letter from Merck. Retrieved June 6, 2007, from http://www.merck.com/newsroom/vioxx/pdf/An_Open_Letter_From_Merck.pdf.

Gilmartin, R. V. (2004b, November 12). For 100 years, patients first. Retrieved June 6, 2007, from http://www.merck.com/newsroom/vioxx/pdf/For_100_years_patients_first.pdf.

Gilmartin, R. V. (2004c, November 18). Summary of prepared testimony. Retrieved March 24, 2005, from http://www.merck.com/newsroom/vioxx_withdrawal/11182004.html.

Guffey, M. E. (2003). *Business communication: Process and product* (4th ed.). Mason, OH: Thomson South-Western.

Hart, P. (1993). Symbols, rituals, and power: The lost dimensions of crisis management. *Journal of Contingencies and Crisis Management, 1,* pp. 36-50.

Hay, C.(1995). Rethinking crisis: Narratives of the New Right and constructions of crisis. *Rethinking Marxism, 8,* pp. 60-76.

Juni, P., Nartey, L., Reichenbach, S., Sterchi, R., Dieppe, P. A., & Egger, M. (2004). Risk of cardiovascular events and rofecoxib: Cumulative meta-analysis. *The Lancet, 364,* pp. 2021-2029.

Locker, K., & Kaczmarek, S. K. (2007). *Business communication: Building critical skills* (3rd ed.). Boston: McGraw-Hill/Irwin.

Mathews, A. W., & Martinez, B. (2004, November 1). Warning signs: E-mails suggest Merck knew Vioxx's dangers at early stage. *Wall Street Journal,* p. A1.

Ober, S. (2006). *Contemporary business communication* (6th ed.). Boston: Houghton Mifflin.

Tenkasi, R. V., & Boland, R. J. (1993). Locating meaning making in organizational learning: The narrative basis of cognition. In R. W. Woodman & W. A. Pasmore (Eds.), *Research in organizational change and development* (Vol. 7, pp. 77-103). Greenwich, CT: JAI.

Venette, S. J., Sellnow, T. L., & Lang, P. A. (2003). Metanarration's role in restructuring perceptions of crisis: NHTSA's failure in the Ford-Firestone crisis. *Journal of Business Communication, 40*, pp. 219-237.

Vioxx, the implosion of Merck, and aftershocks at the FDA. (2004, December 4). *The Lancet, 364*, 1995-1996.

APPENDIX A
Text of "An Open Letter from Merck"

An Open Letter from Merck

By Raymond V. Gilmartin
Chairman, President, and CEO

In the weeks since Merck announced our decision to voluntarily recall VIOXX® (rofecoxib) on September 30, questions have been raised about events and business practices surrounding VIOXX. We have tried to answer those questions in a straightforward way.

However, incomplete and sometimes inaccurate information has been presented by others about Merck's scientific integrity and our commitment to ensuring patient safety. I want to take this opportunity to set the record straight.

Our consistent and rigorous adherence to scientific investigation, transparency and integrity is borne out by the fact that:

We extensively studied VIOXX before seeking regulatory approval to market it.

We promptly disclosed the clinical data about VIOXX.

When questions arose, **we took additional steps, including conducting further prospective, controlled studies** to gain more clinical information about the medicine.

When information from these additional prospective, controlled trials became available **we acted promptly** and made the decision to voluntarily withdraw VIOXX.

We believe that a complete review of the facts will demonstrate Merck's conduct with respect to VIOXX shows both an ongoing commitment to study VIOXX and prompt and decisive action in response to data from prospective, controlled clinical studies.

These actions are consistent with putting the interests of patients first, as well as with faithful adherence to the best principles of scientific discipline and transparency.

Throughout our history, it is those fundamental priorities that have enabled us to bring new medicines to patients who need them.

We will continue to address the facts through letters like this one in the days ahead.

In the meantime, further information on the facts about the withdrawal of VIOXX is available at merck.com.

APPENDIX B
Text of "For 100 years, patients first"

For 100 years, patients first.

By Raymond V. Gilmartin
Chairman, President, and CEO

At Merck, we know that the challenging mission of discovering, developing, and manufacturing new medicines and vaccines brings with it the responsibility to conduct rigorous scientific investigation and maintain high standards of corporate behavior.

We extensively study our medicines both before and after the medicines are approved by regulatory authorities. When we obtain data from our clinical studies, we promptly disclose them. When questions arise about our medicines, we quickly analyze the available data, explore their meaning within the company and in scientific forums, and conduct further studies as warranted.

We strive to ensure that our product communications are properly balanced with benefits and risks.

Our ethical standards are the foundation of our company. We strive to ensure that every Merck employee knows that meeting high ethical standards is at the heart of how we do business. We have clear policies and formal training programs to reinforce these standards.

The value we place on business and scientific ethics is among the reasons why Merck has consistently been recognized as one of the world's most ethical companies.

For more than 100 years, Merck's adherence to these high standards has produced life-saving benefits for countless patients in numerous therapeutic areas. And that longstanding record of achievement continues as our scientists conduct research in areas such as diabetes, obesity, Alzheimer's disease, and cancer.

We believe that our actions surrounding VIOXX® (rofecoxib) are consistent with putting the interests of patients first, as well as a faithful adherence to the principles of scientific discipline and disclosure. Further information about Merck, our values and our actions concerning VIOXX is available at merck.com.

Understanding and Reducing the Knowledge Effect Implications for Writers

John Hayes and Diana Bajzek

CONSIDER AS YOU ARE READING:

Writing does not exist in a vacuum, yet how often do we write as though it does, without consideration of who will read it and what knowledge, values, and experiences they bring? As writers, we need to think not only about what we want to say, but how the cultural and social backgrounds of our readers will contribute to the final shaping of the message. Stepping into the readers' shoes—or, more appropriately, into their minds, memories, culture—may be one of the more significant challenges for writers. In this article, Hayes and Bajzek report on two studies which analyze "the knowledge effect"— the assumption that readers share similar knowledge, memories, and experiences with writers. This reading may advance us towards the course goal of a deeper understanding of how to sculpt an argument for a particular audience.

1. *What did the first study the authors conducted reveal about the likelihood that writers will accurately predict what their audiences know?*

2. *Based on what these authors propose, what are some steps you might take to reduce "the knowledge effect" when you write your next argument?*

3. *Do you agree with the authors' claim that "the knowledge effect" can inhibit clear communication? Why or why not?*

Effective writers and speakers must recognize the knowledge, attitudes, biases, and beliefs that they share with the audience, the "common ground," and just as important, they must recognize what is not shared. If we underestimate audience knowledge, we may be seen as "talking down." If we overestimate audience knowledge, we may confuse the audience. If we incorrectly assume that we share an attitude or belief with the audience, we may fail to provide needed backing for our arguments. Clark (1992) has discussed the importance of understanding common ground in conversation. Understanding common ground is even more critical in writing. If misunderstandings occur in conversation, a question or a blank look can lead the conversational partners to repair the misunderstanding. However, in writing, the reader cannot signal the writer. As a result, writers' misjudgments about the common ground are not easily fixed.

Although it is important that writers have an accurate understanding of the ground they share with their readers, that understanding is not always easy to achieve. Unfortunately, people have a strong tendency to believe that other people are like themselves in knowledge, attitude, and behavior—a tendency that leads them to overestimate, and sometimes strongly overestimate, the ground they share with others. This tendency, called "the false consensus effect," has be extensively studied by social psychologists (for reviews, see Marks & Miller, 1987; Mullen et al., 1985).

Ross, Greene, and House (1977) performed the classic study of the "false consensus effect." In their study, participants were asked to wear a sandwich board sign around campus that said "REPENT." Half of the participants agreed to wear the sandwich board and half refused. Both groups were then asked, "What percentage of your peers do you estimate would be willing to carry the sandwich board around campus?" (p. 290). Those who agreed to wear the sign estimated that 63.5% would wear the sign and 36.5% would refuse. In contrast, those who refused to carry the sign estimated that 23.3% would wear the sign and that 76.6% would refuse. Thus, whichever choice they made, participants tended to estimate that peers would behave as they did. This same phenomenon has been observed in a variety of contexts in which participants predict the opinions, attitudes, and tastes of other people (Marks & Miller, 1987). For example, participants tend to predict that other people will answer as they themselves would if asked questions such as, "Are schools doing a good job?" "Are you an optimist?" or "Do you prefer spicy foods?" In a meta-analysis of 155 studies, Mullen et al. (1985), found that the false consensus effect was reliably observed in a wide variety of studies.

Nickerson, Baddeley, and Freeman (1987) extended the false consensus effect paradigm to include factual knowledge. In the their study, college students were first presented with factual questions about history and sports and asked to estimate for each question the percentage of college students who correctly answered the question. Next, the respondents were asked to answer the questions themselves. The predictions were then compared to norms for college students' answers to these questions. The researchers found that if participants knew the answer to a question, they significantly overestimated the percentage of students who could answer the question correctly. However, if they did not know the answer, they neither systematically overestimated nor underestimated the correct proportions.

Other studies have also demonstrated the effect of people's knowledge on their predictions of other's knowledge and performance (reflecting procedural knowledge). Hinds (1999) showed that individuals who were experienced in performing an assembly task made significantly lower estimates of the time it would take a novice to complete the task than did individuals who had performed the assembly task just once. Bromme, Rambow, and Nuckles (2001) found that laypeople overestimated others' knowledge of concepts if they knew the concepts themselves but did not overestimate others' knowledge of concepts that they did not know themselves.

Hayes, Schriver, Spilka, and Blaustein (1986), described in Hayes (1989), found that providing writers with new topic knowledge immediately reduced their ability to detect parts of an unclear text that would confuse readers who did not have this new knowledge. In the Hayes et al. (1986) study, 88 undergraduates were asked to read two pairs of texts. Each pair consisted of a clear text and an unclear version of the same text. The task was to underline those parts of the texts that they believed would confuse other readers like themselves who were not knowledgeable about the topics. In half the cases, participants read the unclear version before the clear one. In the other half, they read the clear version first. Reading the clear version first provided participants with knowledge that helped them to understand confusing passages in the unclear version. When participants read the clear version first, they identified 40% fewer parts of the unclear text that would be confusing than if they had read the unclear text first. This difference was significant ($p < .001$). It appeared that participants' ability to understand the unclear text, resulting from their special knowledge, led them to believe that other people would also understand the text. Hayes et al. (1986) called this phenomenon the "knowledge effect." The knowledge effect is similar to what Camerer, Loewenstein, and Weber (1989) called "the curse of knowledge," a difficulty that people have in ignoring knowledge that they have but others do not. The knowledge effect may also be seen as a special case of the false consensus effect in which a person's knowledge biases their judgment of another's knowledge.

Because the knowledge effect can lead to problems for writers, it would be useful to have procedures for reducing the effect. Two different theoretical accounts of the knowledge effect suggest different remedial procedures. Nickerson (1999) has proposed that we estimate another person's knowledge as follows:

1. Start with a model of one's own knowledge, Model 1.

2. Use information about the other person (e.g., their age or interests) to adjust Model 1 to produce Model 2, an initial model of the other's knowledge.

3. Adjust Model 2 on an ongoing basis according to new information to produce a current model of the other's knowledge.

As Nickerson (1999) notes, this model can be seen as a special case of Tversky and Kahneman's (1974) general reasoning heuristic of anchoring and adjustment. Here, one's own knowledge is the anchor, and knowledge about the other person is used for adjustment. It has been widely observed that when people use the anchoring and adjustment heuristic, they typically do not adjust enough. This would lead people to estimate that other's knowledge is more similar to their own than it actually is. This account of the knowledge effect would lead us to look for ways to improve people's ability to adjust the representation of their own knowledge so that it better fits the audience.

Another model, discussed by Hinds (1999), is based on the availability heuristic, another of Tversky and Kahneman's (1973) general reasoning heuristics. According to this heuristic, people base their judgments on their most readily available memories. Hinds (1999) suggests that because experts learned their skills long ago, their memory of their own novice experience will not be as readily available to them as their current experience when they make predictions about novices. This will lead them to overestimate the procedural knowledge of novices. This account of the knowledge effect would lead us to look for ways to help knowledgeable people to recall their own experiences as novices.

Hinds (1999) tested this notion by prompting experts to recall their own learning experiences with the tasks being tested and to use that information in making their estimates of novice performance. Although this manipulation failed to produce significant improvements in estimates, other variations of this approach might succeed.

In the present studies, we explored the hypothesis that providing participants with feedback about the accuracy of their judgments would help them to adjust their judgments so they better represented others' knowledge. To do this, we first chose a kind of knowledge prediction that is important for writing: the prediction of vocabulary knowledge. In Study 1, we showed that the knowledge effect was strong when anticipating the technical terms another would likely know. Then in Study 2, we demonstrated that providing participants with feedback about the accuracy of their judgments led them to improve their predictions of others' knowledge.

STUDY 1

Method

Participants. Twenty undergraduate students from a private mid-Atlantic university were selected for the study and were given course credit for their participation.

Materials. Two lists of words were selected from Dale and O'Rourke's (1981) *The Living Word Vocabulary: A National Vocabulary Inventory* that tabulated the percentage of individuals in various populations in the United States (e.g., college freshmen, college graduates) who correctly identified the meaning of each word. The first list consisted of 33 terms for which Dale and O'Rourke provided knowledge norms for college freshmen. This list was called the "freshman list." The second list consisted of 52 terms for which Dale and O'Rourke provided knowledge norms for college graduates. This list was called the "graduate list."

Dale and O'Rourke's criterion for knowing a word was that the participant was able to choose the most appropriate definition of that word from a set of three. Of course, some participants who did not know the word could have chosen the correct definition by chance. Therefore, to obtain better estimates of the percentage of individuals who actually knew the meaning of a term, we adjusted Dale and O'Rourke's data to account for guessing.[1]

Procedure. The study had two phases. In the first phase, participants were presented with the two lists of technical terms, drawn from a variety of scientific and technical fields. For the freshman list, participants were asked to estimate, on a scale from 0 to 100, the percentage of American college freshmen who knew the meaning of each term. For the graduate list, participants were asked to estimate the percentage of college graduates who knew the meaning of each term. For both lists, participants made their estimates by circling numbers on a test form such as that shown in Figure 1.

In the second phase of the study, participants were given these same two lists of words again and asked to rate their own familiarity with the terms on a 4-point scale: (1) *not at all familiar,* (2) *I've heard of it,* (3) *I think I know it,* (4) *I'm sure I know it* (see Figure 2).

Analysis. We compared each participant's estimate of the percentage of people who would know a word, to Dale and O'Rourke's (1981) adjusted data. This provided a measure of overestimation or underestimation of each word by each participant. We then averaged these measures for each participant for each list (freshman and graduate) and for each of the four knowledge categories (*not at all familiar, I've heard of it, I think I know it, I'm sure I know it*). Thus, we obtained eight estimates of overestimation or underestimation for each participant. This allowed us to determine how participants' own knowledge of terms was related to their overestimation or underestimation of college freshmen's and college graduates' knowledge of those terms.

Figure 1

Test Form on Which Participants Estimated Audience Knowledge of Technical Terms

Indicate the percent of first year college students you believe understand this word.

Amalgam	0	10	20	30	40	50	60	70	80	90	100
Amorphous	0	10	20	30	40	50	60	70	80	90	100
Apogee	0	10	20	30	40	50	60	70	80	90	100
Arboreal	0	10	20	30	40	50	60	70	80	90	100
Aurora Borealis	0	10	20	30	40	50	60	70	80	90	100
Boron	0	10	20	30	40	50	60	70	80	90	100
Calorimeter	0	10	20	30	40	50	60	70	80	90	100
Cardinal number	0	10	20	30	40	50	60	70	80	90	100
Centripital	0	10	20	30	40	50	60	70	80	90	100
Cephalic	0	10	20	30	40	50	60	70	80	90	100
Corollary	0	10	20	30	40	50	60	70	80	90	100
Diffract	0	10	20	30	40	50	60	70	80	90	100

Elucidate	0	10	20	30	40	50	60	70	80	90	100
Emulsion	0	10	20	30	40	50	60	70	80	90	100
Finite	0	10	20	30	40	50	60	70	80	90	100
Geodesic	0	10	20	30	40	50	60	70	80	90	100
Igneous	0	10	20	30	40	50	60	70	80	90	100
Kinetic	0	10	20	30	40	50	60	70	80	90	100
Lithium	0	10	20	30	40	50	60	70	80	90	100
Mach Number	0	10	20	30	40	50	60	70	80	90	100

Figure 2

Test Form on Which Participants Estimated Their Own Knowledge of Technical Terms

Indicate how familiar you are with each of these words

Amalgam	not at all	I've heard it	I think I know it	I'm sure I know it
Amorphous	not at all	I've heard it	I think I know it	I'm sure I know it
Apogee	not at all	I've heard it	I think I know it	I'm sure I know it
Arboreal	not at all	I've heard it	I think I know it	I'm sure I know it
Aurora Borealis	not at all	I've heard it	I think I know it	I'm sure I know it
Boron	not at all	I've heard it	I think I know it	I'm sure I know it
Calorimeter	not at all	I've heard it	I think I know it	I'm sure I know it
Cardinal number	not at all	I've heard it	I think I know it	I'm sure I know it
Centripital	not at all	I've heard it	I think I know it	I'm sure I know it

Cephalic	not at all	I've heard it	I think I know it	I'm sure I know it
Corollary	not at all	I've heard it	I think I know it	I'm sure I know it
Diffract	not at all	I've heard it	I think I know it	I'm sure I know it
Elucidate	not at all	I've heard it	I think I know it	I'm sure I know it
Emulsion	not at all	I've heard it	I think I know it	I'm sure I know it
Finite	not at all	I've heard it	I think I know it	I'm sure I know it
Geodesic	not at all	I've heard it	I think I know it	I'm sure I know it
Igneous	not at all	I've heard it	I think I know it	I'm sure I know it
Kinetic	not at all	I've heard it	I think I know it	I'm sure I know it
Lithium	not at all	I've heard it	I think I know it	I'm sure I know it
Mach Number	not at all	I've heard it	I think I know it	I'm sure I know it

Results

Figure 3 shows the effect of participants' knowledge of words on their estimates of the percentage of college freshmen and college graduates who know the terms. The effect of participants' knowledge was significant by repeated measures ANOVA ($F = 19.036$; $df = 3, 19$; $p < .001$). The difference between the estimates for freshmen and graduates was also significant ($F = 93.503$; $df = 1, 19$; $p < .001$). However, the interaction between these factors was not significant.

Figure 3

Percent of Overestimation of College Freshmen's and College Graduate's Knowledge of Technical Terms as Influenced by the Judge's Own Knowledge

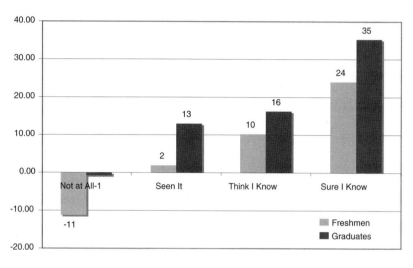

Discussion

As one would expect, participants attributed more vocabulary knowledge to college graduates than to college freshmen. On average, they estimated that the percentage of college graduates who knew the terms was about 10 percentage points higher than the percentage of college freshmen who knew them. This result is consistent with Nickerson's (1999) model, because it indicates that the participants were adjusting their estimates differently and appropriately for the two populations.

More important, participants' knowledge of a term has a very strong influence on their predictions of college freshmen's and college graduate's knowledge of that term. If participants were sure that they knew a term, their estimates, both for freshmen and for graduates, were about 35% higher than if they were not at all familiar with the term. This overestimation is quite substantial. For example, if only one in three college graduates actually knew a term, participants in this study who were sure they knew the term would have estimated that two in three knew it.

STUDY 2

Study 1 demonstrated that participants' knowledge of technical terms led them to overestimate others' knowledge of those terms. As we have suggested, this tendency to overestimate constitutes a problem for experts who have to write to audiences who do not share their expertise. In an effort to alleviate this problem, we created an online tutor (described below) designed to help writers improve their predictions of people's knowledge of technical terms. The tutor presented a sequence of technical terms, asked the student to guess the percentage of people who knew each term, and then provided feedback based on national norms. Study 2 was designed to evaluate the effectiveness of this tutor.

Our hypotheses were the following:

1. The tutor will improve participants' estimates of other peoples' word knowledge.

2. The improvement will be greatest for terms with which the participant is most familiar.

Method

Participants. Twenty undergraduates in a private mid-Atlantic university were given course credit for their participation.

Tutor interface. The interface, shown in Figure 4, was divided into six areas. Instructions to the participants were presented in the upper left. These instructions were present throughout Study 2. Blocks of five technical terms were presented in the lower left; alternative answers from which the participant chose one, in the lower middle; and feedback about each choice, in the lower right. Feedback about the accuracy of the participant's judgments over blocks of five words was presented in numerical form in the upper right and in graphical form in the middle right. The average of the participants' scores was indicated by the vertical bar labeled *you* and the average of the correct answers was indicated by the vertical bar labeled *college grads*.

Materials. The materials were the 52 technical terms from the graduate list used in Experiment 1 plus 13 new technical terms for which Dale and O'Rourke (1981) provided knowledge norms for college graduates.

Figure 4
The Tutor Interface

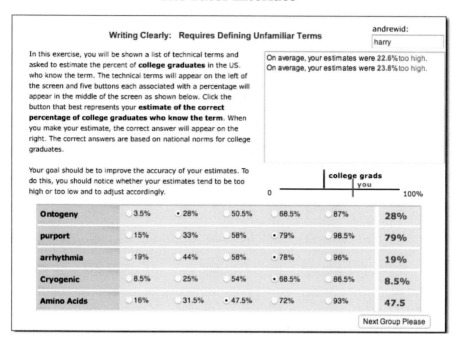

Procedure. Participants were instructed that they were in a learning study and that their task was to try to improve their estimates of the proportion of college graduates who knew specific technical terms. Words were presented in 13 blocks of five words. Figure 4 shows a typical block. The order of the words was randomized separately for each participant. For each word, participants chose one of five alternatives to indicate their estimate. The first percentage was between 0% and 20%; the second, between 20% and 40%; and so on. One of the five percentages was the correct one; the other four were randomly chosen within the appropriate percentage range.

The first group of five words was a pretest and the last group of five words was a posttest. No feedback was provided for these trials. The other 11 blocks were training blocks in which feedback was provided. In the training trials, when the participant chose a percentage, the correct percentage was shown on the right. When the participant finished a block of five words, the average percentage of overestimation or underestimation for the block was shown in the upper right and a graph showing the same information was shown in the middle right (see Figure 4).

Analysis

We hypothesized that the tutor would improve participants' estimates of others'word knowledge. There are two ways in which the tutor could cause improvement. First, the average estimation error might be reduced, and second, the estimates might become more consistent (i.e., they might be clustered more closely together).

We used two measures to evaluate the changes in each participant's estimates. First, we measured each participant's average overestimation. The average overestimation indicates how far the center of the distribution of estimates is from the correct value. In archery, a high average overestimation could mean that most of the arrows passed high over the target. Second, we measured the standard deviation of the estimation errors for each participant. The standard deviation of the errors measures the consistency of the participant's estimates. In archery, consistency, indicated by a low standard deviation, would mean that the arrows were clustered closely together. If the average overestimation was zero and the standard deviation was small, then the arrows would be clustered closely around the bull's eye. Thus, a combination of zero average overestimation and zero standard deviation is best.

We carried out two analyses using these measures. In our first analysis, we compared the average overestimation and the standard deviation of errors in the pretest (the first five trails) with the same measures in the posttest (the last five trials). This provided a test of our first hypothesis that the tutor will improve participants' estimation error. Because there were only five words in the pretest and in the posttest, there were not enough data to test the second hypothesis that the reduction in error will be greater if the participant's knowledge of the terms is greater. Therefore, we performed a second analysis in which we compared estimation errors in the first half (first 28) of the training trials with estimation errors in the second half (last 27) of the training trials. The amount of data available for this analysis is sufficient to differentiate the four knowledge categories. However, we cannot expect this analysis, which measures performance during training, to provide as sensitive a measure of the average reduction in error as does the first analysis, which compares performance before and after training.

Results

Average overestimation and standard deviation of errors for the pretest and posttests are shown in Table 1.

The difference between pretest and posttest scores in average overestimation was significant by one-tailed matched t test ($t = 2.589$, $df = 18^2$, $p < .01$).

Table 1

Pretest and Posttest Scores for Average Overestimation and Standard Deviation of Errors

	Average Overestimation	Standard Deviation of Errors
Pretest	12.35	25.95
Posttest	−1.95	27.95

Table 2

Average Overestimation in the First and Second Half of Training Trials for Four Levels of Participant Knowledge

	Participant Knowledge of Word			
	Not at All	Heard It	Think I Know	Sure I Know
First half	−4.05	−1.74	9.86	20.13
Last half	−6.91	−4.85	−0.15	10.45

The difference in the standard deviation of errors between the pretest and the posttest was not significant.

As shown in Table 2, the average overestimation in the second half of trials was significantly less than in the first half by repeated measures ANOVA ($F = 10.904$; $df = 1$, 16^3; $p = .004$). The effect of participant knowledge on average overestimation was also significant ($F = 18.561$; $df = 3$, 16; $p < .001$). Indeed, when the first half and the second half of the training trials were analyzed separately, the effect of participant knowledge was significant both for the first half ($F = 39.567$; $df = 3$, 15; $p < .001$) and for the second half ($F = 12.615$; $df = 3$, 15; $p < .003$). Contrary to our second hypothesis that improvement would be greatest for the terms that participants knew best, the interaction between the order of trials and participant knowledge was not significant. That is, participants' improvement was not significantly greater for terms they knew well than for terms that they knew less well.

There were no significant effects of these variables on the standard deviation of errors measured during the training trials.

Discussion

The results of both analyses indicate that experience with the tutor significantly and substantially reduced participants' tendency to overestimate others' knowledge of technical terms. Average error declined from 12% in the pretest to −2% in the posttest.

Similarly, average error (across all knowledge categories) declined from 6% in the first half of training trials to about 0% in the last half. The differences between the results may reflect differences in the number of training trials between first and second observation in the two cases (e.g., 55 training trials between pretest and posttest but only half that number on average between first half and second half of the training trials).

Participants' answers to posttest questions were consistent with the results described above. When participants were asked if anything surprised them about their experience with the tutor, the most common answer was that they were surprised that so few people knew terms that they assumed were common knowledge. When asked if they developed a strategy for giving estimates, several participants said that they estimated how many people knew a word as they had done before but then lowered their estimate to create an answer more consistent with the feedback. They appeared to have learned that their initial adjustment was not large enough. This suggests that these participants were changing their adjustments but not their anchors, consistent with Nickerson's (1999) model.

Both analyses also indicate that the standard deviation of the estimation errors was not reduced by the experience with the tutor. That is, the spread of estimates was not changed. For example, a participant whose estimates had ranged, say, from 10% to 50% overestimation before training now ranged from 20% underestimation to 20% overestimation.

The second analysis indicates that participants' knowledge of terms remained an important determinant of overestimation in both the first and the second half of the training trials.

The lack of a significant interaction between participants' knowledge and order of trials does not provide support for our second hypothesis that improvements would be greatest for terms with which the participant is most familiar. However, numerical values in Table 3 suggest that training may yield greater improvement for terms more familiar to the participant. A study involving more extensive training, pretest and posttests with more items, or both might confirm our second hypothesis.

Experience in using the tutor suggested some changes that might make the tutor more effective. First, we found that providing feedback about performance over blocks of five words led a few participants to adopt the following strategy. If these participants received feedback that they had overestimated (or underestimated) the first few words of a block, they would purposely underestimate (or overestimate) the remaining words in the block to obtain a better score for the whole block. Eliminating scoring by blocks would make it less likely that participants would use strategies of this sort.

Second, we observed that some of the participants who benefited most from the tutor adapted the strategy of asking themselves where they had encountered the word. If they read it in popular literature or heard it on TV, then they increased their estimates. If they had only heard it in technical contexts, then they reduced them. Explicitly including this heuristic in the tutor instructions might improve its effectiveness.

Conclusion

We have reviewed four studies, all of which have provided solid evidence for the existence of the knowledge effect (Bromme et al., 2001; Hayes et al., 1986; Hinds, 1999; Nickerson et al., 1987) and now we have added a fifth (Study 1). At this point, the existence of the knowledge effect seems firmly established. It can be viewed as a special case of the false consensus effect, which is even more firmly established.

Our studies provide two points of support for Nickerson's model of the knowledge effect. First, participants adjusted their judgments differently and appropriately for audiences with different educational levels. Second, participants reported that they modified their initial estimates about audience knowledge on the basis of feedback about the audience. Both of these observations would be predicted by the Nickerson model.

The knowledge effect can create serious problems for writers. If a writer does not realize that the words such as *torque* and *maser* are not in the audience's vocabulary, readers are sure to be confused. Therefore, our most important result is that the knowledge effect can be reduced, as Study 2 showed. Before this result can produce practical benefits, however, we need to answer several questions. Will the reduction persist, and will it transfer to the participants' writing? Can methods be developed to reduce the knowledge effect in areas other than vocabulary such as factual or procedural knowledge? Answering these questions could lead to more effective writing instruction.

ENDNOTES

1 To adjust Dale and O'Rourke's (1981) results, we applied the following formula: $C = K + (1-K)*1/3$. C is the percentage of participants who checked the correct answers, and K is the number of participants who actually knew the correct answer.

2   One participant failed to take the posttest.

3   Three participants had incomplete data.

REFERENCES

Bromme, R., Rambow, R., & Nuckles, M. (2001). Expertise and estimating what other people know: The influence of professional experience and the type of knowledge. *Journal of Experimental Psychology: Applied, 7*(4), 317-330.

Camerer, C., Loewenstein, G., & Weber, G. (1989). The curse of knowledge in economic settings: An experimental analysis. *Journal of Political Economy, 97*(5), 1232-1254.

Clark, H. H. (1992). *Arenas of language use.* Chicago: University of Chicago Press.

Dale, E., & O'Rourke, J. (1981). *The living word vocabulary.* Chicago: World Book-Childcraft International.

Hayes, J. R. (1989). Writing research: The analysis of a very complex task. In D. Klahr & K. Kotovsky (Eds.), *Complex information processing: The impact of Herbert A. Simon* (pp. 209-234). Hillsdale, NJ: Lawrence Erlbaum.

Hayes, J. R., Schriver, K. A., Spilka, R., & Blaustein, A. (1986, April). *If it's clear to me, it must be clear to them: How knowledge makes it difficult to judge.* Paper presented at the American Educational Research Association, San Francisco, CA.

Hinds, P. J. (1999). The curse of expertise: The effects of expertise and debiasing methods on prediction of novice performance. *Journal of Experimental Psychology: Applied, 5*(2), 205-221.

Marks, G., & Miller, N. (1987). Ten years of research on the false-consensus effect: An empirical and theoretical overview. *Psychological Bulletin, 102*(1), 72-90.

Mullen, B., Atkins, J. L., Champion, D. S., Edwards, C., Hardy, D., Story, J. E., et al. (1985). The false consensus effect: A meta-analysis of 155 hypothesis tests. *Journal of Experimental and Social Psychology, 21*, 262-282.

Nickerson, R. S. (1999). How we know—and sometimes misjudge—what others know: Imputing one's own knowledge to others. *Psychological Bulletin, 125*(6), 737-759.

Nickerson, R. S., Baddeley, A., & Freeman, B. (1987). Are people's estimates of what other people know influenced by what they themselves know? *Acta Psychologica, 64*, 245-259.

Ross, L., Greene, D., & House, P. (1977). The "false consensus effect": An egocentric bias in social perception and attribution processes. *Journal of Experimental and Social Psychology, 13*(3), 279-301.

Tversky, A., & Kahneman, D. (1973). Availability: A heuristic for judging frequency and probability. *Cognitive Psychology, 5*, 207-232.

Tversky, A., & Kahneman, D. (1974, September 27). Judgment under uncertainty: Heuristics and biases. *Science, 185*, 1124-1131.

Beyond Visual Rhetoric: Multimodal Rhetoric and Newspaper Comic Strips

Dale Jacobs

CONSIDER AS YOU ARE READING:

In 1996 a group of scholars, The New London Group, developed a theory of "multiliteracies," which tries to define how meaning is made not only by words on a page, but in other semiotic (sign) systems as well (such as music and other sound effects, facial expressions, visual stills, moving images, computer screens, etc.). Jacobs' article, originally published in the International Journal of Comic Art, *proposes an application of the New London Group's theories to the multimodal genre of comics. Jacobs' detailed look at the sign system used by comics gives students of rhetoric a systematic approach to analyzing the genre of comics. Jacobs mentions that even something as subtle as the spaces between the comic frames, the "gutters," contribute to the meaning of a comic. Moreover, Jacobs borrows from Aristotle's notion of the enthymeme—a claim whose central premise is shared (often unconsciously) by an audience— to show that readers of comics contribute to the creation of meaning. As writers, we need to think about what readers bring to any argument, whether visual or alphabetic.*

1. *How does the reader/viewer of an image contribute to its meaning? Can you think of an image which might mean something very different to people who come to it with different experiences?*

2. *A comic is most often a multimodal discourse: that is, it usually combines words and images. What other communications have you encountered, or created yourself, that are multimodal? Consider that multimodal communication can include still or moving images as well as audio.*

3. *Comment on Jacobs' claims that comics depend on "enthymemic reasoning" to create meaning. Do you agree? Why or why not?*

> *Just how visual images and visual forms in general can and do communicate propositions, just how the important ancillary concept of context is to be understood and how in practice context is to be interpreted and combined with the visual, and just how text and visuals (and sounds) interact to produce meaning are all questions which strike me as important.*

—J. Anthony Blair
"The Possibility and Actuality of Visual Arguments"

In order to think about how comics act as rhetorical artifacts and environments, we must consider questions other than simply how visual texts communicate. Rather, we must also think about how context affects the meanings that are derived from these texts, and how visuals interact with other semiotic modes such as the spatial, the gestural, and the audio. In pursuing these ideas, I want to introduce the concept of multimodality—how meaning is communicated in texts that combine multiple semiotic modes—as a way to think through these important questions. Building on the New London Groups's idea of design in multimodal texts, this essay lays out a theoretical framework of multimodal rhetoric and uses this theory to explore how newspaper comic strips function as multimodal texts. Through a small number of examples, I seek to illuminate the connections between multimodality, rhetoric, and comics, and to introduce a new theoretical framework for examining the rhetoric of comics.

THE QUESTION OF RHETORIC

As I discuss rhetoric and its relationship to multimodality, I will be considering two different, but related conceptions of the term. First, I will consider rhetoric broadly as purposeful human communication. Such a definition is in accord with scholars such as Sonja Foss, Karen Foss, and Robert Trapp who argue that rhetoric is "the uniquely human ability to use symbols to communicate with one another" (1985:11). In fact, J. Anthony Blair cites this definition in "The Rhetoric of Visual Arguments" (2004) before settling on a traditional definition of rhetoric that focuses on the act of persuasion. Rather than closing off this broader definition, however, I want to explore the ways in which rhetoric as a meaning making activity and rhetoric as persuasion can be put in productive dialogue. That is, let me consider the following question: How does the way we make meaning from texts—and in this case, especially multimodal texts—affect the ways in which we persuade with them and are persuaded by them?

In order to begin to think about how these two conceptions of rhetoric might interact, let me offer another definition of rhetoric. Charles Bazerman writes in *Shaping Written Knowledge,* "By rhetoric I mean most broadly the study of how people use language and other symbols to realize human goals and carry out human activities. Rhetoric is ultimately a practical study offering people greater control over their symbolic activity" (1986:6). Bu studying how we engage in symbolic activity such as reading newspaper comics and how we make meaning through such activity, we can also see how such texts can be used to persuade us and what the available means of persuasion within those comic strips might be. By defining rhetoric as both purposeful communication and as persuasion (one type of purposeful communication), we can consider how multimodal texts operate and how we engage with them as textual producers and consumers.

COMICS IN THEORY AND PRACTICE

Since the appearance of comic strips in the Sunday supplements of newspapers such as William Randolph Hearst's *New York Journal* and Joseph Pulitzer's *New York World* in the late 1890s, comics have endured as a medium in a variety of formats and with a vast array of rhetorical uses. Whether in the short form of a single panel or multiple panel strip, in the longer form of a standard comic book, or in the long form of a graphic novel, comics combine words and images in complex ways to achieve a variety of rhetorical ends, almost always within the commercial context of selling a product. In the case of newspaper comics, since their introduction in the 1890s, comics have been used as means to increase circulation. As Richard Marschall notes in the Introduction to *America's Great Comic-Strip Artists,* "In major cities, but especially in New York, newspapers were fighting mighty battles for readership. The circulation wars were waged with many weapons, including sensationalism, scandal, sex and exposé; women's features, children's pages, and quality fiction; color artwork and, ultimately, the comic strip" (1989: 12). As a fledgling medium, comics were used to draw readers to newspapers and to increase the circulation of individual newspapers.

In trying to increase the circulation of their respective newspapers, press barons such as Hearst and Pulitzer became "patrons for the new art of the comic strip as it was developing in their newspapers, granting cartoonists enormous freedom to experiment" (Marschall, 1989: 12). So intense was the competition and the resulting creative freedom granted to cartoonists as a result that the form of the newspaper comic strip as we know it today came into existence almost overnight. As Maurice Horn writes in the "Introduction" to *100 Years of American Newspaper Comics,* "In a matter of months a new cultural form was born, characterized by a narrative told in a sequence of pictures, a continuing cast of characters, the inclusion of dialogue and/or text within the picture frame, as well as by a dynamic method of story-telling that would compel the eye to travel forward from one panel to the next" (1996: 15-16). The basic multimodal elements that constitute comic strips as we know them today were established early in the history of the form; comics took advantage of the visual as a complex component of a multimodal rhetoric that could be used for multiple rhetorical purposes, including both entertaining and persuading readers and, most importantly from the publisher's perspective, selling newspapers. From the beginning, then, comics employed multiple modes of meaning making as a way to convey ideas to the audience.

As even casual readers of comics know, one element of comic strips that is unique to the medium is the concept of the gutter, the space between panels or conceptual gap that the reader must bridge in order to make sense of the sequence of panels. Through the manipulation of this gap, cartoonists can imply connections between events, people, or objects, speed up or slow down the readers' perception of time, work with or against audience expectation, and, in general, cause the reader to try to make connections between a set sequence of panels. The existence of the gutter in the comics medium increases the involvement of the audience in the creation of textual meaning, pushing them away from passive textual consumption to active textual engagement. For example, in the "Calvin and Hobbes" cartoon (originally published April 6, 1995) shown in **Fig. 1**, the gutters are used as a means of representing the passage of time and as a way to play with the expectations of the audience, to humorous effect. In panel 1, we see Calvin ask to get a drink of water; in panel 2 we see him hurrying (denoted visually by the dust he has kicked up in his wake and the angle of his hair) as his teacher has asked him to do. Finally, in panel 3, we see him at home, telling his mother that he prefers their water. This final panel is not what we expected as readers, either in terms of content (both the words spoken and the image of his home and his mother's reaction) or in terms of time elapsed between panels (the gap in time between panels 1 and 2 is presumably much shorter than the gap in time between panels 2 and 3). Of course, explaining how the gutters operate in this way deflates the humor and childish logic of the strip, but it does begin to get at how we make sense of the spaces between panels and the relation of panels to each other (a process of meaning making that Scott McCloud [1964: 63] calls "Closure") when we quickly scan the newspaper comics page. Though we usually think of newspaper comic strips in terms of humor such as this carton, narrative (as in "Mary Worth" or "Terry and the Pirates"), social/ political commentary (as in "Doonesbury" or "The Boondocks"), or some combination of these genres, the use of the gutter can be employed to virtually any rhetorical end.

Figure 1. Calvin and Hobbes by Bill Watterson

Despite their importance to both comic strips and long-form comics such as comic books and graphic novels, the existence of gutters is only one part of what defines comics, despite the right granted to the idea of sequence in Scott McCloud's often cited definition of comics. Argued through the medium of comics itself, McCloud's influential *Understanding Comics* acts as an extended argument for the possibilities inherent in the comics form. After an extended rumination on possible definitions of comics, he finally comes to see comics as "Juxtaposed pictorial and other images in deliberate sequence, intended to convey information and/or to produce an aesthetic response in the viewer." Or, in shortened form, McCloud simply defines comics as "sequential art" (1994: 9). One problem of such a definition, of course, is that it excludes single panel cartoons. More importantly, however, this definition downplays the interaction of words and images that make comics one of the best examples of multimodal texts. I bring up McCloud's definition not to quibble about the boundaries of the medium, but to show the dangers inherent in a definition that over-privileges the image and the idea of sequencing to the detriment of other important elements in the medium. Much more than simply "sequential art," comics are multimodal texts that serve as sites of imaginative interplay, means of communication, and places of rhetorical practice.

MULTIMODALITY AND DESIGN IN THEORY

Examining comics as multimodal texts not only pushes us to think about comics in more complex ways, but also pushes us to complicate our ideas of visual rhetoric by considering how multiple semiotic modes interact as a reader engages with the text. When we read comics, we engage with the progression of panels and make meaning from the gap that both separates and links these panels, but we do so in a complicated interaction with the visual, linguistic, and spatial content of each of those panels. That is, like many other textual forms that surround us—webpages, newspapers layouts, television news screens, interactive multimedia—comics are a rhetorical medium in which "written-linguistic modes of meaning are part and parcel of visual, audio, and spatial patterns of meaning" (Cope and Kalantzis, 2000: 5). We are constantly reading and often producing multimodal texts as we navigate the world around us in complex ways that go well beyond word-based literacy. To better understand how we communicate with each other, we need to engage with a fully developed notion of multimodality and multimodal rhetoric.

In order to better understand the idea of multimodality, let me turn to the work of the New London Group, a group of ten scholars from Great Britain, the United States, and Australia who first came together in 1994 to discuss the teaching of literacy in a rapidly changing world. Through their discussions and subsequent writing, the New London Group developed the concept of Design, "in which we are both inheritors of patterns and conventions of meaning while at the same time active designers of meaning" (Cope and Kalantzis, 2000: 7). Such a stance not only aligns them with social constructivists in word-based literacy such as John Paul Gee (1996), but with scholars doing similar work in visual rhetoric, such as Charles Kostelnick and Michael Hassett, who argue that "To understand how visual language works, we need to define the social behavior among designers and readers that shapes, stabilizes, and transforms it and that normalizes it as conventional codes" (2003: 3). However, the New London Group goes beyond a focus on either word-based texts or visual texts and instead considers five semiotic systems and the way they interact: "Linguistic Meaning, Visual Meaning, Audio Meaning, Gestural Meaning Spatial Meaning, and the Multimodal patterns of meaning that relate the first five modes of meaning to each other" (2003: 7). The concept of Design is an attempt to mediate between socially constructed patterns of meaning and individual agency in the production of meaning within these multiple semiotic systems. As such, Design addresses David S. Birdsell's and Leo Groarke's concern for context in reading visual texts that "can involve a wide range of cultural assumptions, situational cues, time-sensitive information, and/or knowledge of a specific interlocutor" (1996: 5). A Design approach posits each of us as situated individuals, affected and constructed by the cultures in which we live, but not determined by them.

The concept of Design, as developed by the New London Group, consists of a three stage recursive process that includes Available Design, Designing, and the Redesigned. Available Design includes all resources for Design, including "the grammars of language and the grammars of other semiotic systems," "orders of discourse" (adapted from Foucault by Norman Fairclough), which are "the structured set of conventions associated with semiotic activity (including language) in a given social space," and "a socially produced array of discourses, intermeshing and dynamically interacting" (The New London Group, 2000: 20). As producers and consumers of text, these resources are what we have to draw upon within our multimodal rhetorical environments and can include "discourses, styles, genres, dialects, and voices, to name a few of the key variables" (2000: 21). Designing, then, involves shaping meaning through re-presentation and re-contextualization of the resources available to us as we read and write multimodal texts within specific contexts. In the words of the New London Group, "Designing will more or less normatively reproduce, or more or less radically transform, given knowledges, social relations, and identities, depending upon the conditions under which Designing occurs . . . Transformation is always a new use of old materials, a re-articulation and recombination of the given resources of Available Design" (2000: 22). From this process, the new layer of meaning (always at least slightly different than the Available Design) that results is called the Redesigned. The Redesigned, in its creation of new meanings, provides more available resources for Design (Available Design) that results in what is called the Redesigned. The Redesigned, in its creation of new meanings, provides more available resources for Design (Available Design), thus feeding into the ongoing process of making meaning in which we all engage every day. This recursive process of Design that includes multiple semiotic systems thus gives us a nuanced way to think about comics and other multimodal texts.

MULTIMODALITY AND DESIGN IN PRACTICE: "CALVIN AND HOBBES"

Let me return to the "Calvin and Hobbes" cartoon described above to illustrate how this process of multimodal Design works. In addition to the linguistic element—the words spoken by Calvin, his teacher, and his mother, as represented by the text inside the word balloons—the cartoon also includes not only visual elements, but also spatial, gestural, and audio elements. If, as readers, we relied solely on the words in this cartoon, we would miss much of the meaning and humor that is conveyed through these other multimodal elements; we are able to make sense of these elements because we have access to Available Design, though the pool of resources may differ for each of us based on our experiences, access to a variety of discourse communities, and familiarity with comics conventions. For example, most readers will recognize that the printed words are meant to represent dialogue because they are enclosed within word balloons with directional tags that indicate who is speaking. In the first panel, readers familiar with comics will understand that Calvin is asking, "Can I get a drink of water?" and that the reply, "All right, but hurry up, " is coming from someone who is out of the frame. Further, Calvin is pictured in the center of the frame sitting in a desk; spatially, our eye is drawn to Calvin as the center of the frame, while the visual element places him in school.

Since he is in school, the reader understands (because of his or her familiarity with the discourse and conventions of schooling) that the voice of reply belongs to the teacher even though she (as we know from other "Calvin and Hobbes" cartoons) is out of the frame; her exclusion from the frame centers our attention on Calvin and his request. The audio element of the cartoon helps us to "hear" the manner in which the request and reply are made; that is, textual cues that indicate how the text is meant to be heard stand in for the audio. The words spoken by Calvin and his teacher are at a normal volume and pitch (as indicated by the regularized lettering and standard word balloons) and are free of the stressed intonation we see in panel 3 in which Calvin's mother stresses "you" and Calvin stresses "our": visual elements are here used to represent audio elements. Here we have the linguistic, the visual, the spatial, and the audio working together to set the scene (Calvin asking his teacher if he can get a drink of water) for the punch line that will come in panel 3. In addition, however, as readers we also ascertain meaning from gestural elements that include both facial expression and body language, here evidenced in the form of Calvin raising his hand with an expression on his face that is as neutral as any that Calvin ever displays. Because Calvin raises his hand, uses the expected form of question, and displays a neutral facial expression, as readers we presume that he is simply acting within accepted norms of school behavior as we remember them as part of our Available Design for making meaning from this cartoon; for the regular reader of "Calvin and Hobbes," such behavior on the part of Calvin is at odds with his normal behavior, a part of the Available Design for regular readers of the comic strip. When this setup in panel 1 is combined with the subsequent sequencing of panels, including all of their multimodal elements, and the use of gutters in that sequencing (as discussed above), we are able to understand the humor of the comic strip.

THE QUESTION OF RHETORIC II: COMMUNICATION AND PERSUASION

What I have described here is one of many possible meanings within the matrix of possibilities inherent in the text, but one that approximates how most regular readers of comic strips would interpret it. When we read comic strips such as this one, we actively engage in the process of Designing, drawing on our experiences with discourses, styles, genres, dialects, and voices—Available Design—as we seek to create/negotiate meaning; such a theory of meaning making with multimodal texts acknowledges the social and semiotic structures that surround us and within which we exist, while at the same time recognizes individual agency and experience in the creation of meaning. Knowledge of linguistic, audio, visual, gestural, and spatial conventions within comics affects the ways in which we read and the meanings we assign to texts, just as knowledge of conventions within word-based literacy affects the ways in which those texts are read; for example, lawyers will read legal documents with a different level of comprehension than will people not trained in this type of reading. Similarly, familiarity with these conventions, practice in reading comics, interest, prior experience, and attention given to that reading all come into play in the exercise of agency on the part of the reader (and writer). When we finish reading (or writing) such a comic strip, we are left with the Redesigned, a new layer of meaning that adds to our resources for Available Design. We are influenced by design conventions and grammars as we read, but are not determined by them as our individual agency interacts with the structure of convention; though we are subject to the same set of grammars, my reading of the text is not necessarily the same as that of someone else.

What I have described above is how comics operate as sites of multimodal rhetoric and how writers and readers act rhetorically through the recursive processes of Design in order to create meaning and engage in the act of communication. In other words, comics and other multimodal texts can be seen as rhetorical in that they are part of "how people use language and other symbols to realize human goals and carry out human activities" (Bazerman, 1988: 6). As such, comics can be used to entertain, to sell merchandise, to introduce ideas, to critique people or positions, or to any number of other rhetorical ends. Of course, for many rhetoricians and rhetorical theorists, the end of rhetoric is persuasion and, in the famous formulation of Aristotle, rhetoric is "the faculty of observing in any given case the available means of persuasion" (*Rhetoric*, 1954: 1355b). If comic strips can be used as a rhetorical, audio, and spatial form, they will demonstrate the available means of persuasion that come together in the process of Design outlined above. Clearly, then, writer and producers of comics and other multimodal texts have a complex array of available means of persuasion at their disposal as they create their work, and readers and consumers of these texts need to be able to understand the ways in which these means of persuasion operate as they read these texts. In other words, it is important to think about how a theory of multimodal rhetoric meshes with traditional theories of rhetoric as persuasion.

VISUAL AND MULTIMODAL ARGUMENT IN THEORY

Before I turn to rhetoric as persuasion, let me first address Blair's ideas about visual argument. Blair first addressed the concept of visual arguments in a 1996 article, positing that visual arguments—"propositional arguments in which the propositions and their argumentative function and roles are expressed visually"—are possible but do not often occur (26). He acknowledges that often texts are hybrids of the visual and the verbal and that it is "hard to extract the argumentative force of just the visual dimension of the communication" (38). In his 2004 essay "The Rhetoric of Visual Arguments," however, Blair works through this theoretical problem of hybrid texts, writing that "visual arguments constitute the species of visual persuasion in which the visual elements overlie, accentuate, render vivid and immediate, and otherwise elevate in forcefulness a reason or set of reasons offered for modifying a belief, an attitude or one's conduct" (50). In other words, visual arguments can be seen as a form of multimodal arguments.

In its connection to persuasion, context, and audience, "the visual is above all rhetorical" since "the visual properties of a visual argument must resonate with the audience on the occasion and in the circumstances" (Blair, 2004: 52). Such visual arguments works best within a rhetorical context that is known to both the producer and receiver of the argument "because so much of the argument must remain tacit or unexpressed. Visual arguments are typically *enthymemes*—arguments with gaps left to be filled in by the participation of the audience" (Blair, 2004: 52). Such arguments work rhetorically to add to the persuasive force of a text as the audience participates in the creation of its textual meaning. In this way, visual arguments may be seen as part of a larger multimodal rhetoric in which the reader participates in the creation of textual meaning through the process of Design. How, then, do such visual and multimodal arguments work and how are they dependent upon context and upon the participation of the audience? Let's briefly turn to a recent "Doonesbury" by Garry Trudeau (originally published April 8, 2006), shown in **Fig. 2**, in order to examine Blair's ideas in the context of a specific example.

Figure 2. Doonesbury by Gary Trudeau

VISUAL AND MULTIMODAL ARGUMENT IN PRACTICE: "DOONESBURY"

In this comic strip, Trudeau depicts a television journalist describing the war in Iraq—what he variously calls "Rummyworld," "Throesville," and "Rummyville"—in the course of three panels. These references to Iraq that implicate Secretary of Defense Donald Rumsfeld in Trudeau's critique immediately place the cartoon within the context within which we are living right now; someone reading this cartoon in a collected edition of "Doonesbury" in 50 years would likely have a more difficult time making the immediate connection that most of today's readers would make. Further, the visual arrangement of the correspondent in front of the video screen (in panels 1 and 3) evokes the television coverage of Iraq to which we have been constantly exposed on both network news and cable news channels. The smoke that envelops that screen implies the massive scale of destruction that obliterates everything else that might be included in this internal frame, the importance of which is emphasized spatially by the centrality of this image in the first panel. The second panel depicts the reporter in extreme close-up, forcing the reader to focus on the seriousness of his expression and the words that accompany it. Panel 3 pulls back out to show both the reporter and the scene of destruction as he asks the question, "How do we make sense of a sacrifice with no end?" In these panels, we "hear" the somber, even tones of similar reporters we have seen on television because we are cued by both this intertextual context and by the regularized lettering and standard word balloons. Linguistic, visual, spatial, gestural, and audio elements combine in these three panels to place the reader in the context of a serious news report about the Iraq War. When the reporter sets up the edit to the next shot (as if it were a television report) or next panel (since it is a cartoon) by saying, "For that [answer to his question], the nation turns to the man who understands it best!" the reader (like the nation) expects a valid answer to the question he has posed.

Instead, the final panel gives an answer that, in the context of the comic strip and the current moment, is both humorous and disturbing. In this panel, we see the White House with two dialogue balloons emanating from it. Visually filling the entire panel, the White House stands in metonymically for the office of the President and so, presumably, the first balloon represents the voice of President George W. Bush and the second the voice of one of his advisors (likely Karl Rove, given the place of this particular strip within the recent corpus of "Doonesbury"). Rather than a reasoned answer or justification for the national sacrifices outlined in panel 2, the voice represented in the first word balloon says, "It's hard! 9/11! It's **hard work!** 9/11! Lessons of 9/11! Hard! 9/11!" Not only do the words themselves not inspire confidence, but the way they are said—the visual representation of the audio—also undercuts the ethos of the speaker through the use of bold text and frequent exclamation marks. Further, Trudeau relies on readers being able to draw on their Available Design in order to access the intertext of the previous Bush speeches from which these quotations are drawn; represented as they are in this final panel, the direct connection to Bush's past words is an attempt to undermine confidence in Bush in the context of the comic strip's argument. After the President speaks, the advisor intervenes, as if to calm him down from the stress of the situation. The reader is left to ponder what exactly is coming out of the office of the President and whether or not it should inspire confidence. In the gutter between panels 3 and 4, then, the reader is asked to make connections and draw conclusions about the situation in Iraq and the performance of Bush in light of that situation. Through the arrangement of panels and their multimodal content, Trudeau attempts to push readers to make connections that accord with his view of Bush and his vision for America's involvement in Iraq. In other words, Trudeau uses Design elements to attempt to persuade the reader to his position.

Just as the reader must connect the panels and their multimodal elements through the physical and conceptual gutter, so too does this visual/multimodal argument force the reader to make connections in much the way that Blair described in "The Rhetoric of Visual Arguments." Like an enthymeme, this strip has an unstated but assumed major premise, a stated minor premise, and a conclusion that follows from the linking of the two. To that end, the comic strip might be expressed in verbal terms in this way:

> Without a clear Presidential vision behind America's involvement in Iraq, the national sacrifice is futile and dangerous (unstated major premise).
>
> George W. Bush does not have a clear vision for America's involvement in Iraq (stated minor premise).
>
> The national sacrifice is futile and dangerous (conclusion).

Even the conclusion remains unstated in this strip, though it is clearly implied in the connection that the reader is expected to make through the gutter between panels 3 and 4. Moreover, even the minor premise is stated only in that the kind of incoherent statement Trudeau ascribes to Bush implies that he lacks a clear vision even here, the words we as readers ascribe to Bush emanate in the comic strip from the White House, a metonym for the office of the President. By implying the conclusion, Trudeau attempts to involve the audience in the creation of the argument's meaning. If the reader does come to the conclusion that I stated above, the persuasive the persuasive force is greater because of the involvement of the reader in the comic strip's argument. The danger of this type of argument, however, is that the reader will disagree with the unstated major premise or the obliquely stated minor premise or will not come to the same conclusion that I have outlined above. In fact, in writing this summary, it is not possible to fully capture verbally what this comic strip conveys through all of multimodal elements, even as it operates as a piece of rhetorical persuasion. Though the argument could be put in various verbal forms, none of them is adequate to the rhetorical force that happens when the verbal and the visual combine. As Blair writes, visual arguers create "visual enthymemes thus drawing the viewer to participate in completing the construction of the argument and so in its own persuasion" (2004: 59). Multimodal texts must thus be viewed as complex rhetorical environments in which persuasion occurs through a variety of means.

CONCLUSION

While I have certainly not made an exhaustive case for the ways in which rhetoric operates in newspaper comic strips,

I hope that I have been able to illuminate some important concepts through these examples. As we continue to think about the rhetorical range of comics in all of its forms, I want to encourage us to complicate out thinking by considering the idea of multimodality and multimodal rhetoric. By linking rhetoric as the communicative process of making meaning with rhetoric as persuasive communication, we can better examine how these complex multimodal texts operate and how we are persuaded by them even as we make meaning from them. That is, the concepts of multimodality and Design, when viewed in concert with an expansive definition of rhetoric that includes both communication and persuasion, offer us a powerful lens through which to examine "[j]ust how visual images and visual forms in general can and do communicate propositions, just how, in practice, context is to be interpreted and combined with the visual, and just how text and visuals (and sound) interact to produce meaning" (Blair, 1996: 39). Applied here to a very small number of comic strips, these ideas about multimodality, Design, and rhetoric, can help us to think about how visual and multimodal texts operate in the specific contexts that surround us and how we make sense of them in our daily lives.

REFERENCES

Aristotle. *Rhetoric.* 1954. Trans. W. Rhys Roberts. New York: The Modern Library.

Bazerman, Charles, 1988. *Shaping Written Knowledge: The Genre and Activity of the Experimental Article in Science,* Madison, WI. University of Wisconsin Press.

Birdsell, David S. and Leo Groarke, 1996. "Toward a Theory of Visual Argument." *Argumentation & Advocacy.* 33.1 (Summer): 1-10.

Bizzell, Patricia and Bruce Herzberg, 2001. "George Campbell." *The Rhetorical Tradition,* 2nd Ed. New York: Bedford/St. Martin's.

Blair, J. Anthony, 1996. "The Possibility and Actuality of Visual Arguments." *Argumentation & Advocacy. 33.1* (Summer): 23-39.

Blair, J. Anthony, 2004. "The Rhetoric of Visual Arguments." In *Defining Visual Rhetorics,* edited by Charles A. Hill and Marguerite Helmers, pp.41-61. Mahwah, NJ: Lawrence Earlbaum Associates.

Cope, Bill and Mary Kalantzis, eds. 2000. *Multiliteracies: Literacy Learning and the Design of Social Futures.* New York: Routledge.

Foss, Sonja, Karen Foss, and Robert Trapp, 1985. *Contemporary Perspectives on Rhetoric.* Prospect Heights, IL: Waveland Press.

Gee, James Paul, 1996. *Social Linguistics and Literacy: Ideology in Discourses.* 2nd Ed. London: Taylor & Francis.

Horn, Maurice, 1996. *100 Years of American Newspaper Comics.* New York: Gramercy Books.

Kostelnick, Charles and Michael Hassett, 2003. *Shaping Information: The Rhetoric of Visual Conventions.* Carbondale, IL: Southern Illinois University Press.

Marschall, Richard, 1989. *America's Great Comic-Strip Artists..* New York: Abbeville Press.

McCloud, Scott, 1994. *Understanding Comics.* New York: Harper Perennial.

New London Group, 2000. "A Pedagogy of Multileracies: Designing Social Futures." In *Multiliteracies: Literacy Learning and the Design of Social Futures,* edited by Bill Cope and Mary Kalantzis, pp. 9-37. New York: Routledge.

Trudeau, Garry, 2006. "Doonesbury." Cartoon, April 8.

Watterson, Bill, 1995. "Calvin and Hobbes." Cartoon. April 6

Instrumental And Constitutive Rhetoric In Martin Luther King Jr.'s "Letter From Birmingham Jail"

Michael Leff and Ebony A. Utley

CONSIDER AS YOU ARE READING:

What made Martin Luther King such a powerful rhetor? Leff and Utley answer that question by analyzing King's "Letter from Birmingham Jail." Their analyses reveal the dual functions of ethos: Ethos has an instrumental function which furthers civil rights, and it has a generative function that represents the self, the other, and the scene. Ultimately, ethos plays a role in creating a response to a situation; but it also changes the historical identity of the African American rhetor, and prompts white audiences to accept that new identity. By expanding upon notions of the rhetorical situation, as well as traditional definitions of ethos, Leff and Utley demonstrate the profound social impact potentially unleashed by rhetoric. The complicated dance between writing and identity is one of the important concepts necessary for composing advanced arguments, and this analysis of King's writing demonstrates the sophisticated interplay between writer, identity, the scene of writing, and the audience.

1. *Explain how ethos plays a "constitutive" function in "Letter from Birmingham Jail."*

2. *How does the manner that Leff and Utley describe ethos here shape or inform your identity as a writer of academic essays?*

3. *Do you agree with the authors that character can be constructed as part of the rhetorical process? Why or why not?*

Traditional conceptions of rhetorical ethos treat character exclusively as an instrument of persuasion, but the persona of the rhetor often functions as a means of constituting the self in relation to a complex network of social and cultural relationships. This generative function of character becomes especially important in cases where suppressed groups attempt to find rhetorical means to alter their circumstances. Using Martin Luther King Jr.'s "Letter from Birmingham Jail" as a case study, we argue that the text develops a complex and nuanced construction of King's character. This construct allows King to criticize his target audience without alienating himself from it and also allows the "eavesdropping" black audience to discover a model for reconstructing their own sense of agency. This constitutive dimension of character occurs simultaneously and in intimate connection with its use as an instrument of persuasion concerning specific issues. Based on this case, we argue that rigid distinction between instrumental and constitutive functions of rhetoric are misleading and that rhetorical critics should regard the constitution of self and the instrumental uses of character as a fluid relationship.

Almost 30 years ago, in an essay devoted to the *Autobiography of Malcolm X,* Thomas W. Benson commented that rhetoric is, among other things, a way of constituting the self within a scene composed of "exigencies, constraints, others and the self," and it is also a resource for "exercising control over self, others, and by extension the scene."[1] Thus Benson assigns rhetoric a dual function. It is simultaneously generative and instrumental, because it helps to constitute the identity of self, other, and scene, while it also pulls these identities within the orbit of situated interests. Moreover, once this duality is acknowledged, it virtually forces the critic to expand and complicate the conventional interest in "ethical proof," because the persona of the rhetor emerges not just as an instrument of persuasion, but also as something constituted within the rhetorical medium.

Viewed from our current vantage point, Benson's observations seem prescient. He anticipates a set of pivotal issues associated with recent interest in constitutive rhetoric and with the emergence of "interpretive" or "conceptual" criticism.[2] He also locates a subject—Malcolm X in particular and African American protest rhetoric in general—where these problems arise with special clarity and urgency. In Malcolm's texts, we encounter a persona that, as Benson says, sometimes takes on the aspect of "a magnificent anti-hero, an existentialist saint, or a mythic witness to America's oppressive racism," but that also sometimes seems to display the qualities of a hustler, an opportunist, or a cynical manipulator of words and audiences.[3] Thus, a tension between the constitutive and instrumental functions surfaces almost immediately when examining Malcolm's rhetoric, and although it is generally less obtrusive in other African American rhetors during the civil rights revolution of the 1960s, it is still a prominent feature of their discourse—and for good reason. Their efforts to overcome a system that repressed and demeaned them required rhetorical instruments sufficient not only to serve immediate political ends, but also to constitute a new conception of themselves and their fellow African Americans.

In this essay, we concentrate upon Martin Luther King Jr.'s "Letter from Birmingham Jail" and argue that it displays a subtle and complex interrelationship between construction of self and instrumental appeals through character. On our reading of the text, the "Letter" harmonizes aspects of its author's persona by blending and balancing the representation of the self in relation to what Benson calls "the exigencies, constraints, and others" connected with the scene. King's effort to move through a tangle of events and ideas toward a decorous sense of order contrasts notably with the confrontational rhetoric of Malcolm X,[4] but we hope to demonstrate that in constructing an effective persona, King shares the burden and opportunity of crossing between instrumental and constitutive concerns. Before turning to the text of the "Letter," however, we need to consider the context in which it appeared and some of the circumstances of its composition.

THE BACKGROUND

Early in 1963, the Southern Christian Leadership Conference (SCLC) targeted Birmingham, Alabama, for a nonviolent direct action campaign designed to force the city to modify or eliminate its segregation laws. For a variety of reasons, the campaign was delayed until April 3rd, and when it did begin, it encountered serious problems. Only a handful of protestors proved willing to subject themselves to arrest, and so the effort to force concessions by filling the city's jails was failing. Moreover, white moderates, and even some blacks, thought the campaign ill timed, since the newly elected city government had been given no opportunity to deal with the segregation issue. Worse yet, the city's attorneys obtained a federal injunction forbidding King and other SCLC leaders from sponsoring, encouraging, or participating in a demonstration unless they obtained a permit from the city. In effect, this meant that SCLC either had to abandon the campaign or violate federal court orders.

King decided that it was necessary to violate the injunction and that he himself would lead a march and submit to arrest. This "faith act," he hoped, would invigorate the campaign, and on April 12, 1963 (Good Friday, a day chosen for its symbolic importance), King headed a protest demonstration through the streets of Birmingham and was arrested. Refusing to post bail until April 19, he remained in jail for eight days.[5]

On the morning of the 13th, the day after King was imprisoned; the *Birmingham News* printed a short open letter signed by eight local clergymen. The clergy criticized the direct action campaign as an untimely and unwise effort "led in part by outsiders" and urged the black residents of Birmingham to obey the law, withdraw support from the demonstrations, and resolve their grievances through the courts and the negotiation process.[6] King's "Letter from Birmingham Jail" was a direct response to the clergymen's statement.

The history of the "Letter's" composition is a matter of some interest. According to the conventional story, King began writing his response on the margins of the newspaper that published the clergymen's letter, then on odd scraps of paper provided by a sympathetic prison guard, and finally on a legal tablet provided by King's attorney. While King was engaged in composition, his visitors carried the marginalia, scraps, and pages to SCLC headquarters where a secretary typed the individual bits until the text was completed.

There is no reason to doubt the truth of this story as far as it goes, but it does not seem to be the whole story. Although the "Letter" is dated April 16th, no version of it circulated in public until after the first week of May, and internal evidence rather clearly indicates that the published version of the work could not have been completed until after April 19. Thus, at least some parts of the "Letter" likely were composed and/or revised after King left prison.[7] The tone and content of the document, however, create the impression that the author wrote it from within a prison cell, and as we will note later, this impression greatly contributes to King's self-representation and to the persuasive impact of the "Letter" as a whole.

KING'S "LETTER": THE RHETORIC OF THE TEXT

With this background in mind, we can turn to the text itself and to the construction and representation of agency within it. This interpretative inquiry has an affinity with the neoclassical concern for the rhetor's ethos, but in the neoclassical approach, the tendency is to designate character as a mode of proof, to locate instances where it is invoked, and to isolate it as a discrete element in the persuasive process. In the interpretative frame, the agency of the rhetor refers not just to the use of character appeals, but also to the way that rhetors place themselves within a network of communicative relationships. At minimum, the explication of this process demands attention to: (1) the rhetor's construction of self, (2) the rhetor's construction of the audience (what Edwin Black calls the "second persona"),[8] and (3) the enactment within the text of the relationship between rhetor and audience. In what follows, we will try to explain how King's "Letter" works along all three of these lines and to indicate how they converge to create and represent an identity for King both as writer and as social/political actor.

One of the most prominent features of the text is its extensive use of direct address. Whereas the clergymen's letter is addressed to no one in particular, King begins with the salutation "My Dear Fellow Clergymen," and the first paragraph continues in this vein as King's "I" speaks in response to the "you" who composed the earlier letter. And the dialogic relationship is underscored by the wording of the paragraph's final sentence: "But since I feel that you are men of genuine good will and your criticisms are sincerely set forth, I would like to answer your statement in what I hope will be patient and reasonable terms."[9] This pattern is sustained through the body of the "Letter" as King organizes its content into a seriatim response to claims attributed to the eight clergymen. The following schema indicates this structure:

A. Introduction

B. Refutation

   1. That King is an outsider

   2. That King and his supporters should negotiate rather than demonstrate

   3. That the demonstrations are ill timed (First confession: King's disappointment with white moderates)

   4. That nonviolent direct action precipitates violence

   5. That racial problems will resolve themselves over time

   6. That King and his supporters are extremists (Second confession: King's disappointment with white clergy)

   7. That the Birmingham police deserve praise

C. Conclusion

Save for the fifth point on the list, King introduces every one of his refutations with the use of the second-person pronoun, and most often he fashions a direct response in the first person. (For example, discussion of the second claim begins: "You deplore the demonstrations that are presently taking place in Birmingham. But I am sorry that your statement did not express a similar concern for the conditions that brought the demonstrations into being" [85].) At times, King enhances this interactive sensibility by means of rhetorical questions. (For example, "You may well ask: 'Why direct action? Why sit-ins, marches, etc.? Isn't negotiation a better path?' You are exactly right in your call for negotiation" [86]. In short, King exploits the form of the "Letter" to localize, personalize, and dramatize the issues in the civil rights debate.

Although King's "Letter" literally and directly addressed the eight Birmingham clergymen, it was never delivered to them, nor were they, in fact, his intended audience. The clergymen functioned rhetorically as a synecdoche, as a representation of the larger audience King wanted to reach, and his decision to respond to their statement and his manner of doing so were both strategic. The success of the Birmingham campaign, and of SCLC efforts in general, depended heavily on support from white moderates—Americans already inclined to oppose racial segregation in principle and to feel uncomfortable about the discrepancy between their basic values and the discriminatory policies then practiced in the South, but who were also fearful about direct action campaigns and the threat they posed to public order. When the eight clergymen published their statement, they offered King an opportunity to embody this target audience (and hence to use it as a rhetorical construct) without appearing to manufacture an artificial situation. Equally important, as Richard P. Fulkerson has noted, the invocation of specific individuals as an ostensible audience allowed King to cultivate a personal tone and to project his personality in ways that would have been impossible in a document addressed to no one in particular.[10] The "Letter," then, effectively used an actual event to construct a personalized version of both writer and audience through a double synecdoche. Just as the eight clergy stood for white moderates, so also did King stand for the SCLC and the African Americans engaged in nonviolent direct action campaigns.

While the "Letter's" external structure proceeds in a point-by-point linear order, the rhetoric of the text also develops recurrent themes—repeated ideas, images, and arguments that work through the linear sequence of refutational arguments. These themes represent King as an agent of change who embodies the basic values of his white moderate audience and who acts with restraint and respect even as he attempts to reform glaring injustices. This development, an example of what Kenneth Burke calls "repetitive form,"[11] allows King to disagree with his audience while still remaining consubstantial with it. His dissent thereby seems to arise from within the *habitus* of his interlocutors.

From the opening salutation, King repeatedly emphasizes his status as a Christian minister and his unwavering commitment to the church. This point achieves its most notable articulation in the course of King's "second confession," where he expresses disappointment with white clergymen who "remain silent behind the anesthetizing security of stained-glass windows," and with white churches that stand on the sideline and preach an otherworldly religion. This is strong criticism, but King explains that it comes from a person firmly embedded in the Christian tradition: "In deep disappointment, I have wept over the laxity of the church. Be assured that my tears have been tears of love . . . Yes, I love the church; I love her sacred walls. How could I do otherwise? I am in the rather unique position of being the son, the grandson, and great-grandson of preachers" (97). Here King's figuration overlaps at three levels of embodiment: Christianity is made physical through representation of the church as a walled, physical space; King, coming from a lineage domiciled within those walls, assumes an identity connected with that Christian space, and from this inside position his disappointment with the church can manifest itself only as tears of love. All this figurative work represents King as someone who has the appropriate credentials to criticize the church from within and to recall it to its own ideals.

More generally, King embodies his solidarity with mainstream American values through the use of appeals to authority. The text is peppered with references to venerated figures from American history, Judeo-Christian lore, and the Western intellectual tradition. These include Paul, Socrates, Rheinhold Niebuhr, Thomas Aquinas, Martin Buber, Paul Tillich, Jesus, Amos, Martin Luther, John Bunyan, Abraham Lincoln, Thomas Jefferson, and T.S. Elliot, and King invokes these references to vindicate and explain his own actions. For example, in response to the charge that he is "an outsider," King cites scriptural precedent for his activity: "Beyond this, I am in Birmingham because injustice is here. Just as the eighth-century prophets left their little villages and carried their 'thus saith the Lord' far beyond the boundaries of their hometowns; just as the apostle Paul left his little village of Tarsus and carried the gospel of Jesus Christ to practically every hamlet and city of the Graeco-Roman world, I too am compelled to carry the gospel of freedom beyond my particular hometown." (84-85).

King is obviously concerned to dispel the perception that he is an outsider in Birmingham and a radical who adheres to positions that fall outside the orbit of respectable American opinion. The appeals to authority counter this image at two levels. First, by citing icons of accepted belief and faith, King associates himself with figures who command unquestioned respect from his

target audience, and this helps to establish commonality with
it. Second, the words and deeds of these respected individuals,
insofar as they appear to be the same as or similar to King's words
and deeds, become exemplars that sanction King's position and
open space for it within the conceptual horizons of his audience.
If Amos, Paul, Socrates, and even Jesus behaved as agitators,
then it follows that agitation to expose and overcome injustice
is no threat to the common tradition, but is instead something
needed to renew and sustain its integrity.

King not only constructs his persona through strategies of
embodiment, but he also uses the text to enact the kind of
agency that he wants to have associated with himself and his
movement. By enactment, we are referring not just to what
the text says, but to what it does, and throughout the "Letter"
King's verbal action as writer and advocate presents a complex,
but consistent representation of his character. The manner of
his argument and his style of arguing combine to depict the man
as energetic, active, committed to principles, and committed to
act in accordance with those principles but to do so in a poised,
balanced, reasonable, and restrained manner. The dominant
image is one of restrained energy, and this image is well
calculated to diffuse the accusation that King is a dangerous
radical who lacks prudent judgment and acts without due regard
for practical consequence.

Throughout the sequence of refutations, the text enacts balanced
judgment through what Fulkerson calls a "dual pattern."[12] King
responds to the allegations against him first on an immediate
practical level and then on the level of principle, and as this
unfolds, the reader witnesses King exercising the kind of
judgment most appropriate to deliberation—judgment that
simultaneously encompasses particulars and principles and that
engages questions both of expediency and honor. The first of
King's refutations provides a clear illustration of this strategy. In
responding to the charge that he is an "outsider," King begins by
explaining that the Birmingham affiliate of the SCLC asked for
his assistance, and so he is "here, along with several members
of my staff, because we were invited here." But this is not the
end of the matter, since beyond such particular concerns there
is also a moral imperative that leads King to confront injustice
just as the Hebrew prophets and the apostle Paul did. And,

to place the issue on an even broader ground, King recognizes "the interrelatedness of all countries and states . . . Injustice anywhere is a threat to justice everywhere. We are caught in an inescapable network of mutuality, tied in a single garment of destiny. Whatever affects one directly affects all indirectly" (85). Thus, whether judgment rests on the concrete particulars of the case or on sweeping ethical principle, King should not be regarded as an outsider; his presence in Birmingham is both appropriate and right.

The second, third, and fourth refutational sections also employ this double structure, but it is in the sixth section, where King addresses the charge of extremism, that the technique achieves its most powerful articulation. He begins his response by expressing surprise that anyone would label him as an extremist, since in actuality he stands "in the middle of two opposing forces in the Negro community." On one side, there are those who simply acquiesce to injustice and do nothing, and on the other there are the black nationalists who react to injustice with hatred and bitterness and come "perilously close to advocating violence." Between these extremes of complacency and angry despair, King offers the "more excellent way" of nonviolent protest, and he acknowledges disappointment that this position would be regarded as extremist. King, however, has a second thought on the matter, and he "gradually gained a bit of satisfaction from being considered an extremist. Was not Jesus an extremist in love—'Love your enemies, bless them that curse you, pray for them that despitefully use you.'" This appeal to authority continues through a long list of heroic figures (including Amos, Paul, Martin Luther, John Bunyan, Abraham Lincoln, and Thomas Jefferson) who are also linked to famous quotations expressing extreme ideas. And King concludes that the question is not whether "we will be extremists," but whether we will be extremists for love and justice or extremists for hate and injustice (92-94).

As other commentators have noted, this passage distinguishes between extremism understood as placement along a spectrum of existing positions and extremism understood in terms of intensity of conviction.[13] By the first standard, King is not an extremist but rather a dialectically tempered moderate, since his position comes between and constructively synthesizes the antithetical forces of apathy and violence. By the second standard, however, King is an extremist because he is passionately committed in principle to act against and eradicate injustice, and as King's historical witnesses demonstrate, extremism of this type supports the fundamental values of the society. This passage, then, combines restrained practical judgment with a passionate determination to overcome injustice, and the passion, however strongly it is expressed, still moves along constructive lines, because faith, justice and love channel its energy.

Another notable feature of this passage is King's restraint in choosing the words he uses to address his critics. When labeled as an extremist, King reacts not with an expression of anger or indignity but disappointment. This sort of verbal control recurs throughout the "Letter." Thus, in the two sections that digress from the sequence of refutations, King makes his most critical comments about the inaction of the white community, but he studiously avoids the language of accusation. Instead, he "confesses" his disappointment with them. This restraint not only characterizes King's choice of words, but also, and more powerfully, it is enacted in the structure of some of his sentences.

In one of the most memorable parts of the text, King offers a carefully modulated response to the charge that the demonstrations are untimely. African Americans, he reminds his readers, already have had to wait for 340 years for their rights, and it is no wonder that they are growing impatient. "Perhaps it's easy for those who have never felt the stinging darts of segregation to say, 'Wait'":

> But when you have seen mobs lynch your mothers and fathers at will and drown your sisters and brothers at whim; when you have seen hate-filled policemen curse, kick, brutalize, and even kill your black brothers and sisters with impunity; when you see the vast majority of your twenty million Negro brothers smothering in an airtight cage of poverty in the midst of an affluent society; when you suddenly find your tongue twisted and your speech stammering as you seek to explain to your six-year-old daughter why she can't go to the public amusement park that has just been advertised on television, and see tears welling up in her little eyes when

she is told that Funtown is closed to colored children, and see the depressing clouds of inferiority begin to form in her little mental sky, and see her begin to distort her little personality by unconsciously developing bitterness toward white people; when you have to concoct an answer for a five-year-old son asking in agonizing pathos: "Daddy, why do white people treat colored people so mean?"; when you take a cross-country trip and find it necessary to sleep night after night in the uncomfortable corners of your automobile because no motel will accept you; when you are humiliated day in and day out by nagging signs reading "white" and "colored"; when your first name becomes "nigger" and your middle name becomes "boy" (however old you are) and your last name becomes "John," and when your wife and mother are never given the respected title "Mrs.", when you are harried by day and haunted by night by the fact that you are a Negro, living constantly at tiptoe stance never quite knowing what to expect next, and plagued with inner fears and outer resentments; when you are forever fighting a degenerating sense of nobodiness; then you will understand why we find it difficult to wait. (88-89)

The most obviously remarkable feature of this sentence is it length—331 words, which makes it by far the longest sentence in the text and probably one of the longest sentences in contemporary English prose. But the syntax of the sentence also deserves attention. Because it is structured in left-branching or periodic form, the syntactic complexity of the sentence develops through the accretion of dependent clauses that occur before the main clause. This arrangement suspends the completion of the sentence as a meaningful unit until the end, and so, to understand the sentence, the reader must wait until the final 11 words provide closure. Moreover, since the dependent clauses narrate a series of injuries, insults, and outrages, the whole development iconically represents the plight of the African American.[14] The white readers, who have never directly suffered from the "stinging darts of segregation," must wait while this long list of grievances continues to assault their sensibilities, and so they vicariously experience the frustration of the African

American. The sentence enacts and transmits that experience in a way that no propositional argument could accomplish.

Given the length of the sentence, the tension that mounts through it, and the vivacity with which it represents the effects of injustice, we might expect it to end on a strong note of outrage and anger, perhaps even with an accusation against those who ask African Americans to wait. Instead, however, the climax comes in the form of an understated address to the white audience: "Then you will understand why we find it difficult to wait." The understatement may work to heighten the emotional impact of the sentence, but it is also a striking enactment of King's restraint, and it is difficult to imagine a more appropriate textual representation of King's pledge to proceed in reasonable and patient terms.

Toward the end of the "Letter," when he questions the clergyman's praise of the police, King uses this same verbal technique for building and containing emotional energy:

> I don't believe that you would have so warmly commended the police force if you had seen its angry violent dogs literally biting six unarmed Negroes. I don't believe you would so quickly commend the policemen if you would observe their ugly inhuman treatment of Negroes here in the city jail; if you would watch them push and curse old Negro women and young Negro girls; if you would see them slap and kick old Negro men and young boys; if you will observe them, as they did on two occasions, refuse to give us food because we want to sing our grace together. I'm sorry that I can't join you in your praise for the police department. (98-99)

The loose or right branching construction of the long sentence does not suspend meaning as does the periodic sentence King uses earlier, and partially for this reason, this passage does not have quite the same dramatic impact. Nevertheless, the pattern of energy and restraint is apparent. The long sentence accumulates grievances through its many clauses, and the short sentence that follows offers a controlled, understated response addressed directly to the ostensible audience.

To sum up, in the "Letter from Birmingham Jail" King attempts to reach his target audience by dispelling the perception that he is a radical given to intemperate action and committed to views that fall outside the mainstream of American society. The text consistently works to represent King in a different light, and it does so not just by direct statement, but also by demonstrating balanced, temperate forms of judgment as it engages key issues and by the enactment of restrained energy in the very structure of the prose. At the end of the "Letter," King articulates this theme in two nicely balanced sentences that sum up the position he occupies throughout the text:

If I have said anything in this letter that is an overstatement of the truth and is indicative of unreasonable impatience, I beg you to forgive me. If I have said anything in this letter that is an understatement of the truth and is indicative of my having a patience that makes me patient with anything less than brotherhood, I beg God to forgive me. (100)

PERSONA AND AUDIENCE IN KING'S "LETTER"

Readers of the "Letter from Birmingham Jail" often testify to its powerfully evocative effect. For many Americans, the "Letter" produced an immediate, unified response that restructured and reframed their perception of a complex situation, and E. Culpepper Clark has offered a plausible account for this response. King, he maintains, gathered together an ambiguous set of cultural experiences and expectations and transformed them "into the controlling metaphor for interpreting nonviolent civil disobedience." Writing from the confinement in a prison, King could exercise a prophetic voice that recalled his people to their better selves and that resonated "with the Judeo-Christian struggle against human bondage."[15]

King's actual imprisonment in Birmingham Jail is a necessary condition for the metaphor to work, but the image of a man writing in a cramped, isolated prison cell is in large part constructed by the text itself. And it was not enough simply for King to construct a prisoner's voice, since not all prisoners are prophets. King also faced the more difficult task of embedding himself within a culture that segregated people of his race. The prophetic voice does not come from the outside; it must arise from within the people whom it criticizes. It must incarnate what is highest and best in the culture of that people and summon them to act on standards the prophet embodies and the audience shares.[16] The prophet is a member of the tribe, and so, to be a prophet among the Hebrews, one must be a Hebrew. And what is required to be a prophet among white Americans? That is a role King neither inherits by birth nor gains through any other easy access. He must argue himself into it, and the "Letter" is wonderfully designed to achieve just this purpose. It constructs King as an agent who grounds his identity in the religious, intellectual, and political values of the American tribe, and it enacts a form of agency that sustains connection between author and reader even in the presence of disagreement. King emerges from the "Letter" not just as someone who can argue with a white audience on its own terms, but as an agent who can elevate that audience by forcing it to acknowledge its sins of omission and by demanding consistency between its actions and its highest values.

To this point, our reading of the text has followed the writer-audience ratio that is central to its explicit argument. But while the white moderate surely is the ostensible target audience, King must have known that the text would also circulate among African American readers. A systematic study of the coexistence of this black audience requires more attention than we can give to it in this essay, but we can offer a sketch of how shifting focus to the text's other audience enhances our understanding of the constitutive function of rhetoric.

The black audience for King's "Letter" has a status similar to what James L. Golden and Richard D. Rieke call the eavesdropping audience for the rhetoric of Malcolm X and other militant African American rhetors. While these militants usually speak directly and specifically to a black audience, they are also quite aware of white "eavesdroppers" who are listening even though they are not addressed, and it seems clear that their discourse is intended to have an impact on the whites who "overhear" what is said. This concern about the eavesdropping audience, Golden and Rieke argue, arises from its association with the existing power structure, and so the eavesdropping audience is constructed as an effort to induce people in power to effect change.[17]

As we have shown, King's commitment to writing himself inside the values of mainstream American society enables him to make a direct appeal to the audience of white moderates, but it is the black readers of the text who must be persuaded to risk their bodies. Without their active involvement, nonviolent civil disobedience cannot work, since blacks must exercise their power to protest if they are to force whites to align their professed beliefs with their actions. Thus, even though King places the white audience at the center of his text, his effort to persuade it results from and consequently is constrained by black action. By analogy to the white eavesdroppers on the rhetoric of Malcolm and other militant blacks, we can think of black readers of King's "Letter" as eavesdroppers who are being urged to exercise power to effect change. In this case, the black audience is instructed about how to adopt personae that will make them more effective agents for change and about the means for implementing this agency.[18] If we regard the "Letter" as an appeal to power and conscience and the proper alignment between the two, we must consider it as an appeal not just to the ostensible white audience, but also to the collective power and conscience of black people.

Viewed from this angle, the "Letter" constructs a model for African Americans to adopt and enact. In the opening paragraph, King represents himself in a way that reveals key features of that model. The salutation, "My Dear Fellow Clergymen," sets King on equal footing with the white men he is addressing, and in the sentence that follows; we learn that although King is confined in jail, he is an important and busy man who generally does not have time to answer criticism. In this instance, however, since he thinks the eight clerics are sincere men of good will, he elects to respond to them and to do so in patient and reasonable terms. Thus, even though confined physically, King remains an active agent who exercises choice about when and how to respond to others.

King's immediate situation—his imprisonment—corresponds to the imagery he uses later in the text to characterize the general condition of African Americans. He depicts them as "smothering in an airtight cage of poverty," as forced to sleep "in the uncomfortable corners" of their automobiles, as threatened by the "quicksand of racial injustice," and as prone to fall into the "dark dungeons of complacency." Yet, like King himself, African Americans are beginning to break through these restraints. They are experiencing a new militancy, and they carry the "gospel of freedom," create constructive tension, stride toward freedom, move with "a cosmic energy" toward racial justice, and rise out of the "dark dungeons" to the "hills of creative protest."

By contrast, the white moderate are inert and immobile even though they face no restraints imposed from the outside. They have become, in King's words, stumbling blocks to freedom, dams blocking social progress, silent witnesses of injustice, anesthetized behind stained glass windows, and paralyzed by the chains of conformity. White moderates, then, are passive, while the once passive blacks are becoming agents of change. No longer willing to accept stolid indifference, they demand their rights as American citizens and insist that sincere people of good faith lend them their support. But morally and practically, they are best advised to make these demands in the spirit of King's example. In breaking out of restraints imposed upon them, they should accept a measure of self-restraint. Although white moderates often fail to exercise proper judgment, they can be called to their better selves through actions that force injustice to their attention and through discourse that addresses them in patient and reasonable terms.

For black readers, then, King's "Letter" offers an invitation to adopt a rather specific conception of themselves as they struggle to attain equal rights, and King's placement of himself within the African American community appears in quite a different light than it does when the text is read from the perspective of a white moderate audience. For the white reader, King's assertion that he "stands between" the "'do-nothingness' of the complacent" and "hatred and despair of the black nationalist" (93) appears as a strategy designed to blunt the accusation that he is an intemperate radical, and it thus functions to help unify the writer and the audience. On the other hand, for the black "eavesdroppers," this placement suggests points of differentiation as well as identity; King's position represents an option that some may accept as the "more excellent way" and others may reject. The black audience, in effect, is instructed about how to distinguish the attitudes of its members and invited to make a positive choice in favor of one of the alternatives.

In sum, "Letter from Birmingham Jail" constructs the persona of an author who is critical of his white audience, but not alienated from it. He shares its Christian and democratic values, and recognizes its concern about practical matters, but he also calls upon the audience to acknowledge and act in accordance with its own principles. By insinuating himself within the life-world of his auditors, King can deploy his ethos instrumentally as a means of allaying fears about the immediate scene of social protest, but he can also establish a model of restrained energy that encourages the white audience to reaffirm its basic values as it reconsiders its view of African Americans. At the same time, the text constructs a persona that black readers can use as a model for becoming effective actors on the American scene. Like King, they can view themselves as agents who need not and will not suffer the indifference of white moderates, who can break free of external restraints without losing self-restraint, and who can work from within American society to make fundamental changes in the way they conceive themselves and are conceived by others. Thus at several levels and in respect to different audiences, King's text functions both as an instrument that uses constructions of self to alter attitudes and as a medium for constituting self within a scene composed of "exigencies, constraints, others, and self."

ENDNOTES

1. Thomas W. Benson, "Rhetoric and Autobiography: The Case of Malcolm X," *Quarterly Journal of Speech, 60 (1974): 1.*

2. The terms "interpretive" and "conceptual" are used by James Jasinski to describe what he calls the most important development in rhetorical criticism during the past two decades. This approach, already suggested in Benson's essay, concentrates on providing "thick descriptions" of particular cases rather than the construction or verification of abstract theoretical principles. See James Jasinski, "The Status of Theory and Method in Rhetorical Criticism," *Western Journal of Communication* 65 (2001): 249-70; and also the entry entitled "Criticism in Contemporary Rhetorical

Studies," in James Jasinski, *Sourcebook on Rhetoric: Key Concepts in Contemporary Rhetorical Studies* (Thousand Oaks, Calif.: Sage, 2001), 124-44.

3. Benson, "Rhetoric and Autobiography," 6.

4. On the indecorous nature of Malcolm's rhetoric, see Robert E. Terrill, "Protest, Prophecy, and Prudence in the Rhetoric of Malcolm X," *Rhetoric & Public Affairs* 4 (2001): 34. Terrill's reading of Malcolm's "The Ballot or the Bullet" provides an interesting counterpoint to our interpretation of King's "Letter" presented in this paper.

5. Detailed accounts of these events are provided in Taylor Branch, *Parting the Waters: America in the King Years, 1954-63* (New York: Simon and Schuster, 1988), 673-802; and David Garrow, *Bearing the Cross: Martin Luther King, Jr. and the Southern Christian Leadership Conference* (New York: Vintage, 1986), 231-64.

6. The text of this letter is reprinted in S. Jonathan Bass, *Blessed Are the Peacemakers: Martin Luther King Jr., Eight White Religious Leaders, and the "Letter from Birmingham Jail"* (Baton Rouge: Louisiana State University Press, 2001), 235-36.

7. Concerning the composition and circulation of the "Letter," see Bass, *Blessed Are the Peacemakers,* 110-62; E. Culpepper Clark, "An American Dilemma in King's 'Letter from Birmingham Jail,'" in *Martin Luther King and the Sermonic Power of Discourse,* ed. Carolyn Calloway-Thomas and John Louis Lucaites (Tuscaloosa: University of Alabama Press, 1993), 34-49; and Martha Solomon Watson's essay in this issue of *Rhetoric & Public Affairs.*

8. Edwin Black, "The Second Persona," *Quarterly Journal of Speech* 56 (1970): 109-19. For reasons that will become apparent later in this essay, we think it would be better to consider the rhetor's construction of *audiences* rather than of *the audience,* and so we are introducing an amendment to Black's well-known concept.

9. All references to the "Letter" are from Martin Luther King Jr., *I Have a Dream: Speeches and Writings that Changed the World,* ed. J.M. Washington (San Francisco: Harper, 1986), 83-100. Specific page references to this edition are indicated parenthetically in the text of the paper.

10. Richard P. Fulkerson, "The Public Letter as Rhetorical Form: Structure, Logic, and Style in King's 'Letter from Birmingham Jail,'" *Quarterly Journal of Speech* 65 (1979): 124. Fulkerson's

essay, in our judgment, remains the most systematic guide to the rhetoric of the "Letter" and we have relied upon it throughout our reading of the text.

11. Kenneth Burke, *Counterstatement* (Los Altos, Calif.: Hermes, 1931), 125.

12. Fulkerson, "The Public Letter as Rhetorical Form," 127.

13. See Fulkerson. "The Public Letter as Rhetorical Form," 128.

14. On the structure and rhetorical impact of the sentence, see Mia Klein, "The Other Beauty of Martin Luther King's 'Letter from Birmingham Jail,'" *College Composition and Communication* 32 (1981): 30-37.

15. Clark, "An American Dilemma," 48-49.

16. On the immanent role of prophetic discourse, see Michael Walzer, *Interpretation and Social Criticism* (Cambridge, Mass.: Harvard University Press, 1987), 64-94. James Darsey (*The Prophetic Tradition and Radical Rhetoric in America* [New York: New York University Press, 1997], 111) puts the point somewhat differently when he says that the prophet is "simultaneously insider and outsider." But Darsey's point is fundamentally the same as Walzer's—the prophet must be inside the culture, but must have achieved sufficient conceptual distance from existing practices to be able to note and criticize discrepancies between those practices and the ideals of the culture. On "rhetorical distance," see Michael Osborn's essay in this issue of *Rhetoric & Public Affairs*.

17. James L. Golden and Richard D. Rieke, *The Rhetoric of Black Americans* (Columbus, Ohio: Charles E. Merrill, 1971), 18-19.

18. There is no doubt that King regarded a positive change in black self-esteem as a vital and necessary part of the movement. In other speeches and writings of this period, he maintains that nonviolent direct action precipitated psychological change—it contributed to "something revolutionary" that was occurring in the "mind, heart, and soul of Negroes all over America" (*Why We Can't Wait* [New York: Harper and Row, 1964], 64. Nonviolent direct action, he maintained, challenged stereotypes about blacks, often unconsciously accepted by blacks themselves, that they were inferior and unable to act independently because it gave them a means for peaceful action directed toward their own liberation and for connecting local communities into a national network.

THE VOCABULARY OF COMICS

SCOTT MCCLOUD

CONSIDER AS YOU ARE READING:

Instead of writing an academic essay, McCloud communicates through his principal genre and its form: the comic. By doing so, he is able to demonstrate in every frame the points he is making about the art (and science) of comics. Does the medium imply that his theories are simplistic or that we shouldn't take him seriously? To the contrary, he shows how comics can be the ideal genre for conveying complex concepts as well as appealing to ethos by building a connection with the reader. But what is a discussion of comics doing in a book about rhetoric? McCloud's discussion is instructive in its ability to get us thinking about, as his title implies, the language of his multi-modal form. We study and learn the vocabulary of written rhetoric. Should we not also examine the vocabulary of visual rhetoric, such as cartooning? Doing so may well expand our ability to critically read cartoons, as well as our ability to write multimodal arguments.

1. *Does the format McCloud uses for the delivery of this message harm his ethos or strengthen it? What possibilities does his choice of genre open up to you in composing your own arguments?*

2. *Write down, in a single sentence, a claim or appeal that you made in the last argumentative essay you wrote. Now, translate that claim into a cartoon. What strategies of visual rhetoric are you employing to ensure that your cartoon is persuasive?*

3. *Given McCloud's discussion, what criteria might you use in assessing the effectiveness of any multimodal argument with a visual component?*

WELL, ACTUALLY, THAT'S *WRONG*. THIS IS *NOT* A PAINTING OF A PIPE, THIS IS A *DRAWING* OF A PAINTING OF A PIPE.

N'EST-CE PAS?

NOPE. WRONG AGAIN. IT'S A *PRINTED COPY* OF A DRAWING OF A PAINTING OF A PIPE.

TEN COPIES, ACTUALLY.

SIX, IF YOU FOLD THE PAGES BACK.

DO YOU HEAR WHAT I'M SAYING?

IF YOU *DO*, HAVE YOUR *EARS* CHECKED, BECAUSE NO ONE SAID A WORD.

NOW, THE WORD *ICON* MEANS MANY THINGS.

THIS IS *INK* ON PAPER

THIS IS PAPER

FOR THE PURPOSES OF THIS CHAPTER, I'M USING THE WORD *"ICON"* TO MEAN ANY IMAGE USED TO REPRESENT A A PERSON, PLACE, THING OR *IDEA*.

ICON

THAT'S A BIT BROADER THAN THE DEFINITION IN MY DICTIONARY, BUT IT'S THE CLOSEST THING TO WHAT I NEED HERE.

"SYMBOL" IS A BIT TOO *LOADED* FOR ME.

THE SORTS OF IMAGES WE USUALLY CALL SYMBOLS ARE ONE *CATEGORY* OF ICON, HOWEVER.

THESE ARE THE IMAGES WE USE TO REPRESENT *CONCEPTS, IDEAS* AND *PHILOSOPHIES*.

THEN THERE ARE THE ICONS OF *LANGUAGE, SCIENCE* AND *COMMUNICATION*.

A	B	C	D
1	2	3	4
?	:	!	*
田	森	雨	石
+	=	×	÷
$	%	©	¢

ICONS OF THE *PRACTICAL* REALM.

AND FINALLY, THE ICONS WE CALL *PICTURES*: IMAGES DESIGNED TO ACTUALLY *RESEMBLE* THEIR SUBJECTS.

BUT AS RESEMBLANCE VARIES, SO DOES THE LEVEL OF ICONIC CONTENT.

OR TO PUT IT SOMEWHAT *CLUMSILY*, SOME PICTURES ARE JUST MORE ICONIC THAN OTHERS.

IN THE *NON-PICTORIAL* ICONS, MEANING IS *FIXED* AND *ABSOLUTE*. THEIR APPEARANCE DOESN'T AFFECT THEIR MEANING BECAUSE THEY REPRESENT *INVISIBLE IDEAS*.

IN *PICTURES*, HOWEVER, MEANING IS *FLUID* AND *VARIABLE* ACCORDING TO APPEARANCE. THEY DIFFER FROM "*REAL-LIFE*" APPEARANCE TO VARYING *DEGREES*.

WORDS ARE TOTALLY *ABSTRACT*. THAT IS, THEY BEAR NO RESEMBLANCE AT ALL TO THE *REAL McCOY*.

EYE

BUT IN PICTURES THE *LEVEL* OF ABSTRACTION *VARIES*. SOME, LIKE THE FACE IN THE *PREVIOUS* PANEL, SO CLOSELY RESEMBLE THEIR *REAL-LIFE COUNTERPARTS* AS TO ALMOST *TRICK THE EYE!*

OTHERS, LIKE YOURS TRULY, ARE QUITE A BIT *MORE* ABSTRACT AND, IN FACT, ARE VERY MUCH *UNLIKE* ANY HUMAN FACE YOU'VE EVER SEEN!

LET'S SEE IF WE CAN PUT THESE *PICTORIAL ICONS* IN SOME SORT OF ORDER.

COMMON WISDOM HOLDS THAT THE *PHOTOGRAPH* AND THE *REALISTIC* PICTURE ARE THE ICONS THAT MOST RESEMBLE THEIR REAL-LIFE COUNTERPARTS.

THERE ARE MANY THINGS THAT SET THESE APART FROM ACTUAL *FACES*--THEY'RE SMALLER, FLATTER, LESS *DETAILED*, THEY DON'T MOVE. THEY LACK COLOR-- BUT AS PICTORIAL ICONS GO, THEY ARE PRETTY "*REALISTIC*."

REALITY THIS WAY.

WHY-- --ARE-- --WE-- --SO-- --INVOLVED?

WHY WOULD *ANYONE,* YOUNG OR OLD, RESPOND TO A CARTOON AS MUCH OR MORE THAN A *REALISTIC IMAGE?*

WHY IS OUR CULTURE *SO IN THRALL* TO THE *SIMPLIFIED REALITY* OF THE *CARTOON?*

DEFINING THE CARTOON WOULD TAKE UP AS MUCH SPACE AS DEFINING *COMICS,* BUT FOR *NOW,* I'M GOING TO EXAMINE CARTOONING AS A FORM OF *AMPLIFICATION THROUGH SIMPLIFICATION.*

WHEN WE *ABSTRACT* AN IMAGE THROUGH *CARTOONING,* WE'RE NOT SO MUCH *ELIMINATING* DETAILS AS WE ARE *FOCUSING* ON *SPECIFIC DETAILS.*

BY *STRIPPING DOWN* AN IMAGE TO ITS ESSENTIAL *"MEANING,"* AN ARTIST CAN *AMPLIFY* THAT MEANING IN A WAY THAT REALISTIC ART *CAN'T.*

FILM CRITICS WILL SOMETIMES DESCRIBE A *LIVE-ACTION* FILM AS A "CARTOON" TO ACKNOWLEDGE THE STRIPPED-DOWN *INTENSITY* OF A SIMPLE STORY OR VISUAL STYLE.

THOUGH THE TERM IS OFTEN USED *DISPARAGINGLY*, IT CAN BE EQUALLY WELL APPLIED TO MANY *TIME-TESTED CLASSICS*. SIMPLIFYING CHARACTERS AND IMAGES TOWARD A *PURPOSE* CAN BE AN EFFECTIVE TOOL FOR STORYTELLING IN *ANY* MEDIUM.

CARTOONING ISN'T JUST A WAY OF *DRAWING*, IT'S A WAY OF *SEEING!*

FOLLOW! FOLLOW!

THE ABILITY OF CARTOONS TO *FOCUS* OUR ATTENTION ON AN IDEA IS, I THINK, AN IMPORTANT PART OF THEIR SPECIAL POWER, BOTH IN COMICS AND IN DRAWING GENERALLY.

ONE — A FEW — THOUSANDS — MILLIONS — (NEARLY) ALL

ANOTHER IS THE *UNIVERSALITY* OF CARTOON IMAGERY. THE MORE CARTOONY A FACE IS, FOR INSTANCE, THE MORE PEOPLE IT COULD BE SAID TO *DESCRIBE*.

BUT I BELIEVE THERE'S SOMETHING *MORE* AT WORK IN OUR MINDS WHEN WE VIEW A CARTOON--ESPECIALLY OF A HUMAN FACE-- WHICH WARRANTS FURTHER INVESTIGATION.

WHAT   ARE YOU

REALLY   SEEING?

THE FACT THAT YOUR MIND IS *CAPABLE* OF TAKING A *CIRCLE, TWO DOTS* AND A *LINE* AND TURNING THEM INTO A *FACE* IS NOTHING SHORT OF *INCREDIBLE!*

BUT STILL *MORE* INCREDIBLE IS THE FACT THAT YOU CANNOT *AVOID* SEEING A FACE HERE. YOUR MIND WON'T *LET* YOU!

ASK A FRIEND TO DRAW YOU SOME SHAPES ON A PIECE OF PAPER. THEY SHOULD BE *CLOSED CURVES*, BUT *OTHER-WISE* CAN BE AS *WEIRD* AND *IRREGULAR* AS HE OR SHE *WANTS*.

LET'S SAY THE RESULTS LOOK SOMETHING LIKE *THIS*.

NOW -- YOU'LL FIND THAT NO MATTER WHAT THEY *LOOK* LIKE, EVERY SINGLE *ONE* OF THOSE SHAPES *CAN* BE MADE INTO A FACE WITH ONE SIMPLE ADDITION

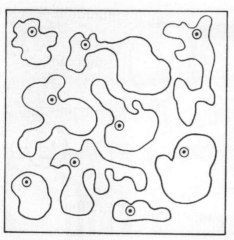

YOUR MIND HAS NO TROUBLE AT ALL CONVERTING SUCH SHAPES INTO FACES, YET WOULD IT EVER MISTAKE *THIS*--

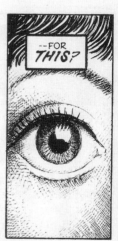

--FOR *THIS*?

WE HUMANS ARE A SELF-CENTERED RACE.

274

ALL SET?

GOOD.

NOW, *SMILE.*

C'MON, NOBODY'S LOOKING.

GOOD. NOW, WHAT *CHANGED* WHEN YOU SMILED? WHAT DID YOU SEE?

NOTHING, RIGHT.

YET, YOU *KNOW* YOU SMILED! NOT JUST BECAUSE YOU FELT YOUR CHEEKS COMPRESS OR THE CRINKLING AROUND YOUR EYES!

YOU *KNOW* YOU SMILED BECAUSE YOU TRUSTED THIS MASK CALLED YOUR FACE TO *RESPOND!*

BUT THE FACE YOU SEE IN YOUR *MIND* IS NOT THE SAME AS *OTHERS* SEE!

WHEN TWO PEOPLE INTERRACT, THEY USUALLY LOOK DIRECTLY *AT* ONE ANOTHER, SEEING THEIR PARTNER'S FEATURES IN *VIVID DETAIL.*

EACH ONE *ALSO* SUSTAINS A CONSTANT AWARENESS OF HIS OR HER *OWN* FACE, BUT *THIS* MIND-PICTURE IS NOT NEARLY SO VIVID; JUST A SKETCHY ARRANGEMENT... A SENSE OF SHAPE... A SENSE OF *GENERAL PLACEMENT.*

SOMETHING AS *SIMPLE* AND AS *BASIC*--

--AS A *CARTOON.*

THUS, WHEN YOU LOOK AT A PHOTO OR REALISTIC DRAWING OF A FACE--

--YOU SEE IT AS THE FACE OF *ANOTHER.*

BUT WHEN YOU ENTER THE WORLD OF THE *CARTOON*--

-- YOU SEE *YOURSELF.*

I BELIEVE THIS IS THE *PRIMARY CAUSE* OF OUR CHILDHOOD FASCINATION WITH *CARTOONS* THOUGH OTHER FACTORS SUCH AS *UNIVERSAL IDENTIFICATION, SIMPLICITY* AND THE *CHILDLIKE FEATURES* OF MANY CARTOON CHARACTERS ALSO PLAY A PART.

THE CARTOON IS A *VACUUM* INTO WHICH OUR *IDENTITY* AND *AWARENESS* ARE PULLED...

... AN *EMPTY SHELL* THAT WE INHABIT WHICH *ENABLES* US TO TRAVEL IN *ANOTHER REALM.*

WE DON'T JUST *OBSERVE* THE CARTOON, WE *BECOME* IT!

THAT'S WHY I DECIDED TO *DRAW* MYSELF IN SUCH A SIMPLE *STYLE.*

WOULD YOU HAVE *LISTENED* TO ME IF I LOOKED LIKE *THIS*??

I *DOUBT* IT! YOU WOULD HAVE BEEN FAR TOO AWARE OF THE *MESSENGER* TO FULLY RECEIVE THE *MESSAGE!*

APART FROM WHAT LITTLE I TOLD YOU ABOUT MYSELF IN *CHAPTER ONE*, I'M PRACTICALLY A *BLANK SLATE!*

IT WOULD NEVER EVEN *OCCUR* TO YOU TO WONDER WHAT MY *POLITICS* ARE, OR WHAT I HAD FOR *LUNCH* OR WHERE I GOT THIS *SILLY OUTFIT!*

I'M JUST A LITTLE VOICE INSIDE YOUR *HEAD.*

A *CONCEPT.*

YOU GIVE ME LIFE BY READING THIS BOOK AND BY "*FILLING UP*" THIS VERY *ICONIC* (CARTOONY) *FORM.*

WHO I AM IS IRRELEVANT. I'M JUST A LITTLE PIECE OF *YOU.*

BUT IF WHO I AM MATTERS *LESS*, MAYBE WHAT I *SAY* WILL MATTER *MORE.*

THAT'S THE *THEORY*, ANYWAY.

SO FAR, WE'VE ONLY DISCUSSED *FACES*, BUT THE PHENOMENON OF *NON-VISUAL SELF-AWARENESS* CAN, TO A *LESSER DEGREE*, STILL APPLY TO OUR *WHOLE BODIES.* AFTER ALL, DO WE NEED TO *SEE* OUR HANDS TO KNOW WHAT THEY'RE DOING?

THERE'S *MORE*, TOO!

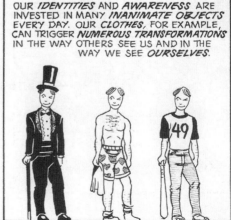

OUR ABILITY TO *EXTEND* OUR IDENTITIES INTO INANIMATE OBJECTS CAN CAUSE PIECES OF WOOD TO BECOME *LEGS...*

PIECES OF METAL TO BECOME *HANDS...*

PIECES OF PLASTIC TO BECOME *EARS...*

PIECES OF GLASS TO BECOME *EYES.*

AND IN *EVERY CASE,* OUR CONSTANT AWARENESS OF *SELF--*

--FLOWS *OUTWARD* TO INCLUDE THE OBJECT OF OUR *EXTENDED IDENTITY.*

AND JUST AS OUR AWARENESS OF OUR *BIOLOGICAL* SELVES ARE *SIMPLIFIED CONCEPTUALIZED IMAGES--*

--SO TOO IS OUR AWARENESS OF *THESE* EXTENSIONS GREATLY *SIMPLIFIED.*

ALL THE THINGS WE *EXPERIENCE* IN LIFE CAN BE SEPARATED INTO *TWO REALMS,* THE *REALM OF THE CONCEPT--*

--AND THE REALM OF THE *SENSES.*

--WE *LEND* TO THEM.

BY DE-EMPHASIZING THE *APPEARANCE* OF THE *PHYSICAL* WORLD IN FAVOR OF THE *IDEA* OF FORM, THE CARTOON PLACES ITSELF IN THE WORLD OF *CONCEPTS*.

THROUGH TRADITIONAL *REALISM*, THE COMICS ARTIST CAN PORTRAY THE WORLD *WITHOUT*--

--AND THROUGH THE *CARTOON*, THE WORLD *WITHIN*.

WHEN CARTOONS ARE USED *THROUGHOUT* A STORY, THE *WORLD* OF THAT STORY MAY SEEM TO *PULSE WITH LIFE*.

INANIMATE OBJECTS MAY SEEM TO POSSESS *SEPARATE IDENTITIES* SO THAT IF ONE *JUMPED UP* AND STARTED *SINGING* IT WOULDN'T FEEL OUT OF PLACE.

BUT IN EMPHASIZING THE *CONCEPTS* OF OBJECTS OVER THEIR *PHYSICAL APPEARANCE*, MUCH HAS TO BE *OMITTED*.

IF AN ARTIST WANTS TO PORTRAY THE BEAUTY AND COMPLEXITY OF THE *PHYSICAL WORLD*--

--REALISM OF *SOME* SORT IS GOING TO PLAY A PART.

281

WHEN DRAWING THE FACE AND FIGURE, NEARLY *ALL* COMICS ARTISTS APPLY AT LEAST *SOME* SMALL MEASURE OF CARTOONING. EVEN THE MORE REALISTIC *ADVENTURE* ARTISTS--

--ARE A *FAR CRY* FROM *PHOTO-REALISTS!*

STORYTELLERS IN *ALL* MEDIA KNOW THAT A SURE INDICATOR OF *AUDIENCE INVOLVEMENT*--

--IS THE DEGREE TO WHICH THE AUDIENCE *IDENTIFIES* WITH A STORY'S *CHARACTERS.*

AND SINCE *VIEWER-IDENTIFICATION* IS A *SPECIALTY* OF CARTOONING, CARTOONS HAVE HISTORICALLY HELD AN *ADVANTAGE* IN *BREAKING INTO WORLD POPULAR CULTURE.*

ON THE OTHER HAND, NO ONE EXPECTS AUDIENCES TO IDENTIFY WITH *BRICK WALLS* OR *LANDSCAPES* AND *INDEED*, BACKGROUNDS TEND TO BE SLIGHTLY MORE *REALISTIC.*

IN *SOME* COMICS, THIS SPLIT IS FAR MORE *PRONOUNCED.* THE BELGIAN *"CLEAR-LINE"* STYLE OF HERGÉ'S *TINTIN* COMBINES VERY ICONIC CHARACTERS WITH UNUSUALLY *REALISTIC* BACKGROUNDS.

THIS COMBINATION ALLOWS READERS TO *MASK* THEMSELVES IN A CHARACTER AND SAFELY ENTER A SENSUALLY STIMULATING WORLD.

ONE SET OF LINES TO *SEE.* ANOTHER SET OF LINES TO *BE.*

IN THE WORLD OF *ANIMATION,* WHERE THE EFFECT HAPPENS TO BE A PRACTICAL *NECESSITY,* DISNEY HAS USED IT WITH IMPRESSIVE RESULTS FOR OVER *50 YEARS!*

IN *EUROPE* IT CAN BE FOUND IN MANY POPULAR COMICS, FROM *ASTERIX* TO *TINTIN* TO WORKS OF *JACQUES TARDI.*

IN *AMERICAN* COMICS, THE EFFECT IS USED FAR LESS *OFTEN,* ALTHOUGH IT HAS CREPT UP IN THE WORKS OF ARTISTS AS DIVERSE AS *CARL BARKS, JAIME HERNANDEZ* AND IN THE TEAM OF *DAVE SIM* AND *GERHARD.*

IN *JAPAN,* ON THE OTHER HAND, THE MASKING EFFECT WAS, FOR A TIME, VIRTUALLY A *NATIONAL STYLE!*

THANKS TO THE *SEMINAL INFLUENCE* OF COMICS CREATOR *OSAMU TEZUKA,* JAPANESE COMICS HAVE A LONG, RICH HISTORY OF ICONIC CHARACTERS.

BUT, IN RECENT DECADES JAPANESE FANS ALSO DEVELOPED A TASTE FOR *FLASHY, PHOTO-REALISTIC ART.*

CLIK!

THE RESULTANT HYBRID STYLES HAD TREMENDOUS ICONIC *RANGE*, FROM EXTREMELY CARTOONY CHARACTERS TO *NEAR-PHOTOGRAPHIC BACKGROUNDS*.

"MONA GOES TOKYO"

BUT JAPANESE COMICS ARTISTS TOOK THE IDEA A STEP FURTHER.

SOON, SOME OF THEM REALIZED THAT THE *OBJECTIFYING POWER* OF REALISTIC ARTS COULD BE PUT TO *OTHER* USES.

FOR EXAMPLE, WHILE *MOST* CHARACTERS WERE DESIGNED *SIMPLY*, TO ASSIST IN *READER-IDENTIFICATION*--

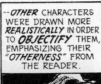

--*OTHER* CHARACTERS WERE DRAWN MORE *REALISTICALLY* IN ORDER TO *OBJECTIFY* THEM, EMPHASIZING THEIR *"OTHERNESS"* FROM THE READER.

A PROP LIKE THIS *SWORD* MIGHT BE VERY *CARTOONY* IN *ONE* SEQUENCE--

--DUE TO THE *"LIFE"* IT POSSESSES AS AN EXTENSION OF MY CARTOON IDENTITY!

BUT SUPPOSE I NOTICE SOME *MYSTERIOUS WRITING* CARVED ON THE SWORD'S *HILT*.

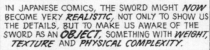

IN JAPANESE COMICS, THE SWORD MIGHT *NOW* BECOME VERY *REALISTIC*, NOT ONLY TO SHOW US THE DETAILS, BUT TO MAKE US AWARE OF THE SWORD AS AN *OBJECT*, SOMETHING WITH *WEIGHT*, *TEXTURE* AND *PHYSICAL COMPLEXITY*.

IN THIS AND IN *OTHER WAYS*, COMICS IN JAPAN HAVE EVOLVED VERY *DIFFERENTLY* FROM THOSE IN THE WEST.

WE'LL RETURN TO THESE DIFFERENCES SEVERAL TIMES DURING THIS BOOK.

I *LIKE* THE MASKING EFFECT, PERSONALLY, BUT IT'S JUST ONE OF *MANY* POSSIBLE APPROACHES TO COMICS ART.

MANY OF MY *FAVORITE ARTISTS* USE IT VERY *RARELY.*

STILL, I HOPE THE JAPANESE PERSPECTIVE ON CARTOONING HELPS DEMONSTRATE THAT ONE'S CHOICE OF STYLES CAN HAVE CONSEQUENCES FAR BEYOND THE MERE *"LOOK"* OF A STORY.

AS I WRITE THIS, IN 1992, AMERICAN AUDIENCES ARE JUST BEGINNING TO REALIZE THAT A SIMPLE *STYLE* DOESN'T NECESSITATE SIMPLE *STORY.*

THE PLATONIC IDEAL OF THE CARTOON MAY SEEM TO OMIT MUCH OF THE *AMBIGUITY* AND *COMPLEX CHARACTERIZATION* WHICH ARE THE HALLMARKS OF *MODERN LITERATURE,* LEAVING THEM SUITABLE ONLY FOR *CHILDREN.*

BUT SIMPLE ELEMENTS CAN COMBINE IN COMPLEX WAYS, AS ATOMS BECOME MOLECULES AND MOLECULES BECOME LIFE.

AND *LIKE* THE ATOM, GREAT POWER IS LOCKED IN THESE FEW SIMPLE LINES.

RELEASEABLE ONLY BY THE READER'S MIND.

THERE'S A LOT MORE TO *CARTOONS* THAN MEETS THE EYE!

MEANING RETAINED.

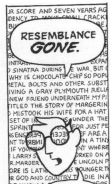

RESEMBLANCE **GONE**.

WORDS--

--ARE THE ULTIMATE ABSTRACTION.

MOST AMERICAN COMICS, NOTABLY COMIC **BOOKS**, HAVE LONG EMPHASIZED THE **DIFFERENCES** BETWEEN WORDS AND PICTURES.

WRITING AND DRAWING ARE SEEN AS **SEPARATE DISCIPLINES**, WRITERS AND ARTISTS AS **SEPARATE BREEDS**--

-- AND "GOOD" COMICS AS THOSE IN WHICH THE **COMBINATION** OF THESE VERY **DIFFERENT** FORMS OF EXPRESSION IS THOUGHT TO BE **HARMONIOUS**.

BUT JUST HOW "DIFFERENT" **ARE** THEY?

WORDS, PICTURES AND OTHER ICONS ARE THE **VOCABULARY** OF THE LANGUAGE CALLED **COMICS**.

A SINGLE UNIFIED **LANGUAGE** DESERVES A SINGLE, UNIFIED **VOCABULARY**.

WITHOUT IT, COMICS WILL CONTINUE TO **LIMP ALONG** AS THE **"BASTARD CHILD"** OF WORDS AND PICTURES.

SEVERAL FACTORS HAVE CONSPIRED **AGAINST** COMICS RECEIVING THE **UNIFIED IDENTITY** IT **NEEDS**.

AND AMONG THEM LIE SOME OF OUR VERY **BEST** INSTINCTS.

287

BOTH ARTIST AND WRITER BEGIN, HANDS JOINED ACROSS THE GAP, WITH A COMMON PURPOSE: TO MAKE COMICS OF "*QUALITY*"

"ARTIE"   "RITA"

FACE

THE ARTIST KNOWS THAT THIS MEANS MORE THAN JUST *STICK-FIGURES* AND *CRUDE CARTOONS*. HE SETS OFF IN SEARCH OF A *HIGHER* ART.

THE WRITER KNOWS THAT THIS MEANS MORE THAN JUST *OOF! POW! BLAM!* AND *ONE-A-DAY GAGS*. SHE SETS OFF IN SEARCH OF SOMETHING *DEEPER*.

IN MUSEUMS AND IN LIBRARIES, THE ARTIST FINDS WHAT HE'S LOOKING FOR. HE STUDIES THE TECHNIQUES OF THE *GREAT MASTERS OF WESTERN ART*. HE PRACTICES *NIGHT AND DAY*.

SHE *TOO* FINDS WHAT SHE'S LOOKING FOR, IN THE GREAT MASTERS OF *WESTERN LITERATURE*. SHE READS AND WRITES *CONSTANTLY*. SHE SEARCHES FOR A VOICE *UNIQUELY HERS*.

FINALLY, THEY'RE READY. BOTH HAVE *MASTERED THEIR ARTS*. HIS BRUSHSTROKE IS NEARLY *INVISIBLE* IN ITS SUBTLETY, THE FIGURES PURE *MICHAELANGELO*. HER DESCRIPTIONS ARE *DAZZLING*. THE WORDS FLOW TOGETHER LIKE A *SHAKESPEAREAN SONNET*.

THEY'RE READY TO *JOIN HANDS* ONCE MORE AND CREATE A *COMICS MASTERPIECE*.

FACE → TWO EYES, ONE NOSE, → ONE MOUTH. *Thy youth's proud livery, so gaz'd on now...*

PICTURES ARE **RECEIVED** INFORMATION. WE NEED NO FORMAL EDUCATION TO *"GET THE MESSAGE."* THE MESSAGE IS *INSTANTANEOUS.*

WRITING IS **PERCEIVED** INFORMATION. IT TAKES TIME AND SPECIALIZED KNOWLEDGE TO DECODE THE ABSTRACT SYMBOLS OF LANGUAGE.

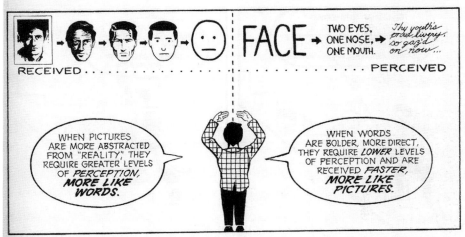

RECEIVED . . . . PERCEIVED

FACE → TWO EYES, ONE NOSE, ONE MOUTH. → *Thy youth's proud livery so gaz'd on now...*

WHEN PICTURES ARE MORE ABSTRACTED FROM "REALITY," THEY REQUIRE GREATER LEVELS OF *PERCEPTION,* **MORE LIKE WORDS.**

WHEN WORDS ARE BOLDER, MORE DIRECT, THEY REQUIRE *LOWER* LEVELS OF PERCEPTION AND ARE RECEIVED *FASTER,* **MORE LIKE PICTURES.**

OUR NEED FOR A UNIFIED *LANGUAGE* OF COMICS SENDS US TOWARD THE CENTER WHERE WORDS AND PICTURES ARE LIKE TWO SIDES OF *ONE COIN!*

BUT OUR NEED FOR *SOPHISTICATION* IN COMICS SEEMS TO LEAD US *OUTWARD,* WHERE WORDS AND PICTURES ARE MOST *SEPARATE.*

BOTH ARE **WORTHY** *ASPIRATIONS.* BOTH STEM FROM A LOVE OF COMICS AND A DEVOTION TO ITS FUTURE.

CAN THEY BE *RECONCILED?*

I SAY THE ANSWER IS *YES,* BUT SINCE THE REASONS BELONG IN A *DIFFERENT CHAPTER,* WE'LL HAVE TO COME BACK TO THIS *LATER.*

289

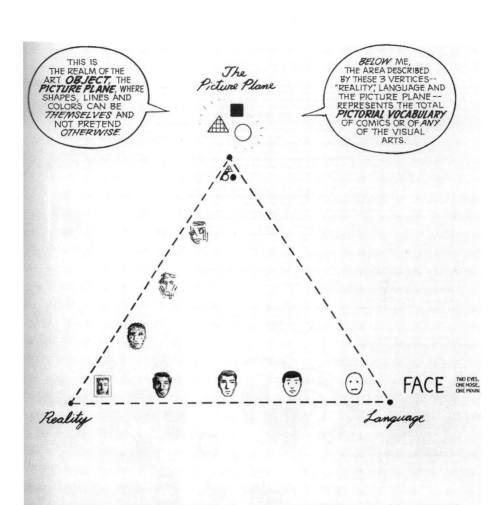

THIS IS THE REALM OF THE ART **OBJECT**, THE **PICTURE PLANE**, WHERE SHAPES, LINES AND COLORS CAN BE *THEMSELVES* AND NOT PRETEND *OTHERWISE.*

The Picture Plane

BELOW ME, THE AREA DESCRIBED BY THESE 3 VERTICES-- "REALITY", LANGUAGE AND THE PICTURE PLANE-- REPRESENTS THE TOTAL **PICTORIAL VOCABULARY** OF COMICS OR OF *ANY* OF THE VISUAL ARTS.

FACE TWO EYES, ONE NOSE, ONE MOUTH

Reality

Language

MOST COMICS ART LIES NEAR THE **BOTTOM**-- THAT IS, ALONG THE *ICONIC ABSTRACTION* SIDE WHERE EVERY LINE HAS A *MEANING.*

NEAR THE LINE, BUT NOT NECESSARILY *ON* IT! FOR EVEN THE MOST *STRAIGHTFORWARD* LITTLE CARTOON CHARACTER HAS A "*MEANINGLESS*" LINE OR TWO!

WATCH THAT *NOSE!*

IF WE INCORPORATE LANGUAGE AND OTHER ICONS *INTO* THE CHART, WE CAN BEGIN TO BUILD A COMPREHENSIVE *MAP*--

--OF THE *UNIVERSE* CALLED **COMICS.**

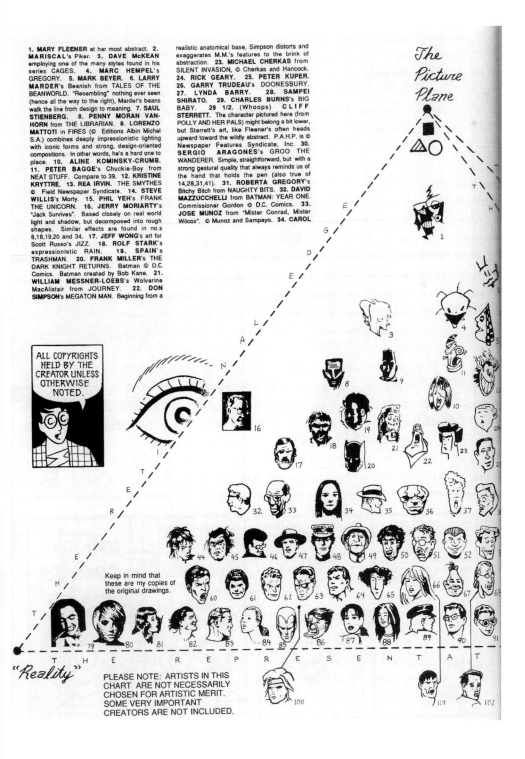

SWAIN. **35.** CHESTER GOULD's DICK TRACY © Chicago Tribune-New York Syndicate, Inc. **36.** JACK KIRBY's Darkseid, © D.C. Comics. **37.** BOB BURDEN. **38.** DANIEL TORRES's Rocco Vargas from TRITON. **39.** PETER BAGGE's Buddy Bradley from HATE. Compare to 11. **40.** SETH. **41.** MARK MARTIN. **42.** JULIE DOUCET. **43.** EDWARD GOREY. **44.** CRAIG RUSSELL's Mowgli from Kipling's THE JUNGLE BOOKS. Russell's characters are as finely observed and realistically based as Hal Foster's or Dave Stevens' but with an unparalleled sense of design that draws them toward the upper vertex. Lately, Russell has been moving a bit higher and toward the right in some cases. **45.** GOSEKI KOJIMA from KOZURE OKAMI

("Wolf and Cub") © Koike and Kojima. **46.** EDDIE CAMPBELL's ALEC. Realistic in tone, but also gestural and spontaneous. The *process* of drawing isn't hidden from view. **47.** ALEX TOTH. Zorro © ZorroProductions, Inc. Art © Walt Disney Productions. (Zorro created by Johnston McCulley). **48.** HUGO PRATT's CORTO MALTESE © Casterman, Paris-Tourmai. **49.** WILL EISNER from TO THE HEART OF THE STORM. **50.** DORI SEDA. **51.** R. CRUMB swings between realistic and cartoony characters, usually staying about this high but occasionally venturing upward. **52.** STEVE DITKO. **53.** NORMAN DOG. **54.** VALENTINO's NORMALMAN sits a bit to the right and up from his current SHADOWHAWK (whose iconic mask made him a bit harder to place). **55.** ROZ CHAST. **56.** JOOST SWARTE's Anton Makassar. **57.** ELZIE SEGAR's POPEYE © King features Syndicate, Inc. **58.** GEORGE HERRIMAN's "Offissa Pupp" from KRAZY KAT. © International feature Service, Inc. **59.** JIM WOODRING's FRANK. **60.** NEAL ADAMS. from X-MEN © Marvel Entertainment Group, Inc. (X-Men created by Lee and Kirby). **61.** GIL KANE from ACTION COMICS © D.C. Comics, Inc. **62.** MILTON CANIFF's STEVE CANYON. **63.** JIM LEE. Nick Fury appearing in X-MEN © Marvel Entertainment Group, Inc. **64.** JOHN BYRNE. Superman © D.C. Comics, Inc. (Superman created by Jerry Siegel and Joe Schuster). **65.** JACQUES TARDI from LE DEMON DES GLACES © Dargaud Editeur. **66.** JEAN-CLAUDE MEZIERES. Laureline from the VALERIAN series. © Dargaud Editeur. **67.** BILL GRIFFITH's ZIPPY THE PINHEAD. **68.** JOE MATT. **69.** KYLE BAKER from WHY I HATE SATURN. **70.** TRINA ROBBINS's

MISTY. © Marvel Entertainment Group, Inc. **71.** RIYOKO IKEDA's Oscar from THE ROSE OF VERSAILLES. **72.** GEORGE McMANUS. BRINGING UP FATHER © International Feature Service, Inc. **73.** CHARLES SCHULZ's Charlie Brown from PEANUTS © United Features Syndicate, Inc. **74.** ART SPIEGELMAN from MAUS. **75.** MATT FEAZELL's CYNICALMAN. **76.** The company Logo. The picture as symbol. **77.** Title Logo. The word as object. **78.** Sound Effect. The word as sound. **79.** TOM KING's SNOOKUMS, THAT LOVABLE TRANSVESTITE. a photo-comic. **80.** DREW FRIEDMAN. **81.** DAVE STEVENS. **82.** HAL FOSTER. TARZAN created by Edgar Rice Burroughs. **83.** ALEX RAYMOND. Flash Gordon © King Features Syndicate, Inc. **84.** MILO MANARA. **85.** JOHN BUSCEMA. The Vision © Marvel Entertainment Group. **86.** CAROL LAY's Irene Van de Kamp from GOOD GIRLS. A bizarre character, but drawn in a very straightforward style. **87.** GILBERT HERNANDEZ. **88.** JAIME HERNANDEZ. **89.** COLIN UPTON. **90.** KURT SCHAFFENBERGER. Superboy © D.C. Comics. **91.** JACK COLE's PLASTIC MAN. © D.C. Comics. **92.** REED WALLER's OMAHA THE CAT DANCER © Waller and Worley. **93.** WENDY PINI's Skywise from ELFQUEST. © WaRP Graphics. **94.** DAN DE CARLO. Veronica © Archie Comics. **95.** HAROLD GRAY's LITTLE ORPHAN ANNIE. © Chicago Tribune- New York News Syndicate. **96.** HERGE's TINTIN © Editions Casterman. **97.** FLOYD GOTTFREDSON. Mickey Mouse © Walt Disney Productions. **98.** JEFF SMITH's BONE. **99.** Smile Dammit. **100.** COLLEEN DORAN's A DISTANT SOIL. **101.** ROY CRANE's CAPTAIN EASY © NEA Service, Inc. **102.** DAN CLOWES. **103.** WAYNO. **104.** V.T. HAMLIN's ALLEY OOP © NEA Service, Inc. **105.** CHESTER BROWN. **106.** STAN SAKAI's USAGI YOJIMBO. **107.** DAVE SIM's CEREBUS THE AARDVARK. **108.** WALT KELLY's POGO © Selby Kelly. **109.** RUDOLPH DIRKS's HANS AND FRITZ © King Features Syndicate, Inc. **110.** H.C. "BUD" FISHER's Jeff from MUTT AND JEFF © McNaught Syndicate, Inc. **111.** MORT WALKER's HI AND LOIS © King Features Syndicate, Inc. **112.** OSAMU TEZUKA's ASTROBOY. **113.** CARL BARKS. Scrooge McDuck © Walt Disney Productions. **114.** CROCKETT JOHNSON's Mister O'Malley from BARNABY © Field Newspaper Syndicate, Inc. **115.** PAT SULLIVAN's FELIX THE CAT © Newspaper Feature Service. **116.** UDERZO. ASTERIX by Goscinny and Uderzo © Dargaud Editeur.

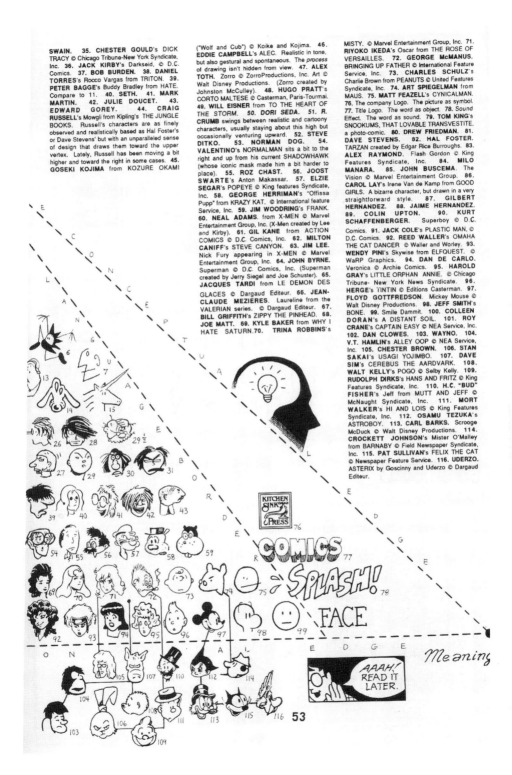

53

293

MOST OF THE PRECEDING EXAMPLES WERE PLACED ON OUR CHART BASED ON THE DRAWING STYLES USED ON *SPECIFIC CHARACTERS.*

EACH CREATOR EMPLOYS A *RANGE* OF STYLES, THOUGH, AND MANY OCCUPY *SEVERAL* PLACES ON THE CHART DURING A GIVEN PROJECT.

SOME, LIKE MATT FEAZELL'S *CYNICALMAN,* KEEP TO ONE AREA CONSISTENTLY.

THE COMBINATION OF *EXTREMELY ICONIC CHARACTERS* AND *ENVIRONMENTS,* MIXED WITH *SIMPLE, DIRECT LANGUAGE* AND A *SOUND EFFECT* OR TWO WOULD GIVE US A SHAPE SOMETHING LIKE *THIS:*

BUT OTHERS *RANGE CONSIDERABLY* FROM ONE END OF THE CHART TO THE OTHER.

WE'VE ALREADY DISCUSSED THE RANGE OF HERGÉ AND OTHERS WHO CONTRAST *ICONIC CHARACTERS* WITH *REALISTIC BACKGROUNDS.*

Sound on!

Vision on!

O.K...Let's roll!

HERGÉ STRETCHES NEARLY FROM *LEFT TO RIGHT*-- FROM *REALISM* TO *CARTOONING*-- BUT VENTURES VERY *LITTLE* INTO THE *UPPER* WORLD OF *NON-ICONIC* ABSTRACTION.

294

MARY FLEENER, ON THE OTHER HAND, VARIES ONLY *SLIGHTLY* IN HER LEVEL OF *ICONIC* CONTENT, WHILE THE LEVEL OF *NON*-ICONIC ABSTRACTION GOES NEARLY FROM *TOP TO BOTTOM!*

ART © MARY FLEENER.

HEY!! COME TA *THINK* OF IT... WHAT *ABOUT* THAT WALKIN' TIME BOMB ??

THAT'S *RIGHT!!* IF HE'S STILL *LOOSE*... THERE'S NO TELLING WHAT'LL HAPPEN !!

IN THE MID-SIXTIES, *JACK KIRBY*, ALONG WITH *STAN LEE*, STAKED OUT A *MIDDLE GROUND* OF *ICONIC FORMS* WITH A SENSE OF THE *REAL* ABOUT THEM, BOLSTERED BY A POWERFUL *DESIGN* SENSE.

ART: JACK KIRBY AND JOE SINNOTT (MY FACSIMILE)
SCRIPT: STAN LEE.

TODAY, MANY AMERICAN MAINSTREAM COMICS STILL FOLLOW KIRBY'S LEAD FOR STORYTELLING, BUT THE DESIRE FOR MORE *REALISTIC* ART AND MORE ELABORATE SCRIPTS HAS PUSHED ART AND STORY *FURTHER APART* IN MANY CASES.

A FIGHT STARTED ON HIS DOORSTEP, HE PUT A STOP TO IT. FAR AS ANYONE KNOWS, ALL THE SURVIVORS ARE PRETTY MUCH OKAY.

WAY YOU TALK, NICHOLAS. FOLKS EXPECT HIM TO START NUKIN' MAMA RUSSIA ANY MOMENT.

IN THE EIGHTIES AND NINETIES, MOST OF THE COUNTERCULTURE OF INDEPENDENT CREATORS, WORKING MOSTLY IN BLACK AND WHITE, STAYED TO THE *RIGHT* OF MAINSTREAM COMICS ART WHILE COVERING A BROAD RANGE OF WRITING STYLES.

THIS FOLLOWS THE LEAD OF THE POST-KURTZMAN GENERATION OF *UNDERGROUND* CARTOONISTS WHO USED CARTOONY STYLES TO PORTRAY ADULT THEMES AND SUBJECT MATTER.

IRONIC THAT THE TWO BASTIONS OF *CARTOONY* ART ARE *UNDERGROUND* AND *CHILDREN'S* COMICS!

PRETTY *FAR APART* AS GENRES GO!

SOME ARTISTS, SUCH AS THE IRREPRESSIBLE *SERGIO ARAGONES*, STAKED THEIR CLAIM ON A PARTICULAR AREA *LONG AGO* AND HAVE BEEN QUITE HAPPY SINCE.

OTHERS, SUCH AS *DAVE McKEAN*, ARE FOREVER *ON THE MOVE, EXPERIMENTING, TAKING CHANCES, NEVER SATISFIED.*

296

ICONS DEMAND OUR PARTICIPATION TO MAKE THEM WORK.

THERE IS NO LIFE HERE EXCEPT THAT WHICH YOU GIVE TO IT.

IT'S *YOUR* JOB TO CREATE AND *RECREATE* ME MOMENT BY MOMENT, NOT JUST THE CARTOONIST'S.

IT'S BEEN OVER *TWENTY YEARS* SINCE McLUHAN FIRST OBSERVED THAT THOSE PEOPLE GROWING UP IN THE LATE TWENTIETH CENTURY DIDN'T WANT *GOALS* SO MUCH AS THEY WANTED *ROLES!* AND THAT'S WHAT VISUAL ICONOGRAPHY IS ALL ABOUT.

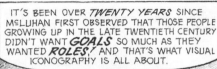

SMILE!

PAF!

AS IT HAPPENS, ONLY *TWO* POPULAR MEDIA WERE IDENTIFIED BY McLUHAN AS "COOL" MEDIA-- THAT IS, MEDIA WHICH COMMAND AUDIENCE INVOLVEMENT THROUGH *ICONIC FORMS.*

ONE OF THEM, *TELEVISION,* HAS REACHED INTO THE LIVES OF EVERY HUMAN BEING ON EARTH--

--AND FOR BETTER OR WORSE, ALTERED THE COURSE OF HUMAN AFFAIRS FROM HERE 'TIL *DOOMSDAY.*

THE FATE OF THE *OTHER* ONE, *COMICS*--

SEQUENTIAL ART

-- IS ANYONE'S GUESS.

Sound Matters: Notes Toward the Analysis and Design of Sound in Multimodal Webtexts

Heidi McKee

CONSIDER AS YOU ARE READING:

Recognizing that we are increasingly immersed in multimodal compositions that include an audio component, McKee poses an important question: How can we begin a conversation about sound in a field that has long privileged the written text and has only recently started seriously considering visual elements of composition? While she acknowledges the difficulties of isolating sound in any analysis of a multimodal composition, McKee identifies vocal qualities, music, sound effects, and silence as four important considerations in analyzing audio in multimodal composition. This essay makes important inroads toward developing sophisticated theories of multimodal rhetoric and providing strategies for analyzing aural texts.

1. *What are the significant elements of each of the four fundamentals McKee considers vital for analyzing audio texts (vocals, music, sound effects, and silence)?*

2. *Listen to a podcast of a news story. How is each element of audio (vocals, music, sound effects, and silence) used to establish ethos?*

3. *Identify two issues—in addition to vocals, music, sound effects, and silence—that shape your response to an aural text.*

"Sound matters. The simplicity of this brief statement could be deceiving"—Gianluca Sergi (2004, p. 3)

As I type this essay, I hear the plasticized, slightly muffled click of the keys and the rhythmic, louder thwick-thwick when my thumb hits the space bar. I hear the whirr of the cooling fan and that odd electronic creaking noise deep in the workings of my computer (a sound that makes me vaguely nervous). When I try to close this document without saving it, the dog help icon woofs at me, jingling its tags and causing my flesh-and-blood dog to rise up and stare eagerly at the screen. Outside I hear the neighbors' children giggling as they run in their yard, and in the distance I hear the faint buzz of a lawnmower.

I chronicle these sounds to emphasize that barring hearing loss,[1] we live immersed in sounds. From the music playing on our stereos and iPods to the rustle of wind through trees, from the voices of people talking, laughing, coughing to the whirr of the electronic devices—we cannot get away from sound. Even in silence, which does not ever truly exist, we hear the sound of our breath and the blood going through our veins. Sound is integral to our worlds.

With the continued development of digitized technologies, sound is also becoming integral to our writing processes as well. Digitization and the increased convergence of computerized technologies enable the integration of visual, aural, and textual elements with unprecedented ease.[2] PowerPoint presentations with soundtracks, Flash works with multiple sound events, webtexts with embedded video and audio—in this multimedia matrix, what is the role of sound in meaning-making? How do we as composition instructors begin to think about and talk about sound design with students? Rhetoric and composition scholars have discussed the visual a great deal, but we haven't as of yet turned our attention to sound. How should we develop understandings of the sounds in which we're immersed and

---

1   An important issue I do not discuss is accessibility. None of the works I analyze follows the principles of Universal Design and the guidelines of such organizations as W3C (e.g., providing subtitles for all sounds, text-reader alternatives for all photographic images).

2   Terminology is, as it always is, a problem. My use of the terms visual, aural, textual implies that text is not visual, for example, or that the aural is not visual (as indeed it becomes so with the interfaces of most sound editing programs). I use textual throughout to refer to the written/alphanumeric, linguistic elements in a webtext.

that increasingly shape how and what we write? Given this move to even greater multiple modalities in composition, what are writers and writing teachers to do?

I first encountered these questions several years ago when I cotaught a writing course focusing on creative multimodal web compositions. As my co-teacher, Brian Houle, and I planned and taught the class and learned with students, we focused a great deal on the visual design of interactive Flash works, but belatedly we realized that we had not discussed sound with students—at least not in theoretical, operational, and critical ways. When students storyboarded their various projects (poetry, virtual world games, literary reinterpretations, hypertextual fictions), they noted timing, sequencing, tweening, various visual behaviors, text placement and the like, but very few noted what types of sounds would accompany their texts and how those sounds would function. Nor did they mark how the sounds would be initiated and how (and if) sounds could be stopped. However, by the time students were finished with their projects, all but two of them had included sound in their work.

For example, one student had slow-paced piano chords play while lines of his poem describing isolation unfurled against a stark, gray landscape. Another student created a drag-in-drop work spoofing his dorm, a work based on "Hangover House" published in *Born Magazine* (Rusen & Dittmar, 2002). When a viewer/user/interacter clicked on characters and dragged them to a different location in the room, dialogue would ensue between the characters, dialogue the student taped one night with his friends and then imported into Flash. Another student, one who co-wrote an article about his project with Brian and me (see Houle, Kimball, & McKee, 2004), wrote a primarily text-based hypertextual autobiographical piece about his female-to-male transgendered transformation. He included sound clips of his higher-pitched voice when he was Bethany and his deeper testosterone-enhanced voice when he was Alex. For the most part, as I hope these brief examples show, students used sound in creative and interesting ways in their Flash compositions, and it seemed as if they were drawing from a variety of web and nonweb genres in doing so. But when discussing their works-in-progress with us and with each other and when we asked them to reflect on their use of sound—and when we ourselves tried to articulate and reflect with them on their use of sound—we found that we lacked cohesive frameworks for doing so.

As Scott Halbritter (2004) noted in his dissertation on sound in the composition classroom (focusing in particular on the concept of voice and the use of music in films, the latter of which he also discusses in an article in this issue), "While our students may have a seemingly inherent felt sense about how to assess the rhetorical effectiveness of an image or a piece of music in an integrated media composition, this felt sense may not guide them productively to make the critical determination necessary to replace, revise, or remediate their integrated media composition" (p. 196). To this I would add instructors, not just students, may not be able to productively make critical determinations. While Brian and I and our students intuitively had a sense of how to use sound and while we could use the basic rhetorical concepts of audience, purpose, and the like, we did not have more detailed frameworks for talking about sound and how it functions.[3]

Figuring out how sound works—both as a single representational mode and, more important, as a mode-in-relation (i.e., how

---

3   This seems self-evident now, but when Brian Houle and I were in the midst of teaching the digital authoring course, we did not think to do the simple and important first step of discussing with students their understandings of sound in multimedia works. Although we had asked them a great deal about their prior experiences and under-standings of the visual design of different interactive web works in preparation for their own design, we just didn't think to talk about the various elements of sound. Questions we could have asked that I think would be helpful for drawing out and articulating students' tacit knowledge of sound include:

- What types of sites do you visit on the Web that include sound?
- How would you describe the function and purpose of the sound on these different sites? Do you notice that there are certain types of sounds that are more commonly used with certain types of sites?
- What terms do you know or have you heard people use when describing sound (either on the Web or in different contexts)?
- What annoys you about sound and its use on the Web? What do you particularly like? Provide some specific examples to share with the class.
- When you compose your multimodal webtext, how might you use sound in your composition? Why?

Obviously this is just a small sample of the types of exploratory questions that could be asked (and none of these questions ask about the role of silence). Regardless of the specific types of questions—some may have a more critical edge, some more rhetorical, others more genre-based—I think it is important that we engage students in these discussions (a) to get them thinking about sound and (b) because they may have a lot more ideas about how to think about sound than we can ever come up with, ideas that can be incorporated into the basic four-part framework I present in this article.

sound, images, texts, not to mention such things as interactivity, work together, forming what Gunther Kress and Theo Van Leeuwen (2001) called *synaesthesia*)—is complicated because of the multiplicity and morphing of genres in which sound occurs and because of the diverse fields upon which to draw when considering sound. As I started to read about sound in other fields, and as I cruised the Web with the speakers turned up, I became a bit overwhelmed. There's a great deal out there with and about sound, but how might writers and writing teachers make sense of it all?

In this essay, I draw from approaches advocated in voice, music, film, theater, and media studies to present a four-part schema for understanding various elements of sound. Sound in multimedia compositions is generally described as including three elements: vocal delivery, music, and special effects. But, as I will explain in more detail below, silence, the almost sound of no sound, also needs to be part of any rhetorical considerations of sound. While it is possible to examine sound and each of its four elements individually—and indeed I will do so in the discussion that follows—it is also important to consider sound (and all the elements of sound) in relation to other modes of representation as well (e.g., textual, visual, kinesthetic/interactive, etc.). Thus, I will first address the often tricky relationship of part-to-whole and whole-to-part when seeking to analyze and compose with multiple modalities.

1. Locating meaning in a multimodal ensemble

One of the first electronic media to combine modes was film, which initially combined text in subtitles with the visual pantomime that was acting and then added sound through the use of "sound effects boys" (Bottomore, 2001) and music players in theaters, then synchronized music tracks, and finally, by the late 1920s and early 1930s, fully synchronized dialogue, music, and special effect soundtracks.[4] As a number of film theorists have noted (see especially Altman, 1992a), it is impossible to talk about a soundtrack of a movie separate from the visual

---

4   For detailed discussions of the incorporation of sound in film, see the following sources: Abel and Altman (2001), Altman (2004), Cameron (1980), Lastra (2000), and Weis and Belton (1985).

images; they each combine to form one communicative event (or a series of communicative events). Sound editor Helen Van Dongen explained it this way:

> Picture and track, to a certain degree, have a composition of their own but when combined they form a new entity. Thus the track becomes not only a harmonious complement but an integral inseparable part of the picture as well. Picture and track are so closely fused together that each one functions through the other. There is no separation of *I see* in the image and *I hear* on the track. Instead, there is the *I feel, I experience* through the grand-total of picture and track combined. (qtd. in Douane, 1985, p. 56)

While it is possible to examine the visual separate from the aural, this practice is incomplete for understanding the grand-total of both combined.

Within the fields of language and communication studies, Kress and Van Leeuwen (2001) have also noted the importance of examining modes in relation. After publishing a number of works examining discrete modes of communication, they prefaced *Multimodal Discourse* by explaining that "discussing the different modes (language, image, music, sound, gesture, and so on) separately was not good enough" (p. vii). By focusing on the relationships of discourse, design, production, and distribution, they argued for an integrated semiosis, one that would recognize the interdependence of the different variables in a communicative event, and one that would recognize that communicative practices "can aggregate and disaggregate in different ways" (p. 122). To illustrate the integrated work of various modes, Kress and Van Leeuwen provide an extended example of a science teacher presenting a lesson on human anatomy where the teacher talks, writes on the board, and manipulates a plastic skeleton. Such an example works well to indicate the potentially seamless integration of multimodal elements into one communicative event.

Yet when working with computerized writing technologies, despite the integration of modes in the final product—for example, animated images and music in a Flash movie—each of those elements still exists separately in the computer. This together-but-separate feature of digitized compositions is one of the defining principles of new media, according to Lev Manovich (2001). In *The Language of New Media*, he identified the second of five principles of new media as modularity (the others being numerical representation, automation, variability, and transcoding),[5] which he explained as follows:

> Media elements, be they images, sounds, shapes, or behaviors, are represented as collections of discrete samples (pixels, polygons, voxels, characters, scripts). These elements are assembled into larger-scale objects but continue to maintain their separate identities. The objects themselves can be combined into even larger objects—again, without losing their independence. (p. 30)

Even though we as end users/viewers/interacters with a web site may experience an integrated composition, the elements of that composition are treated by the computer as separate entities. Given the computer-imposed constraints when composing multimodal works (what Manovich identified as the computer's ontology, epistemology, and pragmatics), writers do then at some level have to consider sound separate from image separate from text, particularly since with most multimedia authoring programs, such as Photoshop and Flash, different modes are best brought in on different layers because of the numerical structuring of computers. Because of the computer's shaping influence on the process of composing and thus on what is produced, it is important for writers of webtexts and those who are analyzing webtexts to consider the various constraints shaping the production and reception of a work.

Thus, in the four-part framework I present below, I will not only discuss the four individual elements of sound in isolation but also in relation to other elements of sound, in relation to other modes of communication, and in relation to technological considerations. I provide brief analyses of creative webtexts

---

5   For an analysis of Manovich's five elements incorporated into a new media pedagogy, see Madeleine Sorapure's (2003) *Kairos* article "Five Principles of New Media, or Playing Lev Manovich," which includes sample student texts.

that illustrate particularly effective uses of sound. Although there are innumerable webtexts that incorporate sound on the Web, I decided to focus on one genre of text so as to facilitate discussion of the examples across the various elements and I decided to focus on works that incorporated multiple modalities. Specifically, I examine multimodal, poetic Flash texts because I found their use of sound particularly interesting and reflective of possibilities transferable to other genres. I focus on webtexts because unlike other media they are readily available; and I try as well to choose texts that are located at stable sites that will, I hope, be around for many more years to come. Integrated into my discussion throughout are implications for teaching both the analysis and design of sound and other modes in multimodal compositions.

2. The element of vocal delivery

In 1762, Thomas Sheridan (1968) pronounced in *A Course of Lectures on Elocution* that "some of our greatest men have been trying to do that with the pen, which can only be performed by the tongue; to produce effects by the dead letter, which can never be produced but by the living voice, with its accompaniments" (p. xii). Sheridan called for there to be an increased emphasis on the nonverbal aspects of vocal delivery, such as the "essential articles of tone, accent [and] emphasis" (p. 10). The essential articles he identified form the core of frameworks for analyzing vocal delivery, whether it occurs in face-to-face or digitally mediated environments.

Theo Van Leeuwen (1999) broke voice down even further into several qualities that carry culturally formed communicative meanings:

- tension—how tight or strained
- roughness—how raspy and throaty (with rougher tones being more associated with men)
- breathiness—how airy or intimate (the more airy, usually in Western cultures, the less authority the voice is deemed to have)
- loudness—how booming or soft
- pitch—how high or low (related to gender)

308

- vibrato—how trembling it sounds (with more vibrato equated with being emotional)

Often when listening to people speak (whether in person or via electronic technologies), we explicitly attend to the words that are stated, but we also implicitly adhere to how those words are said. Thus, meaning is carried not solely by the verbal content but, as oral performers and oral readers continually show, also by the vocal qualities.[6] No matter the web work—be it a radio broadcast archived at NPR, an audioblog on someone's site, a dialogue captured in a streaming video, or the voice-over in a Flash poem—if voice is included, then the terms above can be helpful for analyzing and designing not only the voice alone but also the whole relationship of voice to the rest of the work.

For example, in the poem "Breathing/Secret of Roe" (Carr, 2002), spoken voice and the qualities of that voice shape readers'/ listeners' interactions with the text. The poem's opening page shows lines of text vibrating too quickly to be read while a few somber cello notes resonate briefly. When words that flash in the bottom left-hand corner of the screen are clicked, the Flash movie changes to a stylized, water-washed picture of a man in a room with a partially seen woman watching him as his head hangs down, and his back is slumped. Part of the screen is solid gray, and across both the picture and the gray background, lines and lines of text of different sizes and fonts flash repeatedly across the screen. They move and change so quickly it's hard to focus on them, much less read them, a point the static screen capture in Figure 1 cannot show.

But perhaps even more so than the visual elements, what is most striking about the poem at this point is the man's voice speaking in a deep measured timbre. Whereas the lines of text visually jump and move, the aural reading of those lines sounds heavily in listeners' ears, giving weight and heft to the words that visually feel more impermanent. As I write this essay, seeking to analyze this webtext, I'm struggling with the medium in which I'm working, confined as I am to text and image; it's frustrating because the screen "capture" does not *capture* the impermanence of the written text and the more auditory permanence of the

---

6 David Appelbaum (1990) focused on vocal utterances such as "The Cough," "The Laugh," and "On Breath" in his book, *Voice*.

spoken text. Nor does it show the intricate relationship of the
visual and the aural—how without the aural, the visual resists
focus. For example, when I read the poem with sound muted,
I find it hard to focus my attention on any one line, moving
as quickly as they do. But with the sound turned on, hearing
the speaker's voice focuses my attention so that I am able to
read particular lines and track various words and meanings
as they develop. The rich sonorous texture of the man's voice
steadies and focuses my attention. In addition, the mechanized
reverberating echo of his voice gives the poem even more of a
desolate, resigned feeling: "I did not want you to die alone—
alone, alone. [pause] But there is no cure for that ailment." As
with any spoken performance, the qualities of vocal delivery in
a web composition create tone and convey mood; in this case
it's of someone oddly trapped in "The vessels of this pumping
machine/Breathing: the secrets of roe."

Fig. 1. Screen capture of "Breathing" (Carr, 2002).

In addition to tonal elements to consider in relation to voice,
there are also technological considerations, particularly with the
increased number of tracks available for working with sound.
Just as film and theater sound capabilities moved from monaural
to stereo, from one track to multitrack (see Cameron, 1980;

Sergi, 2004), so too have computerized capabilities evolved (especially with broader bandwidth which makes high-quality 16-bit recording possible along with the inclusion of multiple channels). Of course, there have always been technological considerations when working with sound, especially when seeking to capture and amplify actors' voices in film and on stage. In an article for *Theater Design & Technology*, Richard Thomas (2001) reviewed categorizations of sound in theater and identified one of the primary purposes of a sound designer as being to amplify or otherwise manipulate actors' voices through the use of technology (p. 22) (the other purposes—sound effects and mood setting—I will discuss below).[7] The amplification or modification of voices in theater and on film sets occurs through the strategic placement and use of microphones and mixers to draw out one actor's voice over another or to add reverb and equalization effects. The audience does not necessarily have control over what is being heard and how it is being heard except to turn up or down the volume on their television if watching at home. In a web composition, however, an author can provide controls so that viewers/readers/interacters can control what voices or sounds are heard when and how they're heard.

A good example of this type of use of sound is in the three subparts of the webtext "Conversation" (Nelson, 2003). Each part of the text consists of eight separate voices discussing particular events: injuries, product promotions, and a party among robots. As the author, Jason Nelson, described, "Inspired by Glen Gould, these are sound instruments designed for you to create a corwded [sic] room of verbal composition. There are 8 tracks, each with volume and left and right controls. Play with the voices" (n.p.). Nelson's injunction to play is apt—this is a fun text, one that takes Glen Gould's technique of weaving multiple composers together and applies it to voices. Moving the volume controls on various speakers in the conversation means that the text continually changes—from a monologue by one of the eight, to a dialogue between any two, to a polylogue between several, and finally to a sheer cacophony of sound where it's hard to hear what any one is saying, and words, speech, individuals' voices have been transformed into pure noise, defamiliarizing

---

7 Sarah Kozloff's (2000) *Overhearing Film Dialogue* identified nine functions of dialogue in narrative films and, thus, might be especially useful to writing teachers (pp. 33–34 of the book lists the functions).

any concept of conversation a reader may have had. (I can't help but think as I turn up the volume on all eight voices that the Russian Formalists would have approved of Nelson's text.) For example, in "Injury: a conversation" (see Figure 2), eight different characters tell the tales of their injuries, including a young woman with a shoulder injury, a teacher who stabbed his hand while cutting a kiwi, and a girl who cut her chin when playing Superman with her brother.

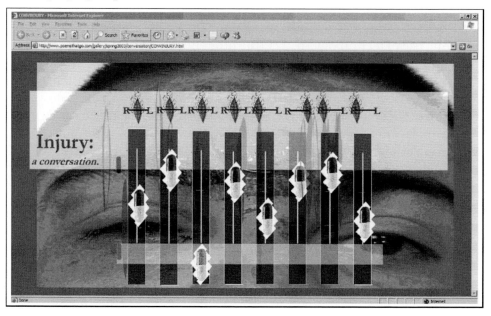

Fig. 2. A screen capture of "Injury: a conversation" (Nelson, 2003).

Moving the equalizers to the left and right, changes the sound from stereo to monaural and makes it so that people sound grouped in conversation, enabling the interacter to pull out different voices in the conversation. Besides being fun to play with, I like how this piece makes evident technical decisions that are often invisible to readers of a final text. That is, when we click "launch" to watch a Flash movie and the sound comes out stereo and at a certain volume and tone level, we may not consider that this was a conscious decision by the author. With it's in-your-face interface of sound controls, "Conversation" makes clear that any analysis or production of sound on the Web must consider technological aspects as well.

"Conversation" also challenges traditional media's approaches for how to splice and play voices together. When working with voices in multimedia texts, our previous models were, as Martin Spinelli (2001) noted, often analog, particularly radio. But whereas in radio the integration of voices often aims to create, in Spinelli's words, "the seamless, invisible, inaudible edit which dislodges nothing, which interrupts nothing, which is in fact deployed to remove interruption, to remove digression and to clarify" (p. 36), digital productions can and, according to Spinelli, *should* seek to disrupt that seamlessness. As he explained (and I quote at length),

> Against the seamless edit, we should posit: the *breathless edit,* which splices two parts of speech unnaturally close to each other in violation of proper spoken rhythm; the *weave edit* where two or more separate lines of thought are cut into various pieces and rearranged in an interlocking manner; the *slow fade to silence edit line cross fade* in which two or more separate lines of thought overlap and interfere with each other; the *jump cut* in which two or more takes of the same speech repeat each other or follow one after another; the *acoustic match edit* in which one piece of speech or sound is transformed into another sound of similar pitch and rhythm; and the *interjection* in which a small fragment of related or unrelated speech interrupts a longer line of thought. (p. 38)

Often when working with voice we are striving for clarity and seamlessness—the digital reproduction of the person speaking needs to be understood,[8] but we also should not forget more postmodern, disruptive approaches. A work like "Conversation" coupled with a schema for voice edits such as Spinelli proposed provide a good framework for teachers and students to analyze both traditional and nontraditional approaches for incorporating voice in multimodal web works.

3. The element of music

Of all the elements of a soundtrack, perhaps music is the one with which most people are familiar, particularly the use of

---

8 See Eberhard Zwicker and U. Tilmann Zwicker (2002) for a discussion on reproducing sounds outside of the human perceptual range.

music to establish tone and atmosphere. The music we listen to is shaped by and shaping of our moods ("I'm in the mood to hear ...." "Play that song. It always cheers me up." "Whenever I hear this song, I think of ...."). Inspirational music plays during lulls in the action at sporting events; music relevant to the production is often used in the stage theatre, to set the scene for audience members; in modern movie theatres, massive speakers boom the crescendo notes of climatic scenes, and, of course, in multimodal web works, music also plays a key role.

Perhaps because music videos are a genre with which students are most familiar, they are often drawn to composing music-like videos when working in Flash or iMovie, synching or juxtaposing ever-changing images to musical soundtracks. While it is interesting to think of music in relation to the visual elements presented in a text, I'm also interested in music in relation to textual elements, which is something, I think, unique to multimodal web works where textual, visual, and aural elements can be integrated most fully (versus, say, movies where the textual is not as easily or as often incorporated).

Whether working with music in isolation or as a mode-in-relation, many of the terms from musical analysis are, not surprisingly, helpful to the discussion. In *What to Listen for in Music* (1957), Aaron Copland claimed that we listen to music on three planes: the sensuous, the expressive, and the sheerly musical.[9] A thorough and useful summary of Copland's work summed these planes up as follows:

[W]hen listening to music on the **sensuous** plane, we focus on

- the medium (i.e., what generates the sound: voice, instrument, ensemble, etc.)

- the quality of sound produced (e.g., tone, uniformity, special effects, etc.)

---

9   In music studies a distinction is often made between hearing (i.e., passively receiving sounds) and listening (i.e., perceiving and understanding sounds in an active way) (Seiler, n.d.). The distinction between hearing and listening parallels discussions of critical perception in new media. In the context of this article, I think hearing equates to the transparency of *looking through* and listening equates to the mirroring of *looking at*. For further discussions of this issue, and related usages of through/at (see Bolter, 2001; Bolter & Gromala, 2003; Lanham, 1993; McKee, 2004; Selfe & Selfe, 1994; Wysocki & Jasken, 2004).

- the dynamics or the intensity of the sound (e.g., loudness, uniformity, and change)

When listening to music on the **expressive** plane, we determine how the music interprets—and clarifies—our feelings. Sounds evoke feelings.

- a busy passage can suggest unease or nervousness
- a slow passage in a minor key, such as a funeral march, can suggest gloom

When listening to music on the **sheerly musical** plane, we focus on

- the movement of the piece (i.e., concentrate on its rhythm, meter, and tempo)
- the pitch (i.e., its order and melody)
- the structure of the piece (i.e., its logic, design, and texture) (Seiler, n.d., n.p.)

Although I think these categories, like all categories, have more overlap than the listing shows, I do think the framework above addresses a number of the key terms for understanding music that could be applied to the use of music in a variety of multimodal compositions. For example, many of the works in the online new media journal *Locus Novus: A Synthesis of Text and Image and Sound and Motion* use music as the only or as the primary sound. "Winter Lyric" (O'Neil, 2005) is a poem that begins with the sound of two domineering tones with two echoing subtones playing over and over like a heartbeat or a distant drum but in a faster rhythm. "Dun-Domm-da-da-Dun-Domm-da-da-Dun-Domm-da-da-Dun-Domm-da-da" is what the reader/viewer/interacter hears before the first words and images appear on the screen and then throughout the rest of the poem. Set to infinitely loop, there is no ending to the music as long as the poem is open. As these notes play, the opening lines animate in over a photograph of a woman's torso, who is standing with her hands clasped in a room full of everyday objects, chairs, tables, a computer. The text reads: "She found as it got colder that it/grew harder to distinguish the/the feeling of her own fingers from/the feeling of what she was/touching with them."

From this first screen, clicking on the snowflake in the lower right-hand corner causes a wiping horizontal slide transition to occur, a movement accompanied by a high-pitched noise like ice rubbing on ice. But even while the new images and words unfurl on the screen, the "Dun-Domm-da-da-Dun-Domm-da-da-Dun-Domm-da-da" continues to pulse and reverberate, creating on the expressive plane a sense of inexorableness and a movement inward to some oddly biological rhythm, a feeling augmented by the text (see Figure 3):

> It wasn't numbness as much as a kind of confusion a
> kind of canceling out of the outside world.
>
> ***
>
> It was kind of like the way blood throbs sometimes
> in your eye
> and reveals in an eerie latticework of bright tendrils
> the inner structure of the eye itself.

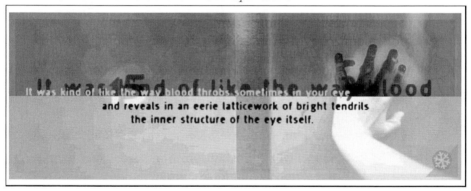

Fig. 3. A screen capture from "Winter Lyric" (O'Neil, 2005).

While other sounds are included in the piece, these notes continue omnipresent, building, even more than the words and images, the feelings of inevitability and isolation that come with the accumulation and loss of living. This poem, as with so many web works with an aural component, is interesting to read first without and then with sound because without the soundtrack, the images and text don't convey the full message.

In addition to considering music in multimodal web works on the expressive and sensual planes, it's also important to consider it on the musical plane, to consider the technology of the music production and how the music is being produced. In "Winter Lyric," I at first thought the "Dun-Domm-da-da-Dun-Domm-da-da" was a recording of drums, but I realized there was too high a tonality in the sound. So then I considered it possibly resulted from strings being plucked on an instrument such as a guitar, but the sound, despite the reverb, was too crisp for that. I now think it's more likely the product of computer-synthesized musical tones, which adds yet another layer of complexity to the meaning of the text. The character in the poem opens with not being able to feel what she's touching, and then as the poem progresses, the character is increasingly divested from the outside world, but moving inward leads to a repetitive, possibly computer-generated rhythm that is maybe meant to convey continuity. Layered in three places in the poem are a few bars of melody played on or synthesized to sound like a xylophone, which adds to the musical complexity of the piece. These short-lived fragments of higher, more hopeful-sounding notes represent, perhaps, another way the character could have lived, but it's a way that cannot be sustained in the face of the relentlessly overpowering and oddly mechanized "Dun-Domm-da-da-Dun-Domm-da-da-Dun-Dumm-da-da."

Music is often used in conjunction with other elements of sound as well, especially dialogue and sound effects, and in the next section I will discuss these three elements of sound and how they interrelate in one particular webtext.

4. The element of sound effects

Sound effects can serve a number of purposes in both stage theater and movies, purposes that also carry over into web compositions (Leonard, 2001). Sound effects

- provide information about a scene (e.g., the rumble of a trainyard)
- serve as a cue reference (e.g., the ring of a telephone or the flush of a toilet when a character emerges from the bathroom)
- help in mood creation (e.g., the wind whistling in an arctic drama)

- act as an emotional stimulus (e.g., the squeal and crash of a car wreck that the audience doesn't see but realizes has killed one of the characters)

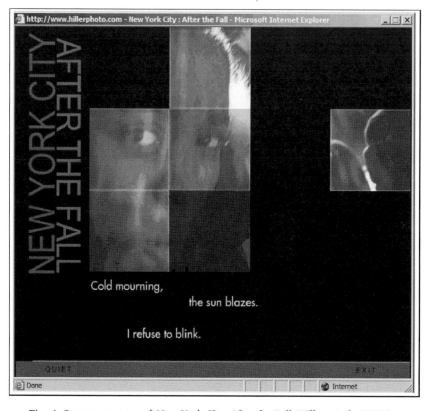

Fig. 4. Screen capture of *New York City: After the Fall* (Hiller et al., 2002).

In computerized environments, sound effects are perhaps most evidentially used in video and computer games. As Glenn McDonald (2001) described in his excellent "History of Sound in Video Games," the soundtrack is often the forgotten element in games because the visuals are so splashy. But, he noted, "oftentimes the mark of superior sound design is that you don't consciously notice it at all. Instead, it goes to work on you subconsciously—heightening tension, manipulating the mood, and drawing you into the gameworld faintly but inexorably" (n.p.). In his chronicle of sound in video games, which begins with Pong and ends with first-person shooter games, McDonald also included links to the sound effects and music in many of the games. Hearing the paranoid thumping of the space invaders marching ever nearer, the high-pitched whir of that tiny killer spaceship from Astroids, and the death squelch from Pacman brought back more memories—visceral memories—of playing those games than just seeing the screen captures did. Jakob Nielson (n.d.) described a study where gamers were asked to play two versions of a game, and they were asked to tell researchers which they thought had the better graphics. What subjects did not know was that both versions had the *exact same* graphics; the only difference between the two was that one had more sound effects and music in the soundtrack. Yet despite the sameness of the graphics, gamers consistently rated the version with the better soundtrack as having better graphics as well. Clearly, sound effects matter, but how can web authors use sound effects effectively?

One lesson for what to avoid can come from early cinema. When sound effects were first used to accompany silent films, there was much outrage in the movie industry and among movie goers about overzealous "sound effect boys" (Bottomore, 2001) who'd see some minor element on the screen, say a cow in a far field when the lead characters were having a romantic kiss under a tree in the shot's foreground, and disrupt the scene with excessive mooing and ringing of a cow's bell. As Stephen Bottomore (2001) described in his detailed (and humorous) account of the early days of cinema, movie goers did not mind sound effects used judiciously and in conjunction with the primary events happening on the screen, but too many effects or effects that were too loud, too frequent, or irrelevant disrupted their theater experience.

One multimodal webtext I found that uses sound effects in particularly striking ways, especially when considered in relation to other modes of representation and in relation to the other elements of sound, is *New York City: After the Fall* (Hiller, Vandel, Perkins, & Sylwester, 2002). In this memorial and reflection upon New York after 9/11, photographs of New Yorkers appear and disappear in grid-like segments against a black screen. Lines of a poem appear beneath each materializing and dematerializing picture as a soundtrack plays (see Figure 4).

This text is of the click-and-play variety. That is, once a reader has clicked the start arrow, the visual, textual, and aural elements of the text unfurl without further action from the reader.

Although I usually get restless being held captive by click-and-play Flash movies, this eight-minute work holds my attention in part because of the power of the images in relation to the text and in part too because of the soundtrack, which is both mesmerizing and jarring. The soundtrack for this webtext is composed primarily of music, but it also includes some sound effects and spoken voices. The music is comprised mostly of electric cellos playing bass chords that fade slowly as another sharper, more dissonant chord strikes, creating a layer of sorrow, both deep and sharp. Punctuating these chords are the sounds of what I can only describe as underwater whale cries, primordial callings or keenings. At first, this seemed really odd to me, but then I noticed the written line "Beneath the surface..." and I realized upon second reading/listening that that line is actually repeated three times in the poem. Because I had been so consumed by studying the people in the photographs, I had only been skimming the text, but the interjections of sounds like underwater cries triggered my attention, working to direct my gaze away from the pictorial images to the textual.

Five or six times in *New York City: After the Fall*, sirens can be heard, sounding as if they are coming closer and then receding. These sirens serve as reminders of the horrors of that day—how no New Yorker can listen to sirens in quite the same way again. Interestingly, the sirens sounded most frequently when the images and text in the work portrayed attempts by individuals to try, for a moment, to withdraw from the events of the world. One screen shows a photograph of people at a sidewalk cafe drinking coffee and reading newspapers. Beneath the photograph are the words, "Too much for two eyes I focus... on my private universe." Another screen shows a man walking, face turned resolutely ahead, accompanied by the text, "I save my eyes and ears...for those close to me. Life's too short to look around." But slicing through this private universe and this attempt to save eyes and ears are the sirens, focusing the readers'/listeners' attention on the fact that there can be no escaping the events of the world.

In addition, human voices are used in *New York City: After the Fall*. On three screens the cellos and underwater keens are replaced by the murmur of numerous voices—none distinct enough that the words can be made out, but the sound of the voices form a questioning chorus that serves to emphasize further the theme of the work, which is perhaps best summed up by the textual elements on the screen: "Related strangers. We step over the cracks in our lives" and "Anonymous. We stand together wonder which way and why. Beneath the surface...." The murmuring of voices that accompany the pictures and text seem to bubble up from beneath the surface, emerging through the cracks in our daily lives, raising the question: Are these the voices of the dead? The murmur of those still living? It's hard to say, but hearing them is disconcerting, emphasizing both the connection and disconnection of the people in the city and of the reader to the text. And, perhaps more disconcerting is the silence that follows the voices.

5. The element of silence

Silence was, until recently, the default setting for any webtext—bandwidth was too dear, playback too fragmented, methods for inserting sound files in texts too complicated. But as these conditions change and as the Web becomes increasingly aural, silence is not necessarily the default setting anymore. Because we can now hear sounds, we can also now hear silences.

Like the art gallery visitors Richard Lanham (1993) described who move from Jean Tinguely's noisy sculpture exhibits back into the quiet of traditional galleries and then question the before-unnoticed quietness of those galleries (pp. 38–40), so too are web users in their moving from multimodal aural texts back to purely visual texts left questioning this absence of sound. Silence is no longer a default but a choice, and web composers and those analyzing web sites need to make conscious use of silence.

As with other elements of sound, silence has been discussed in film, theater, voice studies, and so on. In a discussion of soundtracks for film, theorist François Jost (2001) described silence not initially as the result of an absence but rather as the result of a presence: "[S]ilence does not consist of the absence of all sound. Rather, it results from an action of one of the sound sources over others, an action whose success ends in the reduction to silence" (p. 49). In *New York City: After the Fall*, there are moments when the murmur of voices override all other sounds in the text. Then when those voices cease, returning the viewer to the continuing chords of the cellos and the occasional slicing of the sirens, there is, even amidst that noise, a silence—a presence that is now an absence, and because of that absence its presence is even more fully felt. As Alberto Cavlacanit (1985), another film theorist, explained, "silence can be the loudest of noises, just as black, in a brilliant design, can be the brightest of colors" (p. 111).

I find this consideration of silence as a presence intriguing, and to show how such a *present absence* analysis might work, I am going to analyze two related poems by Jorg Piringer (2003), "Soundpoem one" and "Soundpoem two." Each of these poems revolve around the repetition and silencing of phonetic vocalizations (uttered by a computerized voice reader), like *xa, a, pu, ch, rr*. In "Soundpoem one," users are invited to move circles into squares. When a circle is moved into a square (and a circle may be placed simultaneously and more than once in any square), the utterance on that circle plays repeatedly, enunciated in a computerized voice. Each square represents a different stereo speaker (assuming a four-speaker set), left back, left front, right back, right front. So, for example, in Figure 5 below, the sound resulting from that is as follows (and remember these are all looping and occurring simultaneously):

left front speaker: ch-um-ch-um-ch-um-ch-um-ch-um-ch-um, etc.

left rear speaker: bi-bi-me-bi-bi-me-bi-bi-me-bi-bi-me-bi-bi, etc.

right front speaker: um-ch-um-ch-um-ch-um-ch-um-ch-um-ch, etc.

right rear speaker: me-rr-me-rr-me-rr-me-rr-me-rr-me-rr-me-rr, etc.

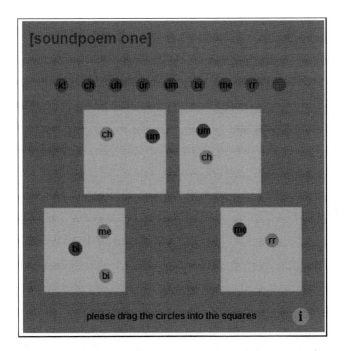

Fig. 5. Screen capture of one "reading" of "Soundpoem one" (Piringer, 2003).

However, this visual and textual rendition of the noises one hears with this configuration does not come close to capturing the crazed busyness of it all. As the editor of *Poems That Go* wrote when describing Piringer's work, "His polite directions, 'please drag the circles into the squares' stand in shocking contrast to the resulting cacophony that is revealed to the user who follows directions" (Sapnar, 2004, n.p.). But it isn't really total cacophony, and that's why I find this piece so interesting to consider in relation to silence. Even with all the overlapping noises created by the many circles already being vocalized, when I add one more to the mix, say I were to add *k!* to the above version of the poem, I would be able to hear its joining because my ears would be attuned to the rhythms, tempos, and tones of those noises already present, and thus something new would be noticed. Were I to take away one of the elements, the *rr*, for example, I would hear its absence as well. Playing with (and I use "playing" here in both the amusement sense and in the musical sense) this poem is helpful for tuning the ear, for listening carefully to both what is present and what is absent, to both the noises and the silences. (And I have shifted to using the term *noise* to distinguish silence from not-silence because, as I argue below, silence and sound are part and whole and should not be set in opposition.) Nelson's "Conversation," which I discussed earlier, is also useful for this, but whereas "Conversation" has merely eight voices, Piringer's poem has the potential, were all circles put just once in all squares, to include at least 36 separate manifestations of these single syllabic utterances, and I wouldn't even know how to begin to calculate all the variations actually possible, particularly knowing that a circle may be put any number of times into the same square, as *bi* is put twice in a square above. I realize I'm discussing this poem in a section on silence and that I've been talking a great deal about noise, but the silence comes in by learning to listen for what is not present so that even when there is noise on the screen there are also silences to be heard.

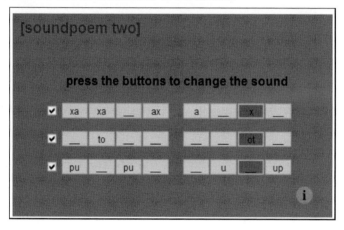

Fig. 6. A Screen capture of one "reading" of "Soundpoem two"
(Piringer, 2003).

xa-xa_ax-a_x_xa-xa_ax-a_x_xa-xa ax-a_x_, etc.
_to_ _ _ _ot_ _to_ _ _ _ot_ _to_ _ _ _ot_, etc.
pu_pu_ _u_up pu_pu_ _u_up pu_pu_ _u_up, etc.

In "Soundpoem two," Piringer (2003) continued to play with syllabic vocalizations, this time providing readers/viewers/interacters the option of silencing or sounding different vocalizations. Perhaps more so than in "Soundpoem one," in this poem the silences and gaps are evident in this poem because of the visual structure of the interface. There are three tracks of utterances possible, and on each track eight spaces which can sound a variety of noises, including silence. If a line is empty, then the computerized voice reader skips over it, leaving a gap in the track. For example, in the rendition of "Soundpoem two" in Figure 6 the resulting sounds and silences are as follows:

As with "Soundpoem one," this poem enables readers to focus explicitly on sound and the element of silence because, unlike with many click-and-play multimedia works (including video and film), the reader can influence what is uttered, when, and how. Now, do these poems illustrate the many complex ways silence can work in conjunction with other elements of sound to create mood and atmosphere, for example? No, certainly not, but what they do enable is a focusing of attention to the layering of sound and silence in a way (in an exercise even) that I think carries over to critically listening to other texts where visual, aural, and textual elements combine in (perhaps) more complicated ways.

Listening for silence is complicated because it involves listening for an absent presence, what is there and *not* there. Jacques Derrida's (1976) concept of *différence* comes to mind here—how language has a play in it that carries traces of other possible meanings. If words are the deferred presence of their meanings, then silence is the deferred presence of noise and noise the deferred presence of silence. Silence *traces* noise and noise *traces* silence in such an interleaving that there cannot, really, ever be a separation, hence the importance of discussions of silence in any discussions of sound. Silence should not be considered separate from sound but rather an integral and important element of sound, one whose relationship to the other elements of voice, music, and sound effects needs to be analyzed, as do each of the elements' relationships to the other modes in a multimodal text.

6. Returning to considerations for an integrated approach

I emphasize the relationships among the elements of sound and among the modes of a multimodal text because in my discussion of the four-part schema and the various relevant terminologies, I fear I may have fragmented elements of sound from each other and from the other modes in multimodal texts. Thus, I would like to close this essay by returning to considerations for developing an integrated approach to sound design and analysis.

Sound is not a fixed, isolated mode, nor should it be considered in isolation. Unfortunately, it often is—a fact that numerous sound designers for film and theater have decried (e.g., Altman, 1992a; Cavlacanit, 1985; Lastra, 2000; Leonard, 2001). To work against this tendency toward isolation, film theorist Rick Altman (1992b) proposed the concept of the *sound envelope* as a way to understand sound-in-relation (p. 18). The sound envelope includes not only the moments when a sound is present but also the moments *before* and *after* as well. By situating sound as an event in time, Altman sought to emphasize the temporality and situatedness of sound so as to be able to consider it within a "multidimensional analysis" (p. 15).

I find Altman's term *sound envelope* not only helpful for analysis but also for guiding design, providing a language for considering how a sound event might occur in a text and helping to shape the design of that text. Writers of multimodal, aural web works need to consider what readers will see and do prior, during, and after a sound event occurs, and they need to consider the rhetorical effects of the before, during, and after of a sound event. Sound is not something to be added as an afterthought. Sound and all the elements of sound play crucial roles in such important areas as setting the mood, building atmosphere, carrying the narrative, directing attention, and developing themes in multimodal works.

I opened this essay by asking how writers and writing teachers should begin to understand sound for both the analysis and design of multimodal, aural texts. To address this question, I have presented a four-part schema examining the main elements of sound—vocal delivery, music, sound effects, and silence—and terminologies for understanding these elements. I have titled this essay "Notes toward the analysis and design of sound in multimodal webtexts" because what I have presented is an opening, an initial frame on which to begin to scaffold and develop more in-depth considerations of sound and how it works in particular contexts for particular writers, audiences, and purposes.[10] That is, our work with sound in the computers

---

10   My title is drawn from Charles Moran's (1995) "Notes Toward a Rhetoric of Email."

and writing field is still at such a nascent period that there is a great deal we need to explore. It is my hope that the terminology and frameworks I have presented will serve as a productive catalyst for our developing more thorough understandings of how and why sound matters.

REFERENCES

Abel, Richard, & Altman, Rick (Eds.). (2001). *The sounds of early cinema.* Bloomington: Indiana UP.

Altman, Rick. (1992). The material heterogeneity of recorded sound. In Rick Altman (Ed.), *Sound theory sound practice* (pp. 15–45). New York: Routledge.

Altman, Rick (Ed.). (1992). *Sound theory sound practice.* New York: Routledge.

Altman, Rick. (2004). *Silent film sound.* New York: Columbia UP.

Bolter, Jay David. (2001). *Writing space: Computers, hypertext, and the remediation of print* (2nd ed.). Mahwah, NJ: Lawrence Erlbaum.

Bolter, Jay David, & Gromala, Diane. (2003). *Windows and mirrors: Interaction design, digital art, and the myth of transparency.* Cambridge: MIT Press.

Bottomore, Stephen. (2001). The story of Perce Peashaker: Debates about sound effects in the early cinema. In Richard Abel & Rick Altman (Eds.), *The sounds of early cinema* (pp. 129–142). Bloomington: Indiana UP.

Cameron, Evan William (Ed.). (1980). *Sound and the cinema: The coming of sound to American film.* New York: Redgrove.

Carr, Jonathan. (2002). Breathing/secret of roe. *Poems that Go,*<http://www.poemsthatgo.com/gallery/ winter2002/ secret.htm>.

Cavlacanit, Alberto. (1985). Sound in films. In Elisabeth Weis & John Belton (Eds.), *Film sound: Theory and practice* (pp. 98–111). New York: Columbia UP.

Copland, Aaron. (1957). *What to listen for in music.* New York: Mentor Book.

Douane, Mary Ann. (1985). The voice in the cinema: The articulation of body and space. In Elisabeth Weis & John Belton (Eds.), *Film sound: Theory and practice* (pp. 162–176). New York: Columbia UP.

Halbritter, Scott A. (2004). Sound arguments: Aural rhetoric in multimedia composition. *Dissertation.* UNC: Chapel Hill.

Hiller, Geoffrey, Vandel, Tom, Perkins, Heather, & Sylwester, Peter. (2002). *New York City: After the Fall.,* <http://www.hillerphoto.com/nyc/#>.

Jost, François. (2001). The voices of silence. In Richard Abel & Rick Altman (Eds.), *The sounds of early cinema* (pp. 48–65). Bloomington: Indiana UP.

Kozloff, Sarah. (2000). *Overhearing film dialogue.* Berkeley: University of California Press.

Kress, Gunther, & Van Leeuwen, Theo. (2001). *Multimodal discourse: The modes and media of contemporary communication.* London: Oxford UP.

Lanham, Richard A. (1993). *The electronic word: Democracy, technology, and the arts.* Chicago: University of Chicago Press.

Lastra, James. (2000). *Sound technology and the American Cinema: Perception, representation, modernity.*New York: Columbia UP.

Leonard, John A. (2001). *Theatre sound.* New York: Routledge.

Manovich, Lev. (2001). *The language of new media.* Cambridge: MIT.

McDonald, Glenn. (2001). History of Sound in video games. *GameSpot*,<http://www.gamespot.com/gamespot/features/video/vg music/>.

McKee, Heidi. (2004). Richard Lanham's The Electronic Word and AT/THROUGH Oscillations. *Pedagogy: Critical Approaches to Teaching Literature, Language, Composition, and Culture, 5.*

Moran, Charles. (1995). Notes toward a rhetoric of e-mail. *Computers and Composition, 12,* 15–21.

Nelson, Jason. (2003). Conversation. *Poems that Go,*<http://www.poemsthatgo.com/gallery/index.htm>.

Nielsen, Jakob (n.d.). Guidelines for multimedia on the Web. *W3C Journal,*<http://www.w3j.com/5/s3. nielsen.html>.

O'Neil, Mark. (2005). Winter lyric. *Locus Novus: A synthesis of text and image and sound and motion,*<http://www. locusnovus. com/lnprojects/winterlyric/>.

Piringer, Jorg. (2003). Soundpoems. *Poems that Go,*<http://www. poemsthatgo.com/gallery/spring2003/joerg/index. htm>.

Rusen, Hartley, & Dittmar, Meredith. (2002). Hangover house. *Born Magazine,*<http://www.bornmagazine.com>.

Sapnar, M. (2004). The sound of new media poetry. *Poems that Go, 15,*<http://www.poemsthatgo.com/gallery/spring2003/print article.htm>.

Seiler, Robert M. (n.d.). *Writing about music,*<http://www.ucalgary.ca/~rseiler/music.htm>.

Selfe, Cynthia L., & Selfe, Richard J., Jr. (1994). The politics of the interface: Power and its exercise in electronic contact zones. *College Composition and Communication, 45,* 480–504.

Sergi, Gianluca. (2004). *The Dolby era: Film sound in contemporary Hollywood.* New York: Manchester UP.

Sheridan, Thomas. (1762/1968). *A course of lectures on elocution: Together with two dissertations on language.* New York: Benjamin Blom (originally London. W. Strahan).

Sorapure, Madeleine. (2003). Five principles of new media, or playing Lev Manovich. *Kairos, 8*(2), <http://english. ttu.edu/kairos/8.2/binder2.html?coverweb/sorapure/ index.htm>.

Spinelli, Martin. (2001). Analog echoes: A poetics of digital audio editing. *UBUWEB,*<www.ubu.com/papers/ object/06 spinelli.pdf>.

Thomas, Richard K. (2001). The function of the soundscape. *Theatre design & technology, 37,* 18–29.

Van Leeuwen, Theo. (1999). *Speech, music, sound.* London: Macmillan.

Weis, Elisabeth, & Belton, John (Eds.). (1985). *Film sound: Theory and practice.* New York: Columbia UP.

Wysocki, Anne Frances, & Jasken, Julia I. (2004). What should be an unforgettable face.... *Computers and Composition, 21,* 29–48.

Zwicker, Eberhard, & Zwicker, U. Tilmann. (2002). Audio engineering and psychoacoustics: Matching the signals to the final receiver, the human auditory system. In Kevin Jeffay & HongJiang Azhan (Eds.), *Readings in multimedia computing and networking* (pp. 11–21). London: Academic Press.

THE MAKER'S EYE

DONALD M. MURRAY

CONSIDER AS YOU ARE READING:

Donald Murray was a professional writer and editor in the public sphere, but he also taught at the university level, so he knew something about the demands on writers in both worlds. This essay was published in a trade magazine, a periodical for professional writers, not an academic journal. The advice he imparts, however, is sound for any writing situation. It may be particularly interesting for student writers because it gives some insight into different attitudes towards revision, which professional writers (and instructors) may value—even delight in—more than some undergraduates do. In working towards our goal to become more aware of our writing process and to try new approaches to composing, we may want to measure ourselves against what Murray describes and try some of the approaches he suggests.

1. *What are the aspects of one's writing that Murray recommends a writer scrutinize when revising?*

2. *When Murray says that writers must be "their own worst enemy" when revising, what does he mean? Are you ever your own worst enemy with your writing? In what way?*

3. *Murray's audience is other professional writers, primarily in the public sphere. To what extent do you think that his advice is applicable to professional or academic writing and student writers?*

When students complete a first draft, they consider the job of writing done—and their teachers too often agree. When professional writers complete a first draft, they usually feel that they are at the start of the writing process. When a draft is completed, the job of writing can begin.

That difference in attitude is the difference between amateur and professional, inexperience and experience, journeyman and craftsman. Peter F. Drucker, the prolific business writer, calls his first draft "the zero draft"—after that he can start counting. Most writers share the feeling that the first draft, and all of those which follow, are opportunities to discover what they have to say and how best they can say it.

To produce a progression of drafts, each of which says more and says it more clearly, the writer has to develop a special kind of reading skill. In school, we are taught to decode what appears on the page as finished writing. Writers, however, face a different category of possibility and responsibility when they read their own drafts. To them, the words on the page are never finished. Each can be changed and rearranged, can set off a chain reaction of confusion or clarified meaning. This is a different kind of reading which is possibly more difficult and certainly more exciting.

Writers must learn to be their own best enemy. They must accept the criticism of others and be suspicious of it; they must accept the praise of others and be even more suspicious of it. Writers cannot depend on others. They must detach themselves from their own pages so that they can apply both their caring and their craft to their own work.

Such detachment is not easy. Science-fiction writer Ray Bradbury supposedly puts each manuscript away for a year to the day and then rereads it as a stranger. Not many writers have the discipline or the time to do this. We must read when our judgment may be at its worst, when we are close to the euphoric moment of creation.

Then the writer, counsels novelist Nancy Hale, "should be critical of everything that seems to him most delightful in his style. He should excise what he most admires, because he wouldn't thus admire it if he weren't…in a sense protecting it from criticism." John Ciardi, the poet, adds, "The last act of the writing must be to become one's own reader. It is, I suppose, a schizophrenic process, to begin passionately and to end critically, to begin hot and to end cold; and, more important, to be passion-hot and critic-cold at the same time."

Most people think that the principal problem is that writers are too proud of what they have written. Actually, a greater problem for most professional writers is one shared by the majority of students. They are overly critical, think everything is dreadful, tear up page after page, never complete a draft, see the task as hopeless.

The writer must learn to read critically but constructively, to cut what is bad, to reveal what is good. Eleanor Estes, the children's book author, explains: "The writer must survey his work critically, coolly, as though he were a stranger to it. He must be willing to prune, expertly and hard-heartedly. At the end of each revision, a manuscript may look….worked over, torn apart, pinned together, added to, deleted from, words changed and words changed back. Yet the book must maintain its original freshness and spontaneity."

Most readers underestimate the amount of rewriting it usually takes to produce spontaneous reading. This is a great disadvantage to the student writer, who sees only a finished product and never watches the craftsman who takes the necessary step back, studies the work carefully, returns to the task, steps back, returns, steps back, again and again. Anthony Burgess, one of the most prolific writers in the English-speaking world, admits, "I might revise a page twenty times." Roald Dahl, the popular children's writer, states, "By the time I'm nearing the end of a story, the first part will have been reread and altered and corrected at least 150 times…Good writing is essentially rewriting. I am positive of this."

Rewriting isn't virtuous. It isn't something that ought to be done. It is simply something that most writers find they have to do to discover what they have to say and how to say it. It is a condition of the writer's life.

There are, however, a few writers who do little formal rewriting, primarily because they have the capacity and experience to create and review a large number of invisible drafts in their minds before they approach the page. And some writers slowly produce finished pages, performing all the tasks of revision simultaneously, page by page, rather than draft by draft. But it is still possible to see the sequence followed by most writers most of the time in rereading.

Most writers scan their drafts first, reading as quickly as possible to catch the larger problems of subject and form, and then move in closer and closer as they read and write, reread and rewrite.

The first thing writers look for in their drafts is *information*. They know that a good piece of writing is built from specific, accurate, and interesting information. The writer must have an abundance of information from which to construct a readable piece of writing.

Next, writers look for meaning in the information. The specifics must build to a pattern of significance. Each piece of specific information must carry the reader toward meaning.

Writers reading their own drafts are aware of *audience*. They put themselves in the reader's situation and make sure that they deliver information which a reader wants to know or needs to know in a manner which is easily digested. Writers try to be sure that they anticipate and answer the questions a critical reader will ask when reading the piece of writing.

Writers make sure that the *form* is appropriate to the subject and the audience. Form, or genre, is the vehicle which carries meaning to the reader, but form cannot be selected until the writer has adequate information to discover its significance and an audience which needs or wants that meaning.

Once writers are sure the form is appropriate, they must then look at the *structure*, the order of what they have written. Good writing is built on a solid framework of logic, argument, narrative, or motivation which runs through the entire piece of writing and holds it together. This is the time when many writers find it most effective to outline as a way of visualizing the hidden spine by which the piece of writing is supported.

The element on which writers spend a majority of their time is *development*. Each section of a piece of writing must be adequately developed. It must give readers enough information so that they are satisfied. How much information is enough? That's as difficult as asking how much garlic belongs in a salad. It must be done to taste, but most beginning writers underdevelop, underestimating the reader's hunger for more information.

As writers solve development problems, they often have to consider questions of *dimension*. There must be a pleasing and effective proportion among all the parts of the piece of writing. There is a continual process of subtracting and adding to keep the piece of writing in balance.

Finally, writers have to listen to their own voices. *Voice* is the force which drives a piece of writing forward. It is an expression of the writer's authority and concern. It is what is between the words on the page, what glues the piece of writing together. A good piece of writing is always marked by a consistent, individual voice.

 As writers read and reread, write and rewrite, they move closer and closer to the page until they are doing line-by-line editing. Writers read their own pages with infinite care. Each sentence, each line, each clause, each phrase, each word, each mark of punctuation, each section of white space between the type has to contribute to the clarification of meaning.

Slowly the writer moves from word to word, looking through language to see the subject. As a word is changed, cut or added, as a construction is rearranged, all the words used before that moment and all those that follow that moment must be considered and reconsidered.

Writers often read aloud at this stage of the editing process, muttering or whispering to themselves, calling on the ear's experience with language. Does this sound right—or that? Writers edit, shifting back and forth from eye to page to ear to page. I find I must do this careful editing in short runs, no more than fifteen or twenty minutes at a stretch, or I become too kind with myself. I begin to see what I hope is on the page, not what actually is on the page.

This sounds tedious if you haven't done it, but actually it is fun. Making something right is immensely satisfying, for writers begin to learn what they are writing about by writing. Language leads them to meaning, and there is the joy of discovery, of understanding, of making meaning clear as the writer employs the technical skills of language.

Words have double meanings, even triple and quadruple meanings. Each word has its own potential of connotation and denotation. And when writers rub one word against the other, they are often rewarded with a sudden insight, an unexpected clarification.

The maker's eye moves back and forth from word to phrase to sentence to paragraph to sentence to phrase to word. The maker's eye sees the need for variety and balance, for a firmer structure, for a more appropriate form. It peers into the interior of the paragraph, looking for coherence, unity, and emphasis, which make meaning clear.

I learned something about this process when my first bifocals were prescribed. I had ordered a larger section of the reading portion of the glass because of my work, but even so, I could not contain my eyes within this new limit of vision. And I still find myself taking off my glasses and bending my nose toward the page, for my eyes unconsciously flick back and forth across the page, back to another page, forward to still another, as I try to see each evolving line in relation to every other line.

When does this process end? Most writers agree with the great Russian writer Tolstoy, who said, "I scarcely ever reread my published writings, if by chance I come across a page, it always strikes me: all this must be rewritten; this is how I should have written it."

The maker's eye is never satisfied, for each word has the potential to ignite new meaning. This article has been twice written all the way through the writing process [...]. Now it is to be republished in a book. The editors made a few small suggestions, and then I read it with my maker's eye. Now it has been re-edited, re-revised, re-read, and re-re-edited, for each piece of writing to the writer is full of potential and alternatives.

A piece of writing is never finished. It is delivered to a deadline, torn out of the typewriter on demand, sent off with a sense of accomplishment and shame and pride and frustration. If only there were a couple more days, time for just another run at it, perhaps then…

THE USE OF PATHOS IN CHARITY LETTERS: SOME NOTES TOWARD A THEORY AND ANALYSIS

MARSHALL MYERS

CONSIDER AS YOU ARE READING:

While academic writing often forestalls any appeal to emotion, it is one of the most commonly used, and abused, appeals in public rhetoric. As participants in the public sphere, it is critical that we understand the appropriate uses and misuses of pathos so that we can use it to our advantage, without abuse, and without becoming victims of manipulative emotional appeals. In this article, Myers looks at what motivates Americans to part with billions of dollars each year primarily through the pathetic appeal of pity. He shows the connection between appeals in modern charity letters and the rhetorical approaches of the ancients (Aristotle and Cicero) as well as the 20th century scholar Kenneth Burke. This article contributes to our goal of understanding the full palette of rhetorical techniques, especially as we engage with public arguments for multiple audiences.

1. *An ongoing debate in the U.S. is whether and to what extent is social good the responsibility of individuals, corporations, or government. Given what Myers concludes about charity letters, what are the pros and cons of each of these approaches to social action?*

2. *At the university you have likely been socialized to avoid appeals to pathos in formal writing. When do you think emotional appeals are appropriate in writing an academic argument? Why?*

3. *We've all been the objects of someone's plea for charity, whether it is our little sister asking for ten dollars, a transient person at the Interstate off ramp, or a representative of an environmental*

*group approaching us on the plaza. How does the analysis of
pathos in this article fit with what you have experienced in your
life outside the classroom?*

Americans are a generous people. In fact, Charles Clark,
writing in *Congressional Quarterly Researcher*, notes that the
"American tradition of philanthropy" is "unique in all the world"
[1]. Along that line, using data from the American Association
of Fund Raising Counsel, Robert Franklin of the Minneapolis
Star Tribune concludes that Americans give away at least $240
billion to charities each year, distributing that money to the
nearly 800,000 charities listed by the Internal Revenue Service
[2].

Besides telephone solicitations, one of the most popular ways
of collecting that enormous amount of cash is through charity
letters. In fact, according to the United States Postal Service,
14 to 15 billion pieces of mail, about 7% of the total volume
of mail, seek donations to a variety of charities in the United
States [2]. One woman in Minnesota, for example, over a
year collected 1430 letters from various charities that included
pleas for money to support heart, cancer, and various religious
organizations, just to name a few [2].

Why do people give to charities?

While that is perhaps a knotty, age-old question, tied to the
various notions of the nature of human beings as a species, recent
research by Ernst Fehr and Suzann-Viola Renniger, published
in *Scientific American Mind*, indicates that popular notions about
why human beings help each other seem to be incorrect. As
these two researcher say, "Recent experiments show that current
gene-based evolutionary theories cannot adequately explain
important patterns of human altruism" [3, p. 15]. Older theories
saw human beings as philanthropists less out of an "expression
of love of humankind than out of the cool calculation of the
entrepreneur who seeks to ensure future profit by clever public
relations," something on the order of "you scratch my back and
I'll scratch yours" [3, p. 17]. And some sociobiologists in the past

340

have suggested that altruistic acts performed "for the benefit of others are really motivated by veiled economic calculations and selfishness or by egoism with an eye to the very long term" [3, p. 15]. Antonio R. Damasio in *Descartes' Error: Emotion, Reason, and the Human Brain* notes, for example, that "In addition to the obvious good that altruists bring to others, they may heap good upon themselves in the form of self-esteem, social recognition, public honor, and affection, prestige, and perhaps even money" [4, p. 176]. Yet Fehr and Renniger dispute those notions. To them, "the strong altruist is one who does good out of motives other than mere nepotism or strategic gain" [3, p. 19]. After a series of intricate scientific experiments that would allow for choices between selfish and selfless behavior, Fehr and Renniger found that "our species is apparently the only one with a genetic makeup that promotes selflessness and true altruistic behavior" [3, p. 21]. Damasio even admits that "Some sublime human achievements come from rejection of what biology or culture propels individuals to do" [4, p. 177]. While it is probably unwise to generalize about the nature of all of humankind's actions based on a limited number of scientific experiments, Fehr and Renniger do offer at least one interesting insight, which, along with older less optimistic theories of altruism, may help to explain why Americans, whether for selfish or altruistic reasons, contribute such large amounts of money to charities each year.

So if billions of letters are sent to prospective donors each year, and if Americans in response contribute billions of dollars to charities, those facts spawn an interesting set of two related questions: In writing such letters, what techniques do charities use to get donors to contribute such large amounts of money? Or, to put it still another way, what is the rhetoric of such letters?

The simple answer to these questions is that these letters appeal to our emotions, particularly to the emotion of pity. Donors contribute money, so the reasoning goes, because they feel sorry for the people this money is supposed to help, an appeal to the readers by what the ancient Greeks called pathos. But the concept of pathos in general and pity in particular as pathetic appeals are complex subjects that can best be understood by tracing their history and development, which, in turn, provides a foundation for a theory of how charity letters use pathos.

In sum, our understanding of pathetic appeals begins with the ancient Greeks, particularly Aristotle, whose painstaking analysis of various emotions, including pity, strongly hinted at the need for an image upon which to project an emotion. Following that, the Roman rhetorician Cicero added to our understanding by reinforcing Aristotle's emphasis on audience analysis and by calling for a strongly emotional peroration. St. Augustine then enriched the concept by injecting Christianity into a pathetic appeal and by his and subsequent generations' emphasis on including style as a persuasive device.

First, definitions are in order. One source, *The Encyclopedia of Rhetoric and Composition,* defines pathos as "an argumentative/persuasive appeal to the emotions of the audience" [5, p. 492]. As one of the three basic appeals (ethos, pathos, and logos), pathos "is based upon the rhetor's ability to arouse certain types of emotions in the audience" [5, p. 493]. Another source, *The Encyclopedia of Rhetoric,* defines pathos in Greek rhetoric as a state which is "allied with the Greek verb *paskhein,* to undergo, experience, suffer, or more generally, to be in a state or condition, and the Greek noun *pathos* preserves this range of meaning" [6, p. 555].

Sharon Crowley and Debra Hawhee in their book *Ancient Rhetorics for Contemporary Students,* go farther, carefully pointing out that "Emotions should be distinguished from appetites, such as pleasure and pain" [7, p. 205]. Damasio, for example, calls these appetites "primary emotions" and concludes that ". . . the mechanism of primary emotions does not describe the full range of emotional behaviors. . . ." Demasio continues, "I believe that in terms of an individual's development they are followed by mechanisms of *secondary emotions,* which occur once we begin experiencing feelings and forming *systematic connections between categories of objects and situations, on one hand, and primary emotions on the other*" (italics in the original) [4, p. 134]. Crawley and Hawhee seem to agree, suggesting these primary emotions "must also be distinguished from values, such as justice and goodness," and add that "people do hold values with more or less intensity, and this intensity is where the rhetorical force of emotional appeals resides" [7, pp. 205-206], for pathos is a very potent persuasive strategy.

In *Classical Rhetoric for the Modern Student,* Edward P. J. Corbett and Robert Connors make another important point about pathetic appeals, warning that pathos, in the minds of many people, doesn't have a very good name. Corbett and Connors say: "People are rather sheepish about acknowledging that their opinions can be affected by their emotions. They have the uneasy feeling that there is something undignified . . . about being stirred into action through the stimulus of . . . aroused passions" [8, p. 77]. Crowley and Hawhee agree, adding that "Of all the ancient kinds of rhetorical proofs, the appeal to the emotions seems the strangest to contemporary rhetors, and perhaps a little bit shoddy as well. That's because of the modern reverence for reason and our habit of making a sharp distinction between reason and emotion" [7, p. 206].

But Corbett and Connors are also careful to note that "There is nothing necessarily reprehensible about being moved to action through emotion; in fact, it is perfectly normal. Since it is our will ultimately that moves us to action and since the emotions have a powerful influence on the will, many of our actions are prompted by the stimulus of our emotions" [8, p. 77]. In other words, many times it is an emotional appeal that pushes people into action. It would be difficult, indeed, for example, to imagine a social cause so great and so appealing to the masses that did not in some way have an emotional element in it. The Revolutionary War, the Civil War, and the Civil Rights Movement in the 1960s, to name just three, all certainly had their persuasive logical arguments, but the leaders in large part used pathetic appeals to motivate their audiences.

As noted earlier, pathos, to be sure, is a concept that has changed over time, nuanced by the age, by the circumstances, and by the rhetorical scholar. As *The Encyclopedia of Rhetoric* is quick to point out, "For some rhetors, the term [pathos] conveys little more than the sense that the auditor's state of mind can cloud or supersede his rational capacities for making decisions. For others, the term invites a thorough analysis of the human soul and its broader relations to language and perception" [6, p. 555]. In the end, a richer understanding of pathos as a concept requires a discussion of how the concept evolved over time.

The concept of rhetorical pathos, an appeal nearly 2500 years old, was employed by, among others in 5th-century Greece, the early Greek rhetorician Gorgias [6, p. 556]. Many scholars say that Gorgias argued effectively on Helen of Troy's behalf and absolved her from blame for the Trojan War because she was persuaded by a powerful pathetic appeal. In "Encomium of Helen," Gorgias says that Helen took her course of action because she was persuaded by emotion. As Gorgias says: "For speech constrained the soul, persuading it which is persuaded, both to believe the things said and to approve the things done.". . . "or if it was love which did all these things, there will be no difficulty in escaping the charge of the sin which is alleged to have taken place" [9, p. 41]. Helen is exonerated, Gorgias argues, because she was persuaded to take her course of action by passion. In Gorgias's mind, the passion of love "has the divine power of the gods, how could a lesser being reject and refuse it?" [9, p. 42]. Yet while Gorgias acknowledges the power of a pathetic appeal, he does not really analyze emotion as an appeal, other than to recognize that it exists and that it is potent.

The idea of pathos grows into the complex appeal it is today beginning with the classical Greek philosophers. Plato, for example, seems, at times, to have little use for an emotional appeal of any kind—particularly in the dialogue *Gorgias*, ironically where he condemns the use of rhetoric in almost any form. Later, though, in several places, including *Phaedrus*, Plato discusses the use of emotion in speech, observing that "the task before rhetoricians is to gain better knowledge of the kinds of souls and the kinds of emotions which appeal to those souls through speech" [6, p. 557]. But Plato's advice is cautious. As Michael J. Hyde says: "By setting up an opposition between emotion and reason whereby emotion is conceived as an irrational impulse destructive of a person's thoughtful judgment, Plato could discredit both the mythopoetic and rhetorical uses of discourse because of their intentional and solitary appeal to this impulse" [10, p. 122]. But as a careful study of Plato's dialogues makes clear, any systematic discussion of pathos would have to wait on a richer understanding of this appeal and its uses.

That wait, fortunately, was not long, for Aristotle, Plato's student, discusses the pathetic appeal at some length in his *Rhetoric*, particularly in Book 2. Aristotle begins by defining emotions as "all those feelings that so change men as to affect their judgments, and that are also attended by pain or pleasure. Such are anger, pity, fear and the like, with their opposites" [11, p. 92]. Aristotle thus delineates what Hyde calls "a more positive conception of emotion and its relationship to rhetorical and poetic discourse than allowed by Plato" [11, p. 122]. As Hyde notes, "For Aristotle, then, the emotional character of human beings plays an important role in their development; it constitutes a person's spirited potential for coming to know what is true, just, and virtuous" [10, p. 123]. In *Rhetoric*, then, Aristotle sets about to define and to discuss the various 16 emotions used by rhetors and to advise rhetors on how to generate each in speech.

For purposes of this discussion particularly, Aristotle defines pity as "a feeling of pain caused by the sight of some evil, destructive or painful, which befalls one who does not deserve it, and which we might expect to befall ourselves or some friend of ours, and moreover to befall us soon" [11, p. 113]. We feel pity for those who are the victims of "destructive evils" like "death in its various forms, bodily injuries and afflictions, old age, diseases, lack of food, . . . the evils due to chance" among them "friendlessness, scarcity of friends and companions, deformity, weakness, mutilation, evil coming from a source from which good ought to have come, and the frequent repetition of such misfortunes" [11, p. 114]. Aristotle adds that "Here too we have to remember the general principle that what we fear for ourselves excites our pity when it happens to others. Further, it is when the sufferings of others are close to us that they excite our pity" [11, pp. 114-115). But, Aristotle says, the "most piteous of all is it when, in such times of trial, the victims are persons of noble character" [11, p. 115].

Then, Aristotle particularly gives advice on how to excite pity in the audience. He suggests, for example, that those who engender the most pity in the audience are those who "put the disasters before our eyes, and make them seem close to us, just coming or just past" [11, p. 115]. This particularly effective technique is called *enargia,* which A *Handlist of Rhetorical Terms* defines as "a generic term for visually powerful, vivid description which recreates something or someone as several theorists say 'before your very eyes'" [12, p. 64]. A *Handlist of Rhetorical Terms* uses phrases to define the concept such as "person-to-person immediacy— the impact we feel, perhaps, in live television at its best" [12, p. 64].

Although Aristotle does not say it directly, the implication is strong that in order for pathos to be effective and to create enargia, there must be something—in this case—to pity, something—in other words—to embody the emotion. Otherwise, the emotion floats in the mind of the audience with seemingly no place to light. As *The Encyclopedia of Rhetoric* says, "Images are particularly effective in arousing emotions, whether those images are visual or direct as sensations, or cognitive and indirect as memory or imagination, and part of a rhetor's task is to associate the subject with such images" [6, p. 555]. And if those images are especially vivid, they are much more likely to persuade the readers and move them to an appropriate action. As Crowley and Hawhee conclude, "it is easier to make people afraid and angry toward a person than it is to make them afraid and angry toward an abstraction" [7, p. 211].

The charity letters for this study, a large shoe box full collected by the author over three months, display these persuasive images in abundance. In fact, almost every letter contained an image as part of its pathetic appeal. For example, a letter from an organization working with children begins with a stark image upon which to cast the reader's pity:

> Eight months into her pregnancy, Lauri [X.] learned that her child would have spina bifida, a serious birth defect. "I didn't know what to do."

The reader is drawn then to pity a particular object; this time it is a person, Lauri. That image, then, provides a place for our pity to light.

A second letter illustrates how writers can project pity itself not just onto a person, but also to an object; this time, appropriately, to a wheelchair:

> If I could say one thing from personal experience . . . a wheelchair is a lonely place if you think no one cares. . . .

Here, while the image is a wheelchair, a non-human object employed by people who are usually the object of pity by many people, all the associations of pity and the victim coalesce around that wheelchair for a very powerful pathetic effect.

The writer for another charity, asking for donations around Christmas time, uses not only images upon which to cast the reader's pity, but employs very vivid description that illustrates enargia at work:

> I'm thinking of a young mother with her 3-year-old daughter who appeared at the door of [the name of the charity] one rainy night. Neither of them had shoes on, and mud caked their feet and legs. The mother's husband had locked them out of their home. They were frightened and desperate for help, but had no friends or family to turn to. They hadn't eaten all day . . . and they didn't have any place to sleep.

Here the images include a rain-soaked, "frightened" and "desperate" mother and child who are locked out of their house one dark night by the husband and father. The images are numerous, striking, and quite pathetic in appeal, and they help build the concept of pity in the reader's mind by giving the reader specific and vibrant objects to pity.

But the ancient Greeks were not the only rhetoricians to try to understand pathos as a concept. In fact, the Romans, particularly Cicero, added significantly to our understanding of the idea by specifically reinforcing the importance Aristotle placed on analyzing the audience in order to create pathos, and by calling for the placement of the most pathetic appeals in the peroration. According to Joseph Colavito, writing in *The Encyclopedia of Rhetoric and Composition,* Cicero keenly understood that "the importance of analyzing the audience and its susceptibility to emotional appeals plays a significant role in the [Cicero's rhetorical] theory" [5, p. 493]. In Cicero's *On Oratory and Orators,* he stresses how important audience analysis is to oratory, for the rhetor "must penetrate the inmost recesses of the mind of every class, age, and rank, and must ascertain the sentiments and notions of those before whom he is pleading" [13, p. 67].

In another place, Cicero again stresses audience analysis, saying the orator must know "what their sentiments and opinions are, what they expect, to which side they incline, and to what conclusion they are likely to be led, with least difficulty, by the force of oratory" [13, p. 134]. But Cicero sees the rhetor's "highest power," however, to be "exciting the minds of men . . ." [13, p. 19]. The source of this strong emphasis on the passions traces back to what *The Encyclopedia of Rhetoric* calls the "Roman taste for theatrical displays of all sorts" [5, p. 560]. Accordingly, Cicero reasons, the best place in the rhetorical artifact for this conscious display of emotion is in the ending of the speech. Cicero, for example, notes that "you must not spring at once into the pathetic portion of your speech, as it forms no part of the question, and men are first desirous to learn the very point to come under the judgment . . ." [13, p. 143]. As Colavito says, "The emotional appeal, according to Cicero, is of significant influence in the construction of the speech's peroration . . ." [5, p. 493].

We can see Cicero's ideas at work in several examples taken from charity letters. In one letter, the peroration pleads with the reader to donate to a charity that supports medical research into heart disease by addressing the reader by name:

> Dr. Myers, please don't give up the fight against America's No. 1 killer. We have not heard from you in some time and your support is missed. It does make a difference. Won't you please send $15 or more today and help us save more lives in Richmond? Think of it as an investment in your own future and in the futures of those you love.

Placed at the end of the letter and addressed to the reader by name, the peroration has a great deal of force, especially since a question is directed at a specific reader and especially since the letter ends in the emotion-packed phrases "in your own future and in the futures of those you love."

Another letter illustrates how the writer has not only ended on a pathetic note, but who also has tied the same image that began the letter with the image that closes the letter, while at the same time underlining key phrases and noting that the reader's donation will not just help one child:

> So please <u>sign your Christmas card and return it with your caring gift today</u>. Your card will give hope and encouragement to a St. Jude patient like Madelyn and her family. And your donation will help ensure that every child at St. Jude continues receiving excellent care, and help us advance our groundbreaking cancer research. Your gift could be the one that tips the scale in favor of Madalyn . . . saving her life, and perhaps the lives of thousands more children fighting cancer.

Another letter ends in a particularly piteous way, calling up the image of Joyce, a homeless girl, mentioned in the opening of the letter, and illustrating the tradition of using extreme emotions that Cicero and his fellow Romans were so fond of through the use of phrases like "say a prayer," "lives in fear of relapse," "I will say a special prayer for you and your loved ones":

> And tonight, if you can do me one more favor, please say a prayer for Joyce. It hasn't been easy for her, and she still lives in fear of a relapse every day. While I'm praying for Joyce tonight, I will say a special prayer for you and your loved ones. The covenant you and I have made with these kids is the best thing—in many cases the only thing—in their lives.

Besides the Greeks and Romans, others have added to our understanding of the concept of pathos. Although he did not invent the concept, in *On Christian Doctrine,* St. Augustine, writing some 500 years later, emphasized something quite significant about pathos, stressing that the orator must "speak sweetly" [14, p. 136], emphasizing that *what* you say and *how* you say something are both part of the pathetic appeal. Of the low, middle, and grand styles, St. Augustine saw the grand style as particularly suited for moving the will, what *The Encyclopedia of Rhetoric* calls using "all linguistic sources" [6, p. 562]. Thus, employing the powerful stylistic device of repeating similar syntactic structures himself, St. Augustine suggests that the listener is convinced if the rhetor realizes that the audience is:

> persuaded if he loves what you promise, fears what you threaten, hates what you condemn, embraces

what you commend, sorrows at what you maintain to be sorrowful; rejoices when you announce something delightful; takes pity on those whom you place before him in speaking as being pitiful, flees those whom you, moving fear, warn are to be avoided; and is moved by whatever else may be done through grand eloquence toward moving the minds of listeners, not that they may do what they already know what is to be done, but that they may do what they already know should be done" [14, pp. 136-137].

What St. Augustine has to say about pathetic appeal is particularly important because the Bishop of Hippo also places rhetoric squarely into a Christian context. In other words, the pathetic appeal for St. Augustine has two engines driving it: the rhetorical knowledge about pathetic appeals and their effectiveness that St. Augustine derived from his secular training in rhetoric, *and* the motivation to use such appeals because they are legitimated by the teachings of Christ who himself used such emotional appeals as pity, for example.

To deal with the latter first, it should not be surprising then that Christian charities make use of some of the suggestions of St. Augustine in their letters. This is not to say that these writers have all read, understood, and implemented what St. Augustine wrote, but the tradition of giving to charities because of pity is deeply seated in the basic tenets of Christianity.

One charity, for example, says that it *"honors the birth of Jesus with gifts throughout the year*—gifts that help children heal" (italics in the original). Later, in the same letter, the writer addresses the reader, saying "Together, we can renew those feelings of wonder and surprise and share in His [i.e., Christ's] peace by heeding His call—to love and protect *all* children, *always"* (italics in the original).

Even charities not affiliated with a church make use of this same linking of religion and pity. The Cancer Recovery Foundation of America focuses on a cancer survivor, Greg, and says that "The truth of Romans 8:28 became real in our lives as God turned Greg's adversity to good by giving him the vision of starting the Cancer Recovery Foundation in 1985." Later in the same letter, the writers affirm that they "have also shed tears over seeing God perform miracles." Still later, the letter says that "Greg is praying that God will provide supporters. . . ." Near the hortatory close of the letter, one of the writers asserts that "As a wife, I pray that God will lead you to be a part in this work by sharing a gift to help change lives."

In its history, such a notion of linking Christianity with pathetic appeal appears again in the Renaissance when rhetoric is seen to be, according to *The Encyclopedia of Rhetoric,* "a tool given by a Christian God, the better to know God's universe and bring the soul into closer communion with God" [6, p. 563].

These rhetors of the Renaissance also reinforce St. Augustine's emphasis on style as a pathetic appeal. Fifteenth-century Dutch Humanist Roelof Huysmann, known as Rudolphus Agricola, for example, recognized that "certain kinds of language have an affinity for certain kinds of emotion, not simply in terms of meaning, but also in tone and in the shape and patterns of language treated in elocutio" [6, p. 564]. By the 1700s, the Slavic rhetorician Feofan Prokopovic even delineated "how different tropes and figures achieve effects appropriate to each affect" [6, p. 565]. In another age, Alexander Campbell, in *The Philosophy of Rhetoric* published in 1776, spent much of that treatise on the role of passion in rhetoric. Campbell saw the passions also intricately related to style, concluding that "the kind of address of which I am treating, attains the summit of perfection in the *sublime* (italics in the original), or those great and noble images, which, when in suitable coloring presented to the mind, do, as it were, distend the imagination with some vast conception, and quite ravage the soul" [15, p. 751]. Just a few years later, in 1783, one popular rhetorician would argue that the passions also assist in generating an appropriate style. In fact, Hugh Blair echoes Campbell, by noting that "passion rouse[s] and kindle[s] the mind, without throwing it out of possession of itself[;] [it] is universally found to exalt all the human powers. It renders the mind infinitely more enlightened, more penetrating, more vigorous, and masterly than it is in calm moments" [16, p. 971]. In *Language as Symbolic Action,* noted 20th-century rhetorician Kenneth Burke concludes that style is also a part of the pathetic appeal. In speaking about the effectiveness of the great Greek orator Demosthenes, Burke observes that the orator's "persuasiveness becomes more like sheer literary appeal . . ." [17, p. 296]. Or as he says later, "'style' becomes 'ritual,'" a part of the "word magic" of a rhetorical artifact [17, p. 301]. Writing in the *Journal of Business Communication* in 1985, Craig Kallendorf and Carol Kallendorf argue that "our speech betrays our feelings when we are angry: connectives are passed over in asyndeton, key words are emphatically repeated in anaphora, clauses become shorter and more direct through parallelism, and so forth" [18, p. 41]. Pathos and style are, then, according to this long line of thinkers, inextricably mixed together.

Several letters illustrate how style can have a persuasive edge to it. One letter, for example, effectively uses a scheme that first begins with a negative sentence and then follows that sentence with its positive counterpart that also includes a repetition of the word *threat:*

> We don't protect species [of animals] because they're cute or appealing. We protect them because, given the interdependence of life on this planet, a threat to any of them is a threat to us all.

Parallelism is also a common stylistic feature in the letters. For instance, one letter sets off three statements in parallel structure, underlines them to increase their power, and arranges the sentences in climactic order with the most important sentence placed last:

> It takes as little as 45 minutes.
>
> It costs as little as $250.
>
> It changes a child's life forever.

Another letter asks the reader a rhetorical question and then follows that with three parallel adverbial clauses with the important noun phrases underlined:

> Why do I believe—as I hope you do—that significant progress can still be made?
>
> Because we've already made great strides through the programs in place . . . because we have the proven

tools that have saved countless children's lives . . .

. . . and because we've seen the extraordinary results that a committed, focused effort can produce.

The charity letters include other long passages that feature parallelism, composed of infinitive phrases, for example, which the writers accentuated by underlining phrases in bold face type to increase their persuasive power:

> **There is always more we all can do:** to protect our basic **right to dignity and choice** in both living and dying, to give **time and space** to reach difficult decisions; to listen, **really listen** to patients, family, and caregivers; to keep each and every patient **pain-free and functional**, and hospice has the medical and nursing knowledge to do that!); and above all, to **'be there.'**

Another letter employs wit rather than structure for its effect. The writers of the letter pun on the word hand:

> My friend, we're not asking for a handout—just a helping hand.

Still another technique is to use an extended string of nouns that climaxes with an adjectival clause at the emphatic last position of the sentence:

> It will mean that we, our loved ones and friends, can have the chance to grow old with dignity rather than with the fear, frustration, suffering, despair and ravaging decline that Alzheimer's brings.

These stylistic devices are persuasive, then, in part because they use language in a clever way, assuming tacitly, that style is a part of the persuasive power of a letter. The reader will donate, supposedly, because the letter in part is cleverly stated and thus attractive to the reader, or because the letter is spoken "sweetly," as St. Augustine would say.

What is obvious from this analysis is that when we look at the rhetorical techniques of charity letters, the writers, consciously or unconsciously, seem to be operating out of a lengthy tradition of scholarship about pathetic appeals. Consequently, understanding how charity letters effectively use pathetic appeals is predicated on understanding how the concept of pathos evolved over 2500 years of scholarship, including the thinking of Aristotle about emotions, Cicero's emphasis on audience analysis and the use of a strongly pathetic peroration, and St. Augustine and a bevy of other rhetoricians' emphasis on style as a part of the pathetic appeal.

It should be pointed out, too, though, that there is a significant use of visual rhetoric in these letters, for visual rhetoric is a consideration in the 21st century in any analysis of the persuasive techniques used in a contemporary rhetorical artifact. These letters are no exception. They make use of such devices as typographical bullets, text underlining, different colors of paper and print, pictures in black and white and in color, and bold type in their total appeal. As John Lannon says in his popular textbook *Technical Communication,* "visuals are a staple of communication today" [19, p. 289]. Mike Markel, in *Technical Communication,* agrees and points out that visuals of various sorts assist in communicating difficult material, help to "clarify and emphasize information," "catch the reader's attention," "help nonnative speakers of English understand the information," and "help communicate information to multiple audiences with different interests, aptitudes, and reading habits" [20, p. 319]. But Lannon quickly notes that that "doesn't mean that verbal messages have become obsolete. Instead, words integrate with shapes and images" to produce the total message [19, p. 289]. Part of the appeal of the letters examined is also derived from the offering of address labels, membership cards, and decorative pins, since they have perhaps some persuasive weight in helping readers decide whether or not to contribute to the charity. But while these same devices are important considerations for any persuasive analysis, they are not, however, the main focus of this present discussion.

Finally, it has also not been the purpose of this analysis of charity letters to disparage them as written documents, to assert or to imply that they make pernicious use of rhetorical tricks that "fool" donors into shelling out hard-earned money for dubious purposes. Charities in the past and do now perform vital services for American society, services that provide food and housing for many well-deserving recipients. Today, politicians of multiple persuasions even support giving governmental funds to what in many instances are "faith-based initiatives" or charities.

Yet, at the same time, understanding better how charity letters work as rhetorical artifacts increases our knowledge of just how those thousands of letters that flood mailboxes all over this country ply their craft and supply money so that charities can perform the important services they do. While, at first, their rhetoric seems simple and straightforward, charity letters, taken as a whole, use sophisticated rhetorical techniques that have a long history, derived from important and influential thinkers who understand and appreciate the usefulness of pathos as an appeal worthy of careful examination and judicious use.

REFERENCES

Congressional Quarterly Researcher, Charitable Giving, 1993. 26 May 2005. <http://www.library2.cqpress.com/cqresearcher/document.php?id=cqresrr>.

Lexis-Nexis, Charities Come Calling, a Lot, 2005. 26 May 2005. <http://www.web.lexis.com/universe>.

E. Fehr and S. Renniger, The Samaritan Paradox, *Scientific American Mind, 14*:5, pp. 14-21, 2004.

A. Damasio, *Descartes' Error: Emotion, Reason and the Human Brain*, Quill, New York, 2000.

J. Colavito, Pathos, *Encyclopedia of Rhetoric and Composition*, T. Enos (ed.), Garland, New York, pp. 492-494, 1996.

Pathos, in *Encyclopedia of Rhetoric*, T. O. Sloane (ed.), Oxford, New York, pp. 554-569, 2001.

S. Crowley and D. Hawhee, *Ancient Rhetorics for Contemporary Students*, Longman, New York, 2004.

E. P. J. Corbett and R. J. Connors, *Classical Rhetoric for the Modern Student* (4th Edition), Oxford, New York, 1999.

Gorgias, Encomium of Helen, in *The Rhetorical Tradition*, P. Bizzell and B. Herzberg (eds.), Bedford, New York, 1990.

M. J. Hyde, Emotion and Human Communication: A Rhetorical, Scientific, and Philosophical Picture, *Communication Quarterly, 32*, pp. 120-132, 1984.

Aristotle, *Rhetoric*, W. R. Roberts (Trans.), Modern Library, New York, 1954.

R. A. Lanham, *A Handlist of Rhetorical Terms* (2nd Edition), University of California Press, Berkeley, 1991.

Cicero, *On Oratory and Orators*, J. S. Watson (Trans. and Ed.), Southern Illinois University Press, Carbondale, 1970.

St. Augustine, *On Christian Doctrine*, D. W. Robertson, Jr. (Trans), Prentice Hall, Upper Saddle River, New Jersey, 1997.

A. Campbell, From *The Philosophy of Rhetoric*, in *The Rhetorical Tradition*, P. Bizell and B. Herzberg (eds.), Bedford, New York, 1990.

H. Blair, From *Lectures on Rhetoric and Belle Lettres*, in *The Rhetorical Tradition*, P. Bizell and B. Herzberg (eds.), Bedford, New York, 1990.

K. Burke, *Language as Symbolic Action*, University of California Press, Berkeley, 1966.

C. Kallendorf and C. Kallendorf, The Figures of Speech, Ethos, and Aristotle: Notes toward a Rhetoric of Business Communication, *Journal of Business Communication, 22*, pp. 35-50, 1985.

J. M. Lannon, *Technical Communication* (10th Edition), Pearson Longman, New York, 2006.

M. Markel, *Technical Communication* (7th Edition), Bedford/St. Martin's, Boston, 2004.

POLITICS AND THE ENGLISH LANGUAGE

GEORGE ORWELL

CONSIDER AS YOU ARE READING:

Bemoaning the apparent degeneration of the English language is not a new phenomenon, nor is it the exclusive purview of English teachers, as this essay by the British satirist George Orwell demonstrates. Those familiar with Orwell's novels may be a little surprised by the formality of this piece, which Orwell composed over half a century ago. Despite its age, however, the advice in this essay is current: today's "modern English" is still plagued by many of the same problems Orwell brings to our attention. Today we may think, even more so than his readers at the time did, that Orwell's complaints are low in the hierarchy of rhetorical concerns we have as writers. But he anticipates this objection when he suggests that sloppy writing is the product of sloppy thinking and the cause of it. How appropriate, in a course which seeks to develop our critical thinking, that we consider the role word choice plays in communicating our thoughts with precision.

1. *What does Orwell's academic tone in this piece imply about its audience and purpose? How might you verify your assumptions?*

2. *Which, if any, of Orwell's complaints do you see in your own writing?*

3. *How much does Orwell's antiquated language in this essay affect your comprehension? How did you work through, or around, passages which were particularly challenging?*

Most people who bother with the matter at all would admit that the English language is in a bad way, but it is generally assumed that we cannot by conscious action do anything about it. Our civilization is decadent, and our language—so the argument runs—must inevitably share in the general collapse. It follows that any struggle against the abuse of language is a sentimental archaism, like preferring candles to electric light or hansom cabs to aeroplanes. Underneath this lies the half-conscious belief that language is a natural growth and not an instrument which we shape for our own purposes.

Now, it is clear that the decline of a language must ultimately have political and economic causes: it is not due simply to the bad influence of this or that individual writer. But an effect can become a cause, reinforcing the original cause and producing the same effect in an intensified form, and so on indefinitely. A man may take to drink because he feels himself to be a failure, and then fail all the more completely because he drinks. It is rather the same thing that is happening to the English language. It becomes ugly and inaccurate because our thoughts are foolish, but the slovenliness of our language makes it easier for us to have foolish thoughts. The point is that the process is reversible. Modern English, especially written English, is full of bad habits which spread by imitation and which can be avoided if one is willing to take the necessary trouble. If one gets rid of these habits one can think more clearly, and to think clearly is a necessary first step towards political regeneration: so that the fight against bad English is not frivolous and is not the exclusive concern of professional writers. I will come back to this presently, and I hope that by that time the meaning of what I have said here will have become clearer. Meanwhile, here are five specimens of the English language as it is now habitually written.

These five passages have not been picked out because they are especially bad—I could have quoted far worse if I had chosen—but because they illustrate various of the mental vices from which we now suffer. They are a little below the average, but are fairly representative samples. I number them so that I can refer back to them when necessary:

1. I am not, indeed, sure whether it is not true to say that the Milton who once seemed not unlike a seventeenth-century

Shelley had not become, out of an experience ever more bitter in each year, more alien (sic) to the founder of that Jesuit sect which nothing could induce him to tolerate.
—Professor Harold Laski (Essay in *Freedom of Expression*)

2. Above all, we cannot play ducks and drakes with a native battery of idioms which prescribes such egregious collocations of vocables as the Basic *put up with* for *tolerate* or *put at a loss* for *bewilder*. -Professor Lancelot Hogben (*Interglossia*)

3. On the one side we have the free personality; by definition it is not neurotic, for it has neither conflict nor dream. Its desires, such as they are, are transparent, for they are just what institutional approval keeps in the forefront of consciousness; another institutional pattern would alter their number and intensity; there is little in them that is natural, irreducible, or culturally dangerous. But *on the other side*, the social bond itself is nothing but the mutual reflection of these self-secure integrities. Recall the definition of love. Is not this the very picture of a small academic? Where is there a place in this hall of mirrors for either personality or fraternity? -Essay on psychology in *Politics* (New York)

4. All the "best people" from the gentlemen's clubs, and all the frantic fascist captains, united in common hatred of Socialism and bestial horror of the rising tide of the mass revolutionary movement, have turned to acts of provocation, to foul incendiarism, to medieval legends of poisoned wells, to legalize their own destruction of proletarian organizations, and rouse the agitated petty-bourgeoisie to chauvinistic fervor on behalf of the fight against the revolutionary way out of the crisis. -Communist pamphlet

5. If a new spirit is to be infused into this old country, there is one thorny and contentious reform which must be tackled, and that is the humanization and galvanization of the B.B.C. Timidity here will bespeak canker and atrophy of the soul. The heart of Britain may be sound and of strong beat, for instance, but the British lion's roar at present is like that of Bottom in Shakespeare's *A*

Midsummer Night's Dream—as gentle as any sucking dove. A virile new Britain cannot continue indefinitely to be traduced in the eyes, or rather ears, of the world by the effete languors of Langham Place, brazenly masquerading as "standard English." When the Voice of Britain is heard at nine o'clock, better far and infinitely less ludicrous to hear aitches honestly dropped than the present priggish, inflated, inhibited, school-ma'am-ish arch braying of blameless bashful mewing maidens. -Letter in *Tribune*

Each of these passages has faults of its own, but quite apart from avoidable ugliness, two qualities are common to all of them. The first is staleness of imagery; the other is lack of precision. The writer either has a meaning and cannot express it, or he inadvertently says something else, or he is almost indifferent as to whether his words mean anything or not. This mixture of vagueness and sheer incompetence is the most marked characteristic of modern English prose, and especially of any kind of political writing. As soon as certain topics are raised, the concrete melts into the abstract and no one seems able to think of turns of speech that are not hackneyed: prose consists less and less of *words* chosen for the sake of their meaning, and more and more of *phrases* tacked together like the sections of a prefabricated hen-house. I list below, with notes and examples, various of the tricks by means of which the work of prose-construction is habitually dodged:

Dying metaphors. A newly invented metaphor assists thought by evoking a visual image, while on the other hand a metaphor which is technically "dead" (e.g. *iron resolution*) has in effect reverted to being an ordinary word and can generally be used without loss of vividness. But in between these two classes there is a huge dump of worn-out metaphors which have lost all evocative power and are merely used because they save people the trouble of inventing phrases for themselves. Examples are: *Ring the changes on, take up the cudgel for, toe the line, ride roughshod over, stand shoulder to shoulder with, play into the hands of, no axe to grind, grist to the mill, fishing in troubled waters, on the order of the day, Achilles' heel, swan song, hotbed* . Many of these are used without knowledge of their meaning (what is a "rift," for instance?), and incompatible metaphors are frequently mixed, a sure sign that the writer is not interested in what he is saying. Some metaphors now current have been twisted out of their original meaning without those who use them even being aware of the fact. For example, *toe the line* is sometimes written as *tow the line*. Another example is *the hammer and the anvil*, now always used with the implication that the anvil gets the worst of it. In real life it is always the anvil that breaks the hammer, never the other way about: a writer who stopped to think what he was saying would avoid perverting the original phrase.

Operators or **verbal false limbs.** These save the trouble of picking out appropriate verbs and nouns, and at the same time pad each sentence with extra syllables which give it an appearance of symmetry. Characteristic phrases are *render inoperative, militate against, make contact with, be subjected to, give rise to, give grounds for, have the effect of, play a leading part (role) in, make itself felt, take effect, exhibit a tendency to, serve the purpose of, etc., etc.* The keynote is the elimination of simple verbs. Instead of being a single word, such as *break, stop, spoil, mend, kill,* a verb becomes a *phrase*, made up of a noun or adjective tacked on to some general-purpose verb such as *prove, serve, form, play, render.* In addition, the passive voice is wherever possible used in preference to the active, and noun constructions are used instead of gerunds (*by examination of* instead of *by examining*). The range of verbs is further cut down by means of the *-ize* and *de*formations, and the banal statements are given an appearance of profundity by means of the *not un*-formation. Simple conjunctions and prepositions are replaced by such phrases as *with respect to, having regard to, the fact that, by dint of, in view of, in the interests of, on the hypothesis that;* and the ends of sentences are saved by anticlimax by such resounding commonplaces as *greatly to be desired, cannot be left out of account, a development to be expected in the near future, deserving of serious consideration, brought to a satisfactory conclusion,* and so on and so forth.

Pretentious diction. Words like *phenomenon, element, individual* (as noun), *objective, categorical, effective, virtual, basic, primary, promote, constitute, exhibit, exploit, utilize, eliminate, liquidate,* are used to dress up a simple statement and give an air of scientific impartiality to biased judgements. Adjectives like *epoch-making, epic, historic, unforgettable, triumphant, age-old, inevitable, inexorable,* *veritable,* are used to dignify the sordid process of international politics, while writing that aims at glorifying war usually takes on an archaic colour, its characteristic words being: *realm, throne, chariot, mailed fist, trident, sword, shield, buckler, banner, jackboot, clarion.* Foreign words and expressions such as *cul de sac, ancien regime, deus ex machina, mutatis mutandis, status quo, gleichschaltung, weltanschauung* , are used to give an air of culture and elegance. Except for the useful abbreviations *i.e., e.g.* and *etc.,* there is no real need for any of the hundreds of foreign phrases now current in the English language. Bad writers, and especially scientific, political, and sociological writers, are nearly always haunted by the notion that Latin or Greek words are grander than Saxon ones, and unnecessary words like *expedite, ameliorate, predict, extraneous, deracinated, clandestine, subaqueous,* and hundreds of others constantly gain ground from their Anglo-Saxon numbers.[1] The jargon peculiar to Marxist writing (*hyena, hangman, cannibal, petty bourgeois, these gentry, lackey, flunkey, mad dog, White Guard,* etc.) consists largely of words translated from Russian, German, or French; but the normal way of coining a new word is to use a Latin or Greek root with the appropriate affix and, where necessary, the size formation. It is often easier to make up words of this kind (*deregionalize, impermissible, extramarital, non-fragmentary* and so forth) than to think up the English words that will cover one's meaning. The result, in general, is an increase in slovenliness and vagueness.

Meaningless words. In certain kinds of writing, particularly in art criticism and literary criticism, it is normal to come across long passages which are almost completely lacking in meaning.[2] Words like *romantic, plastic, values, human, dead, sentimental, natural, vitality,* as used in art criticism, are strictly meaningless, in the sense that they not only do not point to any discoverable object, but are hardly ever expected to do so by the reader.

---

1   An interesting illustration of this is the way in which the English flower names which were in use till very recently are being ousted by Greek ones, snapdragon becoming *antirrhinum, forget-me-not* becoming *myosotis,* etc. It is hard to see any practical reason for this change of fashion: it is probably due to an instinctive turning-away from the more homely word and a vague feeling that the Greek word is scientific.

2   Example: 'Comfort's catholicity of perception and image, strangely Whitmanesque in range, almost the exact opposite in aesthetic compulsion, continues to evoke that trembling atmospheric accumulative ginting at a cruel, an inexorably selene timelessness... Wrey Gardiner scores by aiming at simple bull's-eyes with precision. Only they are not so simple, and through this contented sadness runs more than the surface bitter-sweet of resignation'. (*Poetry Quarterly.*)

When one critic writes, "The outstanding feature of Mr. X's work is its living quality," while another writes, "The immediately striking thing about Mr. X's work is its peculiar deadness," the reader accepts this as a simple difference of opinion. If words like *black* and *white* were involved, instead of the jargon words *dead* and *living*, he would see at once that language was being used in an improper way. Many political words are similarly abused. The word *Fascism* has now no meaning except in so far as it signifies "something not desirable." The words *democracy, socialism, freedom, patriotic, realistic, justice* have each of them several different meanings which cannot be reconciled with one another. In the case of a word like *democracy*, not only is there no agreed definition, but the attempt to make one is resisted from all sides. It is almost universally felt that when we call a country democratic we are praising it: consequently the defenders of every kind of regime claim that it is a democracy, and fear that they might have to stop using that word if it were tied down to any one meaning. Words of this kind are often used in a consciously dishonest way. That is, the person who uses them has his own private definition, but allows his hearer to think he means something quite different. Statements like *Marshal Petain was a true patriot, The Soviet press is the freest in the world, The Catholic Church is opposed to persecution,* are almost always made with intent to deceive. Other words used in variable meanings, in most cases more or less dishonestly, are: *class, totalitarian, science, progressive, reactionary, bourgeois, equality.*

Now that I have made this catalogue of swindles and perversions, let me give another example of the kind of writing that they lead to. This time it must of its nature be an imaginary one. I am going to translate a passage of good English into modern English of the worst sort. Here is a well-known verse from *Ecclesiastes*:

> I returned and saw under the sun, that the race is not to the swift, nor the battle to the strong, neither yet bread to the wise, nor yet riches to men of understanding, nor yet favour to men of skill; but time and chance happeneth to them all.

Here it is in modern English:

> Objective considerations of contemporary phenomena compel the conclusion that success or failure in competitive activities exhibits no tendency to be commensurate with

innate capacity, but that a considerable element of the unpredictable must invariably be taken into account.

This is a parody, but not a very gross one. Exhibit (3) above, for instance, contains several patches of the same kind of English. It will be seen that I have not made a full translation. The beginning and ending of the sentence follow the original meaning fairly closely, but in the middle the concrete illustrations—race, battle, bread—dissolve into the vague phrases "success or failure in competitive activities." This had to be so, because no modern writer of the kind I am discussing—no one capable of using phrases like "objective considerations of contemporary phenomena"—would ever tabulate his thoughts in that precise and detailed way. The whole tendency of modern prose is away from concreteness. Now analyze these two sentences a little more closely. The first contains forty-nine words but only sixty syllables, and all its words are those of everyday life. The second contains thirty-eight words of ninety syllables: eighteen of those words are from Latin roots, and one from Greek. The first sentence contains six vivid images, and only one phrase ("time and chance") that could be called vague. The second contains not a single fresh, arresting phrase, and in spite of its ninety syllables it gives only a shortened version of the meaning contained in the first. Yet without a doubt it is the second kind of sentence that is gaining ground in modern English. I do not want to exaggerate. This kind of writing is not yet universal, and outcrops of simplicity will occur here and there in the worst-written page. Still, if you or I were told to write a few lines on the uncertainty of human fortunes, we should probably come much nearer to my imaginary sentence than to the one from *Ecclesiastes*.

As I have tried to show, modern writing at its worst does not consist in picking out words for the sake of their meaning and inventing images in order to make the meaning clearer. It consists in gumming together long strips of words which have already been set in order by someone else, and making the results presentable by sheer humbug. The attraction of this way of writing is that it is easy. It is easier—even quicker, once you have the habit—to say *In my opinion it is not an unjustifiable assumption that* than to say *I think*. If you use ready-made phrases, you not only don't have to hunt about for the words; you also don't have to bother with the rhythms of your sentences since these phrases are generally so arranged as to be more or less euphonious. When you are composing in a hurry—when you are dictating to a stenographer, for instance, or making a public speech—it is natural to fall into a pretentious, Latinized style. Tags like *a consideration which we should do well to bear in mind* or *a conclusion to which all of us would readily assent* will save many a sentence from coming down with a bump. By using stale metaphors, similes, and idioms, you save much mental effort, at the cost of leaving your meaning vague, not only for your reader but for yourself. This is the significance of mixed metaphors. The sole aim of a metaphor is to call up a visual image. When these images clash—as in *The Fascist octopus has sung its swan song, the jackboot is thrown into the melting pot*—it can be taken as certain that the writer is not seeing a mental image of the objects he is naming; in other words he is not really thinking. Look again at the examples I gave at the beginning of this essay. Professor Laski (1) uses five negatives in fifty three words. One of these is superfluous, making nonsense of the whole passage, and in addition there is the slip *-alien* for akin—making further nonsense, and several avoidable pieces of clumsiness which increase the general vagueness. Professor Hogben (2) plays ducks and drakes with a battery which is able to write prescriptions, and, while disapproving of the everyday phrase *put up with*, is unwilling to look *egregious* up in the dictionary and see what it means; (3), if one takes an uncharitable attitude towards it, is simply meaningless: probably one could work out its intended meaning by reading the whole of the article in which it occurs. In (4), the writer knows more or less what he wants to say, but an accumulation of stale phrases chokes him like tea leaves blocking a sink. In (5), words and meaning have almost parted company. People who write in this manner usually have a general emotional meaning—they dislike one thing and want to express solidarity with another—but they are not interested in the detail of what they are saying. A scrupulous writer, in every sentence that he writes, will ask himself at least four questions, thus:

What am I trying to say?

What words will express it?

What image or idiom will make it clearer?

Is this image fresh enough to have an effect?

And he will probably ask himself two more:

Could I put it more shortly?

Have I said anything that is avoidably ugly?

But you are not obliged to go to all this trouble. You can shirk it by simply throwing your mind open and letting the ready-made phrases come crowding in. They will construct your sentences for you—even think your thoughts for you, to a certain extent— and at need they will perform the important service of partially concealing your meaning even from yourself. It is at this point that the special connection between politics and the debasement of language becomes clear.

In our time it is broadly true that political writing is bad writing. Where it is not true, it will generally be found that the writer is some kind of rebel, expressing his private opinions and not a "party line." Orthodoxy, of whatever colour, seems to demand a lifeless, imitative style. The political dialects to be found in pamphlets, leading articles, manifestos, White papers and the speeches of undersecretaries do, of course, vary from party to party, but they are all alike in that one almost never finds in them a fresh, vivid, homemade turn of speech. When one watches some tired hack on the platform mechanically repeating the familiar phrases—*bestial, atrocities, iron heel, bloodstained tyranny, free peoples of the world, stand shoulder to shoulder*—one often has a curious feeling that one is not watching a live human being but some kind of dummy: a feeling which suddenly becomes stronger at moments when the light catches the speaker's spectacles and turns them into blank discs which seem to have no eyes behind them. And this is not altogether fanciful. A speaker who uses that kind of phraseology has gone some distance toward turning himself into a machine. The appropriate noises are coming out of his larynx, but his brain is not involved, as it would be if he were choosing his words for himself. If the speech he is making is one that he is accustomed to make over and over again, he may be almost unconscious of what he is saying, as one is when one utters the responses in church. And this reduced state of consciousness, if not indispensable, is at any rate favourable to political conformity.

In our time, political speech and writing are largely the defence of the indefensible. Things like the continuance of British rule in India, the Russian purges and deportations, the dropping of the atom bombs on Japan, can indeed be defended, but only by arguments which are too brutal for most people to face, and which do not square with the professed aims of the political parties. Thus political language has to consist largely of euphemism, question-begging and sheer cloudy vagueness. Defenceless villages are bombarded from the air, the inhabitants driven out into the countryside, the cattle machine-gunned, the huts set on fire with incendiary bullets: this is called *pacification*. Millions of peasants are robbed of their farms and sent trudging along the roads with no more than they can carry: this is called *transfer of population* or *rectification of frontiers*. People are imprisoned for years without trial, or shot in the back of the neck or sent to die of scurvy in Arctic lumber camps: this is called *elimination of unreliable elements*. Such phraseology is needed if one wants to name things without calling up mental pictures of them. Consider for instance some comfortable English professor defending Russian totalitarianism. He cannot say outright, "I believe in killing off your opponents when you can get good results by doing so." Probably, therefore, he will say something like this:

> While freely conceding that the Soviet regime exhibits certain features which the humanitarian may be inclined to deplore, we must, I think, agree that a certain curtailment of the right to political opposition is an unavoidable concomitant of transitional periods, and that the rigors which the Russian people have been called upon to undergo have been amply justified in the sphere of concrete achievement.

The inflated style itself is a kind of euphemism. A mass of Latin words falls upon the facts like soft snow, blurring the outline and covering up all the details. The great enemy of clear language is insincerity. When there is a gap between one's real and one's declared aims, one turns as it were instinctively to long words and exhausted idioms, like a cuttlefish spurting out ink. In our age there is no such thing as "keeping out of politics." All issues are political issues, and politics itself is a mass of lies, evasions, folly, hatred, and schizophrenia. When the general atmosphere is bad, language must suffer. I should expect to find—this is a guess which I have not sufficient knowledge to verify—that the German, Russian and Italian languages have all deteriorated in the last ten or fifteen years, as a result of dictatorship.

But if thought corrupts language, language can also corrupt thought. A bad usage can spread by tradition and imitation even among people who should and do know better. The debased language that I have been discussing is in some ways very convenient. Phrases like *a not unjustifiable assumption, leaves much to be desired, would serve no good purpose, a consideration which we should do well to bear in mind,* are a continuous temptation, a packet of aspirins always at one's elbow. Look back through this essay, and for certain you will find that I have again and again committed the very faults I am protesting against. By this morning's post I have received a pamphlet dealing with conditions in Germany. The author tells me that he "felt impelled" to write it. I open it at random, and here is almost the first sentence I see: "[The Allies] have an opportunity not only of achieving a radical transformation of Germany's social and political structure in such a way as to avoid a nationalistic reaction in Germany itself, but at the same time of laying the foundations of a co-operative and unified Europe." You see, he "feels impelled" to write—feels, presumably, that he has something new to say—and yet his words, like cavalry horses answering the bugle, group themselves automatically into the familiar dreary pattern. This invasion of one's mind by ready-made phrases (*lay the foundations, achieve a radical transformation*) can only be prevented if one is constantly on guard against them, and every such phrase anaesthetizes a portion of one's brain.

I said earlier that the decadence of our language is probably curable. Those who deny this would argue, if they produced an argument at all, that language merely reflects existing social conditions, and that we cannot influence its development by any direct tinkering with words and constructions. So far as the general tone or spirit of a language goes, this may be true, but it is not true in detail. Silly words and expressions have often disappeared, not through any evolutionary process but owing to the conscious action of a minority. Two recent examples were *explore every avenue* and *leave no stone unturned,* which were killed by the jeers of a few journalists. There is a long list of flyblown metaphors which could similarly be got rid of if enough people would interest themselves in the job; and it should also be possible to laugh the *not un*-formation out of existence[3], to reduce the amount of Latin and Greek in the average sentence, to drive out foreign phrases and strayed scientific words, and, in general, to make pretentiousness unfashionable. But all these are minor points. The defence of the English language implies more than this, and perhaps it is best to start by saying what it does *not* imply.

To begin with, it has nothing to do with archaism, with the salvaging of obsolete words and turns of speech, or with the setting up of a "standard English" which must never be departed from. On the contrary, it is especially concerned with the scrapping of every word or idiom which has outworn its usefulness. It has nothing to do with correct grammar and syntax, which are of no importance so long as one makes one's meaning clear, or with the avoidance of Americanisms, or with having what is called a "good prose style." On the other hand, it is not concerned with fake simplicity and the attempt to make written English colloquial. Nor does it even imply in every case preferring the Saxon word to the Latin one, though it does imply using the fewest and shortest words that will cover one's meaning. What is above all needed is to let the meaning choose the word, and not the other way around. In prose, the worst thing one can do with words is surrender to them. When you think of a concrete object, you think wordlessly, and then, if you want to describe the thing you have been visualising you probably hunt about until you find the exact words that seem to fit it. When you think of something abstract you are more inclined to use words from the start, and unless you make a conscious effort to prevent it, the existing dialect will come rushing in and do the job for you, at the expense of blurring or even changing your meaning. Probably it is better to put off using words as long as possible and get one's meaning as clear as one can through pictures and sensations. Afterward one can choose—not simply *accept*—the phrases that will best cover the meaning, and then switch round and decide what <u>impressions one</u>'s words are likely to make on another person.

3   One can cure oneself of the not un- formation by memorizing this sentence: *A not unblack dog was chasing a not unsmall rabbit across a not ungreen field.*

This last effort of the mind cuts out all stale or mixed images, all prefabricated phrases, needless repetitions, and humbug and vagueness generally. But one can often be in doubt about the effect of a word or a phrase, and one needs rules that one can rely on when instinct fails. I think the following rules will cover most cases:

1. Never use a metaphor, simile, or other figure of speech which you are used to seeing in print.

2. Never use a long word where a short one will do.

3. If it is possible to cut a word out, always cut it out.

4. Never use the passive where you can use the active.

5. Never use a foreign phrase, a scientific word, or a jargon word if you can think of an everyday English equivalent.

6. Break any of these rules sooner than say anything outright barbarous.

These rules sound elementary, and so they are, but they demand a deep change of attitude in anyone who has grown used to writing in the style now fashionable. One could keep all of them and still write bad English, but one could not write the kind of stuff that I quoted in those five specimens at the beginning of this article.

I have not here been considering the literary use of language, but merely language as an instrument for expressing and not for concealing or preventing thought. Stuart Chase and others have come near to claiming that all abstract words are meaningless, and have used this as a pretext for advocating a kind of political quietism. Since you don't know what Fascism is, how can you struggle against Fascism? One need not swallow such absurdities as this, but one ought to recognise that the present political chaos is connected with the decay of language, and that one can probably bring about some improvement by starting at the verbal end. If you simplify your English, you are freed from the worst follies of orthodoxy. You cannot speak any of the necessary dialects, and when you make a stupid remark its stupidity will be obvious, even to yourself. Political language—and with variations this is true of all political parties, from Conservatives to Anarchists—is designed to make lies sound truthful and murder respectable, and to give an appearance of solidity to pure wind. One cannot change this all in a moment, but one can at least change one's own habits, and from time to time one can even, if one jeers loudly enough, send some worn-out and useless phrase—some *jackboot, Achilles' heel, hotbed, melting pot, acid test, veritable inferno,* or other lump of verbal refuse—into the dustbin, where it belongs.

WRITING FOR THE PUBLIC

MIKE ROSE

CONSIDER AS YOU ARE READING:

Mike Rose has a perspective that is of particular interest to writers trying to cross the bridge from academic to public writing (as is often our objective in writing courses) because he has experience in both worlds. As a professor of English, he is well-versed in academic genres, but he also writes for the public; this is the very topic of this article. While we tend to regard being an academic as an asset to a writer's credibility, Rose reveals how it can be a barrier to entry into the broader world, primarily because experts are often regarded as illiterate in the language of the public. Fortunately for us, he doesn't just identify this problem; he also offers suggestions for overcoming it—essentially by learning to write appropriately for different audiences, which is one of the goals of every advanced writer.

1. *According to Rose, what are the most common differences in conventions between academic and public writing?*

2. *One of Rose's students commented that "...[This] course got me to think of my writing as strategic ...." What do you suppose the student meant by that? How do you, or might you, make your writing more strategic?*

3. *This reading, like many of the others in this book, was not written for undergraduate writers, but rather for other English academics. However, many students have commented that this article is less difficult to read than some of the other essays on rhetoric. Why is this article more accessible, even though you are not necessarily Rose's intended audience?*

For the past twenty years or so, I have been fortunate to write for a fairly broad audience. While I was teaching, or running an educational program, or doing research, I was also composing opinion pieces or commentaries about the work I was doing. This process of writing with part of my attention on the classroom or research site and part of it on the public sphere forced me—would force anyone—out of familiar rhetorical territory. As a result, I've been thinking a lot about both the challenge and the importance of academics and other specialists communicating with the general public—and I certainly have been thinking about how hard it is to do this. Our languages of specialization can be so opaque, and mass media are becoming all the more sound-bite and entertainment oriented. Serious consideration of serious issues is difficult to achieve.

Let me offer two moments from my own writing life that represent some of the tensions inherent in trying to write for a wider readership today.

Lives on the Boundary, a book about educational underpreparation published in 1989, was my first attempt to write about educational issues for the general public. When I began circulating early chapters to publishers in 1987, I received one form-letter rejection after another . . . at least a dozen in all. Then I lucked out and got an agent—though he didn't have much success either until he got a longtime acquaintance, an editor at the Free Press, to sit down with the thing. My agent told me later that the first question he typically got when he told editors I worked at the University of California–Los Angeles (UCLA) and did my research on education and literacy was some variation of, "Okay, but can he write?"

Media need experts in and out of the academy for their knowledge and opinion, but there is an odd relationship here. Those in broadcast media, in trade publishing, in the world of newspapers and magazines are reliant on expertise but, as a rule, are wary, even disdainful, of the expert's ability to communicate it. And not without reason. As so many of all ideological persuasions, in and out of the academy, have hammered home (see Patricia Nelson Limerick's "Dancing with Professors" for a classic treatment), we academic types can be long-winded, reliant on jargon, and given to tangent or an endless loop of qualification and nit-picking. Caught in the linguistic bubble of our specializations, we are often impervious to our inability to connect with a more general audience of listeners and readers. When all those editors knew of me came from a brief professional biography, they had reason to be cautious.

This leads me to my second vignette, which offers another piece of the story.

Not too long ago, I sent a commentary on the No Child Left Behind Act (NCLB) to a magazine of social and political commentary, in which I had published before. So much had been written about NCLB that either dealt with it strictly on the political and policy level, or energetically championed or damned it, that I wanted to try a piece that, though critical, would consider the legislation from multiple perspectives and also explain in plain language the problems with some of its core mechanisms, like the standardized test.

To the editor's credit, I got a quick, personal response, affirming the importance of the topic. But my treatment of it was "too wonky." Could I write something that is "faster" as to what works, what doesn't, and why? The piece I sent was "too cautious."

A "wonk" is someone who is taken by the details of a subject—in this case, educational policy—and the implication is of narrow preoccupation, getting lost in detail, a grind. I was trying to explain the key elements of a piece of public policy and reflect on its implications, but to this editor, what I was doing came across as tedious, boring, the domain of the policy wonk but not the general public. We were at an impasse.

The editor's comments highlight several characteristics of contemporary media's treatment of public policy and social issues, all of which have been much discussed, often by media people themselves.

The first has to do with the definition of *news* itself. The process by which an event gets tagged as newsworthy is influenced by a host of variables, from novelty, conflict, and sensationalism ("If it bleeds, it leads") to an editor's tastes and beliefs. A central issue here involves the scripts or narratives typically used to frame a story. In my case, the editor wanted a "what works/ what doesn't" structure, a kind of ledger sheet that, I'll admit, would make for a quicker read. (The equivalent, if we were looking at the politics of NCLB, would be a "who's winning/ who's losing" story line.) Scripts like these contribute to what gets defined as a good news story. Pertinent here is a troubling finding in the Project for Excellence in Journalism's *The State of the News Media 2008*: the agenda of the American news media continues to narrow, not broaden. This is true, the report adds, for new media as well. Sadly, education gets a tiny percent of total news coverage, and that coverage will tend toward certain kinds of stories rather than others.

The second issue involves the increasing influence of an entertainment orientation on news and commentary. The length of stories is shrinking, as is their informational content. One example of many can be found in the average length of a presidential candidate's television sound bite. During the 1968 election it was 42 seconds; by 2004 it had been clipped to 7.6 seconds.[1] Newspapers and news magazines reflect the same impulse. Sam Zell, the real estate tycoon who owns the *Chicago Tribune* and *Los Angeles Times*, has been slashing and burning his papers to become, in his words, spicier, flashier, and easier to read.[2]

And all this is affected by the explosion of new media. As words decrease, images proliferate, amped up via digital technology. To be sure, images can contribute to powerful inquiry, depending on how they're sequenced and integrated with spoken or written text. But as Glynda Hull, a researcher of literacy and new media, observes, "Instead of examination of an issue, we tend to get simplification. The visual substitutes for narrative and analysis" (personal communication).

---

1   These statistics come from two sources: Thomas E. Patterson's 1994 book *Out of Order* (160) and Erik P. Bucy and Maria Elizabeth Grabe's paper "Image Bite News" (20).
2   Zell is quoted by media reporter Richard Perez-Pena on WNYC's "On the Media," June 13, 2008.

I've also noticed in print media, even in outlets pitched as highbrow, a rising value given to style that is arch or edgy. Liberal columnist Bob Herbert gets slammed in the liberal *Washington Monthly* because, though he's on the side of the magazine's angels, he's "boring."[3] Snap and sizzle. The quick over the deliberative. "Surprise me," an impatient public radio producer tells me as I pitch an idea for a Labor Day commentary.

If academics limit themselves through their specialized language, editors are limited as well by their own definitions of a newsworthy story and can overreact to the mere hint of scholarship, rejecting anything that, as one editor told me, "looks like a study."

*****

I want to suggest some ways for academics to write successfully within this communicative tangle. I'll do so by describing two courses I developed to help graduate students write for broader audiences. These courses are housed in the place where I work, a graduate school of education, but, like education, rhetoric and composition is widely interdisciplinary and has a long reach into practice. The reader will see many parallels.

Education includes areas of study as diverse as history and developmental biology and psychology . . . as well as economics, linguistics, anthropology, political science, sociology, statistics, and more. It is not uncommon for a student to study several of these disciplines, acquiring their vocabularies and modes of argument along the way, acquiring as well the authority of disciplinary membership. But education is also intimately connected to broad public concerns, and the majority of students in education very much want to affect educational policy and practice. How do they turn, and tune, their voices from the seminar room to the public sphere? As they try to do so, they find themselves smack in the middle of a whole set of questions about communication: about writing, voice, audience, and the tension between the language of specialization and the

---

3   See the very title of T.A. Frank's *Washington Monthly* article "Why Is Bob Herbert Boring?" *Washington Monthly*, October, 2007, 16–20.

language of public discourse. The school of education becomes a rhetorical laboratory.

I hadn't been in UCLA's School of Education for very long before these tensions became a focus of my teaching. Student after student in child development, or language policy, or the study of higher education sat in my office expressing a desire to make a difference in the world, to communicate with the public about educational issues that mattered deeply to them. But they didn't know how to do it, or, to be more exact, they worried that the specialized language of learning theory, or critical social thought, or organizational behavior that they had worked so hard to acquire both certified their authority in the academy and tongue-tied them when it came to writing for nonspecialists. Some also worried that these new languages—the syntax and vocabulary, the conventions and stance—left no room for a personal mark, for the deeply felt beliefs that brought them into education, for passion.

The first course I developed helps students become more effective scholarly writers. And while it certainly addresses everything from conventions of citation to summarizing a body of research literature, it also assists students in framing a tight argument and questioning it, in thinking hard about audience, in appropriating stylistic devices and considering the grace as well as informational content of their sentences.

The course is structured like a workshop, and each student begins by reading aloud a piece of his or her writing, even if half of it is charts and statistical tables. Because so many students in education come out of the social or psychological sciences, they have rarely, if ever, had the opportunity to think about their writing as *writing* and not just a vehicle to hold information. I want them to *hear* their writing. I urge them to find other scholarly and non-scholarly writers they like and read them like a writer, noting and analyzing what it is they do that works— and then incorporating those writers' techniques into their own work. At the end of the quarter, I think that the primary thing students acquire is a rhetorical sense of their writing; style and audience are more on their minds. As one student put it so well, "The course got me to think of my writing as strategic.

Who am I writing to? Where do I want to take them with my argument? How can I get them there?" (For a fuller discussion of this course, see Rose and McClafferty.)

The second course shares a good deal with the workshop on scholarly writing, but is designed to help students in education write for the general public. The goal is to produce two pieces of writing: the newspaper op-ed piece and the magazine article. Students can vary these for online media, but the purpose remains the same: to draw on one's studies and research to write for a wide audience a 700- to 800- word opinion piece and a 1,500- to 2,500-word magazine article. Students are also required to familiarize themselves with appropriate outlets and submit to them.

To streamline our discussion here, I'll focus on the opinion piece, though my students and I go through the same process and make some of the same discoveries in writing the magazine article.

On the first day of class, I distribute a variety of opinion pieces—and encourage students to subsequently bring in ones they find that catch their fancy. We operate inductively, reading the selections and looking for characteristics and commonalities. Students immediately notice the brevity and conciseness of the opinion piece (versus the longer, more elaborated writing of their disciplines). Claims and arguments are made quickly and without heavy citation or marshalling of other research relevant to the topic.

Evidence is present in the opinion piece, of course, but it will be one or two key statistics or examples or reports, or a telling and crisp quotation from another expert. The length of this essay won't allow for many examples, but let me offer one here that my students liked. Writing about the plight of temp workers, labor policy analyst Laura Jones warns, "When it comes to benefits, temps better take their vitamins and look both ways before crossing the street: Only 5% receive employer-provided health insurance" (B5). The question that then emerges is, how does one select a sample of evidence that is vibrant yet still representative? Or, more challenging, how does one deal with conflicting evidence within constraints?

Students also notice features of the op-ed genre, particularly the "hook," the linking of the piece onto an event in the news. And, in some pieces, the "turn," that point where the writer, having summarized current policy or perception, turns the tables and offers another way—the way the writer prefers—to think about the issue at hand.

Opinion pieces are written in all kinds of styles and voices—from polemical to didactic to ironic—but students comment on the commonalities in language, the accessible vocabulary, the lack of jargon (or the judicious use of it, always defined), the frequent use of colloquial speech—always for rhetorical effect. Along with diction, they note the syntax of sentences—often not as complicated as they find in scholarly prose—and the short paragraphs (versus paragraphs that in scholarly writing can go on for a page).

This attention to style leads to experimentation: incorporating metaphor, varying sentence length, strategically shortening paragraphs. It also contributes to a heightened appreciation of revision and a commitment to it. "By the time I got done with my piece," one student said, "every sentence was changed. It does you no good to hold onto your precious words."

One thing I love about teaching this course—or the one focused more on scholarly writing—is how easily, readily big topics emerge, topics central to the kind of work the students envision for themselves. We might be talking in class about the kind of evidence to provide, and that discussion balloons to the issue of authority, of demonstrating expertise. Or we're down to the level of the sentence, mixing long sentences with short ones, or even the effective use of the semicolon or the dash, and suddenly we're talking about how someone wants to sound, to come across to a reader.

This concern about how one comes across has a lot to do with identity, a fundamental issue at this stage of a graduate student's development. What kind of work do I want to do? How can I sound at least a little bit distinctive while appropriating the linguistic conventions of my discipline? Whom do I want to write for; how narrowly or broadly will I think of my audience or audiences? Who am I as a scholar?

Another gratifying element of the course is the crossover effect that always emerges: These young scholars begin to apply the lessons learned in this class on popular writing to their academic prose. I encourage a kind of bilingualism, the continued development of facility with both scholarly writing and writing for nonspecialists. But there is playback, as well, from the opinion piece and magazine article onto the writing students do for their disciplines.

They learn, for example, to present their argument quickly, tersely, without the scaffolds of jargon, catchphrases, and a swarm of citations. This honing of language can have a powerful effect on a writer's conceptualization of the argument itself. What *exactly* am I trying to say here? What *is* the problem I'm trying to solve? What is the fundamental logic of my study? Writing the opinion piece, one student observed, "helped me think deeply about my topic. It's so easy to string a lot of fancy words together that look really important, but don't really have substance to them."

I've been writing about the crossover from the opinion piece to scholarly writing, but the crossover works in both directions. Students gain a heightened sense of the potential relevance of their work to issues of public concern. This awareness can vitalize scholarship.

The fostering of a hybrid professional identity—the life lived both in specialization and in the public sphere—is something I think we as a society need to nurture. The more opinion is grounded on rich experience and deep study, the better the quality of our public discourse about the issues that matter to us.

*****

Even as I am helping young scholars write the newspaper opinion piece, newspapers themselves are in flux and being wrenched toward various blends with new media.

381

"How can you convey profundity," a public relations friend of mine asks me, "through Twitter?" Though he used an extreme example with Twitter—the microblogging service where messages are limited to 140 characters—he was pressing a legitimate point. Am I preparing my students for a vanishing world? Is even the 600- to 700-word opinion piece becoming irrelevant?

Though my students are way savvier about new media than I am, I try to provide some guidance in writing for online outlets and in strategically blending image with text. Still, opinion pieces are published online, and many of the abilities students develop working on them carry over to newer genres: the rhetorical sensibility, the linguistic facility, the push toward conciseness.

It *is* hard for specialists to make their way in our complex and evolving media world. Lord knows, this world has handed me my fair share of rejections. But though difficult, it is not closed by any means, and the blogosphere offers its own wide range of options and entry points. One clear thing the history of technology shows us is that while a new technology does change things, sometimes dramatically, it also blends and morphs into existing technologies and social practices.

It is important then to keep in mind that various forms of media are not hermetic, not sealed off from each other. Many users shift from YouTube to a radio podcast, to Google Scholar, to a paperback recommended by a friend . . . possibly on Facebook. And skills learned in one form can transfer to another, and hybrid forms can emerge. A generative interaction. Here are a few quick examples from my own experience.

I mentioned earlier the importance of being concise without sacrificing your core claim or argument. At about the same time I wrote my first opinion piece, I was also beginning to do radio interviews. One medium is print-based and static, the other oral and interactive, but each in its way pushed me to refine the ability to state a point quickly. Also, talk radio—especially those shows with call-ins—really helped me develop a richer, more concrete sense of the audience out there, of possible misunderstandings or elaborations of a claim of mine . . . or counter-arguments to it. And this experience with real and unpredictable audiences was certainly valuable when I sat down to compose something for the unknown readers of the opinion page.

Long inept with all things computeresque, I recently entered the blogosphere, and, probably because I didn't know better, I wrote in a traditional mode for this new medium. Millions of active blogs are out there, of all imaginable content and style, but few in the (admittedly) small sample I saw looked like what I had in mind.

Our national discussion of education has gotten terribly narrow, a discourse of economic competitiveness and test scores. So I wanted a blog that encouraged a more reflective, deliberative discussion of the purpose of education, and the essay more so than the typical blog post seemed the right genre. I wanted to use this new medium to write old-school, small essays about school. What is interesting is the degree to which the readers of the blog have responded in kind. Some of their comments are paragraphs long, crafted and thoughtful. A community college instructor writes a meditation on teaching and the purpose of education: "I love to pull my teaching cart out into the dark, smelling all the trees and flowers that are now only shadows, knowing that I and my students are tired from doing something worthwhile." Essayist literacy a mouse-click away from Twitter.

*****

Rhetoric and composition are deeply connected to matters of broad public interest—literacy, teaching, undergraduate education—and for a while now, some within our field have been seeking public connection through service-learning, courses in civic rhetoric, or involvement in workplace and community literacy projects. There is talk of a "public turn" in composition studies, and several new journals are directly addressing public and community literacy. But the huge, clattering irony is that our field, a field that has rhetoric at its core, offers little or no graduate-level training for public writing or speaking. English and education don't either. Yet many in rhetoric and composition (and in education) are yearning to speak to wider audiences, to insert our various bodies of knowledge and perspectives into the public record.

We academics easily develop a tin ear to the sound of our own language. We talk too much to each other, and not beyond. We risk linguistic, intellectual, and political isolation. Many good things have come of rhetoric and composition's move toward disciplinary status. But with disciplinarity also comes a turn inward, a concentration on the mechanics of the profession, on internal debates and intellectual display, on a specific kind of career building—and it is all powerfully reinforced, materially and symbolically, by the academy.

There's nothing wrong with watching out for one's livelihood, of course not. And there's real value in a tradition that demands intellectual scrutiny within ranks. But, as Lisa Ede smartly observed a while back, there is a tendency for disciplines, for us, to create, or at least amp up, our debates by reducing and reifying one another's positions—then opposing them. This is the academic engine and, yes, it can contribute to more intense thinking. But it also keeps our attention focused on ourselves while all hell breaks loose in public policy and the broader public sphere.

I wonder how we might continue to turn outward through our disciplinary debates. How can we attend to both our field and the public domain . . . and find something generative in considering the two together?

The field of rhetoric and composition is grounded on the art of persuasion, is multidisciplinary, and has a foundational connection to teaching practice and education policy. It is the ideal place, as a number of people have been arguing lately, to imagine a different kind of disciplinary and institutional life.

We could begin in our graduate programs. Here's one small suggestion. We could offer training—through a course or some other curricular mechanism—in communicating to broader audiences, the *doing* of rhetoric. The training could include analysis of public policy and media to heighten sophistication about how they work and how one might find or create an entry point. And such training could also include rhetorical theory and history that enhances the understanding of such public intellectual work—I think here, as one example, of Jacqueline

Jones Royster's *Traces of a Stream,* which offers a rich account of nineteenth-century African American women moving into and affecting public life with a rhetorically attuned public writing. Students would learn a lot about media and persuasion and the sometimes abstract notion of audience. And they would understand rhetoric, the rhetorical impulse and practice, in a way that is both grounded and fresh.[4]

WORKS CITED

Bucy, Erik P., and Maria Elizabeth Grabe. "Image Bite News: An Underappreciated Source of Political Information." American Political Science Association. Marriott, Loew's Philadelphia, and the Pennsylvania Convention Center, Philadelphia. 31 Aug. 2006. Address.

Ede, Lisa. "Reading the Writing Process." *Taking Stock: The Writing Process Movement in the '90s.* Ed. Lad Tobin and Thomas Newkirk. Portsmouth: Boynton/Cook, 1994. 31–43. Print.

Hull, Glynda. Personal Communication. 13 June 2008.

Jones, Laura. "For Temps, There Are No Holidays." *Los Angeles Times* 6 Sept. 1999: B5. Print.

Limerick, Patricia Nelson. "Dancing with Professors: The Trouble with Academic Prose." *New York Times Book Review* 31 Oct. 1993: 3, 23–24. Print.

Patterson, Thomas E. *Out of Order.* New York: Knopf, 1993. Print.

Project for Excellence in Journalism. *The State of the News Media 2008: An Annual Report on American Journalism.* Project for Excellence in Journalism, 17 Mar. 2008. Web. 9 July 2009.

---

4   I would like to thank the following people for their comments on an earlier version of this essay: Richard Lee Colvin, Ellen Cushman, Casandra Harper, Linda Kao, Elham Kazemi, Rema Reynolds, and Kerri Ullucci.

Rose, Mike. *Lives on the Boundary: The Struggles and Achievements of America's Underprepared.* New York: Free Press, 1989. Print.

Rose, Mike, and Karen McClafferty. "A Call for the Teaching of Writing in Graduate Education." *Educational Researcher* 30.2 (2001): 27–33. Print.

Royster, Jacqueline Jones. *Traces of a Stream: Literacy and Social Change among African American Women.* Pittsburgh: U of Pittsburgh P, 2000. Print.

THE CLASSROOM AND THE WIDER CULTURE: IDENTITY AS A KEY TO LEARNING ENGLISH COMPOSITION

FAN SHEN

CONSIDER AS YOU ARE READING:

This essay is a wonderful reminder that the rules of composition, and even the rules of logic that undergird our notions of argument, are cultural constructions directly linked to the values and beliefs that we hold often unconsciously. Shen describes his experience as a Chinese student attempting to learn English Composition in the 1990's. In that historical moment in Chinese culture, the concept of the individual was devalued. In his American Composition classes, however, Shen was pressured to find his "individual" voice and avoid using passive constructions—a direct contradiction with Chinese logic. Shen demonstrates that learning composition requires learning the deeper values and beliefs held by a culture. This essay emphasizes the social nature of our rhetorical choices, and it warns us against considering any rhetorical practice as natural or free of cultural influence.

1. *Shen explains that a writer's identity is closely tied to cultural expectations for language use. How, ultimately, does Shen's identity change as he learned the expectations for English composition?*

2. *Describe an experience in which you found yourself out of touch with the cultural expectations place upon you by a writing situation. (It may be helpful to think about the different cultures in academic departments here.)*

3. *Do you agree with Shen's claims that English composition practices reflect an emphasis on individualism? Why or why not?*

One day in June 1975, when I walked into the aircraft factory where I was working as an electrician, I saw many large-letter posters on the walls and many people parading around the workshops shouting slogans like "Down with the word 'I'!" and "Trust in masses and the Party!" I then remembered that a new political campaign called "Against Individualism" was scheduled to begin that day. Ten years later, I got back my first English composition paper at the University of Nebraska-Lincoln. The professor's first comments were: "Why did you always use 'we' instead of 'I'?" and "Your paper would be stronger if you eliminated some sentences in the passive voice." The clashes between my Chinese background and the requirements of English composition had begun. At the center of this mental struggle, which has lasted several years and is still not completely over, is the prolonged, uphill battle to recapture "myself".

In this paper I will try to describe and explore this experience of reconciling my Chinese identity with an English identity dictated by the rules of English composition. I want to show how my cultural background shaped—and shapes—my approaches to my writing in English and how writing in English redefined—and redefines—my *ideological* and *logical* identities. By "ideological identity" I mean the system of values that I acquired (consciously and unconsciously) from my social and cultural background. And by "logical identity" I mean the natural (or Oriental) way I organize and express my thoughts in writing. Both had to be modified or redefined in learning English composition. Becoming aware of the process of redefinition of these different identities is a mode of learning that has helped me in my efforts to write in English, and, I hope, will be of help to teachers of English composition in this country. In presenting my case for this view, I will use examples from both my composition courses and literature courses, for I believe that writing papers for both kinds of courses contributed to the development of my "English identity." Although what I will describe is based on personal experience, many Chinese students whom I talked to said that they had had the same or similar experiences in their initial stages or learning to write English.

IDENTITY OF THE SELF: IDEOLOGICAL AND CULTURAL

Starting with the first English paper I wrote, I found that learning to compose in English is not an isolated classroom activity, but a social and cultural experience. The rules of English composition encapsulate values that are absent in, or sometimes contradictory to, the values of other societies (in my case, China). Therefore, learning the rules of English composition is, to a certain extent, learning the values of Anglo-American society. In writing classes in the United States, I found that I had to reprogram my mind, to redefine some of the basic concepts and values that I had about myself, about society, and about the universe, values that had been imprinted and reinforced in my mind by my cultural background, and that had been part of me all my life.

Rule number one in English composition is: Be yourself. (More than one composition instructor has told me, "Just write what *you* think.") The values behind this rule, it seems to me, are based on the principle of protecting and promoting individuality (and private property) in this country. The instruction was probably crystal clear to students raised on these values, but, as a guideline of composition, it was not very clear or useful to me when I first heard it. First of all, the image or meaning that I attached to the word "I" or "myself" was, as I found out, different from that of my English teacher. In China, "I" is always subordinated to "We"—be it the working class, the Party, the country, or some other collective body. Both political pressure and literary tradition require that "I" be somewhat hidden or buried in writings and speeches; presenting the "self" too obviously would give people the impression of being disrespectful of the Communist Party in political writings and boastful in scholarly writings. The word "I" has often been identified with another "bad" word, "individualism," which has become a synonym for selfishness in China. For a long time, the words "self" and "individualism" have had negative connotations in my mind, and the negative force of the words naturally extended to the field of literary studies. As a result, even if I had brilliant ideas, the "I" in my papers always had to show some modesty by not competing with or trying to stand above the names of ancient and modern authoritative figures.

Appealing to Mao or other Marxist authorities became the required way (as well as the most "forceful" or "persuasive" way) to prove one's point in written discourse. I remember that in China I had even committed what I can call "reversed plagiarism"—here, I suppose it would be called "forgery"— when I was in middle school: willfully attributing some of my thoughts to "experts" when I needed some arguments but could not find a suitable quotation from a literary or political "giant."

Now, in America, I had to learn to accept the words "I" and "Self" as something glorious (as Whitman did), or at least something not to be ashamed of or embarrassed about. It was the first and probably biggest step I took into English composition and critical writing. Acting upon my professor's suggestion, I intentionally tried to show my "individuality" and to "glorify" "I" in my papers by using as many "I's" as possible—"I think," "I believe," "I see"—and deliberately cut out quotations from authorities. It was rather painful to hand in such "pompous" (I mean immodest) papers to my instructors. But, to an extent, it worked. After a while, I became more comfortable with only "the shadow of myself." I felt more at ease to put down *my* thoughts without looking over my shoulder to worry about the attitudes of my teachers or the reactions of the party secretaries, and to speak out as "bluntly" and "immodestly" as my American instructors demanded.

But writing many "I's" was only the beginning of the process of redefining myself. Speaking of redefining myself is, in an important sense, speaking of redefining the word "I." By such a redefinition I mean not only the change in how I envisioned myself, but also the change in how *I* perceived the world. The old "I" used to embody only one set of values, but now it had to embody multiple sets of values. To be truly "myself," which I knew was a key to my success in learning English composition, meant *not to be my Chinese self* at all. That is to say, when I write in English, I have to wrestle with and abandon (at least temporarily) the whole system of ideology which previously defined me in myself. I had to forget Marxist doctrines (even though I do not see myself as a Marxist by choice) and the Party lines imprinted in my mind and familiarize myself with a system of capitalist/bourgeois values. I had to put aside an ideology of collectivism and adopt the values of individualism.

In composition as well as in literature classes, I had to make a fundamental adjustment: if I used to examine society and literary materials through the microscopes of Marxist dialectical materialism and historical materialism, I now had to learn to look through the microscopes the other way around, i.e., to learn to look at and understand the world from the point of view of "idealism." (I must add here that there are American professors who use a Marxist approach in their teaching.)

The word "idealism," which affects my view of both myself and the universe, is loaded with social connotations, and can serve as a good example of how redefining a key word can be a pivotal part of redefining my ideological identity as a whole.

To me, idealism is the philosophical foundation of the dictum of English composition: "Be yourself." In order to write good English, I knew that I had to be myself, which actually meant not to be my Chinese self. It meant that I had to create an English self and to be *that* self. And to be that English self, I felt, I had to understand and accept idealism the way a Westerner does. That is to say, I had to accept the way a Westerner sees himself in relation to the universe and society. On the one hand, I knew a lot about idealism. But on the other hand, I knew nothing about it. I mean, I knew a lot about idealism through the propaganda and objections of its opponent, Marxism, but I knew little about it from its own point of view. When I thought of the word "materialism"—which is a major part of Marxism and in China has repeatedly been "shown" to be the absolute truth—there were always positive connotations, and words like "right," "true," etc., flashed in my mind. On the other hand, the word "idealism" always came to me with the dark connotations that surround words like "absurd," "illogical," "wrong," etc. In China, "idealism" is depicted as a ferocious and ridiculous enemy of Marxist philosophy. Idealism, as the simplified definition imprinted in my mind had it, is the view that the material world does not exist, that all that exists is the mind and its ideas. It is just the opposite of Marxist dialectical materialism which sees the mind as a product of the material world. It is not too difficult to see that idealism, with its idea that mind is of primary importance, provides a philosophical foundation for the Western emphasis on the value of individual human minds, and hence individual human beings. Therefore, my final acceptance of myself as of primary importance—an importance that overshadowed that of authority figures in English composition—was, I decided, dependent on an acceptance of idealism.

My struggle with idealism came mainly from my efforts to understand and to write about works such as Coleridge's *Literaria Biographia* and Emerson's "Over-Soul." For a long time I was frustrated and puzzled by the idealism expressed by Coleridge and Emerson—given their ideas, such as "I think, therefore I am" (Coleridge obviously borrowed from Descartes) and "the transparent eyeball" (Emerson's view of himself)—because in my mind, drenched as it was in dialectical materialism, there was always a little voice whispering in my ear "You are, therefore you think." I could not see how human consciousness, which is not material, could create apples and trees. My intellectual conscience refused to let me believe that the human mind is the primary world and the material world secondary. Finally, I had to imagine that I was looking at a world with my head upside down. When I imagined that I was in a new body (born with the head upside down) it was easier to forget biases imprinted in my sub-consciousness about idealism, the mind, and my former self. Starting from scratch, the new inverted self—which I called my "English Self" and into which I have transformed myself—could understand and *accept*, with ease, idealism as "the truth" and "himself" (i.e., my English Self) as the "creator" of the world.

Here is how I created my new "English Self." I played a "game" similar to ones played by mental therapists. First I made a list of (simplified) features about writing associated with my old identity (the Chinese Self), both ideological and logical, and then beside the first list I added a column of features about writing associated with my new identity (the English Self). After that I pictured myself getting out of my old identity, the timid, humble, modest Chinese, "I," and creeping into my new identity (often in the form of a new skin or a mask), the confident, assertive, and aggressive English "I." The new "Self" helped me to remember and accept the different rules of Chinese and English composition and the values that underpin these rules. In a sense, creating an English Self is a way of reconciling my old cultural values with the new values required by English writing, without losing the former.

An interesting structural but not material parallel to my experiences in this regard has been well described by Min-zhan Lu in her important article, "From Silence to Words: Writing as Struggle" (*College English* 49 [April 1987]: 437-48). Min-zhan Lu talks about struggles between two selves, an open self and a secret self, and between two discourses, a mainstream Marxist discourse and a bourgeois discourse her parents wanted her to learn. But her struggle was different from mine. Her Chinese self was severely constrained and suppressed by mainstream cultural discourse, but never interfused with it. Her experiences, then, were not representative of those of the majority of the younger generation who, like me, were brought up on only one discourse. I came to English composition as a Chinese person, in the fullest sense of the term, with a Chinese identity already fully formed.

IDENTITY OF THE MIND: ILLOGICAL AND ALOGICAL

In learning to write in English, besides wrestling with a different ideological system, I found that I had to wrestle with a logical system very different from the blueprint of logic at the back of my mind. By "logical system" I mean two things: the Chinese way of thinking I used to approach my theme or topic in written discourse, and the Chinese critical/logical way to develop a theme or topic. By English rules, the first is illogical for it is the opposite of the English way of approaching a topic; the second is alogical (non-logical), for it mainly uses mental pictures instead of words as a critical vehicle.

The Illogical Pattern. In English composition, an essential rule for the logical organization of a piece of writing is the use of a "topic sentence." In Chinese composition, "from surface to core" is an essential rule, a rule which means that one ought to reach a topic gradually and "systematically' instead of "abruptly."

The concept of a topic sentence, it seems to me, is symbolic of the values of a busy people in an industrialized society, rushing to get things done, hoping to attract and satisfy the busy reader very quickly. Thinking back, I realized that I did not fully understand the virtue of the concept until my life began to rush at the speed of everyone else's in this country. Chinese composition, on the other hand, seems to embody the values of a leisurely paced rural society whose inhabitants have the time to chew and taste a topic slowly. In Chinese composition, an introduction explaining how and why one chooses this topic is not only acceptable, but often regarded as necessary. It arouses the reader's interest in the topic little by little (and this is seen as a virtue of composition) and gives him/her a sense of refinement. The famous Robert B. Kaplan "noodles" contrasting a spiral Oriental thought process with a straight-line Western approach ("Cultural Thought Patterns in Inter-Cultural Education," *Readings on English as a Second Language*, Ed. Kenneth Croft, 2nd ed., Winthrop, 1980, 403-10) may be too simplistic to capture the preferred pattern of writing in English, but I think they still express some truth about Oriental writing. A Chinese writer often clears the surrounding bushes before attacking the real target. This bush-clearing pattern in Chinese writing goes back two thousand years to Kong Fuzi (Confucius). Before doing anything, Kong says in his *Luen Yu (Analects)*, one first needs to call things by their proper names (expressed by his phrase "Zheng Ming" XXX). In other words, before touching one's main thesis, one should first state the "conditions" of composition: how, why, and when the piece is being composed. All of this will serve as a proper foundation on which to build the "house" of the piece. In the two thousand years after Kong, this principle of composition was gradually formalized (especially through the formal essays required by imperial examinations) and became known as "Ba Gu," or the eight-legged essay. The logic of Chinese composition, exemplified by the eight-legged essay, is like the peeling of an onion: layer after layer is removed until the reader finally arrives at the central point, the core.

Ba Gu still influences modern Chinese writing. Carolyn Matalene has an excellent discussion of this logical (or illogical) structure and its influence on her Chinese students' efforts to write in English ("Contrastive Rhetoric: An American Writing Teacher in China," *College English* 47 [November 1985]: 789-808). A recent Chinese textbook for composition lists six essential steps (factors) for writing a narrative essay, steps to be taken in this order: time, place, character, event, cause, and consequence

(*Yuwen Jichu Zhishi Liushi Jiang [Sixty Lessons on the Basics of the Chinese Language]*, Ed. Beijing Research Institute of Education, Beijing Publishing House, 1981, 525-609). Most Chinese students (including me) are taught to follow this sequence in composition.

The straightforward approach to composition in English seemed to me, at first, illogical. One could not jump to the topic. One had to walk step by step to reach the topic. In several of my early papers I found that the Chinese approach—the bush-clearing approach—persisted, and I had considerable difficulty writing (and in fact understanding) topic sentences. In what I deemed to be topic sentences, I grudgingly gave out themes. Today, those papers look to me like Chinese papers with forced or false English openings. For example, in a narrative paper on a trip to New York, I wrote the forced/false topic sentence, "A trip to New York in winter is boring." In the next few paragraphs, I talked about the weather, the people who went with me, and so on, before I talked about what I learned from the trip. My real thesis was that one could always learn something even on a boring trip.

The Alogical Pattern. In learning English composition, I found that there was yet another cultural blueprint affecting my logical thinking. I found from my early papers that very often I was unconsciously under the influence of a Chinese critical approach called the creation of "yijing," which is totally nonWestern. The direct translation of the word "yijing" is: yi, "mind or consciousness," and jing, "environment." An ancient approach which has existed in China for many centuries and is still the subject of much discussion, yijing is a complicated concept that defies a universal definition. But most critics in China nowadays seem to agree on one point, that yijing is the critical approach that separates Chinese literature and criticism from Western literature and criticism. Roughly speaking, yijing is the process of creating a pictorial environment while reading a piece of literature. Many critics in China believe that yijing is a creative process of inducting oneself while reading a piece of literature or looking at a piece of art, to create mental pictures, in order to reach a unity of nature, the author, and the reader. Therefore, it is by its very nature both creative and critical.

According to the theory, this nonverbal, pictorial process leads directly to a higher ground of beauty and morality. Almost all critics in China agree that yijing is not a process of logical thinking—it is not a process of moving from the premises of an argument to its conclusion, which is the foundation of Western criticism. According to yijing, the process of criticizing a piece of art or literary work has to involve the process of creation on the reader's part. In yijing, verbal thoughts and pictorial thoughts are one. Thinking is conducted largely in pictures and then "transcribed" into words. (Ezra Pound once tried to capture the creative aspect of yijing in poems such as "In a Station of the Metro." He also tried to capture the critical aspect of it in his theory of imagism and vorticism, even though he did not know the term "yijing.") One characteristic of the yijing approach to criticism, therefore, is that it often includes a description of the created mental pictures on the part of the reader/critic and his/her mental attempt to bridge (unite) the literary work, the pictures, with ultimate beauty and peace.

In looking back at my critical papers for various classes, I discovered that I unconsciously used the approach of yijing, especially in some of my earlier papers when I seemed not yet to have been in the grip of Western logical critical approaches. I wrote, for instance, an essay entitled "Wordsworth's Sound and imagination: The Snowdon Episode." In the major part of the essay, I described the pictures that flashed in my mind while I was reading passages in Wordsworth's long poem, *The Prelude*.

> I saw three climbers (myself among them) winding up the mountain in silence "at the dead of night," absorbed in their "private thoughts." The sky was full of blocks of clouds of different colors, freely changing their shapes, like oily pigments disturbed in a bucket of water. All of a sudden, the moonlight broke the darkness "like a flash," lighting up the mountain tops. Under the "naked moon," the band saw a vast sea of mist and vapor, a silent ocean. Then the silence was abruptly broken, and we heard the "roaring of waters, torrents, streams/Innumerable, roaring with one voice" from a "blue chasm," a fracture in the vapor of the sea. It was a joyful revelation of divine

> truth to the human mind: the bright, "naked" moon
> sheds the light of "higher reasons" and "spiritual
> love" upon us; the vast ocean of mist looked like
> a thin curtain through which we vaguely saw the
> infinity of nature beyond; and the sounds of roaring
> waters coming out of the chasm of vapor cast us into
> the boundless spring of imagination from the depth
> of the human heart. Evoked by the divine light from
> above, the human spring of imagination is joined by
> the natural spring and becomes a sustaining source
> of energy, feeding "upon infinity" while transcending
> infinity at the same time. . . .

Here I was describing my own experience more than
Wordsworth's. The picture described by the poet is taken over
and developed by the reader. The imagination of the author
and the imagination of the reader are thus joined together.
There was no "because" or "therefore" in the paper. There was
little *logic*. And I thought it was (and it is) criticism. This seems
to me a typical (but simplified) example of the yijing approach.
(Incidentally, the instructor, a kind professor, found the paper
interesting, though a bit "strange.")

In another paper of mine, "The Note of Life: Williams's 'The
Orchestra'," I found myself describing my experiences of pictures
of nature while reading William Carlos Williams's poem "The
Orchestra." I "painted" these fleeting pictures and described
the feelings that seemed to lead me to an understanding of
a harmony, a "common tone," between man and nature. A
paragraph from that paper reads:

> The poem first struck me as a musical fairy tale. With
> rich musical sounds in my ear, I seemed to be walking
> in a solitary, dense forest on a spring morning. No
> sound from human society could be heard. I was
> now sitting under a giant pine tree, ready to hear
> the grand concert of Nature. With the sun slowly
> rising from the east, the cello (the creeping creek)
> and the clarinet (the rustling pine trees) started with
> a slow overture. Enthusiastically the violinists (the
> twittering birds) and the French horn (the mumbling
> cow) "interpose[d] their voices," and the bass (bears)

got in at the wrong time. The orchestra did not stop, they continued to play. The musicians of Nature do not always play in harmony. "Together, unattuned," they have to seek "a common tone" as they play along. The symphony of Nature is like the symphony of human life: both consist of random notes seeking a "common tone." For the symphony of life

Love is that common tone

shall raise his fiery head

and sound his note.

Again, the logical pattern of this paper, the "pictorial criticism," is illogical to Western minds but "logical" to those acquainted with yijing. (Perhaps I should not even use the words "logical" and "think" because they are so conceptually tied up with "words" and with culturally-based conceptions, and therefore very misleading if not useless in a discussion of yijing. Maybe I should simply say that yijing is neither illogical nor logical, but alogical.)

I am not saying that such a pattern of "alogical" thinking is wrong—in fact some English instructors find it interesting and acceptable—but it is very non-Western. Since I was in this country to learn the English language and English literature, I had to abandon Chinese "pictorial logic," and to learn Western "verbal logic."

IF I HAD TO START AGAIN

The change is profound, through my understanding of new meanings of words like "individualism," "idealism," and "I," I began to accept the underlying concepts and values of American writing, and by learning to use "topic sentences" I began to accept a new logic. Thus, when I write papers in English, I am able to obey all the general rules of English composition. In doing this, I feel that I am writing through, with, and because of a new identity. I welcome the change, for it has added a new dimension to me and to my view of the world. I am not saying that I have entirely lost my Chinese identity. In fact I feel that I will never lose it. Any time I write in Chinese, I resume my old identity, and obey the rules of Chinese composition such as "Make the 'I' modest," and "Beat around the bush before attacking the central topic. It is necessary for me to have such a Chinese identity in order to write authentic Chinese. (I have seen people who, after learning to write in English, use English logic and sentence patterning to write Chinese. They produce very awkward Chinese texts.) But when I write in English, I imagine myself slipping into a new "skin," and I let the "I" behave much more aggressively and knock the topic right on the head. Being conscious of these different identities has helped me to reconcile different systems of values and logic, and has played a pivotal role in my learning to compose in English.

Looking back, I realize that the process of learning to write in English is in fact a process of creating and defining a new identity and balancing it with the old identity. The process of learning English composition would have been easier if I had realized this earlier and consciously sought to compare the two different identities required by the two writing systems from two different cultures. It is fine and perhaps even necessary for American composition teachers to teach about topic sentences, paragraphs, the use of punctuation, documentation, and so on, but can anyone design exercises sensitive to the ideological and logical differences that students like me experience—and design them so they can be introduced at an early stage of an English composition class? As I pointed out earlier, the traditional advice "Just be yourself" is not clear and helpful to students from Korea, China, Vietnam, or India. From "Be yourself" we are likely to hear either "Forget your cultural habit of writing" or "Write as you would write in your own language." But neither of the two is what the instructor meant or what we want to do. It would be helpful if he or she pointed out the different cultural/ideological connotations of the word "I," the connotations that exist in a group-centered culture and an individual-centered culture. To sharpen the contrast, it might be useful to design papers on topics like "The Individual vs. The Group: China vs. America" or "Different 'I's' in Different Cultures."

Carolyn Matalene mentioned in her article (789) an incident concerning American businessmen who presented their Chinese hosts with gifts of cheddar cheese, not knowing that the Chinese generally do not like cheese. Liking cheddar cheese may not be essential to writing English prose, but being truly accustomed to the social norms that stand behind ideas such as the English "I" and the logical pattern of English composition—call it "compositional cheddar cheese"—is essential to writing in English. Matalene does not provide an "elixir" to help her Chinese students like English "compositional cheese," but rather recommends, as do I, that composition teachers not be afraid to give foreign students English "cheese," but to make sure to hand it out slowly, sympathetically, and fully realizing that it tastes very peculiar in the mouths of those used to a very different cuisine.

"I HAD AN ABORTION.": THE RHETORICAL SITUATION OF A PLANNED PARENTHOOD T-SHIRT

CRYSTAL LANE SWIFT

CONSIDER AS YOU ARE READING:

In this essay Crystal Swift makes practical use of Bitzer's theory of the rhetorical situation to determine if a specific argument is an appropriate response to a given situation. In this case, she is analyzing a t-shirt with the words "I had an abortion" printed on the front. The t-shirt slogan is part of a campaign by Planned Parenthood, and is therefore enmeshed in a particular social and political situation. Swift deploys Bitzer's triad (exigency/audience/constraints) to analyze the rhetorical effectiveness of the t-shirt slogan. It is interesting to note the richness of detail that emerges from this analysis, given that the text under scrutiny is only four words in length. This essay models how much we can glean from a deep reading of the rhetorical situation in which communication takes place.

1. *How, according to Swift, does the Planned Parenthood t-shirt campaign reflect exigence/audience/constraints?*

2. *Create a slogan intended to convince writers to use the rhetorical triangle to analyze rhetorical situations. Now, explain how your slogan addresses the triad of exigence/audience/constraints.*

3. *Do you agree with Swift's assessment that this t-shirt is an effective piece of rhetoric, based on the triad of exigence/audience/constraints that Swift employs? Why or why not?*

"I had an abortion." While most women who have had abortions may not publicly make this declaration, Planned Parenthood has been selling a t-shirt that does so (see Figure 1). The t-shirt itself does not appear controversial, until the words on the t-shirt are read by the viewer; rather, it is a simple burgundy t-shirt with yellow lettering. However, within such a controversial and heated debate (i.e., the abortion controversy), this t-shirt is an incredibly bold piece of rhetoric. Hence, the question arises, Was the "I had an abortion." t-shirt an effective piece of rhetoric given the rhetorical situation surrounding the fight for women's rights? Bitzer's Rhetorical Situation theory leads us to the conclusion that it was. To understand the answer to the research question, we will discuss the women's rights movement, define Bitzer's Rhetorical Situation model, apply Bitzer's theory to the t-shirt, and draw implications from this criticism. Figure 1. "I had an Abortion." t-shirt. Image Retrieved September 18, 2004, from http://store.yahoo.com/ppfastore/ihadabt.html.

BACKGROUND: THE ABORTION DEBATE AND THIS T-SHIRT

The Planned Parenthood Organization was begun by Margaret Sanger in 1930, with the goal of strengthening women's reproductive rights and freedom of choice. The organization's mission is still to provide the tools necessary for managing one's own reproductive rights, regardless of demographics. The shirt is for sale on the Planned Parenthood Web site to provide a way for women to wear their beliefs. The "I had an abortion" t-shirt was released in response to the passage of partial birth abortion legislation in 2004, which escalated the abortion debate in the public's eye.

The t-shirt itself does not promote a specific public event, although it did become available shortly before the National

Organization for Women's March for Women's Lives on April 24, 2004. The timing of the release of the t-shirt is important: while the t-shirt was made available in time to be worn for this march, the homepage for the 2004 event (National Organization for Women, 1995-2007) has no link to this particular shirt, though there are links to other pro-choice t-shirts. The Web page (National Organization for Women, 1995-2007) devoted to the 2004 march declares:

> The March for Women's Lives was an overwhelming success, thanks to the hard work and generosity of hundreds of thousands of supporters like you. But as powerful as the March was, it's not enough that we were heard in the streets of Washington D.C. on April 25. From the day he took office, George W. Bush has treated women's rights as a political bargaining tool, sacrificing women's lives and health to appease the radicals who put him in office. With the March for Women's Lives, we said, "No more."

Coffin (2004) points out that President Bush's decision to sign in to law the ban on partial-birth abortion infuriated many pro-choice activists. This action seems to have escalated the abortion debate in the public's eye. With the 2008 elections fast-approaching, reproductive rights will likely be a central voting issue for many women and men alike. This election could very well indirectly decide who will replace those Supreme Court Justices headed to retirement. The possibilities of replacement justices have encouraged both liberals and conservatives alike to take this election seriously.

Many people have potential exposure to the T-shirt, whether they agree with the shirt's message or not. Anyone can wear the t-shirt at any time and any place. The t-shirt was designed by Jennifer Baumgartner and Amy Richards, founders of soapboxinc.com, who met when they were 22 years old and working for *Ms.* Magazine. The pair has been working to strengthen their perspective on reproductive rights through various projects and have been speakers since the inception of Soap Box Inc, with the joint goal to promote women's rights activism and reach out to communities regarding these issues.

Though the primary rhetors for the t-shirt are the women who created the shirt, any person who wears the shirt is perceived as the rhetor of the message. This parallels any message delivered by someone other than the author of the message: though the person wearing the item may not have written the message, anyone who sees or hears a person associated with that message will most likely deem that person to be in agreement. According to the Soap Box Web site, the T-shirts that state simply "I had an abortion." are part of a project to tell the truth: that women might be sorry to need an abortion, but they aren't sorry that they had access to one (Soapbox, Inc.: Speakers Who Speak Out, 2004).

BITZER'S SITUATIONAL RHETORIC

Bitzer's model of the Rhetorical Situation is concerned with the elements surrounding a piece of rhetoric and enabling critics of rhetoric to determine whether it is an appropriate response to the given situation. Hence, this model serves as an appropriate method of evaluating the abortion t-shirt. Bitzer (1968) claims that "rhetoric is a mode of altering reality, not by direct energy to objects, but by the creation of discourse which changes reality through the mediation of thought action" (p. 4).

The Rhetorical Situation is comprised of three tenets: exigence, audience, and constraints. Bitzer (1968) explains that "any exigence is an imperfection marked by an urgency" (p. 6). Exigence is essentially a call for response. The obstacle in the status quo that the exigence brings attention to must be changeable through some element of discursive response, not solely by other means. Second, there must be a specific audience that is addressed. Bitzer (1968) asserts that rhetoric must be aimed at an audience to influence change. For an audience to qualify as rhetorical, they must be able to influence the situation to make the change that the rhetor is calling for. With an exigence to respond to and an audience to receive that response, the rhetor also faces certain constraints in any rhetorical situation. These constraints consist of the physical, theoretical, and emotional limitations of the situation and audience. Bitzer (1968) argues that these constraints can come from the rhetor, the audience, or the environment in which the rhetoric takes place.

HOW THE T-SHIRT IS RHETORICALLY SITUATED?

Bitzer's model provides an excellent lens to analyze the t-shirt's rhetorical effectiveness and its implications for the abortion controversy. First, there is a clear exigence for this piece of rhetoric. The abortion debate has been in the public eye for decades. Bitzer (1968) tells us that there must be an "imperfection" that calls for an action or at least the spoken word. Throughout the abortion debate, both sides of the issue have consistently identified imperfections that must be addressed. The primary imperfection for the pro-life camp is the fact that abortion remains legal; for the pro-choice camp, the primary imperfection is that abortion rights are constantly being challenged. More immediately, as the 2008 presidential election approaches, this issue is of the utmost importance for many voters because the next president could appoint Supreme Court justices. The women's rights movement generally views the former as a threat to their rights.

While the shirt itself may not have been designed exclusively to address this dilemma, this impending factor may be the catalyst for the shirt as well as the recent mobilization of the women's rights movement. In fact, on April 24, 2004, there was a march for women's lives in Washington, D.C. for which the t-shirt could have been specifically designed to be worn. Suffice it to say, the designers may have intended the t-shirt for the march, but the homepage for the march did not advertise the shirt.

Second, there is a very specific, rhetorical audience that the t-shirt is aimed toward. Bitzer (1968) asserts that this audience must have some ability of attaining agency in the situation and making a change. The t-shirt is aimed at both those who support the availability of abortion and those who oppose it. The specific change to the status quo being sought is to remove all restrictions on abortion rights. While no one person can make any substantive difference in the abortion debate on his or her own, both groups have the power to influence change within the current state of reproductive rights. Through activism and voting, both groups can voice the need for change and collectively make that change happen. Those who support abortion rights, however, are more likely to do so. Therefore, the women who already agree with Soap Box and Planned Parenthood are more valued by the rhetors.

Third, there are many constraints that seem to have been taken into account during the production of the t-shirt. Bitzer (1968) explains that these constraints can be limitations or opportunities. The constraints in this situation are political. For example, a woman wearing the t-shirt clearly identifies herself as pro-choice and as a person who rejects regretting an abortion. This may enrage many pro-life counter advocates and cause extreme emotional reactions. The makers of this t-shirt have clearly taken into account these constraints. On the Soapbox Web site, the explicitly stated purpose of the t-shirt is to get the message across that many women are sorry that they had a need for an abortion, but they do not regret having one (Soapbox, Inc.: Speakers Who Speak Out, 2004). This serves as a limitation for pro-life rhetoric and an opportunity for pro-choice rhetoric. Pro-life advocates rely on the physical and emotional trauma that women experience post abortion as a fundamental part of their evidence for abortion being wrong. If pro-choice advocates can satisfactorily counter these premises, they have an even stronger case. Marketing this t-shirt took place mostly on the Planned Parenthood Web site (http://www.plannedparenthood.org/), which has been a legitimate, trusted source for many women for years. The makers of the t-shirt also took into consideration societal norms for clothing.

The shirt looks like an ordinary piece of clothing: burgundy with yellow lettering in a common font. It does not draw attention to itself through abnormal cut or colors, and t-shirts are commonly worn articles of clothing. Instead it draws attention through the linguistic construct, and perhaps even more because it is so simple. In 2005, Gillian Aldrich and Jennifer Baumgardner made a film, featuring the t-shirt. The Web page which features the film offers the following (Women Make Movies, 2005):

> Underneath the din of politicians posturing about "life" and "choice" and beyond the shouted slogans about murder and rights, there are real stories of real women who have had abortions. Each year in the U.S., 1.3 million abortions occur, but the topic is still so stigmatized it's never discussed in polite company.

The idea is to normalize abortion to the point that it is a procedure concerning a health decision, nothing more. Just like the shirt is ordinary looking, so are the women in the film. They vary in age, race, career path, and lifestyle, but they have a couple of things in common: they all had abortions and none of them are ashamed. As time passes, the advocates of this t-shirt are gaining support and spreading the message further. Only time will tell whether this t-shirt among other efforts can truly erase the shame that society associates with abortion.

The message itself is unique because it makes use of "I" language, forcing the person wearing it to take ownership of their self-ascribed action. The "I" in the t-shirt is given even more power by the film, because the "I" is illustrated and embodied by real women. Most of society, for various reasons, associates a great deal of shame with unwanted pregnancy and even more shame with abortion. The t-shirt suggests that there ought to be no shame associated with this action.

IMPLICATIONS

Through an understanding of Bitzer's rhetorical situation and the way in which this theory applies to the "I had an abortion." shirt, it is possible to draw pragmatic and rhetorical implications from this analysis. Pragmatically, the t-shirt sets a precedent for wearable messages in the future. Rarely is such a simple statement so incredibly powerful as well as controversial. The power lies in the fact that it is displayed in such as simple and acceptable venue. It is not dramatic or grotesque like many pro-life messages are (with pictures of aborted babies and morally condemning messages). While there have been many clothing items with controversial issues addressed on them, not many have been so seemingly popular. At the time I wrote the first draft of this paper, the Planned Parenthood website declared that the t-shirt was sold out, though it was unknown how many t-shirts were available to begin with. However, now there seems to be no place to purchase the t-shirt at all. When there were places to purchase the t-shirt and it was sold out, Planned Parenthood referred the viewer to the Soap Box website to purchase the shirt, though there was no place to purchase the shirt from Soap Box. Instead, Soap Box referred the viewer to the Planned Parenthood website to purchase the t-shirt.

In terms of rhetoric, the t-shirt broadens our society's way of engaging discourse about abortion. While most public discourse about the issue tends to get heated and ugly, this t-shirt shows that subtlety in presentation mixed with pointed commentary may be the most powerful way to express one's views on abortion. While the concept expressed on the t-shirt is bold, the message does not initially draw attention to itself, and it uses simple, common vernacular. Perhaps the pro-life side of the debate may learn from this artifact that pictures of aborted babies merely infuriate, while simple, bold statements encourage discourse. The extreme photos are perhaps effective for the base of the pro-life camp, but are usually placed in arenas where pro-choice advocates will see them. Conversely, the pro-life movement could very well respond with infuriation.

Equally, in terms of rhetoric, the message expressed on the t-shirt may, in fact, be self-defeating. While it seems a step forward for women who have had abortions to be able to disassociate shame from their actions, the message may be negative to some. Many people who support the Roe v. Wade and Doe v. Bolton decisions support them for reasons other than the granted abortion on demand rights. These court decisions also promoted privacy rights to persons which, from the perspective of pro-lifers, are not established by the Constitution alone. However, Greenhouse (2005) explains that Justice Blackmun, arguably the most influential of the justices who voted in favor of Roe v. Wade, did so on the basis that the Constitution does guarantee the right to privacy between a woman and her doctor regarding health decisions. The t-shirt's bold statement, though be it self-imposed, may be interpreted especially by pro-lifers as eliminating any privacy the wearer originally had regarding their abortion, though be it informational and not the intended form of privacy appealed to in the Supreme Court's decision.

Now we must return to our research question: Was the "I had an abortion." t-shirt an appropriate piece of rhetoric to respond to the fight for women's rights? It seems that yes, it was. The exigence of the abortion debate has been in the status quo for a long time. While there are omnipresent arguments and different pieces of rhetoric on both sides of the debate, such as anti-abortion vans parked on street corners or pro-choice bumper stickers, this coming election year has caused the abortion issue to gain prominence. At least some of the audience was ready to receive the message, evidenced by the fact that the t-shirt has been sold out. Additionally, should this t-shirt spur others like it, or should other t-shirts become of interest to rhetorical scholars, it is possible that t-shirts could become an entire genre of rhetorical study. Finally, the way in which the shirt has been manufactured and marketed shows that many constraints were taken into consideration. While the t-shirt itself may not serve as an action to strengthen actual legal abortion rights, it does at least discursively strengthen and support the pro-choice position.

CONCLUSION

With an understanding of some of the background in the women's rights movement, Bitzer's Rhetorical Situation, the application of Bitzer's theory to the T-shirt, and drawn implications from this criticism, it seems clear that the "I had an abortion." t-shirt was an appropriate piece of rhetoric within the rhetorical situation surrounding the fight for women's rights. Only time will tell the degree to which this shirt may influence debate in this arena and the upcoming election. Until that time has passed, the t-shirt remains at the very least a bold statement and vehicle for expression of women who agree with the t-shirt's makers.

REFERENCES

1. Bitzer, L. F. (1968) The rhetorical situation. *Philosophy & Rhetoric* **1**:1 , pp. 1-14.

2. Coffin, S. W. (2004) The abortion distortion. *National Review* **56**:13 , pp. 22-24.

3. Greenhouse, L. (2005) *Becoming Justice Blackmun* Times Books , New York, NY

4. National Organization for Women. (1995-2007). More than a million marched. Now, let's get to work! Retrieved October 29, 2006 from: http://march.now.org/

5. Soapbox, Inc.: Speakers Who Speak Out. (2004). Retrieved September 18, 2004 from: http://www.soapboxinc.com/

6. Women Make Movies. (2005). I had an abortion. Retrieved October 29, 2006 from: http://www.wmm.com/filmcatalog/pages/c693.shtml

Thinking about Multimodality

Pamela Takayoshi & Cynthia Selfe

CONSIDER AS YOU ARE READING:

Takayoshi and Selfe begin with the observation that the field of Rhetoric and Composition must embrace multimodal forms of composition if it is to remain relevant in the coming decades. They see this as both a challenge and a potential windfall: multimodal composition will become essential in an increasingly technological world, composing multimodal texts is engaging to students, multimodal composition meets key pedagogical goals, and working with multimodal texts helps writers focus on basic rhetorical principles of composition. Though this essay is written as a resource to teachers, and it directly addresses concerns about integrating multimodal forms of communication in writing courses, it offers students valuable insight into professionals' arguments about the place of multimodal composition in writing curricula.

1. *What are the reasons that Takayoshi and Selfe feel that teachers of composition must embrace multimodal practices in the classroom? What do they identify as some of the points of resistance to this idea?*

2. *Have you ever analyzed or composed a "multimodal" essay? Do you agree with the authors that this experience was engaging? Why or why not?*

3. *Takayoshi and Selfe are writing to an audience of writing teachers. How might they revise their arguments about the import of multimodal composition for a more general public audience?*

WHY MULTIMODAL COMPOSITION?

It is fast becoming a common place that digital composing environments are challenging writing, writing instruction, and basic understandings of the different components of the rhetorical situation (writers, readers, texts) to change. Such changes are both significant and far reaching—and they promise to be disruptive for many teachers of English composition. For many such teachers at both the secondary and collegiate levels, the texts that students have produced in response to composition assignments have remained essentially the same for the past 150 years. They consist primarily of words on a page, arranged into paragraphs. This flow of words is only occasionally interrupted by titles, headings, diagrams, or footnotes.

These texts resemble—in many ways—other texts that students have been producing elsewhere in the academy (or in other formal educational settings) in response to more conventional assignments like essay tests, lab reports, and research papers. The information within these is conveyed primarily by two modalities—words and visual elements (e.g., layout, font, font size, white space)—and is often distributed in the medium of print. Importantly, however, these texts do not resemble many of the documents we now see in digital environments that use multiple modalities to convey meaning— moving and still images, sounds, music, color, words, and animations—and that are distributed primarily, albeit not exclusively, via digital media (e.g., computers, computer networks, CDs, DVDs). Although composition theories have evolved to acknowledge and study these new **multimodal** texts (texts that exceed the alphabetic and may include still and moving images, animations, color, words, music and sound), the formal assignments that many English composition teachers give to students remain alphabetic and primarily produced via some form of print media. And the papers that students submit in response to these conventional assignments have remained essentially the same: 8.5 by 11 inch pages, double-spaced, 1-inch-margins, 12 or 10 inch fonts. Thus, while time marches on *outside* of U.S. secondary and college classrooms, while people on the Internet are exchanging texts composed of still and moving images, animations, sounds, graphics, words, and colors, inside many of these classrooms, students are producing essays that look much the same as those produced by their parents and grandparents.

Why the astonishing lack of change in both classroom assignments and student-authored writing? It's been many years since Patricia Sullivan (2001) pointed out that, with computer technologies, writers have more control over the page than they've ever enjoyed. Her claims today suggest that authors could expand that notion of control beyond the page, that they could think in increasingly broad ways about texts—not only about pages, words, layout, and design, but also about still and moving visual imagery (photos, photo-editing programs, movie-authoring programs, animation programs) and aural components of communication (music, audio recordings, sounds). Why should composition teachers, researchers, and scholars be interested in taking more advantage of these opportunities?

Agreeing that literacy pedagogy must account for the multiplicity of texts allowed and encouraged by digital technologies, many teacher/scholars and others in fields outside writing studies have articulated compelling arguments for why people concerned with writing and literacy should turn their attention to the cultural shifts in meanings of writing, composing, and texts:

> Cindy Selfe (2004) has elsewhere written: "... if our profession continues to focus solely on teaching only alphabetic composition—either online or in print—we run the risk of making composition studies increasingly irrelevant to students engaging in contemporary practices of communicating" (p. 72).

> "To be responsible teachers,"Anne Wysocki (2003) maintains, "we need to help our students (as well as ourselves) learn how different choices in visual arrangement in all texts (on screen and off) encourage different kinds of meaning making and encourage us to take up (overtly or not) various values" (p. 186).

Arguing that "new communications media are reshaping the way we use language," the New London Group (1996) contends that "effective citizenship and productive work now require that we interact effectively using multiple languages, multiple Englishes, and communication patterns that more frequently cross cultural, community, and national boundaries" (p. 64).

James Gee (2003), writing about video games and literacy, asserts the importance this way: "People need to be literate in new semiotic domains [by which he means any set of practices which relies on multiple modalities to communicate meanings] throughout their lives. If our modern, global, high-tech and science-driven world does anything, it certainly gives rise to new semiotic domains and transforms old ones at an ever faster rate" (p. 19).

In a world where communication between individuals and groups is both increasingly cross-cultural and digital, teachers of composition are beginning to sense the inadequacy of texts—and composition instruction—that employs only one primary semiotic channel (the alphabetic) to convey meaning. In internationally networked digital environments, texts must be able to carry meaning across geo-political, linguistic, and cultural borders, and so texts must take advantage of multiple semiotic channels. At the same time, however, many composition teachers—raised and educated in the age and the landscapes of print—feel hesitant about the task of designing, implementing, and evaluating assignments that call for multimodal texts—texts that incorporate words, images, video, and sound. These teachers understand both the possibilities and the challenges posed by a curriculum that accommodates multimodal literacy practices and students who compose texts from video, sound, still images, and animations, as well as from words. It is a difficult situation, and composition instruction is poised on the precipice of the change.

This collection is designed to provide a beginning point for composition teachers who want to make this theoretical shift in their understanding of literacy and develop effective and sound pedagogical approaches in response. This book provides a basic set of resources for teachers who want to experiment with multimodal composition assignments—particularly those that incorporate video and audio production—in their classrooms.

As we've indicated above, the authors represented in this volume argue for the importance of paying attention to multimodal composing. Our reasoning can be summarized in the following list of claims:

1. **In an increasingly technological world, students need to be experienced and skilled not only in reading (consuming) texts employing multiple modalities, but also in composing in multiple modalities, if they hope to communicate successfully within the digital communication networks that characterize workplaces, schools, civic life, and span traditional cultural, national, and geopolitical borders.**

Whatever profession students hope to enter in the 21st century— game design (Gee, 2003), archeology (Boxer, 2005), science and engineering (Tufte, 1990, 1993, 2001, 2003), the military (D.C. Comics, 2005), the entertainment industry (Daly, 2003), and medicine (Hull, Mikulecky, St. Clair, and Kerka, 2003)—they can expect to read and be asked to help compose multimodal texts of various kinds, texts designed to communicate on multiple semiotic channels, using all available means of creating and conveying meaning. Instructors of composition need to teach students not only how to read and interpret such texts from active and critical perspectives, they also need to teach students how to go beyond the consumption of such texts— learning how to compose them for a variety of purposes and audiences.

In peer-review workshops or studio sessions (where compositions are viewed or heard and responded to), students are simultaneously put in the familiar position of audience member and the perhaps unfamiliar position of critical responder. Many people have argued for a pedagogical commitment to critical and active response, especially to technologies. Grounded in the knowledge that comes from authoring multimodal compositions themselves, students can constructively respond to audio and visual compositions, developing critical perspectives that will serve them well as citizens who respond to any texts.

2. **If composition instruction is to remain relevant, the definition of "composition" and "texts" needs to grow and change to reflect peoples' literacy practices in new digital communication environments.**

Although it may sound like technological determinism to some (i.e., that our professional work and values should take into account changes and developments in communication technologies), the authors of this book believe that it is important to remain in step with the ways in which students, workers, and citizens are communicating, the changing nature of the texts these people produce, and the ways in which such texts are now being used around the world.

The more channels students (and writers generally) have to select from when composing and exchanging meaning, the more resources they have at their disposal for being successful communicators. Aural and video compositions sometimes reveal and articulate meanings students struggle to articulate with words; audio and visual compositions carry different kinds of meanings that words are not good at capturing. It is the thinking, decision making, and creative problem-solving involved in creating meaning through any modality that provide the long-lasting and useful lessons students can carry into multiple communicative situations. In this way, the new composing processes, and problem-solving approaches that students learn when composing with modalities other than words can later serve to illuminate the more familiar composing processes associated with words and vice versa.

Effective technologies often function invisibly in our lives. Think of how visible technologies become when they break down; it's when they are not running invisibly in the background of our work that we become most conscious of them and their roles in our lives. When computers were first introduced to writing instruction, many teachers marveled at how the new writing technologies revealed the processes of writing that over time had become largely invisible to students and teachers of composition.

With the new technologies now mediating composition—the web, digital video, digital photography, digital sound—different aspects of composing meaning, of communicating, have been foregrounded in ways that have encouraged many teachers to take note.

3. **The authoring of compositions that include still images, animations, video, and audio—although intellectually demanding and time consuming—is also *engaging*.** It is certainly true that one of the challenges of teaching multimodal composition is the learning curve involved for both teachers and students new to thinking about different modalities. This learning curve varies, however, depending on whether or not multimodal composing involves computers (many such projects do not, and we provide sample assignments in Chapters 3 and 9 that are nondigital), the size of the project (a 5-minute original video project or an 8-minute montage of still images set to an audio track), the complexity of the compositional elements (still images, audio, or video downloaded from a web source; still images, video or audio recorded by students, downloaded onto a computer, and edited by students; or a combination of these elements), and the time frame (several smaller projects in one semester or one culminating project worked on throughout the semester). In addition, increasing numbers of students coming into composition classes have experience in multimodal composing that teachers can tap.

The collective experiences of the authors represented in this book also indicate that audio and visual compositions are engaging for students. Like the majority of Americans, many students are already active consumers of multimodal compositions by virtue of their involvement in playing and even creating digital music, watching television, shooting home videos, and communicating within web spaces. As a result, students often bring to the classroom a great deal of implicit, perhaps previously unarticulated, knowledge about what is involved in composing multimodal texts, and they commonly respond to multimodal assignments with excitement.

For students, such instruction is often refreshing (because it's different from the many other composing instruction experiences

417

they've had), meaningful (because the production of multimodal texts in class resemble many of the real-life texts students encounter in digital spaces), and relevant (students often sense that multimodal approaches to composing will matter in their lives outside the classroom). Indeed, the teachers writing for this collection have watched students become so engaged in their compositions that they push themselves beyond the boundaries of the assignments and demonstrate learning that goes well beyond teachers' expectations as they begin to understand how multimodal texts look, act, and function. As James Gee (2003) has speculated about the intense engagement some computer gamers experience, "Wouldn't it be great if kids were willing to put in this much time on task on such challenging material in school and enjoy it so much?" Yes, it would be, and this kind of engagement is marvelous to witness.

Additionally, students engage—sometimes very personally and emotionally—with multimodal compositions as readers/ listeners/viewers for their peers' compositions. When was the last time you or anyone in your class was moved to tears by a student composition? Multimodal composition may bring the often neglected third appeal– pathos–back into composition classes (which often emphasize logos and ethos while devaluing pathos as an ethical or intellectual strategy for appealing to an audience). Students authoring multimodal compositions often demonstrate a strong awareness and understanding of how music and images are used as appeals in arguments and, further, how effective these modalities can be in creating and establishing meaning. Maybe classes that draw on such understandings can produce the driveway effect, a state of engagement so strong that radio listeners remain in their cars after they've arrived at their destinations to listen to the end of a program. Wouldn't it be great to re-articulate Gee's question, if students experienced that kind of engagement and connectedness in the peer-response workshops that characterize composition classrooms?

> "There was what they call the 'driveway effect,' Mozetich says. People stayed in their cars in their driveways long after they'd arrived home in order not to miss the ending."
>
> —Hugh Fraser (2001)

4. **Audio and visual composing requires attention to rhetorical principles of communication.** Conventional rhetorical principles such as audience awareness, exigence, organization, correctness, arrangement, and rhetorical appeals are necessary considerations for authors of successful audio and visual compositions. In some ways, many classical rhetorical principles of communication–in which the study of composition is grounded—may be more difficult to ignore in audio and visual compositions. These rhetorical principles of communication–which composition teachers have applied primarily to literate communication–also apply, just as appropriately, to multimodal compositions. Teachers less than willing to make such a leap might be encouraged to remember that the rhetorical principles currently used to teach written composition are, themselves, principles translated from the study of oral communication. To include additional oral and visual elements in composition might be seen as a return to rhetoric's historical concerns.

Further, the authors of this book agree with many contemporary scholars and teachers (Cope & Kalantzis, 2000; Gee, 2003; Hocks, 2003; Kalantzis, Varnava-Skoura, & Cope, 2002; Lankshear & Knobel, 2003; Wysocki, Johnson-Eilola, Selfe, Sirc, 2004) that the study of literacy and composing using a full range of visual and aural modalities can teach students new strategies and approaches which can be productively applied to their efforts at composing more traditional written compositions. Thus, the time spent on multimodal composition, far from being a distraction, will enrich the teaching of composition in general. The following chapters provide suggestions for teachers who want to experiment with multimodal compositions and test this hypothesis for themselves—in both small or more extensive ways.

5. **Teaching multimodality is one pathway to accomplishing long-valued pedagogical goals.** In *Experience and Education,* first published in 1938, John Dewey outlined a vision for "progressive education," as opposed to education in which "the kind of external imposition which is so common in the traditional school limited rather than promoted the intellectual and moral development of the

young" (p. 22). In contrast, Dewey envisioned education as an enterprise involving teachers and students in mutually intellectually satisfying relationships:

> There is, I think, no point in the philosophy of progressive education which is sounder than its emphasis upon the importance of participation of the learner in the formation of the purposes which direct his activities in the learning process, just as there is no defect in traditional education greater than its failure to secure the active cooperation of the pupil in construction of the purposes involved in his studying. (p. 67)

A student's experiences outside the formal educational setting, in other words, should play a significant role in defining the purpose of the educational enterprise. "A student-centered pedagogy asks students to work within their own cultures and discourses by using experimental forms to learn actively from one another and to engage with the world around them," reflects Mary Hocks (2003). Like Dewey, she, too, believes that starting with students' experiences is a pathway into literacy instruction:

> Visual rhetoric–when understood as the dialogical processes of critique and design in contexts that deconstruct the visual world and the technologies surrounding us–goes much further in helping us teach students the rhetorical and compositional abilities that they can use for years to come. (pp. 214 – 215)

In this collection, the authors do not argue that digital technologies (such as audio and visual composing) and an emphasis on multimodal composition are going to be a catalyst in revolutionizing writing instruction. Instead, we argue that *opportunities to think and compose multimodally can help us develop an increasingly complex and accurate understanding of writing, composition instruction, and text.* It is only teachers' learning about new approaches to composing and creating meaning through texts that will catalyze changes in composition classrooms.

Before teachers can begin to explore the possibilities of multimodal composition classes, they must reflect on their pedagogical assumptions about writing instruction generally. What is the goal for composition instruction? With what knowledge/experience/skills/strategies do they want students to leave class? Which meaning-making arenas—academic, civic, private—should they consider for classes? If teachers believe that composition instruction should help students develop and fine-tune the meaning-making strategies and skills they bring with them to classrooms; if they believe it important to teach students to be stronger communicators and meaning makers; if they focus instruction on the many communicative genres, approaches, and forms that people communicate with and through, within and outside the university, then they already share many of the theoretical positions informing multimodal composition instruction. Thinking about multimodality often involves teachers in deep, careful thinking about composition instruction and what matters to communicators in the 21st century.

FIVE KEY QUESTIONS

Thoughtful teachers who are seriously considering whether or not they should expand the range of modalities that characterize their composition assignments do face some realistic concerns— as well as many new possibilities. These concerns are frequently focused on some variation—or combination—of the following five questions. We provide some responses here not to suggest definitive answers, but to offer perspectives that teachers can use as they formulate their own increasingly rich understanding of multimodal composing.

✓ When I teach multimodal composing, am I really teaching composition?

This question rests at the heart of many teachers' concerns about multimodal composing, so it's best to address it directly.

The classical basis of composition instruction involves teaching students how to use *all available rhetorical means of communicating* effectively. For oral cultures, this important phrase—all available means—focused on persuasive oral presentation; for Aristotle and later rhetoricians, *writing* provided an additional means of persuasive communication; for authors after Gutenberg; print text and images were among the resources that could be put to rhetorical use.

At each of these particular points of history, people have expressed sincere concerns about the new technologies of communication and their effects on more conventional forms of literacy. In the *Phaedrus*, for example, Plato has Socrates express the concern that writing weakens the memory and can neither defend itself nor represent truth to others. Indeed, Socrates notes, people are naive if they "believe that words put in writing are something more than what they are" (p. 275). Similarly, in the 16th century, the Church considered the printing press to be a dangerous new communication technology— and one not to be trusted because it supported an increased flow of information to the masses and increasingly vernacular expression (Lea, 1902).

Today, many teachers of English composition worry about the effects of computers and the increasingly vernacular expressions of multimodality that digital environments have encouraged. Multimodality, however, is not limited solely to digital environments; rather, it has been encouraged over a much longer historical period by the advent of various nondigital technologies: engraving, film, photography, recording devices, animation, and television. Indeed, as Sullivan (2001) and Wysocki (2001) have pointed out, print text itself is *already*—at

---

Some English composition teachers might argue:

- Composing with multiple modes takes attention away from writing concerns.

- Multimodal composing is just the newest trendy thing; it won't end up being a sustained concern for writing instruction.

- One semester is barely enough time to teach students to write; how can I possibly also teach them audio and video composition?

- I don't know how to use the technologies to create audio and video compositions; how can I be expected to teach it?

- Audio and visual composing won't teach students important skills like how to construct correct sentences, consistent rhetorical theses; development or organization.

- Literate composition is superior–intellectually, artistically, historically–to audio and video.

some level—multimodal, as any scholar familiar with Laurence Sterne's 18th century novel, *The Life and Opinions of Tristram Shandy*, can attest. Print, in short, carries visual information as well as alphabetic information. This argument can just as easily be extended to other examples of multimodal communication from William Hogarth's 18th century engravings of British life to Ira Glass' 21st century essays on National Public Radio.

So, why *is* multimodal composition such a hot issue *right now*— especially if authors have had a long history of using multiple modalities (words, sounds, visual images) to make meaning, and if media technologies have supported such expressions long before the invention of computers and digital environments? One explanation lies in the convergence of *digital production technologies.* As composition scholars have noted (George, 2002; Wysocki, Johnson-Eilola, Selfe, & Sirc, 2004), the converging inventions of personal computers and the web; photo manipulation, audio-editing, and video editing applications; and digital recorders (still and video cameras and audio recorders) now make it possible for students in many schools to produce a variety of multimodal texts as well as to consume them.

These converging innovations—and the possibilities they help enable—have not gone unnoticed by professional organizations. The National Council of Teachers of English (NCTE), for example, has encouraged teachers to think in new ways about both the *production* and *reception* of multimodal texts. As early as 1996, for instance, the NCTE passed a resolution entitled "On Viewing and Visually Representing As Forms of Literacy," which acknowledged the importance of teaching students how to *produce* and *interpret* multimodal texts in print and nonprint contexts:

> To participate in a global society, we continue to extend our ways of communicating. Viewing and visually representing (defined in the NCTE/IRA Standards for the English Language Arts) are a part of our growing consciousness of how people gather and share information. Teachers and students need to expand their appreciation of the power of print and nonprint texts. Teachers should guide students in constructing meaning through creating and viewing nonprint texts.

And, by 2004, Randy Bomer, then President of the National Council of Teachers of English, had identified multimodal literacy as a key focus of the Council's attention:

> What can NCTE do to advance young people's learning about the multi-modal literacies that are becoming commonplace in a digital environment? How can we create resources that bring the widest possible range of teachers into this conversation? What public policy and public education will prepare the way for the rapid pace of change in these forms of literacy? (personal e-mail communication, Oct. 19, 2004)

By 2005, and the writing of this book, faculty at institutions as diverse as Ohio State, Stanford, the University of Illinois. Michigan State, the University of North Carolina at Chapel Hill, Florida Central University, the University of Massachusetts-Amherst, Georgia Tech, Bowling Green State University, Michigan Tech University, Georgia State University, Kent State University, and the University of Colorado were experimenting with multimodal composition assignments in a variety of courses and curricula.

In each of these cases, organizations, institutions, and individual teachers acknowledge the realities of changing communication practices in which people—in business, science and research contexts, personal correspondence, community work—are increasingly exchanging information in online environments and using a variety of semiotic resources and systems to make meaning as they compose: not only words, but also still and moving images, sound, and color among other modalities. The exigence for changing educational approaches, in other words, has been the recognition that composition instruction must change if it is to remain relevant and fulfill the goal of preparing effective and literate citizens for the 21st century.

✓**Why should English composition faculty teach multimodal composing? Shouldn't we stick to teaching writing and let video production faculty teach video? Art and design faculty teach about visual images? Audio production faculty teach about sound?**

As we have pointed out, a central goal of contemporary education within U.S. colleges or universities is the preparation of literate graduates—intelligent citizens who can both *create meaning in texts* and *interpret meaning from texts* within a dynamic and increasingly technological world. No collegiate unit bears the responsibility for achieving this goal more directly than do composition programs.

Historically, composition teachers have met this responsibility by grounding their instruction firmly in rhetorical theory: making sure that all students are taught how to use all available means to communicate in productive ways and that they are provided a range of strategies and techniques for reaching different audiences, achieving a variety of purposes, and using accepted genres effectively. The belief is that students can take these basic strategies into any disciplinary arena, build on them in more specialized ways, and put them to good use during the remainder of their collegiate programs.

Today, in a world that communicates increasingly via multimodal texts—web sites that include video clips, scientific texts built around visual data displays, radio commentaries, online reference collections—basic composing strategies have changed. Professionals in every discipline—math, physical education, health and medicine, education, science, engineering, the military—are communicating information via multimodal texts: PowerPoint presentations, video tutorials, data displays and animations, educational web sites, and they are expecting students to understand basic strategies for reading and composing such texts. In this context, basic composition instruction, too, must change in order to provide students an introductory, rhetorically focused introduction to a wider range of semiotic resources.

This situation does not mean that English composition teachers, especially in first-year courses, must now assume the responsibility for providing specialized or advanced instruction in animated data displays, video production, art and design, or audio production. Such advanced work, typically, remains solidly grounded in disciplinary contexts in which knowledge of design, production, and exchange is shaped by specialized expectations. The changing nature of communication does suggest, however, that the teaching of rhetorically-based strategies for composition—the responsibility of introducing students to all available means of communicating effectively and productively, including words, images, sound—remains the purview of composition teachers.

✓ When you add a focus on multimodality to a composition class, what do you give up?

One of the main concerns of composition teachers considering the addition of multimodal composition assignments in their courses is that the instruction involved in such projects may take valuable time away from more fundamental instruction on the written word, instruction that many teachers feel is sorely needed among contemporary students.

We, too, would argue that writing is of vital importance to educated citizens. Indeed, it is clear that alphabetic writing—and the ability to express oneself in writing—retains a special and privileged position in the education of contemporary citizens. The fact that alphbetic literacy remains a key responsibility of composition educators is difficult to refute. So, it is not our purpose to suggest that composition teachers should abandon this belief or the practices it suggests. Throughout this book, readers will find that the authors include numerous opportunities for written composition, even within the context of projects that focus on multimodal composition.

The authors of this collection do, however, recognize that other communication modalities—among them, images (moving and still), animations, sound, and color—are in *the process of becoming increasingly important*, especially in a world increasingly global in its reach and increasingly dependent on digital communication networks. We hold that responsible educators will not want to ignore these changes. And we know that in many disciplines, including composition, educators are adapting their instruction to the exigencies of a world characterized by multimodal communication.

We also believe that teaching students to make sound rhetorically-based use of video, still images, animations, and sound can actually help them better understand the particular affordances of written language—that such instruction can, moreover, provide students additional and instructive strategies for communicating in writing. For example, teaching students how to compose and focus a 30-second public service announcement (PSA) for radio—and select the right details for inclusion in this audio composition—*also helps teach* them specific strategies for focusing a written essay more tightly and effectively, choosing those details most likely to convey meaning in effective ways to a particular audience, for a particular purpose. In addition, as students engage in composing a script for the audio PSA, they are motivated to engage in meaningful, rhetorically based writing practice. Further, as students work within the rhetorical constraints of such an audio assignment, they learn more about the particular affordances of sound (the ability to convey accent, emotion, music, ambient sounds that characterize a particular location or event) and the constraints of sound (the difficulty audiences have in going back to review complex or difficult passages, to convey change not marked by sound, to communicate some organizational markers like paragraphs). Importantly, students also gain the chance to compare the affordances and constraints of audio with those of alphabetic writing—and, thus, improve their ability to make *informed* and conscious choices about the most effective modality for communicating in particular rhetorical contexts.

In short, whether instructors teach written composition solely or multimodal composition, their job remains essentially the same: to teach students effective, rhetorically based strategies for taking advantage of *all available* means of communicating effectively and productively, to multiple audiences, for different purposes, and using a range of genres.

✓ **If I teach multimodal composition will the focus on technology detract in significant ways from a focus on rhetorically based composition instruction? Will I have to become a technology expert?**

First, we note that multimodal compositions are not dependent on digital media (although digital tools can often help authors who want to engage in multimodal work).

427

Second, in cases in which multimodal composition does entail the use of digital communication tools and teachers are concerned about the effects of technology on a course, we suggest that teachers start *slowly* and *small*—designing courses that make multimodal composition an option for one *assignment* during a term or creating assignments that make multimodal responses an option *only* for those students who have access to digital equipment (either their own or borrowed from friends) and some experience in using this equipment. These small experiments can help instructors gauge what kinds of assignments are best adapted to multimodal responses; which tasks are most effective in both providing rhetorical instruction and engaging students' interests; how much (and what kind of) assistance students are likely to need as they compose in multiple modalities; and how the teachers' process-based deadlines, conferences, and feedback need to be modified to meet students' needs in such cases.

Third, all teachers have to seek their own level of comfort in digital communication environments. We hope, however, that composition teachers are willing to respect the full range of literacies that students bring to classrooms and build effectively on these literacies, expanding them whenever possible. We also hope that composition teachers serve students as role models in life-long learning— especially with regard to literacy. Teachers who hope to accomplish these goals, we believe, will also accept some level of responsibility for preparing students to communicate in an increasingly global world and one increasingly dependent on networked digital environments.

✓ Does my school have the digital equipment that a composition class might need for multimodal assignments? Can I get access to this equipment?

Each teacher has to answer these questions individually and within the complex and overlapping contexts of their instruction, program, department, institution, and community.

By now, readers should know that multimodal composing tasks are *not dependent* on digital media (even though digital tools can, often, help authors who want to engage in multimodal work).

Later in this collection, we suggest multimodal assignments that students can undertake in nondigital environments (see Chapters 3 and 9). So every teacher, we believe, even those who teach in schools that have very little access to computer technology and digital equipment like video cameras and audio recorders, can still modify some assignments to allow a multimodal option.

Those teachers who do want to work in digital communication environments need to make an early survey of the local instructional resources to which they have access: computer labs within which classes can be scheduled, campus programs or offices that have digital video or audio equipment for loan, informed personnel who might be persuaded to help with instruction; online tutorials and materials available on the web, students who have access to digital equipment or expertise in using such equipment, or community members willing to help. Teachers might also want to read Chapter 13 in this collection: Sustaining Multimodal Composition. In this chapter, Richard Selfe writes about how to form tactical alliances with colleagues, staff, students, other units, and programs in the service of designing not only instructionally effective but also sustainable efforts in multimodal composition.

REFERENCES

Boxer, S. (2005). Digital 'Antigrafitti' Peels Away the Years. Web site review 'Graffiti Archeology,' Arts Section. The *New York Times* web site accessed 22 June at <http://www. nytimes.com/2005/06/21/arts/ design /21boxe.html?ex =1120017600&en=a03801f5a29ef085&ei=5070&emc=e tal>.

Cope, B., & Kalantzis, M. (2000). *Multi-literacies: Literacy learning and the design of social futures*. London: Routledge.

Daly, E. (2003, March/April). Expanding the concept of literacy. *EDUCAUSE*, pp. 33-40.

D.C. Comics. (2005, June). *Harper's Magazine*, p. 22.

Dewey, J. (1938). *Experience and education.* New York: Touchstone.

Fraser, H. (2001, February 27). Hooked on Classics. *Hamilton Spectater.*

Gee, J. P. (2003). *What video games have to teach us about learning and literacy.* New York: Palgrave Macmillan.

George, D. (2002). From analysis to design: Visual communication in the teaching of writing. *College Composition and Communication,* 52(1), 11-39.

Hocks, M. (2003). Teaching and learning visual rhetoric. In P. Takayoshi & B. Huot (Eds.), *Teaching writing with computers:* An introduction, (pp. 202–216). Boston: Houghton Mifflin.

Hull, G., Mikulecky, L., St. Clair, R., & Kerka, S. (2003). Multiple literacies: A compilation for adult educators. A report of the Center on Education and Training for Employment, The Ohio State University, Columbus OH. Retrieved 26 June 2005 from <http://www.cete.org/>.

Kalantzis, M., Varnava-Skoura, G., & Cope, B. (Eds.). (2002). *Learning for the future: New worlds, new literacies, new learning, new people.* Altona, Victoria, Australia: Common Ground Publishers.

Lankshear, C. & Knobel, M. (2003). *New literacies: Changing knowledge and classroom learning.* London: Open University Press.

Lea, H. C. (1902). The eve of the reformation. In A.W. Ward, G.W. Prothero, & Stanley Leathes (Eds.), *The Cambridge Modern History* (Vol. 1, pp. 653-692). New York and London: The Macmillan Company.

New London Group. (1996). A pedagogy of multiliteracies: Designing social futures. *Harvard Educational Review,* 66, 60–92.

On viewing and visually representing as forms of literacy. (1996). A resolution published in the Web site of the National Council of Teachers of English. Retrieved 28 June 2005 at <http://www.ncte.org/about/over/positions/category/literacy/107573.htm>.

Plato. *Phaedrus.* (1956). W. C. Helmbold and W. G. Rabinowitz, Trans. Indianapolis, IN: Liberal Arts Press.

Selfe, C. (2004). Toward new media texts: Taking up the challenges of visual literacy. In A. F. Wysocki, J. Johnson-Eilola, C. Selfe, & G. Sirc (Eds.), *Writing new media: Theory and applications for expanding the teaching of composition* (pp. 67–110). Logan: Utah State Press.

Sullivan, P. (2001). Practicing safe visual rhetoric on the world wide web. *Computers and Composition,* 18(2), 103 122.

Tufte, E. R. (2003). *The cognitive style of PowerPoint.* Cheshire, CT: Graphics Press.

Tufte, E. R. (2001). *The visual display of quantitative information,* (2nd ed.). Cheshire, CT: Graphics Press.

Tufte, E. R. (1990). *Envisioning information.* Cheshire, CT: Graphics Press.

Wysocki, A. F. (2001). Impossibly distinct: On form/content and word/image in two pieces of computer-based interactive multimedia. *Computers and Composition,* 18(3), 207-234.

Wysocki, A. F. (2003) With eyes that think, and compose, and think: On visual rhetoric. In P. Takayoshi & B. Huot (Eds.), *Teaching writing with computers:* An introduction (pp. 182–201). Boston: Houghton Mifflin.

Wysocki, A. F., Johnson-Eilola, J., Selfe, C. L., & Sirc, G. (Eds.). (2004). *Writing new media: Theory and applications for expanding the teaching of composition.* New York: Hampton Press.

FIGHTING FOR OUR LIVES

DEBORAH TANNEN

CONSIDER AS YOU ARE READING:

Because Deborah Tannen is a linguist who has translated some of her research into well received non-fiction for the general public, it is fair to say that she knows how to write for very different audiences. In this piece, which is taken from a larger work, she looks at argument through a feminist lens. Classical rhetoric tends to be constructed using a win-lose model: the sole purpose of an argument is to win. Tannen suggests that argument need not be a battleground dominated by pugilistic metaphors. The purpose of an argument might be deeper understanding, for instance, or compromise, not unlike Rogerian argument (see the article by Richard Young in this volume). In this piece, Tannen suggests that the very language we use to discuss argument is combative and thereby excludes those without agendas of aggression. She believes that words DO matter, that the playground rhyme, "Sticks and stones may break my bones but words will never hurt me," couldn't be further from the truth.

1. Explain what Tannen means by, "When we think we are using languages, language is using us."

2. Reading this piece as a writer, what techniques does Tannen use that you find helpful as a reader and might want to try in your own writing?

3. Did Tannen convince you? Do you look at argument in a different way after this reading? Why or why not?

METAPHORS: WE ARE WHAT WE SPEAK

Culture, in a sense, is an environment of narratives that we hear repeatedly until they seem to make self-evident sense in explaining human behavior. Thinking of human interactions as battles is a metaphorical frame through which we learn to regard the world and the people in it.

All language uses metaphors to express ideas; some metaphoric words and expressions are novel, made up for the occasion, but more are calcified in the language. They are simply the way we think it is natural to express ideas. We don't think of them as metaphors. Someone who says, "Be careful: You aren't a cat; you don't have nine lives," is explicitly comparing you to a cat, because the cat is named in words. But what if someone says, "Don't pussyfoot around; get to the point"? There is no explicit comparison to a cat, but the comparison is there nonetheless, implied in the word "pussyfoot." This expression probably developed as a reference to the movements of a cat cautiously circling a suspicious object. I doubt that individuals using the word "pussyfoot" think consciously of cats. More often than not, we use expressions without thinking about their metaphoric implications. But that doesn't mean those implications are not influencing us.

At a meeting, a general discussion became so animated that a participant who wanted to comment prefaced his remark by saying, "I'd like to leap into the fray." Another participant called out, "Or share your thoughts." Everyone laughed. By suggesting a different phrasing, she called attention to what would probably have otherwise gone unnoticed: "Leap into the fray" characterized the lively discussion as a metaphorical battle.

Americans talk about almost everything as if it were a war. A book about the history of linguistics is called *The Linguistics Wars*. A magazine article about claims that science is not completely objective is titled "The Science Wars." One about breast cancer detection is "The Mammogram War"; about competition among caterers, "Party Wars"—and on and on in a potentially endless list. Politics, of course, is a prime candidate. One of innumerable possible examples, the headline of a story reporting that the Democratic National Convention nominated Bill Clinton to run for a second term declares, "DEMOCRATS SEND CLINTON INTO BATTLE FOR A 2nd TERM." But medicine is as frequent a candidate, as we talk about battling and conquering disease.

Headlines are intentionally devised to attract attention, but we all use military or attack imagery in everyday expressions without thinking about it: "Take a shot at it," "I don't want to be shot down," "He went off half cocked," "That's half the battle." Why does it matter that our public discourse is filled with military metaphors? Aren't they just words? Why not talk about something that matters—like actions?

Because words matter. When we think we are using languages, language is using us. As linguist Dwight Bolinger put it (employing a military metaphor), language is like a loaded gun: It can be fired intentionally, but it can wound or kill just as surely when fired accidentally. The terms in which we talk about something shape the way we think about it—and even what we see.

The power of words to shape perception has been proven by researchers in controlled experiments. Psychologists Elizabeth Loftus and John Palmer, for example, found that the terms in which people are asked to recall something affect what they recall. The researchers showed the subject a film of two cars colliding, then asked how fast the cars were going; one week later, they asked whether there had been any broken glass. Some subjects were asked, "About how fast were the cars going when they bumped into each other?" Others were asked, "About how fast were the cars going when they smashed into each other?" Those who read the question with the verb "smashed" estimated that the cars were going faster. They were also more likely to "remember" having seen broken glass. (There wasn't any.)

This is how language works. It invisibly molds our way of thinking about people, actions, and the world around us. Military metaphors train us to think about—and see—everything in terms of fighting, conflict, and war. This perspective then limits our imaginations when we consider what we can do about situations we would like to understand or change.

Even in science, common metaphors that are taken for granted influence how researchers think about natural phenomena. Evelyn Fox Keller describes a case in which acceptance of a metaphor led scientists to see something that was not there. A mathematical biologist, Keller outlines the fascinating behavior of cellular slime mold. This unique mold can take two completely different forms: It can exist as single-cell organisms, or the separate cells can come together to form multicellular aggregates. The puzzle facing scientists was: What triggers aggregation? In other words, what makes the single cells join together? Scientists focused their investigations by asking what entity issued the order to start aggregating. They first called this bosslike entity a "founder cell," and later a "pacemaker cell," even though no one had seen any evidence of the existence of such a cell. Proceeding nonetheless from the assumption that such a cell must exist, they ignored evidence to the contrary: For example, when the center of the aggregate is removed, other centers form.

Scientists studying slime mold did not examine the interrelationship between the cells and their environment, nor the interrelationship between the functional systems within each cell, because they were busy looking for the pacemaker cell, which, as eventually became evident, did not exist. Instead, under conditions of nutritional deprivation, each individual cell begins to feel the urge to merge with others to form the conglomerate. It is a reaction of the cells to their environment, not to the orders of a boss. Keller recounts this tale to illustrate her insight that we tend to view nature through our understanding of human relations as hierarchical. In her words, "We risk imposing on nature the very stories we like to hear." In other words, the conceptual metaphor of hierarchical governance made scientists "see" something—a pacemaker cell—that wasn't there.

Among the stories many Americans most like to hear are war stories. According to historian Michael Sherry, the American war movie developed during World War II and has been with us ever since. He shows that movies not explicitly about war were also war movies at heart, such as westerns with their good guy—bad guy battles settled with guns. *High Noon*, for example, which became a model for later westerns, was an allegory of the Second World War: The happy ending hinges on the pacifist taking up arms. We can also see this story line in contemporary adventure films: Think of *Star Wars*, with its stirring finale in which Han Solo, having professed no interest in or taste for battle, returns at the last moment to destroy the enemy and save the day. And precisely the same theme is found in a contemporary low-budget independent film, *Sling Blade*, in which a peace-loving retarded man becomes a hero at the end by murdering the man who had been tormenting the family he has come to love.

PUT UP YOUR DUKES

If war provides the metaphors through which we view the world and each other, we come to view others—and ourselves—as warriors in battle. Almost any human encounter can be framed as a fight between two opponents. Looking at it this way brings particular aspects of the event into focus and obscures others.

Framing interactions as fights affects not only the participants but also the viewers. At a performance, the audience, as well as the performers, can be transformed. This effect was noted by a reviewer in the *New York Times*, commenting on a musical event:

> **Showdown at Lincoln Center**. Jazz's ideological war of the last several years led to a pitched battle in August between John Lincoln Collier, the writer, and Wynton Marsalis, the trumpeter, in a debate at Lincoln Center. Mr. Marsalis demolished Mr. Collier, point after point after point, but what made the debate unpleasant was the crowd's blood lust; humiliation, not elucidation, was the desired end.

Military imagery pervades this account: The difference of opinions between Collier and Marsalis was an "ideological war," and the "debate" was a "pitched battle" in which Marsalis "demolished" Collier (not his arguments, but him). What the commentator regrets, however, is that the audience got swept up in the mood instigated by the way the debate was carried out: "the crowd's blood lust" for Collier's defeat.

This is one of the most dangerous aspects of regarding intellectual interchange as a fight. It contributes to an atmosphere of animosity that spreads like a fever. In a society that includes people who express their anger by shooting, the result of demonizing those with whom we disagree can be truly tragic.

But do audiences necessarily harbor within themselves a "blood lust," or is it stirred in them by the performances they are offered? Another arts event was set up as a debate between a playwright and a theater director. In this case, the metaphor through which the debate was viewed was not war but boxing—a sport that is in itself, like a debate, a metaphorical battle that pitches one side against the other in an all-out effort to win. A headline describing the event set the frame: "AND IN THIS CORNER..." followed by the subhead "A Black Playwright and White Critic Duke It Out." The story then reports:

> the face-off between August Wilson, the most successful black playwright in the American theater, and Robert Brustein, longtime drama critic for The New Republic and artistic director of the American Repertory Theatre in Cambridge, Mass. These two heavyweights had been battling in print since last June...

> Entering from opposite sides of the stage, the two men shook hands and came out fighting—or at least sparring.

Wilson, the article explains, had given a speech in which he opposed Black performers taking "white" roles in color-blind casting; Brustein had written a column disagreeing; and both followed up with further responses to each other.

According to the article, "The drama of the Wilson-Brustein confrontation lies in their mutual intransigence."[1] No one would question that audiences crave drama. But is intransigence the most appealing source of drama? I happened to hear this debate broadcast on the radio. The line that triggered the loudest cheers from the audience was the final question put to the two men by the moderator, Anna Deavere Smith: "What did you each learn from the other in this debate?" The loud applause was evidence that the audience did not crave intransigence. They wanted to see another kind of drama: the drama of change—change that comes from genuinely listening to someone with a different

---

1   **intransigence** refusal to compromise.

point of view, not the transitory drama of two intransigent positions in stalemate.

To encourage the staging of more dramas of change and fewer of intransigence, we need new metaphors to supplement and complement the pervasive war and boxing match metaphors through which we take it for granted issues and events are best talked about and viewed.

MUD SPLATTERS

Our fondness for the fight scenario leads us to frame many complex human interactions as a battle between two sides. This then shapes the way we understand what happened and how we regard the participants. One unfortunate result is that fights make a mess in which everyone is muddied. The person attacked is often deemed just as guilty as the attacker.

The injustice of this is clear if you think back to childhood. Many of us still harbor anger as we recall a time (or many times) a sibling or playmate started a fight—but both of us got blamed. Actions occur in a stream, each a response to what came before. Where you punctuate them can change their meaning just as you can change the meaning of a sentence by punctuating it in one place or another.

Like a parent despairing of trying to sort out which child started a fight, people often respond to those involved in a public dispute as if both were equally guilty. When champion figure skater Nancy Kerrigan was struck on the knee shortly before the 1994 Olympics in Norway and the then-husband of another champion skater, Tonya Harding, implicated his wife in planning the attack, the event was characterized as a fight between two skaters that obscured their differing roles. As both skaters headed for the Olympic competition, their potential meeting was described as a "long-anticipated figure-skating shootout." Two years later, the event was referred to not as "the attack on Nancy Kerrigan" but as "the rivalry surrounding Tonya Harding and Nancy Kerrigan."

By a similar process, the Senate Judiciary Committee hearings to consider the nomination of Clarence Thomas for Supreme Court justice at which Anita Hill was called to testify are regularly referred to as the "Hill-Thomas hearings," obscuring the very different roles played by Hill and Thomas. Although testimony by Anita Hill was the occasion for reopening the hearings, they were still the Clarence Thomas confirmation hearings: Their purpose was to evaluate Thomas's candidacy. Framing these hearings as a two-sides dispute between Hill and Thomas allowed the senators to focus their investigation on cross-examining Hill rather than seeking other sorts of evidence, for example by consulting experts on sexual harassment to ascertain whether Hill's account seemed plausible.

SLASH-AND-BURN THINKING

Approaching situations like warriors in battle leads to the assumption that intellectual inquiry, too, is a game of attack, counterattack, and self-defense. In this spirit, critical thinking is synonymous with criticizing. In many classrooms, students are encouraged to read someone's life work, then rip it to shreds. Though criticism is one form of critical thinking—and an essential one—so are integrating ideas from disparate fields and examining the context out of which ideas grew. Opposition does not lead to the whole truth when we ask only "What's wrong with this?" and never "What can we use from this in building a new theory, a new understanding?"

There are many ways that unrelenting criticism is destructive in itself. All of society loses when creative people are discouraged from their pursuits by unfair criticism. (This is particularly likely to happen since, as Kay Redfield Jamison shows in her book *Touched with Fire*, many of those who are unusually creative are also unusually sensitive; their sensitivity often drives their creativity.)

If the criticism is unwarranted, many will say, you are free to argue against it, to defend yourself. But there are problems with this, too. Not only does self-defense take time and draw off energy that would better be spent on new creative work, but any move to defend yourself makes you appear, well, defensive. For example, when an author wrote a letter to the editor protesting a review he considered unfair, the reviewer (who is typically given the last word) turned the very fact that the author defended himself into a weapon with which to attack again. The reviewer's response began, "I haven't much time to waste on the kind of writer who squanders his talent drafting angry letters to reviewers."

The argument culture limits the information we get rather than broadening it in another way. When a certain kind of interaction is the norm, those who feel comfortable with that type of interaction are drawn to participate, and those who do not feel comfortable with it recoil and go elsewhere. If public discourse included a broad range of types, we would be making room for individuals with different temperaments to take part and contribute their perspectives and insights. But when debate, opposition, and fights overwhelmingly predominate, those who enjoy verbal sparring are likely to take part—by calling in to talk shows, writing letters to the editor or articles, becoming journalists—and those who cannot comfortable take part in oppositional discourse, or do not wish to, are likely to opt out.

This winnowing[2] process is easy to see in apprenticeship programs such as acting school, law school, and graduate school. A woman who was identified in her university drama program as showing exceptional promise was encouraged to go to New York to study acting. Full of enthusiasm, she was accepted by a famous acting school where the teaching method entailed the teacher screaming at students, goading and insulting them as a way to bring out the best in them. This worked well with many of the students but not with her. Rather than rising to the occasion when attacked, she cringed, becoming less able to draw on her talent, not more. After a year, she dropped out. It could be that she simply didn't have what it took—but this will never be known, because the adversarial style of teaching did not allow her to show what talent she had.

POLARIZING COMPLEXITY: NATURE OR NURTURE?

Few issues come with two neat, and neatly opposed, sides. Again, I have seen this in the domain of gender. One common polarization is an opposition between two sources of differences

---

2   **winnowing** separating the good from the bad, the valuable from the worthless. The original process involved throwing grain into the air so that the wind would blow away the lighter chaff, or covering, while the heavier and valuable grain fell back to the ground.

between women and men: "culture," or "nurture," on one hand and "biology," or "nature," on the other.

Shortly after the publication of *You Just Don't Understand*, I was asked by a journalist what question I most often encountered about women's and men's conversational styles. I told her, "Whether the differences I describe are biological or cultural." The journalist laughed. Puzzled, I asked why this made her laugh. She explained that she had always been so certain that any significant differences are cultural rather than biological in origin that the question struck her as absurd. So I should not have been surprised when I read, in the article she wrote, that the two questions I am most frequently asked are "Why do women nag?:" and "Why won't men ask for directions?" Her ideological certainty that the question I am most frequently asked was absurd led her to ignore my answer and get a fact wrong in her report of my experience.

Some people are convinced that any significant differences between men and women are entirely or overwhelmingly due to cultural influences—the way we treat girls and boys, and men's dominance of women in society. Other are convinced that any significant differences are entirely or overwhelmingly due to biology: the physical facts of female and male bodies, hormones, and reproductive functions. Many problems are caused by framing the question as a dichotomy: Are behaviors that pattern by sex biological or cultural? This polarization encourages those on one side to demonize those who take the other view, which leads in turn to misrepresenting that work of those who are assigned to the opposing camp. Finally, and most devastatingly, it prevents us from exploring the interaction of biological and cultural factors—factors that must, and ca1 only, be understood together. By posing the question as either/or, we reinforce a false assumption that biological and cultural factors are separable and preclude the investigations that would help us understand their interrelationship. When a problem is posed in a way that polarizes, the solution is often obscured before the search is under way.

AN ETHIC OF AGGRESSION

In an argument culture aggressive tactics are valued for their own sake. For example, a woman called in to a talk show on which I was a guest to say, "When I'm in a place where a man is smoking, and there's a no-smoking sign, instead of saying to him 'You aren't allowed to smoke in here. Put that out,' I say, 'I'm awfully sorry, but I have asthma, so your smoking makes it hard for me to breathe. Would you mind terribly not smoking?' Whenever I say this, the man is extremely polite and solicitous, and he puts his cigarette out, and I say, 'Oh, thank you, thank you!' as if he's done a wonderful thing for me. Why do I do that?'

I think this woman expected me to say that she needs assertiveness training to learn to confront smokers in a more aggressive manner. Instead, I told her that there was nothing wrong with her style of getting the man to stop smoking. She gave him a face-saving way of doing what she asked, one that allowed him to feel chivalrous rather than chastised. This is kind to him, but it is also kind to herself, since it is more likely to lead to the result she desires. If she tried to alter his behavior by reminding him of the rules, he might well rebel: "Who made you the enforcer? Mind your own business!" Indeed, who gives any of us the authority to set others straight when we think they're breaking rules?

Another caller disagreed with me, saying the first caller's style was "self-abasing" and there was no reason for her to use it. But I persisted: There is nothing necessarily destructive about conventional self-affacement. Human relations depend on the agreement to use such verbal conventions. I believe the mistake this caller was making—a mistake many of us make—was to confuse *ritual* self-affacement with the literal kind. All human relations require us to find ways to get what we want from others without seeming to dominate them. Allowing others to feel they are doing what you want for a reason less humiliating to them fulfills this need.

Thinking of yourself as the wronged party who is victimized by a law-breaking boor makes it harder to see the value of this method. But suppose you are the person addicted to smoking who lights up (knowingly or not) in a no-smoking zone. Would you like strangers to yell at you to stop smoking, or would you rather be allowed to save face by being asked politely to stop in order to help them out? Or imagine yourself having broken a rule inadvertently (which is not to imply rules are broken only by mistake; it is only to say that sometimes they are). Would you like some stranger to swoop down on you and begin berating you, or would you rather be asked politely to comply?

As this example shows, conflicts can sometimes be resolved without confrontational tactics, but current conventional wisdom often devalues less confrontational tactics even if they work well, favoring more aggressive strategies even if they get less favorable results. It's as if we value a fight for its own sake, not for its effectiveness in resolving disputes.

This ethic shows up in many contexts. In a review of a contentious book, for example, a reviewer wrote, "Always provocative, sometimes infuriating, this collection reminds us that the purpose of art is not to confirm and coddle but to provoke and confront." This false dichotomy encapsulates that belief that if you are not provoking and confronting, then you are confirming and coddling—as if there weren't myriad other ways to question and learn. What about exploring, exposing, delving, analyzing, understanding, moving, connecting, integrating, illuminating...or any of innumerable verbs that capture other aspects of what art can do?

WHAT OTHER WAY IS THERE?

Philosopher John Dewey said, on his ninetieth birthday, "Democracy begins in conversation." I fear that it gets derailed in polarized debate.

In conversation we form the interpersonal ties that bind individuals together in personal relationships; in public discourse, we form similar ties on a larger scale, binding individuals into a community. In conversation, we exchange the many types of information we need to live our lives as members of a community. In public discourse, we exchange the information that citizens in a democracy need in order to decide how to vote. If public discourse provided entertainment first and foremost—and if entertainment is first and foremost watching fights—then citizens do not get the information they need to make meaningful use of their right to vote.

Of course it is the responsibility of intellectuals to explore potential weaknesses in others' arguments, and of journalists to represent serious opposition when it exists. But when opposition becomes the overwhelming avenue of inquiry—a formula that requires another side to be found or a criticism to be voiced; when the lust for opposition privileges extreme views and obscures complexity; when our eagerness to find weaknesses blinds us to strengths; when the atmosphere of animosity precludes respect and poisons our relations with one another; then the argument culture is doing more damage than good.

I do not believe we should put aside the argument model of public discourse entirely, but we need to rethink whether this is the only way, or always the best way, to carry out our affairs. A step toward broadening our repertoires would be to pioneer reform by experimenting with metaphors other than sports and war, and with formats other than debate for framing the exchange of ideas. The change might be as simple as introducing a plural form. Instead of asking "What's the other side?" we might ask instead, "What are the other sides?" Instead of insisting on hearing "both sides," we might insist on hearing "all sides."

Another option is to expand our notion of "debate" to include more dialogue. This does not mean there can be no negativity, criticism, or disagreement. It simply means we can be more creative in our ways of managing all of these, which are inevitable and useful. In dialogue, each statement that one person makes is qualified by a statement made by someone else, until the series of statements and qualifications moves everyone closer to a fuller truth. Dialogue does not preclude negativity. Even saying "I agree" makes sense only against the background assumption that you might disagree. In dialogue, there is opposition, yes, but no head-on collision. Smashing heads does not open minds.

There are times when we need to disagree, criticize, oppose, and attack—to hold debates and view issues as polarized battles. Even cooperation, after all, is not the absence of conflict but a means of managing conflict. My goal is not a make-nice false veneer of agreement or a dangerous ignoring of true opposition.

I'm questioning the automatic use of adversarial formats—the assumption that it's always best to address problems and issues by fighting over them. I'm hoping for a broader repertoire of ways to talk to each other and address issues vital to us.

ROGERIAN ARGUMENT AND THE CONTEXT OF SITUATION: TAKING A CLOSER LOOK

RICHARD E. YOUNG

CONSIDER AS YOU ARE READING:

In the 1950's, psychologist Carl Rogers published a work which would become the basis of a new approach to rhetoric, and foundational to modern rhetorical theory—although that probably wasn't the application he had in mind. Rogers proposed a new approach to conflict resolution after seeing clients unable to resolve differences because they were incapable of talking and listening to one another. In this article, Young applies Roger's theories to rhetoric; the result is an approach to argument very different from Aristotelian rhetoric, which, he claims, is carried out among people who, while they might not agree on a particular issue, share common goals and values. Rogerian argument may better address conflicts between more disparate individuals or groups. As advanced writers who are working to hone our awareness of audience, this reading challenges us to think of whether our audience would even be willing to enter a conversation with us and, if not, how we might construct an argument that avoids confrontation and enhances mutual understanding.

1. *Apply Young's theories to the rhetorical strategies used in this essay. How might the structure of Young's argument be considered Rogerian?*

2. *Think of the last argument you had with someone close to you. How might the principles of Rogerian rhetoric have changed the dynamics of that argument?*

3. *Young mentions six purposes, other than winning, for argument. Name as many of those purposes as you can. If you can think of other reasons that Young doesn't mention, include them as well.*

In his "Argument as Emergence, Rhetoric as Love," Jim Corder remarks that "the arguments most significant to us are just where threat occurs and continues, just where emotions and differences do not get calmly talked away," where "contention generates that flushed, feverish, quaky, shaky, scared, hurt, shocked, disappointed, alarmed, outraged, even terrified condition" that characterizes value-laden dispute (1985, p. 25). I quote Professor Corder's description because I want to make clear at the start what kind of experiences are at issue in the discussion that follows and, by implication, what kinds are not. Whatever other features instances of such conflicts may have, all are dyadic (that is, they involve two people or two groups of people), and, in all, strongly held values are at issue, values that are perceived by the participants as essential to their well-being, so much so that often the primary goal of the participants is the defense of these values.

Twenty years ago, conflicts of this kind prompted Alton Becker, Kenneth Pike, and me to develop a suggestion by Carl Rogers in his "Communication: Its Blocking and Its Facilitation" (1951)[1] and introduce it into modern rhetorical theory and pedagogy. Since then, what we called *Rogerian argument* has prompted a surprisingly wide range of reactions: it has been seen as a promising basis for a modern rhetoric (Bator, 1980)—a much more expansive function than the one we had proposed; as aiding real-world problem solving (Teich, 1987); as impairing our ability to deal effectively with the socioeconomic dimensions of conflict (Pounds, 1987); as an extension of, or at least consistent with, Aristotelian rhetoric (Lunsford,) 1979); as fundamentally inconsistent with Aristotelian rhetoric (Mader, 1980); as inappropriate for written communication (Ede, 1984); as appropriate for written communication and its teaching (Hairston, 1982); as not really a kind of argument at all (Mader, 1980); and as a misguided and potentially harmful innovation (Ede, 1984). The diversity and incompatibility of the reactions alone suggest the need to take a closer look, not only at how we presented Rogerian argument at the time, but at the possibilities that we saw as well, since it would be a mistake to reject the idea because our effort to realize it may have been flawed. In taking a closer look here, I hope I can persuade others to do the same. Until we have looked amore closely, we ought, I think, to defer making claims about what Rogerian argument can and cannot do, or for that matter what it could do if it were modified in the light of what we know now. A more tentative, inquiring stance seems most appropriate to the situation we find ourselves in today.

"Rogerian argument," we said, "rests on the assumption that out of a need to preserve the stability of his image [i.e., his system of beliefs], a person will refuse to consider alternatives that he feels are threatening, hence that changing a person's image depends on eliminating this sense of threat" (Young, Becker, & Pike, 1970, p. 274), thus making it possible to consider another position. Hence, the efforts of this kind of argument are strongly directed toward reducing the opponent's feeling of threat: e.g., by avoiding highly evaluative language, by demonstrating that the opponent's position has been understood in a way that is sensitive to its personal meaning and implications, by indicating that the opponent's position is seen as reasonable, by acting out of an assumption of similarity and identifying shared features that could become possible bases for further interaction. (Such efforts are functions or subgoals of the discourse, not parts of its structure.) *Winning* the argument, if that word can be appropriately used in this context, means making it possible for the opponent to consider alternatives, or establishing and maintaining communication, or creating a willingness to enter into a common effort to solve a common problem—in general expanding the possibilities for cooperation beyond those that had hitherto been available in the dispute.

Even though classical argument does effectively address conflicts in the courts and other public forums, relatively little has been said by classical rhetoricians about conflicts of the sort I have described, despite their being so intrusive and often so important in our lives. The whole orientation of the great classical tradition has been toward the conduct of public affairs; it is a rhetoric that presupposes communities with widely shared beliefs and conflicts in which opponents are willing and able to communicate. It has not spoken directly to dyadic situations where a sense of threat makes it difficult and at times impossible for one or both of the participants to even consider adopting another position; where fundamental beliefs are often not shared; where there is a greater sense of diversity than of community, indeed, where in some cases say an Amish pacifist and a Pentagon hawk, the differences are so extreme that one questions whether mutual understanding is possible; where confrontation often veers toward coercion and violence. This is not to say that classical argument is either irrelevant or unimportant in modern society or that Rogerian argument can replace it. They were invented for quite different kinds of situations, and many of their distinctive features derive from the differences in these situations.

In our thinking about value-laden situations, however, Becker, Pike, and I were preoccupied with how they differed from situations in which traditional argument can be effective.[2] We did not pay enough attention to the considerable variation in actual dyadic situations; and we did not see that both the use and the usefulness of Rogerian argument seem to vary as the situation varies. The peculiarities of the particular situation affect, or should affect, the choices one makes in addressing it; not understanding this leads to inappropriate and ineffective choices.

II

If we examine some of the suggestions for using Rogerian argument, we see several kinds of situations that can be differentiated on the basis of how willing and able the parties are to address their differences. For example, Nathaniel Teich (1987) argues for the use of Rogerian argument in situations that are quire different from the highly conflicted one I have been describing:

> As a prerequisite for achieving Rogers' goal of "real communication," however, the parties must share a common interest in resolving a problem or dispute by a mutually satisfactory solution. (p. 53)

And further,

> All aspects of Rogerian communication—intent, purpose, and product—are governed by the presupposition that the parties are willing to compromise. (p. 55)

450

In the writing class this assumption affects the student's choice of topic:

> If you cannot adopt Rogers' Rule [that the other's position must be restated satisfactorily before you may state your own] or risk changing your views... [Teich cautions his students], then you should reconsider your choice of topic. Consequently, students tend to avoid arguing about such potentially loaded topics as abortion, gun control, nuclear power, world disarmament, religious preferences, and political partisanship, because these problems are usually bound up in categorical issues of belief and value. (pp. 57-58)

Here Rogerian argument is used as a way of encouraging a willingness to communicate and cooperate that already exists. Becker, Pike, and I were interested in quite a different kind of situation, the very sort of situation that Teich excludes, that is characterized by defensiveness and antagonism on the part of one or both the parties, where communication is impaired and as yet no common desire to cooperate exists. In noting this difference, I do not mean to imply that Teich is wrong; Rogerian methods are quite likely to be useful in the situation he describes. And it is easier to address the situation Teich describes, certainly easier in the classroom, than the situation we were interested in.

A very different sort of situation is apparent in Maxine Hairston's proposal that Rogerian argument can be helpful in creating a classroom atmosphere that is low-risk, nonthreatening, and hence encouraging to the novice writer. Hairston remarks that *few students write well out of fear.* They do not do their best work or develop as writers as long as they feel they are in a high risk situation, and all too often they perceive the writing classroom as an extremely high risk situation" (1982, p. 51, emphasis in original). The relation between the teacher and the students is obviously dyadic and, no doubt from many students' point of view, often laden with strong emotions. Notice, though, that the situation is not a conflict; the situation is much more like that between therapist and patient. Like the therapist with a patient, the teacher does not feel threatened or antagonistic and has an understanding of the situation and a control over it that the student lacks.

In contrast to Hairston's proposal, Jim Corder's "Argument as Emergence" does address powerful dyadic conflicts. He states that in this sort of situation, "the arguer must, with no assurance, go out, inviting the other to enter a world that the arguer tries to make commodious, inviting the other to emerge as well, but with no assurance of kind or even thoughtful response." "How," he asks, "does this happen? Better, how can it happen?" His answer is that "it can happen if we learn to love before we disagree." "Usually," he says, "it's the other way around: if we learn to love, it is only after silence or conflict or both" (1985, p. 26). If I understand what Corder is saying, one of the opponents is not wholly captured by the conflict, but has, rather, in some sense transcended it, or at least has enough control over his own feelings that he can reach out to the other and try to understand. Although a participant in a dispute in which the stakes are perceived as being very high, he, also, is different from the shocked, disappointed, alarmed, outraged combatant Corder described earlier.

III

Consider now still another form that value-laden dyadic conflict can take, one in which *both* of the arguers are zealous in the preservation of their own values and unbending in the pursuit of their own goals. "We have not," Corder says with considerable understatement, "fully considered what happens in argument when the arguers are steadfast" (1985, p. 23). That is probably reason enough to take a closer look, even though at first its extremeness makes the situation appear to be an unpromising subject for inquiry. But it is at least that the situation only appears to be unpromising because we approach it with fixed assumptions.

If our goal is the resolution of conflict, the great difficulty when both arguers are steadfast is that neither is very interested in reducing the other's sense of threat or in controlling antagonistic feelings. Self-control and conciliation are not what we desire when we find ourselves in such situations, though they appear to be what is necessary if the conflict is to be resolved. We may well know what we could do to quiet the conflict and transform it into something more constructive: Rogerian argument certainly offers a way of preceding that is both ethically and pragmatically attractive. But we may not be willing or, at that time, even able to make the effort necessary to understand the other's position in any but the most superficial sense— just enough understanding of the position, that is, to give us something to attack. Carl Rogers describes the usual outcome of such arguments when he remarks that "the stronger our feelings the more likely it is that there will be no mutual element in the communication. There will be just two ideas, two feelings, two judgments, missing each other in psychological space" (1951, p. 331). The threats and commands that erupt in such conflicts— Henry Johnstone calls them "degenerate" forms of argument (1978, p. 108)—tend to replace more conventional forms. One peculiar, and disheartening, feature of Rogerian argument, then, is that when we need it most, we are least inclined to use it. In the situation in which both parties are steadfast, it can be a method for reaching a goal that, at the appropriate moment, we as often as not have no desire to reach. In fact, in this particular situation, we often seek contrary goals: i.e., not to conciliate but to attack, not to understand another but to protect ourselves, not to cooperate but to dominate—or, in Corder's more general terms, not to love but to oppose.

In this kind of situation, as Corder has pointed out (1985, p. 21), the strategy Becker, Pike and I outlined seems inappropriate, because it presupposes that at least one of the antagonists has the courage and the desire to use it. We did not attend to that inconsistency, nor have others since then, and the result has been proposals for instructional methods which in *that particular kind of situation* are unlikely to be effective. The methods may well be effective in other situations, such as those described earlier by Teich (1987) and Hairston (1982), but not when both arguers are steadfast in their own positions.

One important question to ask, before we consider any further the situation in which both arguers are steadfast, is whether we, as students of rhetoric, *should* consider it. It certainly occurs frequently, we may feel that it is important in our lives, and as Corder says, it is rhetorical? Of necessity, any discipline draws a line around itself, deciding what sorts of issues are appropriate for it to examine and what sorts are beyond its interest. So we can reasonably ask whether what happens when opponents are steadfast is an issue that falls within the domain of rhetoric.

In his "Functional Communication: A Situational Perspective," Lloyd Bitzer argues that certain problems though real are beyond our control (e.g., a friend dying of an untreatable disease); other problems do not require communication with someone else in order to be solved (e.g., finding a way of reconciling a contradiction in one's own thinking). Some problems, however, require or invite communication addressed to audiences whose actions can bring about the desired change; such problems, Bitzer says, are rhetorical (1980, pp. 26-27). Unless such a problem is present, Bitzer argues, a rhetorical situation never develops, and, hence, a rhetorical act never occurs. Something else may happen, but not a rhetorical something.

Value-laden dyadic conflict appears to fall within the category of rhetorical problems, as Bitzer conceives of them, i.e., problems that arise out of a human difference, the solution to which requires a change in belief or behavior on the part of at least one of the parties in the dispute. But suppose the parties are steadfast in their beliefs. Is the problem still rhetorical? Bitzer observes that "the person who speaks in order to modify a nonrhetorical exigence—one which discourse cannot possibly change—is engaged in a futile venture" (1980, p. 27). With steadfast opponents, communication would certainly appear to be futile. But does it follow that the problem is nonrhetorical? Does at least one of the two antagonists initially have to be willing to change before change is possible and hence before a rhetorical situation can develop? If so, the situations of the sort that Teich and Hairston discuss and the situation with steadfast opponents are not variant forms of the same concept but are, instead, different in nature; and the latter would appear to be immune to argument, Rogerian or otherwise.

There are, however, reasons to pause before saying that the apparently intractable situation we are examining lies outside the domain of rhetoric. Rogers himself offers one reason: the case in which a third party, using Rogerian methods, mediates the conflict. As Rogers, says, the movement toward understanding "can...be initiated by a neutral third person, providing he can gain a minimum of cooperation from one of the parties" (1951, p. 336). In discussing the role of facilitator in groups where conflict runs high, James Zappen observes that "the movement from often bitter expression of personal feelings toward collective consideration of issues, collective decision making, and constructive action is documented in Rogers' own and others' experiences, not only with oppressed minorities but with other groups as well, including even such bitter opponents as Catholics and Protestants in Northern Ireland" (1980, p. 104).

Or consider disputes in which the antagonists not only refuse to communicate, but literally or figuratively walk away from the confrontation. Is walking away the end of the dispute? Corder shrewdly observes that "we must pile time into argumentative discourse...in our most grievous and disturbing conflicts, we need time to accept, to understand, to love the other. At crisis points in adversarial relationships, we do not, however, have time; we are already in opposition and confrontation" (1985, p. 31). But is walking away, at least sometimes, a very undemanding kind of rhetorical act, and, precisely because it is undemanding, a valuable one? It requires no great courage or generosity, and it can pile time into argument. In doing so, it perhaps holds out some hope that change may eventually become possible.

Even though inconsistent with the common view of an argument as a polished performance (a finished piece of writing or a carefully constructed speech), is it unreasonable to think of a single argument as a groping, intermittent effort—whether written or spoken or both—made up of several utterances and extending over what might turn out to be a substantial span of time? Though we can no doubt find instances in our own experience, our art ignores the possibility of argument as a continuing though discontinuous dialogue in which the emphasis is on the intent and effects of the statements rather than on features of the statement itself (its truth or falsity, its stylistic distinction). If in actuality some arguments are of this unconventional sort, then simply holding open the possibility of change becomes an important rhetorical goal.

The effectiveness of Rogerian argument seems to depend much more heavily than Becker, Pike, and I had assumed not only on timeliness, but on duration of time. It has been only in the last generation that the ancient notion of *kairos* and such related notions as situational context and rhetorical situation have begun to play a significant role once again in rhetorical theory and pedagogy (Kinneavy, 1986). In the contexts we have been exploring, knowing when not to try to communicate would appear to be as important as knowing when to try; however, time and timeliness have seldom been subjects for sustained discussion in composition texts.

Or, again, consider disputes that erupt into actual violence of some sort: getting into a shouting match, for example, and then suddenly realizing what one is doing and apologizing; the fist fight you had with the neighbor kid and the subsequent friendship; the reconciliation between husband and wife after a bitter fight; Corder's example of the memorial service for American and German troops at the Remagen Bridge in 1985 (1985, p. 27); the moving ending to the recent film "Children of a Lesser God," where the pattern I am describing is in fact the plot of the film. All dyadic, all freighted with powerful values, all full of language. We can, of course, also come up with plenty of examples of violence that do not evolve into their opposites. But that does not negate the point I am trying to make. Somehow the dynamics of conflict can at times alter the willingness of the participants to come to new understanding and reach some sort of accommodation.

Henry Johnstone has remarked that "in general the risk a person takes by listening to an argument is that he may have to change himself. It is the self, not any specific belief or mode of conduct, that the arguer's respondent wishes to maintain. But his interest in maintaining it cannot be absolute, for if it were he would be presenting a closed mind to the argument." (1978, pp. 109-110). There is always a tension in the participants in an argument between the desire to maintain themselves and their worlds and the necessity of exposing themselves to the risk of change implicit in the argument. However, suppose both are steadfast out of conviction and fear change. Out of a desire to preserve the stability of their images, they resist opening themselves to alternatives that they feel threaten fundamental beliefs. When opponents are steadfast and fear change, neither permits himself any choice or, more accurately, has any choice, at least at the moment, except to persist in his beliefs. And, as Edward Corbett points out, "where the choices are arbitrarily pared down or eliminated, rhetoric begins to disappear" (1969, p. 293).

Change as a psychological goal is clearly central to any conception of rhetoric. But in order to be considered rhetorical, must the change always entail persuasion, in the sense of a significant alteration or abandonment of the audience's position as the result of argument? We can, I think, accept Johnstone's observation that the absolutely closed mind is beyond rhetoric (assuming that there is such a thing as an absolutely closed mind) and still acknowledge the possibility of modest though nonetheless important changes in the situation where the opponents hold steadfastly to their beliefs. For example, we might consider extending our notion of rhetorical change to include dialogical exchanges in which the opposing positions retain their integrity while being strengthened and deepened by the opposition. Since our beliefs are fully revealed and understood only in contrast to other beliefs, a possible outcome of a dispute in which the arguers are steadfast can be greater understanding of one's own position and perhaps, at least gradually, the opponent's as well. Dialogical exchanges of the sort I have in mind might result in altered conceptions of the world in which both disputants have a place, though not the same place; or perhaps a heightened awareness of each other as *Thous*, to borrow Buber's term; or an emerging mutual respect and, as a consequence, a willingness to continue the dialogue. Such growth of understanding need not mean abandoning beliefs regarded as important, though it may well qualify them and introduce new complexities; and it might soften harsh attitudes toward those who believe something else. Resisting change and a deepening of commitment may well be desirable, since to change a position is not necessarily to make it more adequate (Pike, 1961, pp. 272-273). Unfortunately, beyond discussions of fallacious reasoning, the rhetorical tradition has had little to say about resisting change and what the effort of resisting change in order to preserve one's own system of beliefs does to thinking, argument, and conduct.[3]

It appears, then, that the situation in which the opponents are steadfast constitutes some sort of boundary condition. In talking about it, are we still talking about rhetoric? I have tried to suggest reasons for thinking that we are, though traditional conceptions of rhetoric, certainly those that have been dominant in English departments, would have to change to accommodate them. The intractable situation I have been exploring is a very general description of innumerable concrete situations that, in the past, would have been considered un-rhetorical or, perhaps more accurately, pre-rhetorical, because, traditionally, a rhetorical situation presupposes a sense of community and shared values and a tacit agreement to enter into an exchange that may significantly alter beliefs. But conflicts in which the opponents are steadfast are so common and unavoidable, so characteristic of a diverse and rapidly changing society, and world, that we must learn to address them. Aristotle observed that it is easy to praise Athenians to Athenians. But it is very hard to praise Greeks to Turks, or Israelis to Arabs, or Irish Catholics to Irish Protestants, or pro-choice advocates to pro-life advocates...

If serious investigation of Rogerian argument and its situations can open up new questions for rhetorical study, it can also reintroduce, in a particularly insistent way, questions that have been neglected in the rhetoric that has dominated English departments for the last century. As we have seen, it raises questions about the scope of rhetoric, rhetorical situations, and appropriate action. It also encourages us to think again about *logos, ethos, and pathos* as persuasive appeals. For generations, the rhetoric taught in the schools, particularly in composition classes, has tended to valorize the logical appeal, treating issues of personal authority and the emotions as, relatively speaking, peripheral. What were originally conceived of as mutually reinforcing appeals have been sharply separated in this tradition, with *ethos* and *pathos* being for the most part relegated to the margin of our attention.[4] The effort by Becker, Pike, and me, and by others since then, to extend Rogers' suggestions into rhetorical theory and practice can be seen, in part at least, as an effort to breathe new life into the ancient concepts of *ethos* and *pathos* and to position them within an enriched conception of rhetoric, which, like its ancient counterpart, addresses the question of how one invents arguments under the constraints of actual situations.

Rogerian argument, in so far as it is an effort to respond to intense dyadic conflict, seems to offer a means for reasserting the dialogue character of rhetorical argument in its long slide toward dialectics. "Take a dialogue," M.M. Bahktin remarks, "and remove the voices (the partitioning of voices), remove the intonations (emotional and individualizing ones), carve out abstract concepts and judgments from living words and responses, cram everything into one abstract consciousness—and that's how you get dialectics" (1986, p. 147). The artificial and highly questionable separation of the study of writing from the study of speaking in academic institutions has encouraged a view of written as *logos*; as presented in our writing texts, rhetorical argument has moved very close, too close I think, to logic. Rogerian argument might well be one means of reintroducing a notion of rhetorical argument as addressed by someone in particular to particular individuals at particular times in particular places and for particular purposes.

NOTES

1 "Can we," Rogers asked, "take this small scale answer [to conflict and breakdowns in communication], investigate it further, refine it, develop it and apply it to the tragic and well-nigh fatal failures of communication which threaten the very existence of our modern world" (1951, p. 337).

For example, we noted three kinds of situations that classical rhetoric addresses effectively: (1) low-value dyadic situations (i.e., two-party conflicts in which differences are not perceived as fundamental or threatening and hence are resolvable by traditional means, which presuppose that the possibility of communication and change already exists), (2) love-value triadic situations (i.e., conflicts in which the argument is directed to a third party who is not a participant in the conflict but who decides the outcome of the argument, e.g., two lawyers arguing a routine case before a judge); and (3) high-value triadic situations (e.g., two lawyers in a court case that involves issues perceived as fundamental to the welfare of the participants). A fourth kind of situation contrasts with these, i.e., high-value dyadic situations. This very general set of situations, contrasted in a two-by-two matrix, was a convenient way of explaining the differences in distribution of classical and Rogerian argument: in retrospect, however, it seems a bit too tidy.

2. James Baumlin (1987) discusses some of the rhetoric implications of steadfastness in "Persuasion, Rogerian Rhetoric, and Imaginative Play."

Making a similar point about the emphasis on critical thought, Alice Brand (1987) has sought to raise the issue of emotion as a counterpart to cognitive activity in the process of writing, linking it to the writer's motivation; it is interesting to see this as an effort to expand the meaning of *pathos* to include a concern with the psychology of the writer as well as the reader. Recent work on *ethos*, particularly that of Jim Corder (1978), Michael Halloran (1982), and Nan Johnson (1984), demonstrates the value of scholarly inquiry into the notion of *ethos* and the complexity of the task. For a discussion of this work, see my article entitled, "Recent Developments in Rhetorical Invention" (Young, 1987), especially pages 18-20.

REFERENCES

Bakhtin, M.M. (1986). *Speech genres and other late essays.* (V. McGee, Trans.; C. Emerson & M. Holquist, Eds.). Austin, TX: University of Texas press.

Bator, P. (1980). Aristotelian and Rogerian rhetoric. *College Composition and Communication,* 31, 427-432.

Baumlin, J.S. (1987). Persuasion, Rogerian rhetoric, and imaginative play. *Rhetoric Society Quarterly,* 17, 33-43.

Bitzer, L. (1980). Functional communication: A situational perspective. In E. White (Ed.), *Rhetoric in transition: Studies in the nature and uses of rhetoric* (pp. 21-38). University Park, PA. Pennsylvania State University Press.

Brand, A. (1987). The why of cognition: Emotion and the writing process: *College Composition and Communication,* 38, 436-443.

Corbett, E. (1969). The rhetoric of the open hand and the rhetoric of the closed fist. *College Composition and Communication,* 20, 288-296.

Corder, J.W. (1978). Varieties of ethical argument, with some account of the significance of *ethos* in the teaching of composition. *Freshman English News,* 6, 1-23.

Corder, J.W. (1985). Argument as emergence, rhetoric as love. *Rhetoric Review,* 4, 16-32.

Ede, L. (1984). Is Rogerian rhetoric really Rogerian? *Rhetoric Review,* 3, 40-48.

Hairston, M. (1976). Carl Rogers' alternative to traditional rhetoric. *College Composition and Communication,* 27, 373-377.

Hairston, M. (1982). Using Carl Rogers' communication theories in the composition classroom. *Rhetoric Review,* 1, 50-55.

Halloran, M. (1982). Aristotle's concept of ethos, or if not his somebody else's. *Rhetoric Review,* 1, 58-63.

Johnson, N. (1984). Ethos and the aims of rhetoric. In R. Connors, L. Ede, & A. Lunsford (Eds.), *Essays on classical rhetoric and modern discourse* (pp. 98-114). Carbondale, IL: Southern Illinois University Press.

Johnstone, H. (1978*). Validity and rhetoric in philosophical argument: An outlook in transition.* University Park, PA: Dialogue Press.

Kinneavy, J. (1986). Kairos: A neglected concept in classical rhetoric. In J. Moss (Ed.), *Rhetoric and praxis: The contribution of classical rhetoric to practical reasoning* (pp. 79-105). Washington, DC: Catholic University of America Press.

Lunsford, A. (1979). Aristotelian vs. Rogerian argument: A reassessment. *College Composition and Communication, 30,* 146-151.

Mader, D. (1980). What are they doing to Carl Rogers? ETC.: *A Review of General Semantics, 37,* 314-320.

Pike, K.L. (1961). Stimulating and resisting change. *Practical Anthropology, 8,* 267-274.

Pounds, W. (1987). The context of no context: A Burkean critique of Rogerian argument. *Rhetoric Society Quarterly,* 17, 45-59.

Rogers, C. R. (1951). Communication: Its blocking and its facilitation. In C.R. Rogers, *On becoming a person* (pp. 329-337). Boston, MA: Houghton Mifflin.

Teich, N. (1987). Rogerian problem-solving and the rhetoric of argumentation. *Journal of Advanced Composition, 7,* 52-61.

Young, R. (1987). Recent development in rhetorical invention. In G. Tate (Ed.), *Teaching composition: Twelve bibliographic essays* (pp. 1-38). Ft. Worth, TX: Texas Christian University Press.

Young, R.E., Becker, A.L., & Pike, K.L. (1970). *Rhetoric: Discovery and change.* New York: Harcourt, Brace.

Zappen, J.P. (1980). Carl R. Rogers and political rhetoric. *PRE/ TEXT,* 1, 95-113.

CITATIONS

Baildon, Mark and James S. Damico. "How Do We Know?: Students Examine Issues of Credibility With a Complicated Multimodal Web-Based Text." *Curriculum Inquiry* Vol. 39, No. 2 (Mar., 2009), pp. 265-285.

Bitzer, Lloyd. "The Rhetorical Situation." *Philosophy and Rhetoric* 1.1 (1968): 1-14. Print.

Blair, J. Anthony. "The Possibility and Actuality of Visual Arguments." *Argumentation and Advocacy* 33.1 (1996): 23-39. Print.

Christoph, Julie Nelson. "Reconceiving Ethos in Relation to the Personal: Strategies of Placement in Pioneer Women's Writing." *College English* Vol. 64, No. 6 (Jul., 2002), pp. 660-679.

Ede, Lisa, and Andrea Lunsford. "Among the Audience: On Audience in an Age of New Literacies." *Engaging Audience* Ed. Weiser, Fehler, and Gonzalez, NCTE 2009. 42- 69.

Ede, Lisa, and Andrea Lunsford. "Audience Addressed/ Audience Invoked: The Role of Audience in Composition Theory and Pedagogy." *CCC* 35.2 (1984): 155-71. Print.

Foss, Sonja K. and Cindy L. Griffin. "Beyond Persuasion: A Proposal for an Invitational Rhetoric" *Communication Monographs*, volume 62, March 1995

Griffin, Frank. "Merck's Open Letters and the Teaching of Ethos." *Business Communication Quarterly* 72.1 (2009): 61-72. ERIC. EBSCO. Web. 30 Mar. 2011.

Hayes, J.R.; & Bajzek, D. (2008). "Understanding and reducing the knowledge effect: Implications for writers." *Written Communication*, 25(1), 104-118.

Jacobs, Dale. "Beyond the Rhetoric: Multimodal Rhetoric and Newspaper Comic Strips." *International Journal of Comic Art,* Spring 2007 pp. 502-14.

Leff, Michael, and Ebony A. Utley. "Instrumental and Constitutive Rhetoric in Martin Luther King Jr.'s 'Letter from Birmingham Jail'." *Rhetoric and Public Affairs* 7.1 (2004): 37-51. MLA International Bibliography. EBSCO. Web. 30 Mar. 2011.

McCloud, Scott. "The Vocabulary of Comics." *Understanding Comics: The Invisible Art.* New York: Harper Collins, 1994. 24-37. Print.

McKee, Heidi. "Sound Matters: Notes Toward the Analysis and Design of Sound in Multimodal Webtexts." *Computers and Composition* 23.3 (2006): 335-54. Print.

Murray, Donald M. "The Maker's Eye: Revising Your Own Manuscripts." *Language Awareness.* 10th ed. Ed. Paul Escholz, et al. New York: Bedford/St. Martin's, 2009. 161-165. Print.

Myers, Marshall. "The Use of Pathos in Charity Letters: Some Notes Toward a theory and Analysis." *Journal of Technical Writing & Communication* 37.1 (2007): 3-16. Academic Search Premier. EBSCO. Web. 30 Mar. 2011.

Orwell, George. "Politics and the English Language." *Language Awareness.* 10th ed. Ed. Paul Escholz, et al. Bedford/St. Martin's, 2009. 156-170. Print.

Rose, Mike. "Writing for the Public." *College English* 72.3 (2010): 284-92. Print.

Shen, Fan "The Classroom and the Wider Culture: Identity as a Key to Learning English Composition." College Composition and Communication Vol. 40, No. 4 (Dec., 1989), pp. 459-466.

Swift, Crystal Lane. "'I Had an Abortion': The Rhetorical Situation of a Planned Parenthood T-Shirt." *Qualitative Research Reports in Communication* 8.1 (2007): 57-63. Print.

Takayoshi, Pamela, and Cynthia Selfe. "Thinking about Mul-
timodality." Ed. Cynthia L. Selfe. *Multimodal Composition:
Resources for Teachers.* Cresskill, NJ: Hampton, 2007.1-12.
Print.

Tannen, Deborah. "Fighting for Our Lives." *The Argument
Culture: Stopping America's War of Words.* New York:
Ballantine, 1998. 3-26. Print.

Vatz, Richard. "The Myth of the Rhetorical Situation."
Philosophy & Rhetoric, Vol. 6, No. 3. The Pennsylvania
State University Press, University Park, Pa. and London

Young, Richard. "Rogerian Argument and the Context of
Situation: Taking a Closer Look." *Rogerian Perspectives:
Collaborative Rhetoric for Oral and Written Communication.*
Ed. Nathaniel Teich Norwood, NJ: Ablex, 1992. 109-21.
Print.